My Family's Keeper

Brad Haddin

My Family's Keeper

HarperCollins*Publishers*

HarperCollins*Publishers*

First published in Australia in 2016
by HarperCollins*Publishers* Australia Pty Limited
ABN 36 009 913 517
harpercollins.com.au

HarperCollins*Publishers*
Level 13, 201 Elizabeth Street, Sydney NSW 2000, Australia
Unit D1, 63 Apollo Drive, Rosedale, Auckland 0632, New Zealand
A 53, Sector 57, Noida, UP, India
1 London Bridge Street, London SE1 9GF, United Kingdom
2 Bloor Street East, 20th floor, Toronto, Ontario M4W 1A8, Canada
195 Broadway, New York NY 10007, USA

National Library of Australia Cataloguing-in-Publication entry:

Haddin, Brad, author.
  My family's keeper / Brad Haddin.
  ISBN: 978 1 4607 5249 4 (hardback)
  ISBN: 978 1 4607 0732 6 (ebook)
  Haddin, Brad.
  Cricket players — Australia — Biography.
796.358092

Cover design by HarperCollins Design Studio
Cover images by Phil Hillyard / Newspix
All photographs are from Brad Haddin's private collection unless otherwise noted
Typeset in Sabon LT by Kirby Jones
Printed and bound in Australia by Griffin Press
The papers used by HarperCollins in the manufacture of this book are a natural, recyclable product made from wood grown in sustainable plantation forests. The fibre source and manufacturing processes meet recognised international environmental standards, and carry certification.

To my beloved parents Anne and Ross,
brothers Michael and Christopher,
wife Karina, and children Zachary, Mia and Hugo.
In the end, nothing else matters.

Contents

FOREWORD BY

RICKY PONTING

SOMEBODY ONCE TOLD ME that loyalty is more than just a word: it's a way of life. No-one epitomises this more than Brad Haddin. Fiercely loyal to his friends, fiercely loyal to his teammates and, most important of all, fiercely loyal and completely devoted to his family.

I am very honoured to write the foreword to Brad's book, which gives us an insight into his life and, in particular, the challenges he and his remarkable wife, Karina, confronted head-on when Mia became ill. Brad and Karina's story is one of great determination and strength of character; a story of unrelenting sacrifice and commitment; and, above all, a story of a beautiful family that deserve a long and happy life together.

Brad, or Hadds, as he is more affectionately known to me, is one of our country's best-ever wicketkeeper–batsmen. He's right up there in every statistic across all three forms of the game, as well as for his longevity, playing 66 Test matches and 126 One Day Internationals (ODIs) for Australia. From the first time we played against each other in a Tasmania vs Canberra Comets game in the late 1990s to our very last Test match together in January 2012 at the Adelaide Oval, Hadds never stopped impressing me. He had an unbelievable work ethic and his preparation was second to none. Hadds's attacking style stood out, whether it was with the bat, looking to aggressively take control of every ball, or by pushing his teammates to find a way to win a game, no matter what situation we were in.

He was extremely competitive on and off the field. He was what I like to call a winner. At training, he was always working at full pace with his keeping drills, or wanting bowlers to try and knock his head off in the nets. Hadds gave it 100 per cent all the time.

I used to enjoy standing at second slip and listening to his friendly banter when we were in the field. His glove work was outstanding too. He was also one of the very best at celebrating a victory, and I have so many wonderful memories of those moments shared with Hadds and our teammates. I will also never forget sharing a 151-run partnership with Hadds in an ODI against New Zealand in 2010. We had a lot of fun that day, and Hadds went on to score 110, which was his highest-ever international ODI knock.

But this story is not so much about cricket as it is about a family that was thrown a curve ball with Mia's diagnosis in 2012. Reading these pages, you will be deeply moved as you go back in time with Brad and Karina and follow their family's private journey through Mia's treatment and everything that came with that. You will be inspired by their resilience and strength of character. You will be touched by the raw emotion of dealing with a seriously sick child, and I know that you will finish this book feeling like you know a very special family in Brad and Karina Haddin and their three gorgeous children, Zac, Mia and Hugo.

DR LUCIANO DALLA-POZZA

IN CARING FOR CHILDREN confronting illness and facing a future under threat, there are moments — many in fact — when you pause and reflect on their strength and tenacity. Yet, as great as the challenges are for them, a substantial, sometimes overwhelming, burden falls squarely on the shoulders of their families, who are thrust without warning or preparation into a setting outside their influence or control. On the morning I first met Brad Haddin, before I introduced myself, I could only speculate what was going through his mind. He sat quietly in a chair, shadowed by his wife, Karina, both keeping an anxious, exhausting vigil over their restless daughter, Mia — a perfect little girl in an imperfect world. In the next few moments both were poised to make a choice in her care — to run from this dire situation or meet the challenges head-on.

Over the ensuing months and years, when the cancer ward became a resented and unwanted second home, Brad and Karina, supported by a loving extended family, navigated the fog of uncertainty that is a part of the care of critically ill children, with a clarity that constantly impressed. They faced many difficult decisions. The choices they made reflected an approach that in turn served to inspire other families and staff. In all of this, I cannot think of Brad without also thinking of Karina, locked together in a desire to extract from uncertainty a strategy that offered hope for their daughter.

It is clear that the same unique qualities Brad brought to cricket, which characterised and moulded his approach as a player, proved crucial in the clear, unambiguous, family-focused choices he and Karina made together, and that these choices define him as a person, a partner and, crucially, as a parent. Choices maketh the man.

Brad's impressive achievements and choices in cricket are dwarfed by the profound influence that he and Karina have had on the lives of their children. Mia has simply been the most obvious beneficiary of their love and attention. They nurtured and sustained the hope in their family and friends that an unwavering effort would yield results, allowing Mia to reach and participate in a future full of promise and possibilities.

Together, Brad and Karina have since extended their efforts and influence outside their immediate world, reaching into areas that will serve to improve the outcome and care of children with cancer through research and support. They have moved from confronting challenges to seeking solutions that make a genuine difference.

If luck has anything to do with life, then Mia was unlucky in having to confront a serious illness at such a young age. Yet rainbows can only be seen with the sun at your back. Standing behind Mia were two people who secured her health and welfare and allowed her to blossom. She was hugely fortunate in having Brad and Karina as her parents.

Dr Luciano Dalla-Pozza
Senior Staff Specialist
Cancer Centre for Children
The Children's Hospital at Westmead

CHAPTER 1

DOWN THE RABBIT HOLE

'IS SHE GOING TO *die? Is Mia going to die?'*

The instant my phone buzzed at 6.30 a.m. Caribbean time I knew something was wrong back at home. The display showed it was Karina calling. For more than a decade she had been waving me off on tour to play cricket around the world. Remembering time-zone differences was second nature to her. She would never have rung at this time unless there was bad news that couldn't wait. My stomach tightened as I reached over to the bedside table.

In theory it could have been anyone in the family who was in crisis — one of our parents or siblings or our three-and-a-half-year-old son, Zac. It could have been Karina herself, 30 weeks' pregnant with our third child. But my mind went straight to Mia, our funny, cheeky, adorable 16-month-old daughter. I was sure even before Karina spoke that it was our little girl she was calling about. I braced myself for what I was about to hear, but what Karina told me was worse than anything I could ever have imagined.

It was 15 March 2012 and I was in Kingstown, St Vincent, on a two-month Australian cricket tour. The tour took in five One Day Internationals (ODIs), two Twenty20 Internationals (T20Is) and three Test matches. The first game, a one-dayer, was scheduled for the following day. I was very unlikely to be playing in it, after not being picked for recent limited-overs games, but come the first Test in Bridgetown, Barbados, in two weeks' time, I'd be doing the job I loved and had worked so hard to earn — keeping wicket for my country. I knew I could perform well enough both behind the stumps and with the bat to silence the critical chatter that had been directed at me for months. I'd done the hard work to fix the grip problems that had affected my batting. Let people say what they liked; my performance on the pitch would be my answer. That's what I'd been thinking as I went to bed the night before, but what Karina was about to tell me would change everything.

The reason I was so certain the call was going to be about Mia was because Karina and I both felt that something hadn't been quite right with her for a while. We'd talked about it before I'd flown out for the West Indies at the end of February. It was hard to put a finger on what was wrong, just that something seemed … off. Mia had been progressing through the various stages of life as a toddler in leaps and bounds, but recently it was almost as if she was regressing to babyhood: wanting to walk less on her own, becoming much more clingy, and sleeping more. Having pretty much dropped to one nap a day, she now often went back to having two, and she didn't have to be persuaded, she'd just curl up and drop off. She was often paler and more irritable than usual too and had produced some spectacular projectile vomits. But despite all this she wasn't obviously crook. She'd have good days when she was her usual perky, adventurous self and nothing seemed wrong at all, then she'd have days when she wasn't quite so bright. We'd taken her to the GP, but he'd reassured us that she probably just had a virus. That made sense and, sure enough, she would bounce back a few days later, but then she'd start to seem unwell again.

Because her symptoms came and went, it was hard to say how long it had been going on for, but when we really tried to pin it down we thought maybe the first signs that something was amiss had been at the beginning of February or maybe even a little bit earlier. Taken on its own, each 'symptom' fell within normal childhood experience. As we knew from Zac and the other little ones among our family and friends, kids of that age always seem to be coming down with one lurgy or getting over another. (I once heard a doctor explain it by saying that this period in their life is all about building up the catalogue in their 'germ library': every cold or tummy bug they have teaches their immune system more about how to fight back the next time. So apparently going from one thing to the next is normal.) Then there was her lack of energy and colour. Well, growth spurts can make kids a bit more tired than usual and tired kids tend to look pale. Besides, Mia was a strawberry blonde with a pale complexion at the best of times.

But when we stepped out of the hustle and bustle of busy family life and really started to look at the pattern of her 'good days' and 'bad days', it was obvious she was struggling with something. Karina and I discussed it before I left. Maybe Mia had developed an allergy or food intolerance, or maybe she'd picked up some bug that was a bit more hard-hitting than the usual common cold.

Not long after I'd flown out of Sydney, Karina had taken the kids a couple of hours north to Nelson Bay for a week away to celebrate her mum's 60th birthday. As well as Karina's sister, Danielle, and parents, Margaret and Phil, her aunt, uncle and cousins and their families were there, all staying in one big house they had rented for the occasion. It was planned as a really nice break for everyone. Karina and I reasoned that if Mia was just fighting something off, this holiday would give her a chance to rest up and be spoiled. Karina would keep a close eye on her and if she didn't seem to be improving they would see our family doctor when they returned home.

As always when I was away, most days I'd spoken to Karina and the kids via phone or occasionally Skype. I knew they were having a really lovely holiday in general but Mia wasn't picking up the way we'd hoped, so a couple of days into the break, accompanied by Danielle, Karina took her along to a doctor at a nearby medical centre. Mia was so drowsy she was almost asleep in Karina's arms when they were called in. The doctor examined Mia, paying special attention to her abdomen. He said he thought her liver might be a bit enlarged, but it didn't seem to be a great concern. He advised Karina to wait until she returned home the following week, then see our usual family GP, saying, 'He might do some blood tests and request a few things like that, if you're worried about her.'

When they did arrive back in Sydney it was easier, with me away, for Karina and the kids to go to her parents' house in Killara for the night rather than back to our place, an extra 20 minutes' drive away in Tennyson Point. When I called them, Karina told me that she'd made an appointment to take Mia to the doctor the following day. She was determined to find out what was wrong and her dad, who runs his own business, had offered to free her up by taking Zac to work with him. Our usual GP wasn't available, but one of his colleagues in the same excellent practice was, and Karina promised to give me an update when we spoke 24 hours or so later. But instead of waiting until the evening, my time, to call, she was ringing first thing. I realised Mia must have something serious, maybe an infection.

'Karina, hi. What's up? Are you okay? Is it Mia? What happened at the doctor's?'

'Brad, I'm ringing from the Children's Hospital. She's got a tumour. Mia has cancer.'

We both reeled through the rest of that conversation in a state of shock, but I later found out exactly how a day that had started out in Sydney with an 11.30 a.m. check-up had unfolded, sending us all into freefall.

As soon as the GP, Dr Amrit Hingorani, had seen Mia he'd remarked with concern on her lack of colour. When we looked back on the photos from the holiday, it's striking how pale she was, but because it had happened little by little, and came and went, Mia's lack of colour hadn't alerted the people closest to her the way it did to a new person seeing her for the first time. Dr Hingorani said Mia looked anaemic and, feeling her abdomen, he echoed the verdict of the Nelson Bay doctor that her liver was enlarged.

He decided to send her for a blood test to check various key measures, including the level of her haemoglobin (the substance in red blood cells that carries oxygen around the body). He said it would be fine for this to happen the following day, Friday, but in the meantime he asked Karina to take Mia for an ultrasound. He made the call himself, requesting it as a matter of urgency to make sure they got an appointment that afternoon. Karina is a radiographer, so she understands very well the workings of the human body and, despite the doctor's reassuring manner, her concern level had risen sharply at the turn things were taking. He tried to calm her fears as she and Mia were heading out, saying, 'Don't worry, I'll get a call from the ultrasound clinic if there's anything wrong and call you straight away; otherwise I'll ring you when the blood test results are back.'

Wanting information as soon as possible, and with just about enough time to get it done, Karina decided not to wait until the next day for the blood test. She squeezed it in, then raced Mia to her 2 p.m. ultrasound. Despite being too young to understand what was happening, Mia lay down on the ultrasound table and stayed there patiently as the procedure went on for what Karina knew was an unusually long time.

Generally the sonographer does the ultrasound and then later a specialist doctor, a radiologist, checks the scans and writes the report that will go back to the referring GP. But in Mia's case the sonographer went and got the radiologist and asked her to look at what he was seeing on his screen. Karina tried not to read too much into this — sometimes they just want a little extra clarification, or they're starting out and need guidance. But then the sonographer asked as casually as he could manage if she was taking Mia back to the doctor that afternoon. Karina told him they weren't; the doctor had advised he would contact her if there was a problem. When the sonographer didn't say anything further she knew something was definitely wrong.

The radiologist said they would like to do a CT scan to get a better picture of what was happening with Mia. As CT scans are a kind of x-ray, everyone but the patient has to leave the room, so Karina could not sit by Mia's side holding her hand as she had done during the ultrasound. Mia got so upset when Karina left the room that they called off the procedure, saying the best plan would be to make an appointment at the Children's Hospital, Westmead, where everything was set up to make the process easy for children. That made sense.

It was after four when Mia and Karina left, carrying the oversized envelope containing the scans and the written report for Dr Hingorani. Throughout the day Mia had been too tired and unwell to walk, so Karina had either carried her or used the pram, as she did now, going back to the parked car. With Mia buckled into her child-seat, dozing, Karina opened the sealed envelope and pulled out a report that was headed 'Confidential'. She read on, skipping ahead to what they'd found: 'There is a large, lobulated, solid mass arising from the medial upper pole of the right kidney ... There is a mass effect exerted on the right kidney ... The liver is also displaced by the mass ... The findings would be most consistent with a Wilms tumour.' It would have all been gobbledygook to me, but Karina understood exactly what it meant. It meant our beautiful daughter had cancer.

On the one hand Karina felt stunned by this news, but on the other at least we now had an answer as to what was going on, and once you have a diagnosis a treatment plan can follow. Both of the GPs who had seen Mia had thought her liver was enlarged but the scans had revealed that wasn't the case; it was the large mass pushing the liver forward that deceptively made it seem bigger. Karina's medical training really kicked in and she comforted herself with the fact that if it had to be cancer at least it was a Wilms tumour, a rare disease that mostly affects children under five and has a very high survival rate — in fact, if it's caught early and it's not aggressive the survival rate is over 95 per cent.

Before she drove off, Karina called her friend Rebecca, also a radiographer. She remained fairly calm at first but it all hit her as she said the words out loud: 'Mia's got a Wilms tumour.' Rebecca let her cry it out then offered some practical comfort, reminding her how good the cancer treatment for children is in Australia. They were talking about what Karina needed to do next when another call came in. It was Dr Hingorani, ringing because he had just received a copy of the report via email. He also reassured Karina that Mia would get the very best of treatment and that all would be well. He said he would arrange for her to be seen by a paediatric specialist as an outpatient at Westmead, either the following day or Monday. The specialist would carry out further investigations and advise about treatment. All that Karina could do until then was to keep Mia as comfortable as possible.

Before she set off for her parents' house to break the news to them face to face, Karina called my mum and dad in Queanbeyan. They were, of course, stunned and upset and offered to come up to Sydney straight away. Karina suggested they hold off until Mia had seen the specialist. She told my dad, Ross, that she hadn't yet rung me because it was still the middle of the night where I was and she was going to wait just a little longer. She also said that maybe I'd be able to stay on with the team until we knew exactly what we were up against. Hearing in Karina's voice that she was still in shock, Dad gently said to her that he was certain that I would want to come home right away. They finished the call and she steadied herself for the drive home.

Karina was on the road when Dr Hingorani called again. He'd just received the results of Mia's blood test and it showed that her haemoglobin was dangerously low; in fact, it was only half what it should have been. The plan needed to be changed: she had to go to the Children's Hospital that evening for a blood transfusion. When she reached her folks' house, Karina quickly packed a bag for herself and Mia and anxiously waited for her parents and sister to get home. It was a very emotional scene when they arrived. Having been with Mia non-stop for the previous week, they all knew that something wasn't right, but like everyone else they were knocked sideways by the news that it was cancer. Karina's mum offered to go with them to the hospital for support. So Karina, Marg and Mia set out for the hour-long trip, leaving Phil and Danielle to look after Zac. Meanwhile Dad and my mum, Anne, having been updated on the transfusion development, also hit the road for the hospital, 280 kilometres away.

As instructed, Karina, Marg and Mia went to the busy Emergency Department and waited to be assessed by a triage nurse. The nurse went through the standard questions of the child's name and date of birth. But everything suddenly changed when she asked, 'And why have you brought her in today?' and Karina answered, 'We've just found out she's got cancer and we've been told to come here so she can be admitted and receive a blood transfusion.' The next minute they were ushered through to a single treatment room, where one of the Emergency doctors told Karina that Mia was being admitted under oncologist Dr Luciano Dalla-Pozza, who would come and see her the following morning. Karina told me later that the moments she came closest to breaking during these strange, awful hours were the ones when she had to say aloud — to our parents, her friend Bec and to the triage nurse — that our baby girl had cancer.

By around 9.30 p.m., the doctors had gathered all the information they could, various tests had been done and there was a lull while preparations were made for the transfusion. This gave Karina a chance to leave Marg with Mia and duck out to find a corridor where she could get phone reception and call me.

I felt sick in the guts as she told me what was going on and I choked on my words when I asked, 'Is she going to die? Is Mia going to die?' Karina reassured me that Wilms tumours were very treatable and children had an excellent survival rate. She told me we would know a lot more when the results of the various tests came back over the next seven days. I said, 'Right, I'll jump on a plane.' Karina said, 'Well, you probably don't have to. How about I ring you in the morning after I've spoken to more people and we have a better idea what to expect?'

Looking back, this was a pretty amazing thing for her to have said. No doubt she was still affected by shock, but her response mostly came from her incredible strength and her deep knowledge and respect for all the effort involved for me to become an elite athlete playing at the highest level. It requires an unbelievable amount of dedication and determination to earn and keep a spot in the Australian Test team. Karina knew precisely what it had taken for me to get to where I was because she was the other half of the story. I couldn't have been a family man *and* achieved what I had done if she hadn't been there, willing to be basically a single parent for months at a time, picking up all the other pieces so I could concentrate on cricket. As she had done so often before with other things involving the kids, she was offering to shoulder the immediate load with Mia.

But this was so different from anything we had ever faced before that there was no question in my mind, not a flicker, not a particle of doubt: I needed to be there with my family, not 16,000 kilometres away on the other side of the planet. I said, 'No, I'm coming. I'll be there as soon as I can. Kiss Mia for me. I love you. I'll send you the flight details as soon as I have them.'

I jumped up, threw on some clothes and went straight to the room of our team manager, Gavin Dovey. He wondered who the hell was knocking on his door so early but one look at my face told him there was a good reason for it. I said, 'Mate, I've got to go home. Mia's just been to the doctor, she's got a tumour. Can you get me on a flight as soon as possible?' Gav quickly expressed his concern and told me he'd get it sorted.

I went back to my room in a state of numbness and changed into clothes I could fly in. When we travelled as a team we wore specially marked gear but I wasn't a cricketer anymore, I was a husband and a father. I pulled on my own civvy clothes, threw a few things in a bag and left everything else as it was. I stared sightlessly around. My suit was hung with the tie knotted around it, ready for the next official function. There was a pair of bright orange running shoes on the floor and three cricket bats leaning against the wardrobe. None of it seemed to have any connection to me — I might never have seen any of it before for all the sense it made. I went straight past my kitbag. I even left my toiletries bag behind as I walked out of the room on automatic pilot.

In the few minutes since I'd spoken to him, Gav had filled in the team captain, Michael Clarke, and the coach, Mickey Arthur. I saw them both in the team room and they wished me all the best, as did the other players who were now up and at breakfast had heard the news. The guys I was closest to on the tour — Peter Siddle, Nathan Lyon, Mitchell Johnson and fitness trainer Stuart Karppinen — sought me out to see how I was doing. There wasn't much I could say beyond the fact that I was going home because Mia had a tumour. They were all naturally upset for me.

Gav updated me on the travel situation: there was a spot on the next available flight, which departed in four hours. But, he explained apologetically, it involved going the long way round. Normally we returned from the Caribbean via Miami then LA and back across the Pacific. I could take that shorter route if I was prepared to wait until the next day to depart. But I just couldn't; I had to be there with my little girl. So instead I would fly St Vincent to Barbados, where there was a six-hour wait before the next flight, from Barbados to London's Gatwick Airport. From there I would transfer by cab to Heathrow, then fly back to Australia via Singapore. In all, it would be 42 agonising hours before I landed in Sydney.

A car had been arranged to get me to the airport, but first Gav asked me to speak to the Cricket Australia media liaison personnel travelling with us. They started talking about putting out a media release saying I was leaving the tour because my daughter had been diagnosed with a tumour. That snapped me out of my daze. I said, 'No, you're not doing that. You just say, "Brad Haddin has gone home for personal reasons."' They weren't happy with that, saying that there would be intense media scrutiny unless all the facts were explained. I said again, 'No.' They tried to convince me that revealing the fact that I had a sick child would lead to less intrusion in the end. I said, 'No, absolutely not. You don't understand. My grandmother doesn't know yet. Karina's grandmothers don't know. They cannot hear it on the news. Just say "personal reasons" and "we ask everyone to respect their privacy at this time".' My insistence carried the day and that's how the release was worded.

I got in the car and headed for the airport. There was still three hours until the flight and Gav had asked if I would prefer to wait at the hotel rather than sit on display in the basic little terminal building. But even though St Vincent is a very small island, less than 30 kilometres long, I didn't want to risk any delays that might make me miss the flight. I needed to feel that I was on my way.

I knew that Karina would be back in the room with Mia and unable to talk but I sent her a copy of the itinerary for my flights. I called Dad. It was nearly 11 p.m. Sydney time and he and Mum had almost reached Westmead. There wasn't much we could say to each other, but we said it. I gave him my arrival details and he said he'd be there to pick me up.

Around the time my plane was taking off, Mia's four-hour blood transfusion began. I spoke to Karina again during the long wait at Barbados and she said it had had a huge effect on Mia. The doctors had said she would feel much better after it and they were right. Karina described how she had rosy little cheeks for the first time in what we now realised was weeks and weeks. As well as her low haemoglobin, the doctors were very concerned about Mia's high blood pressure, a direct result of the tumour, but they were giving her medication for that. I hated being so far away but she was in expert hands and it seemed as if the outlook was positive. Little did we know.

While I was still at the airport at Barbados my phone rang: it was the radio 2UE sports team calling for one of the interviews I regularly did with them. Playing and training is a huge part of the working life of a professional athlete, but you also have many other obligations and responsibilities in your packed schedule: sponsor commitments, public engagements and media appearances. I'd always been able to fulfil all these commitments, maintaining intense focus on the game itself while also keeping on top of all the other details. But by the time I hung up from that initial call from Karina I had completely switched off from everything cricket. It was like stepping through a doorway. The thing that had taken up such a huge part of my life for so many years was gone in an instant.

There was no room for it when every single part of me was occupied with the knowledge of the fight we had on our hands with Mia.

I answered the phone, saying, 'Mate, can't talk. I'm on my way home. My daughter's sick. Bye,' and hung up. To its huge credit, the station didn't exploit this bit of inside knowledge over the following days and weeks when speculation about why I'd left the tour was running wild. Along with everyone else (including the close friends Karina emailed in the middle of the night from Mia's bedside) they did what we'd asked in the media release and respected our privacy. It made a big difference.

The flight from Barbados to London is eight and a half hours. Normally I would pass the time by watching movies but I couldn't focus on anything outside my own swirling thoughts and feelings and I felt too sick with worry to really eat or drink. The hours crept by as I lay there trying to tell myself not to leap ahead until we had all the facts.

While I was high above the Atlantic, Friday morning arrived in Sydney and Mia's oncologist (that phrase made my heart clutch) had come to see her for the first time. Dr Luciano Dalla-Pozza is actually the head of Westmead Children's Hospital Oncology Department but there's nothing formal or stuffy about him. He's known to one and all as Dr Luce (he gently corrected us every time we called him Dr Dalla-Pozza) and, as we were to discover, he has a wonderful way with both cancer-stricken children and their fear-stricken parents. Dr Luce told Karina that as well as causing her haemoglobin to be low, the tumour was pressing up on the bottom of Mia's lungs, making it hard for her to breathe. It was awful to think about how long this thing might have been growing inside her before its presence became clear enough for a diagnosis, but he told Karina it was best not to focus on things we couldn't change or control. He reassured her that we couldn't have been expected to guess Mia had a serious problem any earlier than we did.

He also said that while many of the signs pointed to Mia's disease being a Wilms tumour there was the possibility it might be another type of cancer that commonly starts in the adrenal glands, neuroblastoma. Not wanting to cause unnecessary alarm, he didn't say much about neuroblastoma, but Karina remembered enough from university to know that it was a very different and much more aggressive cancer. We had well and truly fallen down the rabbit hole: still in shock at the news her child had cancer at all, Karina now found herself hoping and praying that it was the 'good' kind.

Later that day a CT scan, done under general anaesthetic, revealed the size and location of the tumour but didn't clarify the diagnosis, although there were worrying signs pointing to neuroblastoma. We wouldn't know any more until a biopsy was done to remove a little of the tumour tissue and some of her bone marrow and these samples were analysed. These procedures also had to be done under a general anaesthetic. It was almost the weekend, and even though Mia was on an emergency list, the earliest they would happen was Monday — and it would take several days after that to get the pathology results. In the meantime, the doctors were trying to stabilise Mia's heart rate, which often raced dangerously, and her still-high blood pressure.

Karina had to break all this to me after I landed in London, during the hour-long transfer from one airport to the other. She did a great job of staying calm and upbeat about it, not wanting to make the next 24 hours even worse for me than she knew they already would be. Protecting my family was such a huge part of my role in life, but right now I couldn't do a single thing to help any of them.

I hadn't really taken in the name 'Wilms tumour' in Karina's first phone call, but now I scribbled it down along with 'neuroblastoma' and when we said our goodbyes I Googled them one after the other. I found out what Karina already knew about Wilms tumours: that they had a very high survival rate and required relatively straightforward treatment — as much as you can say that about treating any young child for cancer. If caught early enough, the cancer could be removed by surgery, and even though this usually meant also removing the affected kidney, this treatment was not considered very drastic. And, if the cancer was in the very early stage, it might not even be necessary to follow up with chemo or radiation therapy.

Then I searched 'neuroblastoma' and what I saw scared the hell out of me. The 'blastoma' part meant that it was a disease that affected cells that were still developing (that's why this term appears in the name of many childhood cancers). 'Neuro' didn't mean to do with the brain; it meant to do with the nervous system. In two-thirds of cases this type of cancer has already spread to other parts of the body by the time it is found. As with any cancer, there are different stages of tumour growth for neuroblastoma, but there are also differences in the tumour itself and some forms of it are much worse than others, with survival rates as low as two children in five. Feeling like I was going to throw up, I quickly shut down the browser on my phone.

Despite keeping to myself and not wearing any Cricket Australia logos, a few people did recognise me over the course of that hellish trip and some of them came up to talk to me, either while we were waiting to board or during the flights. Normally those sorts of approaches, often with a request for a selfie, are just part of the deal when you play for your country. You're not high profile in the way a pop star is, but you are a public figure and for people who are big cricket fans you're definitely a drawcard. My policy is to appreciate the interest and whenever possible give people the bit of conversation or the photo they're hoping for. I have no idea how I behaved with the people who approached me during this journey. I hope I was polite. I know I tried to be, even when I was attempting to end the encounter as quickly as possible. In answer to why I was no longer in the West Indies, I think once or twice I blurted out, 'My daughter's sick. I'm on my way home.'

As soon as I could after we'd taken off from Heathrow I swallowed a couple of sleeping pills. It was an attempt to knock myself out so I could avoid having to talk to other people and, more importantly, avoid having to think about what lay ahead. I woke up as we were coming into Singapore and immediately felt my entire body tense up in fear of the news that might await me when I turned my phone back on. No matter how much I tried to tell myself it wasn't going to happen, I couldn't shake the thought that there could be a message from Karina telling me Mia had died while I'd been in the air. Even after I'd double-checked to make sure there was no such message, I felt shaky, with what seemed like a million and one emotions sweeping over me.

I'm always happy to come back to Australia but I've never felt anything like the intense relief shot through with dread I felt when we touched down in Sydney at 8.10 that Saturday night. As well as the anxiety about what state Mia would be in, I was worried about the prospect of media waiting at the airport. I'd often been on flights where our arrival was supposed to be kept private and yet we'd land and find photographers and journalists waiting. It would be bad enough for me to have to deal with that, but what would it be like for Dad? How would he react?

Fortunately there were no media, just Dad, my youngest brother, Christopher, and my manager and friend, Peter Lovitt, anxiously scanning the arriving passengers. When I joined them they each shook my hand and we hurried out to the car for the last leg, a 45-minute drive to Westmead, calling Karina to let her know we were on the way. Dad had been at the hospital, along with Mum and Karina's mum, for most of the past 48 hours, leaving only to catch a few hours' sleep at our place. He told me Mia was doing fairly well, considering, but tried to prepare me for the sight of her hooked up to tubes and wires in her room in the cancer ward.

Dad dropped me at the main entrance while he went to park the car. I had to fight the urge to run full pelt along the corridors that led to Oncology. I walked into the ward and before I had even reached the nurses' station or opened my mouth to say who I was here to see, they were showing me where to go. They knew exactly which child I was here for and how far I'd had to come.

Finally I was where I needed to be, walking through the door saying, 'Daddy's here, Mia Moo. Daddy's here now.'

CHAPTER 2

SPORT, SPORT AND MORE SPORT

EVEN BEFORE MIA'S ILLNESS, my kids were having very different childhoods to my own. Like me, they've been raised on a bedrock of love, in a tight family unit at the centre of a close group of relatives. But that's where the similarities end. They're city kids who know never to play on the road and are comfortable sitting chatting to the barista in our favourite local coffee shop. My young days were very different. Mine was a classic country-town childhood, spent outdoors as much as possible, roaming free.

I was born in 1977 in Cowra, in what's known as the Central West of New South Wales (although it's only a bit over 300 kilometres southwest of Sydney). It's an area with strong family ties — my mum and dad had each grown up nearby and both sets of grandparents and aunts, uncles and cousins were within easy reach. Dad's parents were on the south side of the town itself and Mum's, who we called Mar and Pa, were just 50 kilometres away in the village of Wyangala.

Nearby Wyangala Dam is a really beautiful place, like a great sprawling lake. (In fact I remember being very impressed as a kid by the fact that it holds twice as much water as Sydney Harbour. Take that, Big Smoke!) People come from all around to enjoy the area's fishing, water sports and natural landscape, including two State Parks, and there's room for everyone. I have very fond memories of our Christmases at Mar and Pa's place. Mum's whole clan would gather there and we kids were in our element, swimming, chasing rabbits across the paddocks, exploring the bush and playing impromptu games of cricket and footy.

At that stage we were a family of four, including my brother Michael, who is 18 months younger than me (the youngest child, Christopher, wouldn't make his appearance until I was seven). In 1982 we moved a couple of hundred kilometres south. Dad decided to make a career and lifestyle change from being a builder to being a publican, and he and Mum bought the Criterion Hotel in the main street of Gundagai, the town famous for the Dog on the Tuckerbox monument. With a population under 10,000, Cowra was hardly big, but it was a bustling metropolis compared to Gundagai, which was home to fewer than 2000 people. That suited me just fine.

Although Michael and I were quite young, the safety of a small-town environment meant we were given the freedom to take off on our bikes or skateboards and be out and about all day with our new friends, popping back home if we got hungry. If we didn't feel like riding we'd head down to the back of the pub where there was a bridge over a creek offshoot of the Murrumbidgee River. We could walk across to the town's playing fields, including the footy ground at Anzac Park, and run around to our heart's content, or we would take the back lane to the local tennis courts. The only rules were we had to finish our chores or homework before we left and we had to head home when the streetlights came on.

The Criterion is a two-storey red-brick and tile Art Deco pub, and we lived upstairs. We had a nice backyard with a trampoline and jungle gym gear, and our mates often wanted to come over and hang out there. Mum, who helped Dad run the pub and managed the bistro, enjoyed having kids around and was happy to have what often seemed like a cast of thousands romping around the place.

We kids were aware that while a lot of the regulars came to the pub for a few low-key drinks with their mates, some of the Criterion's customers took it too far. But Dad had the perfect temperament for running a pub: he was popular but he knew how to take charge and defuse the situation if something looked like it might get out of control. Most of the time, the place had a really good atmosphere. From when I was about seven or eight, if it was a slow Sunday, Dad would occasionally sit me up on a stool behind one end of the bar near a beer tap. The locals would come over and order a beer and I would proudly pour it for them, feeling very grown up.

If I wasn't off with Mike or my mates, I'd be hanging around with Dad — wherever he was, that was where I wanted to be. People used to smile about me being his little shadow. In different times he might have been a professional sportsman himself. As a young man in Cowra, he loved rugby league and would line up for three games on a Saturday, playing in the Under-19s, then sitting on the bench for the Reserves and First Grade. In fact, he was so good as a half-back that just before I was born he was noticed by a talent-spotter who put an offer on the table for him to play a season in England then come home and play first grade in Sydney. But he and Mum were settling into married life and looking forward to having a family. In the 1970s you couldn't make a living playing league: you had a full-time job and trained and played in your 'spare time'. If he had taken up the offer, they would have had to move away from family support and he would have traded the certainty of his skilled work as a builder for an unknown future in football. His priorities lay elsewhere, so he turned down the opportunity.

You hear about some parents who didn't get the chance to fully explore their own talents and so channel all their unfulfilled ambitions into their children. There was never even a hint of that from Dad. He was absolutely content with the decision he had made. When it eventually became clear I was serious about cricket and wanted to see how far I could take it, both he and Mum were wholeheartedly there for me. But they would have been every bit as encouraging if I'd decided to follow him into the building trade or become a teacher. Both my parents have offered unconditional support to all three of us boys our whole lives. There's no-one's opinion I respect more than my father's when it comes to just about everything, sports included. He is an astute observer and an acute analyst. But he's not the one I get my competitive nature from — that would be Mum, a talented athlete in her own right and a take-no-prisoners netballer in her day.

We kids played whatever sport was on offer, depending on the season, and Dad did too. In summer it was swimming, tennis and cricket and in winter it was rugby league. Even on freezing cold nights when Dad went out to footy training with the first-grade Gundagai team, I wanted to be there with him. Other people found the fact that a young kid would sit there by choice for hours unusual enough to warrant a comment, and I guess it was. But I was always interested in whatever was happening on the sporting field, even if it was just blokes running around doing drills. I'd be all rugged up; Dad would sit me under the goalposts with some Minties and I'd be absorbed for the whole session. On game days I'd serve as ball boy, Mike too when he got old enough, and Mum would turn up at half-time with a sausage roll or hot-dog to keep us going. In 1983, the Gundagai team made the whole town proud by winning the Riverina Division premiership for the first time in 20 years.

When it came to cricket, Dad was an all-rounder, happy to bowl and then go out and try to whack a four or six at bat. His team got together through the pub and took its name. I was thrilled to bits when as a very young kid Criterion made me their 12th man, listing me as the number 11 batsman. Of course, according to the rules of cricket, the 12th man can never bat (or bowl, or do anything other than come on as a substitute fielder). But I didn't know that at the time; I just felt hugely pleased to be part of the team.

We would listen to the cricket or footy calls on the radio or watch them on TV. However, I wasn't really interested in plonking myself in front of the telly after school or on weekends when I could be running around instead, so I took part in whatever was going. At age six or seven I started playing Kanga Cricket on Saturday mornings. It was a fun introduction to the game, but cricket didn't stand out to me at that age and wouldn't for a few years. I was really small for my age, but it was obvious from very early on that I had above-average hand–eye co-ordination. So, despite my small stature, there wasn't really a sport I didn't enjoy or do well in, be it tennis, rugby league, cricket or squash. In fact Mum recalls taking me to a district school holiday tennis clinic where, at age nine, I was the youngest player. The other kids were mainly teenagers but I won the award for best player and when the coach was making the presentation of a cool new tennis racquet Mum remembers him saying, 'I want to be there when this young fella plays Wimbledon.'

Dad says he already knew early on that sport would be the focus of my adult life. At the request of my brothers and me, he spent untold hours kicking balls around with us or throwing to us in the cricket nets. His work made a lot of demands on him, but he'd give us his free time without complaint. If he wasn't available and I couldn't scare up a brother or mate to play with, I would kick a ball around the park by myself, hit tennis balls against the pub wall endlessly or bowl against it to practise catching.

I didn't mind school, but sports day was far and away my favourite day — I was never too sick to go to school then. As long as I was active I never got bored; even my parents used to shake their heads in wonder at me sometimes. Dad, for instance, hated doing footy training; he went through with it because he knew it needed to be done but he loathed it. I loved training and when even the keenest of the other kids had reached the point where they just wanted to get home, I'd still be going hard at it, asking the coach to give me more. I was that way when I was seven and I'm still the same now.

Michael and Chris were also above-average athletes, with Chris talented in cricket and Michael in both cricket and rugby union. (They would each go on to captain their high school First XI cricket teams but Chris, who was a fast bowler, stopped playing after he got stress fractures in his back. Michael was good enough in rugby to have had opportunities to go on and play the game at a high level after he finished school, but he chose to study instead.)

We were raised to have a very clear sense of sportsmanship. A lot of people these days seem to feel that kids should be discouraged from being competitive, that they should be told it doesn't matter who wins, that it's enough simply to participate. I understand the intent and I think there are certain contexts where that is probably a good approach, but it's not how we grew up. We were taught that it was okay to want to win. For me, competitiveness is one of the great things about sport. I enjoyed challenging myself to get better — better than the opposition and better than my own previous level. There's nothing abstract or subjective about the scoreboard at the end of a game: it's a clear, objective result. Being on the winning side on that scoreboard feels good, and the desire to repeat that feeling motivates you to push yourself harder to be the best you can be. But — and it is a very important but — as competitive as we were, we took it as a fundamental truth that a win was only ever worth something if you played the game in the right spirit. For us, respect was crucial: you had to respect the game, respect the coaches, umpires, referees, linesmen and any other officials, and respect the opposition. (Later I had to find a way to make that work within the often confronting atmosphere of professional sport.)

Every now and then, a kid I was playing with or against would throw down their cricket bat or kick a goalpost when things weren't going their way. My brothers and I knew that if we ever did anything similar it would have been the end of our involvement: our parents simply wouldn't have tolerated it. We understood that it was important that you always played fairly and, whether it was a win or a loss, at the end of the game you thanked the ref and you shook hands with the other team's players as you looked them in the eye. If you won, you celebrated it without acting like an idiot. If you lost, it was okay to feel disappointed, but you had to accept the simple truth that you'd been beaten by a better team, end of story. I learned those values at Anzac Park in Gundagai and they took me all the way to some of the most cherished sporting grounds in the world, including the home of cricket, Lord's. They are values Karina also grew up with and they're ones we are passing on to our own children.

Unfortunately not everyone felt the same. Over the years I've seen more than enough of the ugly side of parental involvement in kids' sport. It's definitely the minority who don't know where to draw the line, but it can easily sour the experience for everyone else. Fortunately I was too young to even realise what was going on the day nasty sideline behaviour turned into a real threat to me. It started out as just a normal game of footy with the Gundagai Tigers Under-8s. I was easily one of the smallest kids on the field but I was used to that. I was also one of the fastest. A kid on the opposing team got the ball, saw an opening and made a break for it. I took off after him, ran him down and tackled him. Unfortunately, he fell awkwardly, breaking his collarbone in the process.

He was much bigger than me, the tackle was legal; it was one of those unfortunate things that happens from time to time in contact sports. But in an instant the atmosphere turned very nasty indeed. His teammates moved in, surrounding me, and their parents got up and started to make a beeline for me, more intent on heaping abuse on me than on helping the injured boy. The ref tried to settle things, but it was all going downhill fast. Dad walked over, seemingly casually. He checked that the boy would be okay, then put his hand on my shoulder and, turning to the nearby ref, who he knew well, said to him quietly but with an unfamiliar intensity, 'How much time to go?' The ref said, 'Five minutes.' Dad said, 'I think you'd better call it now.'

Still oblivious to the menace in the air I said, 'Gee, Dad, those other parents are carrying on a bit, aren't they?' Continuing to project absolute calmness but walking me off the field with him as he talked, he said, 'Yes they are. Tell you what, let's go up to the pub. I'll get you a lemonade and a packet of chips.' Chips were a pretty usual treat for us but we hardly ever got soft drinks. I was very tempted, but my usual routine after I played was to stay and watch every other grade play right through till the late afternoon men's game with Dad's team. I told him I'd rather do that, but he said again, 'No, I think we need to head up home.' Finally I said, 'Well all right, but I can come back down with you later, can't I?' Because Dad maintained such a calm, unworried façade during this whole event, it took me a long, long time before I realised what had really happened.

Even before that occurred, whenever he watched any of us play sport Dad preferred to stand apart from all the other parents. He never made a big show of it; he would just quietly walk to a place where he could concentrate on the game without hearing any bitching or overbearing commentary from the sidelines. He still does it to this day, and I do the same.

Moving up through my primary school years, I was increasingly selected for advanced tennis clinics or to play in regional tournaments and do rep trials in cricket or league. This often meant driving an hour or so to Wagga Wagga and Cootamundra, but somehow my parents always seemed to manage it so one of them could get me there. Family logistics got a bit trickier when they decided it was time for a change and sold the pub in mid-1987. They rented a house in town so Michael and I could see out the school year and Dad went back to work 'on the tools' in Canberra, where building jobs were plentiful. He would spend weekends with us, leaving in the early hours of Monday morning for the two-hour drive and returning on Friday evenings. It could be a treacherous road, especially in winter, and one sleety morning his ute hit an oil slick and span out of control into a tree. He was lucky to walk away from the crash, which split the ute in two, and everyone was relieved that our move a few months later to Queanbeyan meant he no longer had to make that trip.

Canberra and Queanbeyan are neighbours, but the fact that my parents chose to live in one rather than the other was one of the greatest strokes of luck I could have had. I might never have become an Australian Test cricketer otherwise.

The CBDs of the two cities are less than 15 kilometres apart and at the closest point of their boundaries if you weren't paying attention to road signs you might almost assume you were driving from one neighbouring semi-rural suburb to the next, not realising you'd passed from one city to another. But an arbitrary line on the map marks a crucial distinction between them. Canberra sits snugly in the Australian Capital Territory while Queanbeyan is in New South Wales. That means that as close as they are geographically, there is a massive difference between them — and it was even more marked back then. Canberra gets the kind of investment and attention you'd expect for a nation's capital, while Queanbeyan often gets forgotten. Things have improved a lot, but in the 1980s the city's nickname was Struggletown and Canberrans looked down on it from a great height (too many still do).

A lot of that stuff passes kids by, at least until they're teenagers, and I was no exception. For me, living in Queanbeyan was brilliant because it meant that I had twice as many competitions to play in — NSW school comps and the ACT club comp that, for logistical reasons, the Queanbeyan Cricket Club was part of.

At age ten I went along to an open cricket trial at the National Exhibition Centre (as it was called then) in Canberra. There were quite a lot of kids there and after a bit of introductory talk the organisers started sorting us out to see what we could do in the five nets they had set up. They asked first, 'Who's an opening batter?' My hand shot up, along with a load of others. Four got picked to form the first group and were told to pad up and head over to the nets; I wasn't one of them. The next question was, 'Who's a fast bowler?' Well everyone's a fast bowler at that age, so again my hand went up, but again I wasn't one of the ones picked. Then they asked, 'And who's a wicketkeeper?' The closest I'd come to wicketkeeping was those hours of catching balls in the backyard, but I'd give anything a go. Up went the hand again. This time, mine was the only one. I got sent over to catch for one of the bowlers and that's how my career as a keeper was born.

It was pure chance in one sense — if I'd been selected for one of the other groups I wouldn't have begun to see myself as a keeper at that early age. But I believe that keeping would have found me in the end, one way or another. It suited me perfectly because the wicketkeeper is always in the game. There's no waiting around for your turn; you're right there in the middle of the action. (Now I see that same desire to be in on everything in my son Zac when he plays — he'll be fielding off to one side but if he can see the ball heading to an unguarded spot he'll hare after it no matter how far it is, and plenty of times he'll get there, too. He wants to be as involved as he can. My parents look at him and shake their heads with a smile, saying, 'He's just like you were at that age.')

The other part of the keeper's role that suited me was that I could handle the scrutiny and the weight of other people's expectations. Like goalkeeping in soccer, wicketkeeping is a pressure position — it's easy for people to take for granted all the things you do right, while every miss is highly visible. I was okay with that. I didn't let my misses get to me and I didn't carry them over to the next ball. Instead I just tried to figure out how I could avoid it happening again.

We had an old cricket kit at home that Dad's younger brother Paul had given to us when he no longer needed it and it included a pair of red keeper's gloves. They were adult-size, which meant they came pretty much up to my elbows but I didn't complain. We were all used to making do in my family and I was able to make use of them until I could get something better, by which time they had all but fallen apart.

When I did upgrade, it was Rod Marsh-branded gloves I wanted, not because I knew anything much about the man who had kept wicket for Australia for an amazing 14 years through the 1970s and into the mid-1980s. No, the reason I wanted them was because they were the kind I saw my new hero, Ian Healy, wearing. Heals had made his *test* debut the month before I turned ten. My introduction to wicketkeeping came just as he was really making his mark on the game and it was his work I focused on when we watched cricket on the telly and his poster I had on my wall. You could get Marsh Golds or Silvers, depending how much money you had to spend. The answer for us was, not much.

Like my brothers, I had to work to get the money to buy 'extras' like this. In school holidays we would go and pitch in on Dad's building sites. He paid us $20 a day and despite much complaining about 'slave labour' rates as we got older, the amount never did seem to increase. (The sites also provided Dad's answer when in due course we expressed interest, as teenage boys often do, in going to the gym. He felt we were a bit young when it first came up, but he had the perfect alternative: 'See those pavers?' 'Yes.' 'Well move that lot 'round the back. That'll build your muscles.' He was unmoved by the 'Aw, jeez, Dad!' response.) When I finally did get those coveted gloves I had them for four years, getting them resurfaced before the start of each season and only buying a new pair when they were almost in pieces.

By 1990 I was in my first year at Karabar High School, still playing every sport I could, standing out more each year not just for the medals and trophies I brought home but because I stayed so small while my classmates grew. In Year 8 I was chosen to play as wicketkeeper in the school's senior competition team but I was so undersized that after I took a particularly big diving catch one of my teammates lifted me right above his head in celebration, saying, 'Look at this little kid go!' Because being small didn't hinder me in sport, it didn't worry me too much in general. I thought I'd eventually get to somewhere around Dad's height of 175 centimetres (5 feet 9 inches) and in fact I ended up at 178 centimetres, although it took many years.

I continued my move up through rep and district sides, was chosen for the regional South Coast schools teams in both cricket and rugby league, and won a place in the overall state Combined High Schools (CHS) team for cricket. I played after-school cricket within the ACT clubs system and I also rose through the ranks in that system. Playing within both the NSW and ACT systems gave me a big advantage. Not only was I building up experience more quickly, but because ACT had a tiny population to draw on (even when you included players who lived in Queanbeyan), it was easier for me to be noticed than if I'd been vying with the many thousands of kids playing in the NSW system. So many different comps meant a lot of travelling for Mum in particular, as Dad was often working as far away as the Snowy Mountains, but both parents were happy to support us boys in any way they could.

As a player within the NSW comps, being from Queanbeyan meant I flew under the radar. I remember talking with Dad about what to expect one day as we made the long drive down the South

Coast for one of the CHS trial matches that he was able to take me to. He said, 'You have to realise, nobody there knows you.' I understood that I needed to be strategic about showing what I could do, both with a bat and behind the stumps. My size meant I didn't yet have as much power batting as I wanted, but, even so, I had a big, straight drive down the ground. We arrived early and I sat down to watch the bowlers warm up in the nets. I figured my best chance of making an impression was to take a crack at one of the best bowlers straight away. I spotted a contender and made a beeline for him. I hit a couple of beauties: *whack, whack.* That got people's attention, and I followed up by showing what I could do behind the stumps. There were a couple of other players in contention for the keeper position in the team that was being chosen, including one who was older and more experienced than me, having held the position the previous season. But I was the one who got picked.

My profile continued to build and I was picked to play in the ACT team in a national Under-17s championship series in Hobart in January 1992. That was a pretty good achievement for a 15-year-old, even if I was still so small I looked like the mascot in the team photo. This tournament is part of the development pathway that potentially leads from kids' local cricket all the way through to the Australian Test team. I was already dreaming of one day being chosen to wear the fabled Baggy Green cap, but so was every other cricket-mad kid. (Or rather, back in those days, every other cricket-mad boy. It's great that girls can now also dream big, thanks both to the strides that have been made in bringing them into the sport and to the international triumphs of the Australian women's cricket team.)

Despite my daydreams, the only exposure I had to professional athletes was the Canberra Raiders rugby league team. One of the team's biggest stars, Ricky Stuart, came from Queanbeyan and when we went to Raiders games I watched him and that other great talent Laurie Daley closely, observing how they performed on a big stage, how they handled pressure and lifted their team when things were going against them. I wasn't consciously amassing knowledge for my own future, but it was all being stored away somewhere.

The ACT Under-17s team finished last in Hobart, pretty much in line with expectations, but I performed well. In fact, so well that Rod Marsh asked to have a photo taken with me. I thought that was very cool, but I'm not sure I fully appreciated it at the time. He was doing it as a gesture of encouragement, in his capacity as the man who oversaw the development of up-and-coming players as director of the Australian Cricket Academy rather than as a wicketkeeping great, but that certainly added something extra special to the moment.

My parents wanted me to do my final years of high school at the Catholic boys' school St Edmund's College in Canberra. Mum in particular felt that it would raise my education to a new level and set me up well for whatever career I decided to pursue. It had been all planned for some time and, knowing about my rep team selections for cricket and footy, the school was keen to have me (although being a private school they played rugby union, not league). They'd even invited me along to do a bit of cricket training and to let me see their facilities. It all looked great and I was keen, but then out of the blue came a golden opportunity, courtesy of Greg Irvine.

Greg was a satellite coach for the Australian Institute of Sport's Cricket Academy. While the AIS was headquartered in Canberra, the Academy was in Adelaide, but it had an arrangement with coaches around the country to scout talent in their area. Greg's remit was to identify promising ACT cricketers. I'd been on his radar for a while and when I was 15 he had chosen me to take part in the winter coaching clinic he ran. He obviously thought I'd done pretty well because now he had an extraordinary offer to make: would I like to join the club he played for, Australian National University (ANU), as wicketkeeper on the first-grade team?

I wouldn't turn 16 until three months into the upcoming season. I'd played in the Queanbeyan club youth competition the whole time we lived there, but for the past two years I had also been in the fifth-grade men's team. On a Saturday I'd play alongside the other kids all morning, then Mum would pick me up and I would scoff lunch in the car while she drove me to the men's match. Now here I was being given the chance to leap straight from fifth grade to first grade — something that *never* happened. It came with a caveat: I had three games to prove myself. If I hadn't performed by then I'd be dropped to a lower grade. That was totally fair. It was an incredible offer.

But I couldn't accept it if I was going to go to St Edmund's. The school administration told us they wanted me to commit to every school game including at weekends. My parents said that while I would happily play every game I could, on Saturdays I was going to take the chance to extend myself with the ANU Cricket Club (ANUCC). For the school it was a deal breaker, so in the end we had to say I wouldn't be going there after all. (I believe they have now changed the policy.) I didn't mind much. I wanted to join ANUCC more than I'd wanted anything before. But for my parents it was a more serious decision. First there was the issue of my education: would they be letting me follow a path that might limit my future career choices, just so I could play weekend cricket? Second, was it reckless to send a kid of my size and age out on the field against men playing tough, unforgiving, first-grade cricket?

To their huge credit, they decided the risks were worth it. They could see how passionate I was and they knew that whatever I took on I would give it my all. But Dad said I couldn't just walk away from the club I was already part of; I should find out what plans they had for me. I spoke to my Queanbeyan club coach and asked where he thought I'd be playing in the upcoming season. He said he planned to put me in fifth grade again. I said in that case I was afraid it was time for me to move on. We called Greg and told him that ANUCC had a brand new wicketkeeper.

CHAPTER 3

NO LONGER A NORMAL FAMILY

DESPITE THE EFFORTS DAD had made on the way to the hospital to prepare me for Mia's appearance, I was so shocked to see how sick she looked that my stomach dropped. It was hard to take in. It was difficult to believe she could have deteriorated this much in three months let alone in less than three weeks, which is all it had been since I'd last seen her. She had a tube going into her nose, with tape on her face to keep it from moving, and a contraption on her right hand that consisted of a padded rectangular piece of plastic strapped to her palm to keep her from dislodging other tubes coming out of her wrist. But I barely registered the equipment. All I could take in at first was her huge, misshapen tummy. She lay starfished on her back in the cot, monitors all around, wearing only her nappy. Her stomach was so distended it was painful to look at.

Mia opened her eyes when she heard my voice and, ill as she was, gave me one of her beautiful cheeky grins. She sat up and I reached into the cot and held her as tight as I dared without putting any pressure on her abdomen. Karina and I hugged and wiped away tears. Emotions rushed through me in waves. The relief at being home, being able to see and touch Mia, and be there for Karina was immense. My worst fears hadn't been realised: Mia hadn't died before I could get to her. I was back where I needed to be. But now there was a different sense of helplessness: I couldn't take away her pain or get rid of her cancer.

My whole life I've felt that it doesn't matter how bad things are, the unknown is always worse. Once you accept the reality, you can start to deal with the situation. You just take it one step at a time and do what needs to be done, no matter how hard that may be. My parents raised me with that philosophy. They taught me to never avoid the truth or try to kid myself. Bad or good, it was always better to face up to the situation and do what you could to handle it. That approach got me to the top in the world of cricket and kept me there in the face of injuries and being out of favour with selectors and every other setback I faced. But it was one thing to feel that way about my own challenges and quite another to have our baby girl dealing with something so unimaginably big. It broke my heart not to be able to make everything better for her.

It all felt head-spinningly surreal. The feeling wasn't helped by jetlag; after more than three and a half days of continuous travel, it felt like someone had attached invisible weights to my limbs. I'd been to children's hospitals on goodwill visits many times over the years. I'd been out here to Westmead. Hell, I'd even been to this ward, Camperdown, and met little kids in the throes of cancer and tried to serve as a bit of a distraction for them and their anxious families during those long, long hospital days. But now here we were, and it was my child wearing the medical ID wristband and my wife sitting by her side. It felt like there'd been some kind of a mistake somewhere and we'd slipped through the TV screen into someone else's story.

Of course I knew this happened to people just like us every day. Cancer in children is the ultimate leveller. Rich or poor, black or white, cruising or struggling, it makes no difference. It can happen to anyone. The kids I'd seen and met on those visits didn't walk around with an 'X' on their foreheads before they got sick. Life just rolled along for those families day by absolutely ordinary day right up until the moment it didn't. I knew all that. But again, knowing it in my head did nothing to help the sickening, inescapable reality of it deep in my guts.

It didn't take long after I arrived to get Mia settled again with her favourite blanket for comfort. Her body was so whacked that she barely moved after she had drifted off. It looked more like unconsciousness than sleep and she was making an unfamiliar panting noise that I found disturbing. Karina explained it was the result of the tumour pushing up against her little lungs.

Karina and I talked for an hour or more. I had so many questions: 'What do we know? What kind of cancer is it? Is she going to live?' Karina said gently, 'We don't know anything yet. They're still hoping it's a Wilms tumour, but we won't know for a couple more days, until after she's had the scans on Monday.' I found this hard to accept. 'There must be something we can do to move things along. We can't just sit here and let her get worse while nothing happens.' What Karina said next set the tone for the rest of our journey through Mia's cancer. 'Brad, Mia is in the best possible hands, getting the best possible care. Dr Luce is an expert and when you meet him you will see how much he genuinely cares about each and every one of the kids in here. If we second-guess him and his team we'll drive ourselves crazy and we won't help Mia. They've explained to me that another 36 hours or so until the scan won't make any difference in her condition. I'm confident they know what they're doing.'

As much as the protective father part of me wanted to see Mia having the scan right that second, what Karina said made a lot of sense. I recognised that hospitals were places that made me feel deeply uncomfortable. I always went into them for surgery on an injury anticipating the unpleasant woozy feeling after a general anaesthetic and the pain during recovery. The only positive associations this kind of place had for me were the births of Zac and Mia, and even then they were caesarean births so I'd been in an operating theatre seeing Karina get cut open. I'd always entered hospitals unwillingly and walked out with a sigh of relief.

It was completely different for Karina. Her whole professional life had been spent in these environments. For her there was nothing threatening or foreboding about them — just the opposite. She saw them as good places where people got the information they needed and treatments designed to heal them. In fact she didn't even register one of the things that I hated most — that characteristic hospital odour. I suppose it's the disinfectant they use or something, but it makes my skin crawl. I said to Karina at one point, 'I can't stand that smell!' She sniffed the air and said, genuinely puzzled, 'What smell?'

As well as being completely comfortable in the environment and familiar with medical terminology and human anatomy, Karina was incredibly well organised. By the second morning after she'd brought Mia in, she had asked her sister, Danielle, to bring her a journal so she could keep a day-by-day diary of exactly how Mia was feeling and how her symptoms were changing hour by hour; who was in her medical team and the updates they were giving about her condition and treatment; detailed diagnostic results and readings of things like Mia's blood pressure and haemoglobin levels; and more. As upset as she was, she was staying on top of it all. I put my trust in Karina, so if she put her trust in the medical team that was good enough for me.

Karina had been with Mia every moment since they'd set out for the doctor on Thursday morning, with Zac being looked after by her parents. Now that I was back we could take turns switching between home and hospital. As the clock neared 10 o'clock that Saturday night, we held one another again and reassured each other that everything would turn out okay and then Karina went home for the night.

When she had gone I stood by Mia's cot, stroking her head, and took in the room for the first time. Like the rest of the Camperdown oncology ward it had been painted and decorated with purples and yellows and other bright colours to make it as child-friendly as a hospital could be. This room had a light-hearted police theme with flashing lights the kids could activate and lots of murals. The ward catered for children aged anywhere from tiny babies to 16-year-olds. They often spent long stretches in here and they almost always had an adult with them, so the rooms were set up to accommodate that. At the moment Mia was in a single room but there were also shared wards. Either way, a fold-out bed was provided for each child's parent or carer. Before she left, Karina had explained the set-up: what looked by day like a comfortable low armchair folded out to become a bed, and linen and pillows were provided. Given that there wasn't a lot of space to begin with, the staff asked that you had it all folded up by 9 a.m. each day so the nurses and doctors could move around freely.

The room had an ensuite toilet that normally was for the patient's use only, but which in our case they kindly allowed Karina to use, given her advanced pregnancy. There was a small fridge in the room where we could keep food, and another shared one in the parents' lounge. There was a tea room where you could help yourself to a cuppa and a biscuit and even, if needed in the long night hours, find something to eat in the freezer stocked by a wonderful charity called Cure Our Kids.

Even though I was exhausted, it was hard to sleep, despite the fact that Mia was now resting peacefully. I did eventually nod off, although I woke each time the nurses came in to do their observations by torchlight. In the morning, despite seeming to have slept quite well, Mia woke up tired. Her tummy also looked even larger to me. She was having daily blood tests and the first one I was there for was hard to watch. It took four attempts for them to find a vein that worked and the poor baby got very upset.

During the morning her heart rate started racing and her blood pressure reading was low, which concerned the doctors. They gave her something for the pain she was obviously in, but said that for the moment they wanted to just keep an eye on the heart rate. Again, I found it hard to understand that some kind of immediate action wasn't being taken, but Karina, who had come back to the hospital, bringing Zac with her, reassured me that observation is often the best approach to start with.

I handed over to Karina and took Zac home for a few hours. Zac always felt my absence acutely when I was away on tour and he was extremely excited to have me back home. It was such an innocent excitement — he was simply too young to understand what was going on with Mia — and on the one hand it was beautiful to see him bouncing around in all his lively, three-year-old good health, but on the other it made the contrast with Mia's current state all the more painful. Emotions were running high. My brother Michael called from his home in the United Arab Emirates (UAE), where he runs a really successful fitness company. When Mum had first called him with the news, while I was still in the West Indies, he'd thought he could get by with just daily phone updates. But he was ringing to say he couldn't stand to be away from the family at such a time — he, his wife Amy and their daughter Molly, the same age as Mia, were jumping on a plane and would arrive later that night. Knowing how busy he was running his business over there in Abu Dhabi I would never have asked him to come, but I was very glad he had decided to.

Happy to have been able to spend some time with Zac, I left him in the capable hands of Karina's mother, Marg, and returned to the hospital. I stayed there for the afternoon and evening before reluctantly saying goodbye to Mia and Karina and heading back home again about 8 p.m. The idea had been that I would get a decent sleep then be back out at Westmead again the following morning in plenty of time for the procedures Mia had scheduled, including the CT scan. But things didn't quite go to plan. I went to bed all right but I tossed and turned, my mind racing. I finally gave it up as a bad joke in the early hours. The hospital asked that only one adult stay overnight, but I needed to be there with my girl. So I got dressed as quietly as possible, crept out of the house, trying not to wake Zac and Marg, got in my car and drove to the Westmead car park. My intention had been to stay in the car, dozing if I could, until daylight and then go into the ward. But I just couldn't take not knowing what was happening and at 3.30 a.m. I texted Karina to let her know where I was.

Karina was awake because Mia was having a rough night with worrying symptoms. Her heart rate had continued to have alarming spikes, hitting 175 beats per minute at some stages. Her temperature was also too high and she was clearly in discomfort. Paracetamol had given her temporary relief and when I texted she was having yet another blood sample taken. I waited until that was all done and went in about 4 a.m. By that point Mia was sitting up in her cot happily watching *In the Night Garden* on a portable DVD player — you'd never have guessed the night she'd had. Karina got no sleep at all, but Mia nodded off for a couple of hours between 6 a.m. and 8 a.m., when one of Dr Luce's team came in to say that the blood test had shown her haemoglobin was down, which is why her cheeks were once again pale. The level wasn't as bad as it had been when she was admitted, but it was low enough to warrant another blood transfusion.

Dr Luce Dalla-Pozza came to see us himself a little later. I immediately saw what Karina had meant about his caring, compassionate manner and calm professionalism. He explained to me what he had previously told Karina about the types of cancer Mia might have, he spoke reassuringly about the depth of experience the hospital's staff had in treating children's cancer and he outlined the procedures she would be having that afternoon. There was a lot to absorb, although he made it all as simple as possible. But one thing he said stood out so clearly that I will never forget it as long as I live. He said, 'You have a child with cancer. You're no longer a normal family. There's no such thing as a "normal day" anymore.' His words echoed in my head long after he had left.

The second transfusion, which brought Mia's rosy cheeks back yet again, was finished well before her 2 p.m. CT scan. For kids who are too young to understand they have to lie perfectly still, scans like this are done under general anaesthetic, and while Mia was under they were going to do several other procedures, to help with diagnosis and to tailor her treatment. The state of bone marrow can tell doctors a lot about whether cancer is spreading through the body and how much damage it is doing. Mia would have two kinds of bone marrow samples taken: an 'aspiration' of the cells, which means they suck up some of the marrow into a syringe, and a core biopsy, which means they punch out a 1cm or so section of the marrow in a single piece. In Mia's case they took the core biopsy from the top of her pelvis. They have to push through the bone to get to the marrow, and it can feel sore for days afterwards, but, under a general anaesthetic, at least Mia wouldn't feel any pain while it was being done.

The doctors were also going to do a biopsy of the tumour itself. This would give the answer to what kind of cancer it was — a Wilms tumour or the feared neuroblastoma. They do this by using ultrasound to position a hollow needle, into which they then pull tissue. All of this would be done in Radiology. Then Mia would be taken to the operating theatre where they were going to insert something called a central line — a thin tube that went in under the skin and was fed into one of the veins that goes down near the heart. It's used to supply drugs, fluids and even nutrients, and to take blood samples without the painful repeated attempts Mia had previously gone through as they tried to find a vein in her hands and arms. One end of the tube is left outside the body, on the chest, and when it's not having something injected into it or blood extracted from it, it's kept capped and covered with a dressing.

It was confronting to think of such a little girl needing to have so many things done to her before the actual treatment even started. Again I heard Dr Luce's words. Normally, Mia would have spent the day playing with her friends from Karina's mothers' group or visiting a local park, but there was no point thinking about 'normal'. We were on a fast-moving train, with no option to turn back. Instead of pushing her on the swings or catching her as she came down the slide, Karina and I were walking beside Mia as she was wheeled in a cot down to a radiology suite for the two-hour procedure.

One of the medicos in Dr Luce's team, Oncology Fellow Dr Santosh Valvi, came in to see us a few hours after it was all done. Karina had met him soon after Mia's admission, when he told her she'd need to remember his name because he'd be coming in to check on Mia as many as four times a day in these early stages of treatment. He hadn't been exaggerating. Dr Santosh explained that he didn't yet have any results to give us; the samples were being analysed but it would be at least 24 hours before we had any findings. In the meantime they were going to perform another, different scan the following day, an MIBG. Apparently CT scans, like the one Mia had already had, are a kind of sophisticated X-ray, good at showing what's going on in soft tissues, including organs. An MIBG scan, performed in the nuclear medicine department, uses a radioactive liquid in the search for a couple of really specific cancers, including neuroblastoma. MIBG is actually shorthand for the name of the liquid — iodine-123-meta-iodobenzylguanidine. It's put into the body on one day, and on the next day it can be picked up on a special kind of camera.

The MIBG is injected into a vein, but in order to protect the thyroid from being damaged by it the patient has to swallow a special kind of iodine, so we had to get Mia to drink this mixed into milk each day for four days before and three days after the scan. It has a reputation for tasting disgusting and judging by her reaction the reputation is spot on. But as horrible as it must have been, she got it down. One thing that stood out about Mia right from the start of those first few days in hospital all the way through her treatment was how incredibly compliant she was and how she would do just about whatever was asked of her, no matter how hard it was.

I left in the evening to go home and see Zac. Once again the plan was that I would come back the following morning, but again I just couldn't sleep and couldn't bear being away, so I was back in Mia's room before 5 a.m. on the Tuesday. Despite my restlessness I felt the first real surge of optimism I'd had since Karina's initial phone call. I said to her as soon as I arrived, 'Whatever results we get from the scan, she can be cured.'

That good feeling lasted only a few hours as by early afternoon Mia was once again running a fever and her heart rate had shot up to 180. She'd been sleepy all morning but now she wasn't moving at all. The nurse checking her vital signs hit the button for the emergency response team, bringing six doctors hurrying to her side. They had various theories about what might be causing her to deteriorate and none of them sounded good. The two that I grasped were that she might have a collapsed lung as a result of the general anaesthetic and that she might have developed an infection from the central line. It was a foreign object inside the body so this was always a possibility. They investigated a bit further and realised that there was a tiny hole in part of the central line. (I hadn't realised, but it wasn't just a single hollow tube but was split into separate channels. One of these had somehow — no-one knew how — become damaged.) They had to fix it then and there, not under another general, and it was really, really upsetting to watch as one young doctor tried and failed before handing over to a senior colleague.

I thought that had been tough, but the day got much worse when Drs Luce and Santosh came to see Karina and me to tell us what they knew so far. All the signs were that Mia had neuroblastoma, not a Wilms tumour. It was so hard to take in anything after that, but these two kind doctors were used to parents reeling in the face of terrible news and they took it slowly and gently, breaking it down into chunks of information we could understand. Even so, I'm not sure I would have retained anything very much, but fortunately Karina took diary notes that we could check later as we started to absorb the information.

They told us that neuroblastoma was rare: there were only about 40 cases diagnosed a year in Australia. Dr Luce sees about 14 cases a year, which was some kind of comfort. We learned that there were four different categories, depending on the age of the child at diagnosis, how far the cancer had spread around the body, what a microscopic analysis (a 'histology') of the tumour showed, and whether or not it had extra copies of a particular MYCN gene — having that put you into the category with the lowest survival rates. I knew about human beings having genes but didn't really understand how a tumour could have them. It didn't make sense. I was drowning in all this information, but thankfully Karina looked like she understood most if not all of it. There was just one bit of good news: the bone marrow sample that had been aspirated was clear. But it would still be two more days before the results of the tumour and marrow core biopsies came through. In the meantime, the following day's MIGB scan would tell us a lot more.

When the meeting was over, Karina and I couldn't do much more than look at each other. We reminded ourselves that there was plenty we still had to find out and it was important not to jump to conclusions. We had to stay strong for Mia and deal with whatever came next. But we were both still feeling shaky when Karina went home to spend the night with Zac, and she told me later she cried herself to sleep. I don't think I got any shut-eye at all.

The following morning Mia's heart rate and blood pressure were both up and her distorted stomach had grown 1.5 centimetres larger in just 24 hours. She was sedated for an hour and a half for the MIGB procedure and Karina stayed with her while I went home to collect Zac. He had been to the hospital for two brief visits since Mia had been admitted, but he hadn't liked it much. From a three-and-a-half-year-old's perspective, hospitals are challenging places at the best of times — people are always telling you not to run and not to yell and not to open things. And despite all the efforts to make the Camperdown ward child-friendly, seeing Mia hooked up to tubes and monitors and so clearly unwell upset him.

Previously, Marg and Danielle had brought Zac in, giving him just a little time in Mia's room before a chance to burn off some steam either in the playground outside or in the Starlight Express Room. This is a place where the kids being treated and their brothers and sisters can go to play video games or do some craft or just unwind. To help them relax as much as possible, it's officially a 'doctor-free zone'. But this time we didn't have to take Zac out of Mia's room to be entertained because, with Mia recovered from her sedation, the Clown Doctors made a visit.

You've probably seen the Clown Doctors on TV. They're performers who dress up in white coats and red noses and silly wigs and face-paint and go by names like Dr Silly Billy and Dr

Colourfool. Their whole job is to go around cheering up sick kids and they do it brilliantly. Depending on the age of the child, they might tell jokes or play silly tunes on a ukulele or do what they did for Mia, which was to sing songs and blow lots of bubbles. She was entranced by that initial visit and Zac was too, and it was wonderful to see them laughing as if everything was normal. I did, however, see Karina discreetly wipe away a tear at one point and I understood her feelings perfectly — this was not a scene from a TV show or a fundraising brochure; this was real, we were here, and it was our baby girl they were visiting.

The following hours passed in a jumble of visits. First came my brother Chris and his then girlfriend (now wife), Jenna; then Michael, who came straight from the airport; then Mum and Dad, who took Zac home with them when they went. There was someone from the Cure Our Kids charity (these days visits are from Redkite) bringing a care basket of toiletries, vouchers for the car park and the hospital's cafes, and little toys. In between there were nurses coming in to check on Mia and take observations. It all made my head spin.

We'd been told that Karina, being pregnant, shouldn't pick Mia up after the MIBG because she would still be 'radioactive' until the nuclear-medicine solution had passed from her body. But when our little girl got tired or distressed or when she vomited, as she did a lot during the days following the scan, and I wasn't immediately on hand, Karina couldn't help herself and I don't blame her one bit. How could you not pick up your child and comfort her? How could Mia possibly understand that in order to find out about her disease we had to pump chemicals into her that were so dangerous they might pass from her body into ours? All we could do was what we'd done all her life — cuddle her and stroke her and reassure her everything would be okay, even though we had no idea whether that was true or not.

When everyone had left and Mia was resting, Dr Luce came by to tell us the results of the MIGB scan. It was the news we'd been dreading: Mia did have neuroblastoma. Even though he and Dr

Santosh had said the signs were pointing that way, we had hoped against hope that it would turn out to be something else. The space that hope had been occupying inside my chest emptied with every sentence Dr Luce spoke. A sick, cold feeling came over me as the news got even worse.

Not only did Mia have this dreaded form of cancer, the scan showed it had spread to different parts of her body ('metastasised' is the technical term). The tumour wasn't content to surround her kidney, shove her liver out of place and push her aorta, the body's main artery, sideways; it wanted even more of her and had sent cancer cells to set up colonies. It was in her shoulders, knees, hips and leg bones. That's why she had stopped wanting to walk and had lifted her arms out to Karina to be carried every time she had to climb stairs. As well as the big mass inside her making it hard for her to breathe and eat and get comfortable, the cancer in her bones had made them tender and sore.

It was a grade 4 tumour. There is no grade 5. This was the most advanced stage with the lowest survival rate. Dr Luce tried his best to comfort us, telling us it was all too easy to focus on the negative side of the survival rates and overlook the children who were successfully treated. In fact he urged us not to torture ourselves by going online to look up survival rates or other families' experiences but instead to keep our focus firmly on Mia. He said there were clear protocols for treatment, and a plan to follow that gave her the best possible chance. He also said there was one more piece of the puzzle to come — whether the tumour had the MYCN gene or not. We wouldn't know that until the following day.

If her tumour didn't have that gene she would be treated with a combination of chemotherapy, eight rounds most likely, plus surgery. The chemo would aim to shrink the tumour in her abdomen so that it could be taken out surgically, and it would hopefully kill off all the remaining cancer cells, including the ones that had spread into her bones. If she did have the gene, the treatment would be much longer and more intense. The chemo would be a higher dose, and it and the surgery would be just the start. Hope flickered to life again: *Please let the pathology not show the gene. What she's facing already is so much more than enough, please let hers be the less terrible kind of tumour.* As upset and stunned as Karina and I were by what we'd learned, we couldn't show it in front of Mia. We had to do our best to hold it together and pretend to be happy for her sake. There were a lot of deep breaths and plenty of turning away for a moment.

When the time came for me to head home to Zac, my brother Michael and Amy and Molly, Mia seemed content watching DVDs and playing on an iPad, although she'd had a couple more vomits. The medical team had put her on two different kinds of medication designed to get her blood pressure under control, one fast-acting and one long-term. She was also on antibiotics to get rid of the suspected infection, painkillers to relieve her discomfort and laxatives because all the other medications had blocked her up. Her cancer treatment hadn't even started yet.

In the middle of the night she went suddenly and rapidly downhill and her heart rate shot back up to 180, bringing the emergency response team racing in. They stabilised her and she eventually got a few hours' sleep, but she was awake when I arrived at 6 o'clock on Thursday morning. Karina filled me in on what had happened, including the fact that even though Mia was hungry and showing us she wanted food, we weren't allowed to give her anything. She had to fast in case she needed another scan to find out what was causing her vital signs to fluctuate so wildly and what had caused her haemoglobin to drop again to the point where they had started yet another transfusion.

It was exactly one week since Karina had strapped Mia into her car-seat and headed to our GP. Dr Santosh came in with the results of the core biopsy. The news was exactly what we didn't want to hear: Mia's tumour had the MYCN gene. To give her any chance of beating it, they had to treat her in the most aggressive way possible. That meant high-dose chemo, surgery, more chemo, a bone marrow transplant, radiation therapy and something called immunotherapy. This brought long-term risks that started with infertility and radiation-induced secondary cancers and went on from there. But without it our beautiful daughter would certainly die.

Mum and Dad came to visit before heading back home to Queanbeyan and we told them where things stood. Karina phoned her parents and filled them in. We all told each other that this kid was a fighter and if anyone could make it she would, and the doctors were the best, and she was definitely going to get through this, and we would deal with it all one step at a time. But I couldn't get the metallic taste of fear out of my mouth.

Dr Santosh had also told us that the drop in Mia's haemoglobin made them suspect she might have a slow internal bleed so they would be going ahead with the scan, a CT this time, under general anaesthetic of course.

Some time after Mia had been taken in for the scan, Dr Luce came back to see us and, finding Dad and I there, asked to speak to us. He said hospitals weren't always very nice places and despite the best efforts everyone made, things didn't always work out and the doctors weren't able to save everyone. I took what he said to be a follow-on from what he and Dr Santosh had told Karina and me previously — about Mia having the gene that made everything worse. Only much later did I realise that wasn't what he meant at all.

He knew the scan was confirming the team's suspicions. Apart from all the other effects it was having, the tumour was surrounding and damaging blood vessels inside Mia's body, weakening them and making them leak. That's why each transfusion they had given her only fixed the problem temporarily. Even as blood was being put into her veins, it was leaking out somewhere else. They were going to perform surgery to try to stop it. However, far from it being another simple procedure like a transfusion or a biopsy, this was an incredibly complicated all-or-nothing roll of the dice. At the time, I didn't twig to any of this.

I hugged my parents goodbye and told them to drive safely, then went back and passed on to Karina what Dr Luce had said. We didn't have a clue that he was preparing us for the worst and that, as we talked, Mia was a hair's-breadth away from death.

CHAPTER 4

FINDING MY POWER

WHILE EACH DAY BROUGHT us more news about what Mia was up against, the West Indies vs Australia one-dayers had got underway in the Caribbean. I often passed TVs tuned to the matches in the patient lounges or heard scores on the radio in the car as I was driving back and forth to the hospital, but it was as if it was all happening on the other side of a thick glass wall. It didn't seem to have much connection to me at all — a very strange thing, when cricket had occupied so much of my mind for so many decades.

Certainly at 15 I'd thought about little else, especially after my parents agreed to let me play first grade for the ANU Cricket Club in the 1993–94 season (back then, no girl could hold a candle to a great day's play). I'd convinced them that I could handle it but there was a part of me that still wasn't entirely sure. I felt confident that if I was given enough time I would make it, but the sliver of doubt remained because I knew I had only three games to prove myself and I wasn't sure how quickly I'd be able to switch from fifth-grade cricket to this whole new level.

Despite the club's name, players didn't have to have any connection with the Australian National University to join; anyone who wanted to play grade cricket could sign up and aim to get on a team. So I wasn't playing with uni students just a few years older than me, I was a 15-year-old playing with experienced men, many in their late twenties or thirties. They'd been playing first grade for years, in one case for over a decade, and they expected me to get up to speed quickly. They were taking a big risk on me — I hadn't earned the right to be there in the usual way, hadn't done my time and worked my way up through the grades. Was I really good enough to deserve this exceptional opportunity? The only thing I could do to shrink those inner doubts was train even harder to try to eliminate any weaknesses. Then I'd just have to walk out there and give it everything I had.

Being so small meant that, while I had form with the bat, I lacked power. In addition to the rest of my training, I worked at strengthening my forearms using a simple but effective piece of equipment Dad made for me. It was a cricket bat handle attached to a rope which had a weight at the other end. With my hands parallel, I would dip and raise one side then the other in a smaller version of the kind of motion you'd use to paddle a kayak. As the handle dipped and rose, the weighted rope would wind up around it and then wind down again. I spent hours training on it in my bedroom, picturing myself strong enough to smash sixes out of the ground.

My first match with the club in September 1993 — my first-grade debut — was always going to be memorable, but it proved to be an absolute baptism of fire. We bowled first. While they had signed me up for my wicketkeeping skills, one of the very first balls revealed a flaw that no amount of training could overcome: my lack of height.

There was some handy talent on the team including a big West Indian called Ken McLeod. Ken, who was 29 when I joined, had played first-class cricket for a solid five years in the 1980s, first with his home team, Jamaica, then with English side Lancashire in the year they made it to the county championship final. Now living in Canberra, he'd been playing for ANU for four or five years before I joined them. He could do some pretty good work as a right-handed batsman (I recall one match where he got five sixes in a score of 63 not out) but it was as a left-arm quick he really made his mark. Ken opened the bowling and one of the first shots he delivered was a bouncer that went clean over my head, well above my outstretched hands. 'Ah gee,' he grumbled to our captain, Greg Irvine, 'where'd you get this kid!' That wasn't the most comfortable feeling in the world, but I knew others on the team had faith in me so I didn't dwell on it. I just tried to keep my head in the game, and got through the rest of the innings without too many problems.

Then it was our turn to bat. My forearm strength-building notwithstanding, I was unsurprisingly listed at number 11. Despite my excitement at being in the game, the longer the innings went on, the worse I felt. I tried to ignore it and tell myself it was just nerves, but that didn't ring true. When I stopped to think about it I realised that as well as my limbs feeling heavier than usual, I was itching like crazy, especially on my upper half. I had a look under my shirt and saw I was starting to develop an angry rash across my chest. I quietly went over to Dad, who was sitting nearby, and told him about it. He took a quick look and said, 'They're sweat pimples. Go back over there and get ready to get on the field.' I said, 'Dad, are you sure? I feel pretty weird.' He said, 'Yes, it's just a sweat rash. Time to focus now.'

Our number 9 got out and I was on. We needed 30 to win. The opposition team included a guy who had played at state level for South Australia and was known to be a bit of a hothead. He was fielding in slips and at one point he scooped up a ball I'd hit and as he went past me he said, 'If I get a chance at you, young fella, I'm gunna knock your head off, I'm gunna make you wish that ...' I tuned out at this point.

Dad and I had talked a lot about the fact that blokes would undoubtedly try to intimidate me and agreed I just could not let it get to me. In fact if I wasn't going to be able to let it roll off me like water off a duck's back, he and Mum weren't prepared to let me be in the team. Now, standing there and copping this stuff for real, I found I didn't have to make any big pretence of not being bothered. I genuinely wasn't thrown by what this hothead was saying. I let him finish then said, 'Righto,' and gave him a shrug that meant,

What do you want me to say to you, mate? I'm here to play, so let's play.

I didn't end up getting a run, but much more importantly I didn't get out. I was too small to whack away and take the game forward, but I could stand up to whatever came my way, so that's what I did. I gutsed it and got behind the ball and wore a couple and in the end stayed out there long enough for my batting partner to get the runs we needed for victory. (Dad, who has seen me play hundreds, maybe thousands of matches over the years, says it's still among his favourite innings.)

Things might not have gone exactly the way I'd have scripted them for the match — the rash turned out to be chicken pox and I ended up in bed for nearly a week afterwards — but it was a good start. I'd shown my team that I was there to compete and I'd shown my parents that I could handle the pressure. I'd also, inadvertently, shown myself that I could push on through even more discomfort and pain than I'd have guessed. I still felt pretty ordinary the following Saturday, but, with the doctor confirming I was no longer contagious, I was determined to get back out there. I felt keenly that every one of the first three games counted.

In reality I'd already done enough to convince Greg his intuition about me was correct, and recovering from chicken pox would have been an absolutely valid reason for missing a week. But even back then I never, ever wanted anyone to make allowances for me on the cricket field. There were to be no excuses, no reasons why I couldn't deliver. From my first match on, I'd worked as hard as anyone on the team. I was determined to reward my teammates' faith in me. I knew I had to earn my stripes, otherwise I was gone, and the only way to do that was to perform — so I did. They recognised that and respected it.

There would be plenty of memorable moments during my time with ANU but one that's still vivid is my first dismissal, which was of a kind that's rare at any level of the game. Ken bowled, the batsman took a swipe and missed and I caught the ball. That's when things got interesting. In trying to have a go at it, the batsman had actually stepped out of his crease. Registering his lapse instantly, I rolled the ball onto the stumps and turned to the umpire with a big, 'Howzat!' The umpire signalled 'out' and both sides turned to look at me. The opposition looked both startled and annoyed, while my teammates just looked amazed. They started to compliment me on my match awareness in spotting the opportunity. I waved the comments away, saying as casually as I could manage, 'Oh well, I just saw it and went for it. Now let's get another.' But inside I was feeling pretty great.

ANU had undertaken a big recruitment drive for that season, signing a number of new players, some of whom, like me, came from just across the ACT–NSW border. They included Simon Mann and Peter Solway. Peter was a mentor to me, helping me out in more ways than I can count. He also lived in Queanbeyan and drove me to training and matches, gave me bats and much more. He came from a wonderful family with very deep connections to cricket in general and in particular to the Queanbeyan Cricket Club, which he'd joined in 1980 as a 16-year-old. He'd played for Queanbeyan for 13 seasons before making the switch to 'University'. There was an undercurrent of hostility whenever the two clubs went up against one another but one match really stands out in my memory.

It was a twilight game at the Queanbeyan ground. Mum took me to this one and the idea was for her to stay and watch for a while then leave. Dad would come by after work, catch the end of play and drive me home. But this day the aggression from the sidelines was particularly intense and it all seemed to be focused on me. The Queanbeyan supporters had a reputation for having some fairly hard men among them and they were going for it, calling me everything under the sun in the foulest language. At the mild end was, 'You're on the wrong field, sonny. You should be at the kiddies' game. Where's your mummy?' Then it amped up to, 'There's the little traitor — g'arn, get him,' and got worse from there.

It was so bad that when Mum realised what was happening she decided to stick around to keep an eye on me and, just as importantly, make sure Dad didn't catch wind of it. She contacted him and told him not to bother coming; she was there and would stay and bring me home. He said no, that was fine, he was running a bit behind but he wanted to see some of the game and he wouldn't be too much longer. Fearing the abuse I was copping was so bad it would send even my mild-tempered father over the edge, she tried again to talk him out of it without actually saying why. But Dad just said again he was happy to come by and he'd be there soon. I think Mum had a very tense time until Greg Irvine went over to the loudmouths. He said to the ringleader, 'Oy, what do you think you're doing? He's just a kid. Calm it down.' It seemed to work and fortunately by the time Dad arrived the sideline commentary had dropped back to the usual level of one-eyed barracking.

That was among the worst examples, but a fair bit of aggro came my way that entire season, one way and another. As I always did when something surprised or confused me, I talked it over with my father and took my cue from his unruffled reaction. I'd say, 'Gee, Dad, you should have heard this guy today. He said this, this and this.' Dad would say, 'Well, you know why they're doing it. They're trying to win. You're going to have to deal with that. If they're directing all that energy into trying to put you off your game, you must be doing something right.' That made sense to me.

My teammates were also there for me. They took what you might call direct action, especially when I was copping it from the opposition players rather than their supporters. Week in, week out, men from the teams we were playing against would stand over me, trying to intimidate me and get in my head. I just laughed it off, but every now and then it got a bit out of hand. The guys I was playing with appreciated the fact that I didn't rise to the bait but, even so, most of them took a protective attitude towards me: I was their pet project, especially that first year. If they thought the opposition's tactics had gone beyond gamesmanship into something nastier, they took it personally and did what they could to fix things.

Generally that meant making things uncomfortable for the other side until they backed off a bit. If they didn't back off, things got very uncomfortable indeed. There was one mouthy guy who couldn't take a hint. He was batting and he just would not let up. It got so bad that I felt myself start to get rattled. Ken McLeod said in that wonderful West Indian accent, 'Don't you worry, Bradley, I'll fix this,' and he sent down a ball so fast that the batsman could barely see it, let alone play it. The bloke took a punt and moved one way, instantly realising his mistake when the ball connected with his hand — from memory, breaking his thumb. People tended to lay off if they knew you had that kind of support behind you. That is, of course, unless they were actually part of your own team.

Simon Mann, seven years older than me, was an absolutely lovely bloke off the field but an explosive cricketer. We put it down to him being a fiery redhead, but, whatever the explanation, he underwent a personality change between the change room and the pitch. And he didn't discriminate: if he didn't like what you were doing, you'd cop it from him, teammate or opposition alike. Looking back on some of his classic blow-ups, he once said to me with a shake of the head, 'It really never bothered you, did it, when I was abusing one of the blokes on our team? Even if it was you, it never seemed to faze you. Other people would crack it but you'd just laugh or give me some cheeky comment back or say, "Shut up, Simon, and get on with your job" and that was that.'

At the time, beyond those occasional conversations with Dad, I didn't think too much about this aspect of my game. But even though I wouldn't have been able to articulate it, I recognised that only a handful of the many other players I saw in action in schoolboy and state rep teams had a similar sense of inner focus. For instance, Brett Lee, even at 16 or 17, stood out from everyone around him, even though some of the other kids were very skilled. Phil Jaques did too. Drive was a big part of it, but it was more than that. The way they looked at the game and handled pressure was different from other people. From a young age they had the mental capacity to stay focused, no matter what. Physical ability is the base-level requirement for achievement in sports but it's nowhere near enough. If you don't also have exceptionally strong mental control you won't get much past 'promising'.

In December it was time for the 1993 Under-17s national championships. Having only turned 16 two months previously, I still qualified for that age group. Not only was I once again chosen as part of the ACT squad, I was named captain. I headed down to the carnival, held this time in Adelaide, with two things at the forefront of my mind: leading the team in a way that would do ACT proud and performing well enough to win a place in the Australian Under-17s development squad.

As a keeper, getting into this 'merit team' posed the usual problem: numerous contenders for just a couple of spots. Once again it was a matter of being strategic to ensure I made an impression. I took decisions during games based on what would produce the best results for the team I was captaining. But I also made sure I knew who all the selectors were, and if one came near when we were fielding, whenever possible I brought on my medium-pace bowlers and told them to send balls down the leg-side — giving me the best shot of making a stumping or two when it mattered.

It all worked brilliantly. The previous year the ACT had come seventh out of seven teams, just as expected. This year we made it to the semi-finals, coming fourth. As well as that, I got offered one of the coveted merit team spots and so did two other players from the team, batsman Paul Gambale and bowler Jesse Edwards. It was the first time the ACT had ever managed to have so many players selected. Everyone involved was over the moon.

Being chosen not only put the three of us on the national cricket talent radar, it also offered us the invaluable experience of a week at the Australian Cricket Academy when the season was over. There we would get to meet and be coached by some of the biggest names in the history of cricket in this country, including Rod Marsh, who was chair of the selection panel for the development squad in addition to running the Academy. I couldn't wait to get back down to Adelaide and pit my skills against the very best of my peers.

When the time came it was just as much fun as I'd hoped it would be. They worked us quite hard, which I loved. Much of the week was devoted to the specific skills that had earned us our place, with a 'camp' for each speciality. I was keen to test myself against the most talented keepers from around the country and when I did I thought, *Hang on a minute, I'm not out of place.* Objectively I saw that I was as good as, if not better than, anyone there. It was a significant step in making the mental shift from being one of those thousands upon thousands of kids daydreaming about wearing the Baggy Green cap to realising that, although there was a hell of a long way to go, it was a realistic goal.

Apparently other people also saw my potential — well, that was the point of the camp, after all. Many years later I was talking to Paul Ryan, who played in the NSW Second XI and in first grade for Sydney club St George. It turned out he had been in Adelaide for the wicketkeepers' camp too, although I didn't know him at the time. He asked me if I remembered the experience. When I said yes, he said, 'You made quite an impression. I went back to the NSW team and said, "I've just seen the next NSW keeper. He's a young kid from Canberra."'

Back home I continued to go from strength to strength with the ANU first-grade team. I learned so much during my time there, including how important senior players are in setting the tone for any team, knowledge that would turn out to be crucial for me years later with both the NSW and Australian sides. I honed my skills with every game and learned about the unmatched satisfaction of delivering solid performances and earning the respect that comes with that. Both Greg Irvine and Peter Solway had told me not to worry too much about the lack of power in my batting. They knew that would come as I developed physically. In the meantime, they said, I should just focus on technique. It was great advice. Over the course of that first season I moved from bottom of the batting order up to number eight, having only got out something like three times. The following season started strongly, and I was keen to push things and see what I could really do. But my summer was not the one I'd planned.

As Year 11 came to an end in 1994, I was one of two Queanbeyan schoolboy players who had done well enough in the South Coast

Combined High Schools (CHS) competition to be chosen to play for the state CHS team. The other, Nathan Reid, borrowed a car and we went to Sydney together for the competition, splitting the driving. All the players were billeted out in accommodation that had been provided not too far from Penrith, where the games were being played. The two of us and a few others were being put up above a pub. The evening before the first game some of the guys wanted to go downstairs and have a beer. I knew that a couple of them had already turned 18 but I didn't know about the others. I'd only just turned 17 and I felt really uncomfortable about the whole thing. I didn't want to be a wowser, but I didn't want be down there illegally drinking, either. In the end, two of the guys decided to go to Kings Cross, getting the okay from Nathan to borrow the car we'd driven up in. That gave me my out: I'd recently got my P-plates so I volunteered to be the designated driver (I had no idea it was 74 long kilometres from Penrith to the Cross).

My plan worked just fine for the first half of the night. The two of them had beers at a few different places but didn't pressure me to drink. Finally, around 3 a.m. they were ready to head back. Forty-five minutes later we were still driving, but I was feeling fine, thinking to myself, *Nearly there now. How good's this? I've dodged a bullet tonight.* At this point the windows started to fog. Even though I wasn't totally familiar with the car, the central window controls were in the usual place. I pressed what I thought was the button for my window but one of the ones in the back went down instead. I looked down at the buttons, trying to get my finger on the right one. It was only for a few seconds, but it was just enough of a lapse of attention to send us off the road and down into a gully. The car smacked into a tree and the front end concertinaed in on me, snapping my brake foot back. Still careening forward, we skidded between two huge boulders. I have no idea how we didn't smash into them.

Finally, we stopped. The entire crash had probably only taken a matter of seconds, but it seemed to go on forever. Incredibly, my two passengers weren't hurt, but they were in shock and yelled,

'Get out, get out, the car's going to blow!' They both jumped out and started running. I got my door open and stepped out to follow them, but as soon as I put my foot down I knew I'd done some damage. Still thinking the petrol tank might go up, I tried to take another step and felt the bones move inside my ankle in a way that was badly wrong. I sank to the ground. The other guys came back to help me and the next thing I knew everything was being lit up by flashing police and ambulance lights.

I was taken by ambulance to Nepean Hospital. I phoned Dad and didn't get much more out than, 'I've been in a car accident' before he said, 'Where are you? I'm coming now.' The emergency doctor looked at my foot and confirmed it was a bad break. It was still pre-dawn so nothing could happen for a few hours, but they gave me more pain relief and scheduled me for orthopaedic surgery that afternoon, when two metal pins would be inserted to hold everything together. I must have slept for a couple of hours, then the nurses came in and started going through the pre-surgery procedures. That was, until Dad arrived.

Dad had already got onto our family GP, an ex-sportsman himself. They talked about what was likely to happen in the hospital and came up with a plan to bring me home and have me treated by a specialist in Canberra. When Dad arrived at the hospital, the staff discussed what they were planning to do, but Dad said, 'No, he's not going to have that procedure. Could you please just immobilise the ankle; I'm going to take him back to Canberra for treatment.' The doctor in charge wasn't at all happy, but Dad was quietly insistent and eventually they did as he asked. He got me out to the car, not saying much. I really was not looking forward to the conversation that I knew was coming, so we were barely out of the car park before I pretended to fall asleep. I kept up the act for the whole three-hour trip home.

When we did finally talk, Dad certainly wasn't pleased about what had happened, but he and Mum were mostly relieved the outcome hadn't been much, much worse. They knew it was a genuine accident, with my inexperience behind the wheel mostly to blame. They never held the thousands of dollars they paid out for my share of costs from the accident against me.

After a couple of days, when the swelling had gone down, Dad took me to the ankle specialist the GP had recommended and explained that I was a wicketkeeper showing enough talent to get me noticed at the national level. We talked about the specifics of how I needed to be able to crouch and move and the surgeon came up with an approach that still used two pins but placed them in such a way that, if I did the post-surgery physical rehab as prescribed, I would have no problem continuing as a keeper.

I took what he said very seriously. The surgery went well and then I threw myself into rehab. It was the school holidays but I really didn't have time for my mates or the girl I'd started seeing, I was too focused on getting my ankle right. I needed to build up strength and flexibility without too much weight-bearing. Hydrotherapy was the answer and I had a bright idea about how to make it happen. Friendly neighbours across the street had an above-ground backyard pool which they agreed to let me use. I woke at 6 a.m., got myself across there on my crutches and walked around that pool for hours. I'd come home to get something to eat and do different physio exercises, then I'd head out again for yet more pool walking.

This went on for the entire six-week summer break. I didn't have to be talked into doing it and I didn't complain. It was me pushing myself, driven by my need to get back to cricket at the level I'd been playing at. Looking back, Mum and Dad said something changed in me after that accident. I became not ruthless exactly, but laser-focused about what I wanted to achieve and what I was willing to do to get there. The fear that I might never get full movement back in my ankle drove me to push myself as hard as I could to make sure that didn't happen.

The accident ruled me out of the annual national youth teams' competition, which felt like a terrible blow at the time but turned out to be a blessing in disguise. Because I'd been doing so well, the ACT selectors had been keen for me to go up to the next age division, the Under-19s, even though I was eligible for one more year in the Under-17s. Going to the higher age group would have given me three years in the Under-19s, which seemed like a wonderful opportunity to advance. But, as it happened, the players in that age group at that particular time tended to be more interested in partying than playing, or at least playing at the level I wanted to. And when it comes to team sports you can only achieve your individual best when you're part of a team that shows hunger and commitment. Missing out on becoming a part of that peer group turned out to be a good thing for me.

Eight or nine weeks after the crash, the surgeon checked the ankle and pronounced it healed and indeed it felt pretty good again. ANU had suggested I return in second grade to give me time to get back up to speed. I said no, I would rather take a bit more time, tell them when I was completely ready and then go straight back into first grade, and that's what happened. I found form very quickly on my return. Having started that season as eight on the batting order, the combination of the match experience I'd accumulated, the extra power delivered by an adolescent growth spurt and my intense post-crash single-mindedness saw me rise to become one of the side's best batsmen, playing at number four. The whole team lifted that season and we ended 1994–95 as winners of both the twilight and one-day competitions as well as minor premiers and overall premiership winners — the first time ANU had held the trophy since 1986.

By the start of my third season with the club I felt like I was firing on all cylinders, and I found I'd developed the ability to change the rhythm of a game. In the process of coming into my own with the bat and finding how far I could push things, I definitely made mistakes, taking chances that wiser heads might have resisted. But I also scored at a rate that got people talking, and my teammates were happy to let me go for it. We would go up against teams with players who had given me a hard time a year or two earlier and they literally didn't recognise me now when I came out to bat. One of them was a bowler who looked at me in surprise when I whacked one of his first balls for four and said to him, 'Payback time. I'm not that kid anymore.' He had no idea what I meant. He turned to his keeper and asked, 'What's this guy on about?' The keeper just shook his head, so I answered instead, 'Today we're going to play,' and proceeded to hit him all over the ground. It was a powerful feeling and I wanted more of it.

CHAPTER 5

BACK FROM THE BRINK

DAY 7 IN THE hospital with Mia brought us terrifyingly close to losing her, although we had no idea at the time. All day there had been signs that her condition was deteriorating dangerously. Her stomach, for instance, was huger than ever. In fact it was so big it was becoming hard to get her nappies done up. She didn't have much interest in anything; she just slept for hours at a time, barely moving. But in the context of how sick she was already, none of these symptoms especially stood out to me. Even Karina didn't realise just how bad things were.

Mia had gone in for the CT scan at 3.30 p.m. and was out by 4.30 p.m. It was the fourth general anaesthetic she'd had in less than a week but she didn't recover from this one the way she had done after the previous scan. She was in the Post-Operative Recovery ward for two hours, far longer than expected. When she did finally start to wake up it took ages and apart from opening her eyes she didn't move. She'd had to fast all day before being put under, but she showed no interest in food. Instead, she fell back into a sleep so deep and motionless she looked like she was still anaesthetised. She also had a rash on her body that the doctors thought might have been a reaction to the 'packed cell' blood transfusion she had received earlier in the day.

I'd become aware over the previous 24 hours that I was coming down with something, most likely a bug picked up on one of the legs of my journey home. I knew that Karina would have company and help from her dad, Phil, and sister, Danielle, and my brother Chris and his partner, Jenna, who were coming to visit over the course of the morning, so I'd taken the opportunity to go to our family GP. He confirmed that as well as a head cold I had a throat infection, for which he prescribed me antibiotics. I felt the lurgy really take hold over the course of the day. Even though I'd started wearing a face mask in the hospital, I was still worried about the possibility of passing my germs on to Mia (and maybe even to other vulnerable children in the ward). So Karina and I arranged that I would sit in the car park for the evening and she would keep me updated by phone.

But when Mia didn't respond the way she should have in Recovery, Dr Luce asked Karina where I was. She told him and he said, 'Do you want to get him in here?' She explained that I was unwell and didn't want to take the chance of making Mia sicker. Dr Luce then said to Karina, 'How do you think Mia is at the moment?' Suddenly starting to feel nervous, she replied, 'She's not waking up properly, is she?' 'No, she's not,' he said. He knew what we didn't — that our daughter was already as sick as she could possibly get. He said kindly, 'Why don't you ring Brad and tell him to come in?' She phoned me and I started to repeat my concerns. Karina said, 'I know, Brad, but Dr Luce said just come.'

Even at this point we still didn't realise how dire Mia's situation was. The doctors and nurses were so professional and so caring that we felt that whatever was going on they would handle it. We figured they knew what they were doing and anything that could happen would be something they'd seen before. We were worried, but no more than we had been a few hours earlier. We were still in the mindset of assuming there was a way of treating every problem that could arise. When he'd told me and Dad a few hours earlier that hospitals weren't nice places, Dr Luce had said specifically, 'Prepare yourself for the idea that things don't always go to plan.' I'd listened and nodded and thought I knew what he meant: not every cancer can be cured, not every single child will make it, so despite all the treatments they were going to throw at Mia over the next few months, they couldn't guarantee the outcome. I was oblivious to the real warning in his words.

While we were still in Recovery, with Mia unable to stay awake, we got a visit from an interventional radiologist called Dr David Lord. Interventional radiologists do complicated invasive treatments within the body without the need to open up the patient as in traditional surgery. They inject a special dye to 'light up' the blood vessels and then, using scans and x-rays to guide them, insert a needle into an artery and push tiny tubes through the blood vessels until they get to the part they're going to treat.

It's an amazing process, but Dr Lord was very matter of fact about it all. In strict technical terms, people in his job aren't classified as surgeons but he had the same off-hand manner surgeons often have. He said, 'Mia is bleeding internally. Her abdomen is filling up with blood. I'm going to try to stop that by doing a procedure called an embolisation.' Karina was familiar with the process but for my benefit Dr Lord explained that it involved trying to find the origin of the bleed in order to block up the leaking blood vessel or vessels. This is sometimes done with a special kind of glue or putty or even miniature metal coils, but in Mia's case he was planning to use tiny plastic beads. He drew a sketch to demonstrate how the beads would be placed in every affected vessel.

When he'd gone I phoned my parents to tell them what was happening. They hadn't even made it back to their place yet, having stopped at the home of my cousin Peter and his wife, Michelle, who live a few minutes away from them in Queanbeyan and with whom we're all really close. They were having a bite to eat when I rang but their immediate response was, 'We're on our way.' They got straight in the car to drive more than three and a half hours back to Westmead.

Mia was still sleeping when she was taken down to Radiology for the embolisation. Karina and I walked beside her cot as it was being wheeled along. We turned a corner and I stepped back to let the cot get around. As I did so I saw a couple of players from the Parramatta Eels rugby league team who I knew a little. They were at the hospital on a goodwill visit, just like the kind I'd made many times before. They assumed I was there for the same reason. They said hello and, knowing my connection with the ACT, started chatting to me about the Canberra Raiders. I made a response then indicated Mia and said, 'I'm here with my daughter.' Looking shocked and concerned as they took it all in, they wished us well and stepped aside. The gulf between us felt a mile wide.

At 7.30 p.m., with Mia in having the procedure, Karina and I went back up to the Camperdown ward, where we waited and waited. The minutes crawled by. It was after 11 p.m. when Dr Lord appeared to tell us how it had gone. He had none of Dr Luce's warm manner but projected aloof self-assurance and ate from a packet of barbecue-flavoured chips as he spoke. He said, 'It went well, I'm really happy.' *Munch, munch.* 'I couldn't find the site of the bleeding but I embolised all the vessels leading into the tumour, while hopefully keeping the gates open on the blood vessels that supply the kidney.' *Munch, munch.* 'So I think I may have stopped the bleeding and hopefully she improves from here. Any questions?' I said, 'No, you're the expert. If you're happy, we're happy.' He gave us a farewell nod and walked out, still munching away.

Mia was in the Paediatric Intensive Care Unit (PICU). Two parents or carers were allowed in at a time (though only to sit with the child, not to sleep there), but it was definitely not a good idea for me to be there when I wasn't completely healthy, so Karina went in alone. Mia was still out of it, lying flat on her back, and Karina said her tummy looked bigger than ever. She had two tubes in her nose: one carrying oxygen to help her breathe and a nasogastric (NG) tube running down the back of her throat to deliver much-needed nutrients in the form of liquid straight to her stomach.

Not until the following Monday, five days later, were we able to appreciate what an incredible thing had happened. One of the surgical team saw Karina in a corridor and said, 'Dr Lord did an amazing job saving Mia's life the other night.' Karina started to nod then said, 'Hang on, sorry, what do you mean?' The surgeon, Dr Tori Lawrence, said, 'Oh, if he hadn't been able to stop the bleeding the way he did, Mia wouldn't have survived the night. Going into the procedure we feared she was gone. He did an absolutely amazing job.'

When Karina told me about the conversation I felt my knees almost buckle and I could see it had hit her just as hard. I was relaying what the surgeon had said to Dad when it suddenly came to me: *Oh my god, that's what Dr Luce was saying. He was warning us we were right on the point of losing our little girl.* I started to say to Dad, 'Do you remember that conversation in that room with …' but before I got out any more he said, 'Yes, he was telling us that …' We finished the sentence at the same time, in the same shocked tone: 'Mia was going to die.'

(We finally got the chance to personally give our thanks to Dr Lord almost four months later, when Karina passed the miracle-worker in a corridor. Thinking she recognised him, but not a hundred per cent sure since he was in a suit and looked very different to when we'd last seen him, all kitted out in his theatre scrubs, she said, 'Dr Lord?' He stopped and said, 'Yes?' She said, 'My daughter, Mia Haddin, you saved her life.' He said, 'Yes.' Karina said, 'Thank you.' He gave her a friendly pat on the shoulder and kept walking. Who knows how many lives he had saved since we had seen him last? That level of skill was literally all in a day's work for him, taking place in a public hospital where anyone who needed his help gets it. It's mind-blowing.)

After the operation, Mia remained in PICU where she had one-on-one nursing. Her stomach was slightly larger than it had been the day before but all the other signs were very positive: her haemoglobin remained steady and her temperature didn't fluctuate as much. Encouraged by Mia's nurse, Karina went down to the

Camperdown ward to get some sleep, while I remained nearby in the parked car. I was very relieved when she called first thing in the morning from PICU to tell me that Mia was half sitting up in her cot and looking much better.

The previous day Drs Luce and Santosh had explained the course of the treatment they planned to give Mia to try to cure the neuroblastoma. They outlined the risks and potential side-effects of each element of the treatment, the outcomes they hoped to get at each stage and how they could tell if it was all working. It would begin with intensive chemotherapy. Partway through the chemo, some of Mia's stem cells would be extracted via her central line and stored. All being well, following chemo she would have major abdominal surgery to remove the tumour.

When she had recovered sufficiently she would have one more cycle of chemo — an extremely high dose to kill off any remaining cancer cells (and inevitably many of her precious good cells too, making this a particularly dangerous stage of the treatment). Then her own stem cells would be put back into her body in a bone marrow transplant. Following that she would have radiation therapy and finally a very painful treatment called immunotherapy. In all, the process would take 14 months. But she wouldn't have to stay in Westmead that whole time. Certain treatments required hospital stays (for instance, five-day blocks during each chemo cycle, and six weeks in isolation after the bone marrow transplant) but in between she could come home and be treated as an outpatient.

The information they gave us was a huge amount to absorb. I felt like I was being pumped so full I had no chance of taking in the details. I'd be relying on Karina to explain it to me as we went along. But Drs Luce and Santosh outlined everything patiently and clearly, and they welcomed our questions. The first question Karina and I had was why had it taken seven days to get a diagnosis? The tumour was growing the whole time and Mia had become much worse over the week since she'd been admitted, so why hadn't they just got her on the operating table and cut the thing out? The doctors explained that surgery to remove the tumour still wasn't an

option because it was so large and was intertwined with her right
kidney and adrenal gland as well as blood vessels. One of the main
aims of the chemo was to shrink it enough so that it could be taken
out surgically. The other was to kill off the cancer cells that had
spread to different parts of the body.

Karina then asked about something that I knew was causing
her a lot of anguish. She said, 'Looking back, we think Mia was
showing symptoms as long ago as January. Would she have been
all right if I'd brought her in back then? Would that have prevented
this?' In his kind but straightforward manner Dr Luce said, 'You
can't let yourself think that way. You couldn't have been expected
to know what was going on. You've got to draw a line, accept that
you did your best for Mia then and you're doing your best for
her now. You need to focus on what lies ahead and you can't do
that if you're trying to rewrite the past.' That was a big thing to
do but we could both see that it made sense. Dr Luce then added
something that really helped us let go of the dark fear that we had
failed Mia by not seeing what was going on sooner. He told us that
this particular type of tumour would either respond to chemo or
it wouldn't, regardless of its size. He added that they would know
quite quickly which way it was going to go.

I asked what might have caused the cancer. I was wondering
if there was something we could have done to prevent it, but I was
also thinking about Zac and the baby growing in Karina's belly and
whether they were at risk. Drs Luce and Santosh explained that
so much about neuroblastomas is still unknown. A great deal of
research is being done to try and figure out if the tumour is somehow
triggered by a faulty gene that the person is born with. There's also
lots of work underway to try to improve treatments. But progress
has been incredibly slow compared to some other childhood cancers,
including particular forms of leukaemia, for which survival rates are
now very high. Dr Luce did, however, say that it was very unlikely
that the other two children would develop it.

The treatment protocol they were going to give Mia was being
used in other countries including France and Germany. It was very

clearly laid out and they would be following it precisely, but it was also still being refined. Data from every child who received this treatment went back into a central database. Researchers could then see what kinds of side-effects were associated with what doses and adjust the protocols, improving things for kids who came after. They were also able to keep track of how many children's lives were saved and in how many the cancer had returned.

Dr Luce and his team were always careful not to state anything as an absolute certainty, so as not to make people lose hope: parents are much better able to help their kids through treatment if they can cling to optimism instead of giving way to despair. So when they talked to us about relapse they phrased it very carefully. Even so, what we learned was chilling. Basically, if everything worked just as it should do and Mia was cleared of cancer, she still wouldn't be out of the woods. That's true of anyone with the disease — if, after treatment, you are cancer-free, the doctors don't say you're cured; they say you're 'in remission'. This period begins when all the treatment is complete and it lasts for the following five years. The concern is that during that time you might relapse. If the cancer does come back, they again try to get rid of it. But with Mia's particular type of neuroblastoma the first two years after treatment were critical. Research showed that if a child relapsed within this period there was very little chance of a cure.

We needed to get a sense of the big picture at the start of the process, but Dr Luce urged us to always keep our focus on whichever stage of treatment Mia was having rather than trying to predict an outcome we couldn't control. As he knew very well, the lack of control is one of the hardest things to accept when you find yourself in the position we were in. As a parent, you want to protect your kids and do everything you can to give them the best possible chance in life. But when your child has a life-threatening illness, there is nothing you can do. Karina, me, her parents, my parents — every single one of us would have taken Mia's illness on ourselves if we'd been able to spare her. But we couldn't.

Instead, we had to place our trust in strangers. Admittedly, these were people who were at the top of their field, but still, they were people we had barely met. Looking back on it now, I can see that part of the reason I trusted them was that they were such a cohesive team. Teamwork has been the heart of my whole life in sport and I know good teamwork when I see it. I could sense immediately that Dr Luce and his team were a tight group who worked well together. Whether that would be enough, only time would tell. We had no choice but to let go and put our faith in them.

That meant following Dr Luce's advice to take it all step by step, and the first step was chemo. Even though less than 24 hours had passed since Dr Lord had performed the embolisation, Mia had improved so much they were going to start chemo that very day, 23 March 2012, right there in intensive care.

Karina called me and, wearing a surgical mask, I came up from the car park for the formal briefing and permission process. Dr Santosh and Oncology Clinical Nurse Consultants Erin Sheehan and Virginia Greene explained that Mia would have six rounds of chemo, each one running for almost four weeks. They would do a scan after the first two rounds. That would tell them if the chemo was working — if it was, the tumour would have shrunk. Mia would then have three more chemo cycles and more scans, after which they would operate.

When they felt she'd recovered enough from surgery, the final cycle would begin. She would only need to stay in hospital until she had recovered from the surgery, probably for a week or so, and then we could take her home. She would be an outpatient for most of the final chemo cycle before being readmitted for the bone marrow transplant stage. That was the plan, anyway.

The chemo would be delivered in two-day blocks, with each block involving a different combination of drugs (and different likely side-effects for each block). But the overall pattern remained the same: four days of receiving the drugs intravenously (along with lots of fluids to flush them through the system), followed by a three-week break. During this time Mia's platelets (or clotting cells) and her white blood cells (including neutrophils) would fall to almost nothing, thanks to the chemo, then gradually build back up just in time for the next hit.

I didn't get it. White blood cells are the ones that fight infection, right? So why kill them off? Dr Santosh explained it's an unfortunate side-effect of the fact that chemo is designed to specifically target the cells in your body that divide fast, like cancer cells. Unfortunately, white blood cells are also in that category. They are collateral damage. So people on chemo lose their immunity and become vulnerable to every passing bug. It's even worse if they're young children, since the drugs also erase the immunity they've gained from normal childhood vaccinations for things like diphtheria and measles. The awful truth, we learned, was that it might not be the cancer that would kill Mia; it might be the treatment.

The hard news kept coming. The type of chemo Mia was getting and her young age meant that if she did make it through she was likely to be left with a bunch of very serious side-effects. Permanent hearing loss, damage to the heart, slower cognitive processing and problems with puberty and reproduction were the ones I took in. Those things all sounded bad, but we'd just have to face them if and when they happened. As it was, we would consider ourselves blessed to get Mia to her second birthday, never mind to puberty and beyond.

Again, the amount of information was overwhelming, but Dr Santosh and Erin broke it all down in a way we could understand and when it was time for us to sign the consent forms we were as well informed as we could possibly be. They gave us a handbook that covered everything they'd told us, a treatment diary and a textbook on childhood cancers that answered any other question we might think up. Any question except the unanswerable one: will this save our little girl's life?

Even at this point we didn't fully appreciate what we were up against — we hadn't seen the tumour. It had never occurred to me to look at a scan because I wouldn't have been able to make head or tail of it anyway, but Karina leapt at the chance. Through her work she had seen many, many tumours and she'd been expecting Mia's to be maybe the size of an apricot. The reality shocked her so much she struggled for the words to describe it to me. The tumour was enormous, taking up the majority of the right side of Mia's abdominal cavity. Karina had never seen anything like it.

Over the next few days I felt even more helpless than I already had. I was still crook with the throat infection, which meant that I couldn't do the one thing I wanted to — go into PICU and take my turn sitting with Mia as she started chemo. Instead, Karina, Marg and my mum took it in shifts.

Chemo drugs are toxic — that's how they kill cancer cells — and that means there are tons of precautions around them, as we'd learned in the briefing. Any item that has anything to do with the drugs is identified in purple: the nurses who administer it wear purple gowns and gloves, the bags and bins for contaminated chemo waste are purple, the warning signs are purple. This is so no-one forgets the danger and becomes careless at any time, because even after the drugs have been administered, they stay in the patient's bodily fluids for up to a week following the treatment. We'd been warned that we had to be careful not to let any of Mia's fluids touch our skin; however, in one of her phone calls to me, Karina told me that was just impossible. When I was well enough to return to the hospital room, a few days after Mia's first treatment, I could see what she meant.

The drugs made Mia vomit and gave her diarrhoea, so there were lots of clean-ups and the nurses couldn't do all of them. We were supposed to put on a gown and gloves to wipe her down when she got sweaty with fevers or even to dry her tears. But the number one thing we all wanted to do was to make her a bit more comfortable. How could you expect such a tiny child to understand she would just have to wait while you put on a whole load of gear? You couldn't. So often the best we could do was to quickly grab a pair of gloves. I did worry about this at first, especially for Karina with the unborn baby, but she was totally pragmatic about things. Her view was that we should be careful and follow procedure as much as possible, but that Mia's needs came first.

What was happening to Mia had hit Karina just as hard as it did me, but she adapted exceptionally quickly. Even the staff commented on it. After we'd been there a while, one of the senior nurses looked back on those early days and said that while I was like a deer in headlights for ages, as most parents are in this situation, Karina somehow managed to absorb it all and get completely into the rhythm of our new reality. In fact, by the time Mia started chemo Karina was not just maintaining her diary, she was also keeping track of events by taking photos with her phone-camera all through the day.

It's not something that would have occurred to me to do in a million years. But Karina has always loved taking pictures; she does it all the time. She organises the photos and makes up albums to mark special occasions. I was used to her doing it, but why on earth would we want photographs of Mia looking desperately sick? Karina, however, took this amazing long view. She said, 'This whole 14 months is going to go by really quickly. If we don't record it now, we'll look back and it will all be a blur and if Mia later asks us what happened in detail we won't be able to tell her.'

I didn't know about that; every day seemed to sear some horrible new image into my memory and I couldn't imagine forgetting any of it. I also wasn't quite sure whether taking photos was something we should be doing in a hospital. Karina told me that she had felt awkward about it the first few times, especially in Intensive Care, but she said, 'No-one minds, honestly. In fact the nurses have started offering to take the photos for me.' Fair enough. Anything that helped Karina cope, including taking photos and keeping a diary, was fine with me.

Ten days had passed and, after initial speculation in the media about why I'd flown home, things had gone quiet — news of Mia's diagnosis hadn't leaked. It just showed the honourable nature of the people we encountered at the hospital and of our inner circle, who knew the basics. It also illustrated the tightness of the Australian Test team. On one of her brief breaks at home, Karina had ducked up to the local supermarket, where she bumped into Mark and Judi Taylor.

Tubby, as he is affectionately known, is about as well connected as you can get in Australian cricket. Not only is he a former Test captain and a current Nine Network commentator, but he's also a director on the board of Cricket Australia. His playing career was coming to an end just as mine was starting and we'd only played together in one game, for Northern Districts, so Karina hadn't met him. But standing right next to Mark and Judi, she felt she ought to introduce herself. The first thing Tubby said was, 'How is Brad? Is he okay?' Karina said, 'Yes, it's actually not Brad who ... It's Mia, our daughter. She's in hospital at Westmead. She's got cancer.' They expressed shock and sympathy and it was clear from the look on their faces that they hadn't heard even a whisper about it.

We didn't want to start talking in public at length about what was going on, but now that we knew more and Mia had started treatment we figured we could give people a one-sentence update and leave it at that. Following his Test career, Michael Slater had found success in the media, including on Sky Sports Radio's *The Big Sports Breakfast* program, to which I was also a regular contributor. I told Slats that it was okay for him to tell his listeners that Mia had cancer, which he did, sending us his best wishes. A sports columnist then texted me to see if I was okay with him running a small item and asked if there was anything else he could do. A few days later, on 1 April, the one-paragraph piece ran in one of the Sunday papers, and that was pretty much that. Karina and I have never been people to seek the spotlight or court publicity. We were already dealing with so much it would have been incredibly stressful to have to fend off the media as well (and I couldn't imagine anything worse than inviting the world into your life at a time like this). So it was a huge relief when everyone took the high road.

We kept visitors to the hospital to an absolute minimum — we couldn't take any risks with Mia's suppressed immune system — but those close to us sent us wonderful messages of support and thoughtful gifts and found ways to give us practical help. The people Karina had emailed on her first night in hospital got back to her sending love and kind thoughts. That included the mothers' group she'd been part of for the three years since Zac was born. They all saw each other every week with the kids and were very close. Without having to be asked, these lovely ladies swung straight into action. They were all very familiar with our house and knew we had a chest freezer in the laundry, which was separate from the main house and accessible even when the house was locked. So they cooked up a storm and stocked the freezer with comforting, healthy meals for us and Zac that we could warm up at home or microwave at the hospital. (In fact, taking turns, they kept it topped up for the next 18 months, a mammoth and hugely appreciated effort.)

Meanwhile the chemo got underway. The drugs were delivered straight into Mia's central line. Each bag took around an hour and a half to empty, and while it was going on she had to try to not move around too much. A bit of visual distraction went a long way. Before she got sick she had just reached the age where she was starting to speak and now, as kids do, she was saying more words every day. The two best ways of keeping her entertained during chemo were the DVD and iPad — 'DDD' and 'Hipad' in Mia-speak. Karina's sister, Danielle, was great at sourcing discs and loading up the iPad with Mia's favourites, like *In the Night Garden*, *Playschool*, *The Wiggles* and *Barbie*, and keeping the selection updated so that there was always something new for her to discover.

But it was hard for Mia to get into a comfortable position where she could see the screen. The hospital had those over-bed tables on wheels, the ones that have a top that can swing around, but they didn't fit the cots. No sooner had Dad seen the problem than he came up with a solution. He measured the cot then and there and drew up a design for a wooden table that would slot onto its rails at just the right height. But he wasn't about to solve the problem for Mia alone if he could also help other little ones. So he went home and got the joiner who does work for him to turn out half a dozen of them and then quietly donated them on his next visit to the hospital, making each day just slightly better for the children who had to be in there. It was a typically kind and practical gesture.

Many friends, from cricket and other parts of our lives, sent flowers or food baskets or other gifts. We found it was especially touching when people included Zac, as many did; the ones who did this tended to be parents themselves. Most of the time we weren't able to get back in touch with people to thank them individually because we were just too consumed with caring for Mia, but we truly appreciated every one of those gestures.

I couldn't let go of my worry about the baby who was on the way despite the fact that there had been clear scans all the way through the pregnancy. But even though Karina felt that the chances of anything being wrong were absolutely tiny, she was happy to get a referral and go for an ultrasound just to ease my mind. It came back all clear, to my relief. Whatever we could do to make things a little easier for each other we did. We had a battle on our hands now for Mia's life, and the more distractions we could remove the harder we'd be able to fight.

CHAPTER 6

THE APPRENTICE

UNTIL SOMETHING AS DRASTIC as a child with cancer changes all the rules, a lot of us think of life as a linear path — if you work hard enough you'll progress from point A to point B. That's certainly how I looked at things and it had been as far back as I can remember.

Throughout my teenage years I felt like I was moving up a staircase towards my goal and by 1995, my final year of high school, I was more single-minded about cricket than ever. I did what I needed to get through Year 12 and pass all the subjects in my Higher School Certificate — despite having cheekily told my parents a year or two earlier that you didn't need to be good in school to play for Australia.

I'd copped the first of the injuries that are a constant of any wicketkeeper's career: fracturing a thumb while playing in a CHS carnival. I didn't realise it was actually broken for a week or so afterwards, despite it swelling up like a sausage. I was much more worried about the front tooth I had lost when a ball came off a pad at just the wrong angle. Dad would soldier on through most things himself and he expected us boys to do the same. When one of us got an injury on the sporting field he was a great one for saying, 'Just ice it; it'll be right,' or, if it was a graze, 'Put some zinc on it.' But no amount of ice or zinc would fix my scary new smile. I was sure I was disfigured for life. (At the time, even though I knew an enormous amount about cricket, there were huge parts of life I had no clue even existed. Reconstructive dentistry was one of them.)

Meanwhile I had really come into my own with the bat, scoring my first century for ANU right around the time of my 18th birthday, that October. (I would go on to get another and a 90 before the season was over, ending on an average of 48.6.) There were fantastic opportunities on every front. Both NSW and ACT had a Colts youth development side and I played in both; I captained the ACT team in the 1995 national Under-19s championship. I got the chance to captain ANU's First XI, and acquitted myself well. I was then selected as wicketkeeper-batsman for the Australian Under-19s team, which would cap off the season playing New Zealand at various ACT and NSW grounds throughout March 1996. Cricket even brought me into the Prime Minister's orbit for the first time.

The Prime Minister's XI game is an annual Canberra tradition. It is an invitation match between an Australian team, which consists of established names plus up-and-coming players, and an overseas team here to tour for the summer — this time round, the West Indies. It's customary that the captain of the ACT Under-19s gets to be 12th man, so there I was on the team sheet along with the likes of Dean Jones, Brad Hogg and local boy made good Michael 'Bevo' Bevan. The Windies side we would face included the famed (and feared) Curtly Ambrose and Courtney Walsh.

In the lead-up to the game there is a function for both teams at the prime ministerial residence, The Lodge. I knew Canberra like the back of my hand but the closest I'd come to The Lodge was driving past it on the way to a cricket ground. I was so young and green that even wearing a suit and tie was an unfamiliar experience. We were put up in a hotel the night before the game and taken on a team bus to the function. It was exciting and daunting to see so many great talents up close and nerve-racking to work out how I could talk to them without making an idiot of myself. And then there was the etiquette of meeting the PM, Paul Keating. Fortunately, we were given a protocol briefing on what to say when he shook our hand, how to mingle and what to do when it was time to go. It was a thrilling experience and my parents were filled with quiet pride. Unfortunately, the match itself had to be abandoned just after the toss without a ball being bowled, thanks to torrential rain, but even so it was a very memorable couple of days for a teenager.

During my final two years of school I'd been considering what I'd do after graduation. Getting chosen for the Australian Institute of Sport (AIS) Cricket Academy was my number-one goal, but players often weren't picked for it until they were in their early twenties and maybe had a few first-class games under their belt. So I needed other short-term options. I thought about following my father into carpentry or playing to my interests by doing an Education degree and becoming a PE teacher or doing a Sports Science degree and seeing where that led me.

But I hadn't inherited Dad's aptitude for working with my hands and any uni study was going to be frequently interrupted by my sporting commitments. I figured the best thing I could do was give cricket a crack: get any kind of job that would pay the rent and focus all my energy on working my way up towards the state and hopefully national level. Not everyone shared my enthusiasm. My then girlfriend's father told me flatly that playing cricket for a living was a totally unrealistic plan, that I'd never be able to keep a family that way and that the sooner I came to my senses the better. But my parents were totally supportive. The way they looked at it, I'd be doing the equivalent of completing an apprenticeship.

When it comes to state cricket, it doesn't matter where you were born; you can, of course, play for any state. The two territories, ACT and NT, don't field teams in the Sheffield Shield, but all six states do and there's a solid tradition of players moving interstate in the hope of increasing their chances of getting into a high-level team. That's especially true of wicketkeepers, whose opportunities are so limited. Adam Gilchrist is a prime example. He grew up in New South Wales and played grade cricket in Sydney but was unable to break through into the state side thanks to Phil Emery's lock on the keeper's role, so he moved to Perth to play for Western Australia.

Talent-spotters from other states had made approaches to me, but I wasn't prepared to even consider the option of going elsewhere. I'd grown up idolising the NSW team, with players like the Waugh twins, Glenn McGrath, Bevo and so many other greats who showed just as much pride playing for the Blues as they did for Australia. I was intent on following in their footsteps. Playing first-class state-level cricket was already a pretty lofty ambition, but it wasn't enough for me. My single-minded goal was to play for NSW and NSW alone, to be able to call the hallowed turf of the Sydney Cricket Ground home.

So, with the blessing of my parents, my plan was to move to Sydney in the winter of 1996 and get myself set for the following season when I could start to work my way up. But then something even better came along: the coveted invitation to the Cricket Academy in Adelaide — not in four or five years' time but now, as soon as the playing season was over. Of all the high-performing young players around the country, only a squad's worth, 15, were chosen. It was very rare for a player who'd come up through the ACT system to win one of these places and almost as rare to be accepted at such a young age. I was on cloud nine.

It was a 12-month scholarship that started when the cricket season finished and consisted of nine months' intensive training and development, followed by three months travelling around playing. Everyone who went there was hoping they would ultimately end up playing for their country, but the Academy's official role was as a kind of finishing school for potential state cricketers. You were provided with full board, supervision and a packed weekly schedule, which included a few hours' compulsory work, arranged for you, to earn a bit of spending money.

I was champing at the bit to get going, but before I departed I had some memorable firsts: my international Youth Test and Youth One-Day debuts as part of the Australian Under-19s team, which also included Nathan Bracken and Chris Rogers. We were to play three Tests and three one-day Youth Internationals against the New Zealand Under-19s. First up was a four-day Test. My parents and brothers would have travelled anywhere around the country to see this game but it just happened to be at Canberra's Manuka Oval, a 15-minute drive from our place. The location meant that the whole extended family was able to come and watch, along with a bunch of my schoolmates and ANU teammates.

In a Hollywood movie I would have had a heroic game. But life isn't a movie. New Zealand won the toss and sent us in to bat. After an abysmal start, we were 5 for 173 by the time I walked out in the first innings, nervous but determined. Unfortunately, I only added six before being sent back to the pavilion. Things didn't improve much over the next three days for me or the team, and New Zealand beat us by five wickets. It wasn't the show I was hoping to put on for all those supporters, but I was too excited and proud to be representing Australia and too eager for the next match to worry about it. The initial one-dayer was played at Bowral at the historic Bradman Oval. We fielded first and while I did fine behind the wicket, I got bowled for a duck. (Would you believe it was my tribute to The Don's final Test score? No, me neither.) By the end of New Zealand's tour they had taken out the limited-overs series while we'd won the Youth Test series. It was great experience, and the perfect precursor to the start of my time at the Academy.

When I got down to Adelaide I was pleased to see that Brett 'Binga' Lee had also been chosen. It was good to have at least a somewhat familiar face around the place, this being my first time living away from home. (Perth boy Simon Katich was another in the intake.) After we'd been shown around the facilities and found our spot in the dormitory, Rod Marsh welcomed us in his role as director of the Academy. He emphasised what a special opportunity we'd been given; he then told us he would be working us harder than we'd ever worked and he expected each one of us to give it everything we had. I thought, *Yep, yep, bring it on!*

Bring it on they did. We were up early and we went hard all day. One day would consist of a weights or general fitness session in the morning and a skills session in the afternoon; the next day we might do a swimming session in the morning and work in the nets after lunch. We had lectures on nutrition. We were given media training with mock interviews. We learned about cricket history by having to do assignments on influential people or important Test series. Legends of the sport, including Dennis Lillee and Ian Chappell, came to talk to us and work on specialist skills.

Ian Healy, whose poster I'd had on my bedroom wall, came down to do a week on wicketkeeping. I was in heaven. I tried to take in his every movement and store images away to mentally replay later. I thought then — and still do — that he's the best technician Australia has ever had behind the stumps. I was in awe of him and wanted my style to follow his as closely as possible. I was nervous even opening my mouth at first, but he was so friendly and focused and encouraging that I soon forgot about my nerves. I was drawn to his outstanding work ethic and his incredible attention to detail. He was a true role model.

Even though Rod Marsh had been a wicketkeeper, I didn't spend much time catching balls or looking at footwork with him one on one. Instead he provided us all with an invaluable education in the rich tradition of the game. He helped us see what the Australian way of playing cricket means and how the great players have left the game in a better place than they found it. He taught us to understand the importance of teamwork while still looking at what each player could do to move the game forward, and he instilled in us the importance of playing to win every single time. But I think the single biggest thing he drilled into us was discipline.

He was a hard taskmaster, no doubt about it. He knew exactly how much was required of a first-class cricketer and he was going to use everything in his arsenal to force us to dig deep. No excuses, no half measures. He warned us in advance what would happen if we messed around or screwed up, and these weren't empty threats. We were young blokes, many of us having our first experience of not being under the parental roof, and we pushed the boundaries a bit when it came to the weekends. But Rod made sure we didn't get too out of hand on a Friday night by scheduling a full-on weights session every Saturday morning. We soon learned to find the tipping point between a good night out and one that just wasn't worth the next day's pain.

It was our responsibility to bring the gear to training. We trained at Adelaide Oval, both in the indoor centre and on the Oval itself. I was blown away the first time we got to go out onto that beautiful, famous ground. But it didn't take long to develop other feelings about it, thanks to regular punishments for misdemeanours such as forgetting to bring the cricket balls along with the rest of the gear. Rod would have us run around the pitch in the freezing rain for what felt like hours until he thought we'd learned our lesson. If we missed a training session without explanation or came seriously late, he took it to the next level, making us pile in a mini-bus so he could take us to the beach at Glenelg and send us out to swim wearing just our Speedos. If that doesn't sound too bad, remember: this is winter in Adelaide we're talking about.

Rod had an almost spooky way of knowing exactly what we'd been up to. If some of the blokes got a bit carried away drinking at the Hindley Street clubs on a Saturday night, he would know the full story even before they woke up the next day. It didn't occur to us, or to me anyway, that the vehicles we were allowed to drive around in were AIS-owned Taragos with distinctive number plates and that Adelaide was a pretty small place where Rod knew a ton of people. We thought we looked just like any other young guys out on the town, but we must have stuck out like the proverbial.

Icy dips at Glenelg were one thing, but occasionally there was a really serious loss of privilege, just like we'd been warned. Some of the guys went up into the Adelaide Hills to play golf, had a few beers too many and caused some kind of ruckus that got back to Rod immediately. They were banned from going on the end-of-year tour to South Africa. That was a huge thing to miss out on. It really made us understand what was at stake. We couldn't act like rowdy kids on a school camp — a big part of the preparation for becoming professional cricketers was behaving as if we already were.

At the same time, Rod and his staff understood that life at the Academy was a major adjustment, particularly for the youngest members of the group, including me and Shannon Tubb, a Tasmanian bowler who was just 16. They knew that even though we were excited to be there, we did get homesick, and they organised for us to go home every couple of months for short visits. During these visits, especially early on in my time at the Academy, I would complain to Dad about how much they were pushing us and how hard it was. As always, he had a clear, calm perspective on it all. He reminded me that I'd made a commitment and needed to see it through, and that the course wasn't meant to be easy; it was designed to weed out people who couldn't hack life as an elite athlete. He also reminded me that if I turned out to be one of the people who couldn't hack it, I would have to go and get a regular job. There was no pressure in it, just a whole lot of common sense, and I always got back on the plane more determined than ever not to let myself or anyone else down.

I was true to that promise when it came to the learning and training part of the course, but not so much when it came to the job that went with it. Some of the older guys did their hours labouring on building sites where there wouldn't have been much chance to slack off, but Shannon (who was, inevitably, nicknamed Tubby) and I were sent to Adelaide Oval for two four-hour shifts a week with the grounds staff. To earn the $2.50 an hour, or whatever nominal rate we were being paid, we were supposed to do whatever needed doing: mowing lawns, cutting back bushes, sweeping up or anything else that needed zero skills. But in a big place like that there are a lot of spots where you can be out of sight, and we found most of them.

We were still getting used to the demands put on our bodies by the training regime. The Academy staff were absolutely flogging us and it was a quantum leap from anything either of us had ever experienced, even though, like me, Tubby was already playing first grade. It wasn't unknown for us to do the first task we'd been given and then go and find an obscure place where we could catch some zzzs. One of these spots was a little mezzanine balcony that overlooked the nets in the indoor cricket centre. Standing up there you were visible to everyone, but lying down you were out of sight. Tubby and I were resting up there one day when we heard something that sent us into a frozen panic. It was the unmistakable voice of Rod Marsh, talking to a group of visiting dignitaries as he led them around.

His voice got louder and louder as he approached the balcony, telling them all what a great program the Academy offered. Standing next to the bottom of the steps that led up to us, he said, 'We put these boys through the mill. They work really hard, I'm telling you.' Lying there, not moving a muscle, I kept thinking, *That's it, it's all over. I've got about two seconds left and then he comes up and we're done.* I knew without a shadow of a doubt we'd get sent home if he found us. But, by some miracle, one of his tour group asked Rod a question about some other part of the centre and he turned away from the steps and led them off to show them the answer. Tubby and I got a lot more industrious after that close shave.

In August 1996, we went to South Africa for three weeks to play two three-day games and two one-dayers against an equivalent team from their cricket academy. It was my first overseas trip and it felt pretty great to walk out onto grounds I'd seen so often on TV: Johannesburg's Wanderers and Durban's Kingsmead, the latter where Allan Border played his last Test. Rising stars Andy Bichel and Michael Kasprowicz joined the team to lend us some experience — they would both make their Test debuts for Australia a few months later. I'd learned a lot over the past months and I was able to put it all into practice, taking some choice catches and top-scoring in two games, with a 97 and a 75 not out. The momentum continued after we came back to Australia and embarked on a national tour, playing each state's Second XI team and a couple of the Firsts as well. Beating the WA and Queensland First XIs made us feel 10 feet tall and bulletproof. Both trips also left me wanting more of the lifestyle: for an 18-year-old country boy, which is essentially what I was, living out of hotels and going to a different city every few days was pretty damned appealing.

In December I got my first taste of the game at a true international level. It began in Canberra with my second appearance as the 12th man in the Prime Minister's XI game. Once again the opposition was the West Indies and this time the line-up was even more awe-inspiring on both sides. Allan Border captained a team that included Matthew Hayden, Adam Gilchrist and Stuart MacGill, and the Windies line-up, captained by Courtney Walsh, now included the legendary Brian Lara. I'd grown up watching the dominant, aggressive Calypso brand of cricket from the comfort of my couch or occasionally the stands, but this was my first daunting exposure to the real thing under pressure, in front of a big crowd.

They always try to give the 12th man a bit of time in the field and towards the end of the West Indies' innings I was sent out for a stint by the long-on fence. Walsh hit a sky ball like nothing I'd ever seen. It travelled seemingly miles up before descending at speed. In a fraction of a second my fantasies about blowing everyone away with an incredible catch were replaced by the urgent desire to protect my head. Positioning myself out of impact range meant I didn't even get a hand on the ball, but I was almost too awed by the power and speed I'd just seen to be embarrassed. And Walsh wasn't even a batsman! (Fortunately, my miss didn't do any damage — we won by 58 runs.)

Three days later I was back in Adelaide for the annual one-day match in which the Academy team took on the season's international touring team when they passed through town. This year it happened to be Pakistan. It was the first match of the tour for them, a warm-up to facing Australia two days later, and they didn't hold back. In the lead-up to the game there was a lot of talk in the media about one of their new fast bowlers, Mohammad Zahid. He'd made his Test debut a couple of weeks earlier and had drawn a lot of attention by taking 10 wickets.

Pakistan won the toss and sent us in to bat. Michael Dighton and I had been chosen to open. He was only six months older than me but he had an air of authority about him (maybe helped by the fact that at 193 centimetres he looked down at me from a great height). Walking out with Dighta, I'd assumed that since he was listed first on the sheet he'd be on strike. However, he wanted a chance to see what he would be up against, and as we approached the wicket he said, 'No, you're facing.' I wasn't in a position to argue.

As the bowler was getting himself ready, I thought, *That doesn't look like the bloke in the paper*, and I took a quick look around the field. I spotted Zahid and figured, correctly, that he'd most likely be bowling the following over. The bowler I was facing was Shahid Nazir, another recent addition to the team but not in Zahid's league. I got a single off him towards the end of the over and Dighta ended up facing Zahid. The first ball he sent down was quicker than anything I'd ever had to hit. We were playing with the big boys now. I was quite happy to reach 45 before I was nabbed by Saqlain Mushtaq, who was known at the time for what he called the 'doosra', a leg-break delivery bowled with an off-break action. But I was even happier that Dighta and I put on 103 before I got out, a very good contribution to our overall score of 248.

The whole team was feeling pumped up when we took the field. Pakistan started reasonably well, but we stuck to our game plan and wickets started to fall. I contributed a couple of solid catches and a run out and we got them all out for 235. We'd beaten Pakistan and I'd been an integral part of the victory. Wow! The Academy's tough love approach certainly produced results, at least for me.

My time down in Adelaide had reached an end but the opportunities just kept coming. I was asked to captain both the ACT Colts (who were part of the NSW Country competition) and the overall NSW Country Colts (which played against a City Colts side that included players such as Brett Lee) for the 1996–97 season. As I'd still been 18 when the season started, I was eligible to play one more Under-19s National Championship. Once again I was made captain of the ACT team. By chance, that year the tournament was held in Canberra, which was special. I played well, scoring a century in our games against Tassie and WA, and 90 against South Australia, and finishing as one of the leading batsmen despite missing a game to play for the ACT (seniors) against NSW. In fact, I performed well enough not only to be named in the Australian Under-19s team for a second year, but to be made captain. Captaincy is always a great honour, but it was particularly special in this case because it was a first for an ACT player.

The previous season Australia had been the home team; this time we would travel all the way to Pakistan for a month-long tour, taking in three Youth Tests and three Youth One-Dayers. The squad included several of us who had been at the Academy together, including Simon Katich, Brett Lee, Marcus North and Chris Davies. Before we left for the tour there were many briefing sessions about security and cultural sensitivities and the protocols that went along with representing your country. However, this was the pre-YouTube era and I was a fairly naïve 19-year-old: no amount of briefings prepared me for the confronting sights of life in a developing nation, even just through the windows of our coach from Karachi airport to the hotel.

I also had no preparation for what happened during our first match, a three-day practice game that began on 3 March 1997. I went out for the toss with the Pakistan Under-19s captain, Ahmer Saeed. He won and decided to bat and we both headed back to our change rooms. When my guys were ready I said a few words, reminding them that the conditions might be different to anything we'd experienced before, but we were playing for Australia and we just needed to stick to our plan and play the kind of cricket we knew we were capable of. Then we went out to take the field ... and so did Pakistan. Wait, what? I took a second to try to work out what I was seeing but I couldn't come up with anything that made sense. I must have given Saeed a look of complete puzzlement, because he just shrugged his shoulders and said, 'We changed our minds.' The umpire seemed unfazed by this, so there was nothing to do but say, 'Ah, right. We'll bat then.' *Something tells me we're not in Queanbeyan anymore, Toto.*

We won that game by a very comfortable margin of 145 runs and I was pleased to have led by example, doing pretty well with the bat and taking 10 catches across their two innings. We continued to perform creditably and by the end of the month we had one Test win, one loss and a draw, as well as a one-day loss and a tie (the other one-dayer was called off before we even tossed the coin). We had travelled from Karachi on the Arabian Sea across to Quetta on the Afghan border and right up to Lahore. It was here, in the memorably named Gaddafi Stadium, that we played our final match — this was the down-to-the-wire tie — and I hit 117.

I learned so much over the four weeks, both on and off the field. It was the first time I'd been exposed to those kinds of turning wickets, so different from anything we played on in Australia. And I started to create a mental catalogue of opposition players, including bowler Imran Tahir, who went on to play for South Africa; wicketkeeper-batsman Kamran Akmal; and batsman Hasan Raza, who had already made his Test debut for Pakistan the year before, aged just 15. I found that as captain I was able to set clear standards and expectations for the team so that we could have an enjoyable time while doing the job we were there to do. Part of the role was giving speeches at the formal dinners on the itinerary, including at the Australian High Commission. That was new to me and intimidating at first, but it was also a valuable part of my development.

Every bit as important as all that match time and the associated experiences was the informal education I got off the field from Brian Taber, who managed the team, and Allan Border, who coached us. For an ambitious young keeper, Brian was someone to look up to, having filled the role for NSW and Australia. As a young man he had learned at the feet of revered keeper Bert Oldfield and he had played with Bill Lawry and Doug Walters. He'd managed the Under-19s the year before, too, when we'd toured New South Wales, but it was in Pakistan that I really got to hear his stories, along with those of bona fide legend AB.

For all the obvious reasons, this wasn't a tour where you could go out at the end of the day and sample the local nightlife. In fact, security concerns were so high that we were not permitted to make any forays at all on our own. We travelled as a group from whatever hotel we were staying in to the ground and back again, and that was pretty much it. But somehow Brian managed to have a slab of Foster's waiting for us at the end of each day's play. He would fill the bath in his room with ice and after dinner the whole squad would go up there and listen as he and AB told us stories from their careers. We young players would scatter ourselves around the room on whatever bit of furniture or floor we could find, and sit absolutely rapt, with the same drink in our hand for three hours, as they talked. We had plenty of questions and they were happy to answer them.

Their stories about specific games and memorable innings were fascinating, but what really stayed with me was the passion they each showed when they spoke about the relationships they'd formed through cricket. They both had good yarns about their own memorable individual moments, but it was clear that those moments would have meant nothing without teammates to share the highs and lows. Playing for Australia was a huge honour for both of them, and the experience had been immeasurably heightened by sharing it. That resonated deeply with me. When I was young I enjoyed playing tennis and I liked doing well at it, but the reason I didn't stick with it is because it was all about individual achievement. Apart from my family, sport was pretty much everything to me. But it was never about ribbons or trophies or getting my name in the paper. It was about that unique, profound feeling of shared effort and achievement that is the absolute heart of team sport — or should be, anyway.

I'd boarded the plane to Pakistan keen to do well. By the time we returned I was not only more polished as a player, I'd deepened my understanding of what the Baggy Green truly means and I was determined to do everything I could to be worthy of it.

CHAPTER 7

WITHOUT FAMILY THERE'S NOTHING

IF KARINA AND I thought that having Mia start chemo would put her on a steadier, more predictable medical path, we were wrong. Her condition continued to fluctuate wildly, not just from morning to night but often within a few minutes. In addition to the chemo drugs themselves, she was on an incredible amount of medication, including three different antibiotics, something to steady her blood pressure, a laxative, an anti-nausea drug, another drug to try to prevent bleeding in the bladder caused by the chemo, a diuretic to prevent sodium build-up, an antihistamine and increasingly heavy-duty pain relief. (This began as paracetamol but was ramped up all the way to morphine and then, when she reacted badly to that, fentanyl.)

Her blood was analysed several times a day and as soon as a problem showed up it was treated — if her potassium levels were low, she was given a dose of that; when she developed a thrush-like infection in her mouth, she was given anti-fungal medication to deal with it; when a rash sprang up on her back, anti-viral medication was added. ('Itchy' became one of her new words.) Combinations and doses were constantly being tweaked.

Despite all of this, it was sometimes the simplest, most old-fashioned things that brought her the quickest relief. Mia's temperature spiked into the fever zone (above 38°C) so often that when it didn't do so from 7 o'clock one night all the way to 5 o'clock the next morning, Karina noted it in her diary with the comment, 'That's a record.' When her temperature was up, giving her a sponge bath and changing her cot sheets for clean cool ones always eased her, at least for a little while, until the next fever spiked.

Some of what she was experiencing was a direct result of the chemo drugs, some was a side-effect of the drugs given to counter the effects of the chemo drugs and some was a side-effect of the tumour breaking down and releasing its toxins into her bloodstream. Her stomach shrank a little then increased in size again, and with the mass pressing against her lungs she struggled to breathe. She was put on oxygen, but when her levels remained worryingly low the decision was made to intubate her (insert a tube down her windpipe under anaesthesia), although fortunately she picked up enough for it to be called off at the last minute. Her haemoglobin dropped again, as did her platelets, requiring transfusions of both. She spent a lot of time in PICU.

Karina got a puzzled look from Dr Luce when she said one day she wished Mia would just go to sleep and stay that way for the next 24 months, but I understood exactly what she meant. Many things were hard to deal with in our new reality, but the worst thing of all was seeing Mia in terrible pain and discomfort and not being able to help her. At least when she was asleep she mostly looked serene, as though she wasn't suffering.

I couldn't believe what my poor little girl had to endure, but the really incredible thing was how tough and stoic she was. She didn't understand much more than that she was sick and everyone was trying to help her. She wasn't even 18 months old, so she had no capacity to grasp the big picture, which was that her life was at stake and we hoped that if she endured some very hard months now she would have many, many years of life in the future. She had no concept of time or how long all this was going to go on for. And yet, when she wasn't tossing in a fever or crying with pain, she was smiling and laughing and looking curiously around, taking it all in with those beautiful blue eyes.

Mia had been a wonderfully cheeky, spirited kid from the moment her personality first started to show. Just ask the priest at her christening. She kept readjusting his glasses for him the whole way through the ceremony. At first everyone tried to stifle their amusement, but by the end, the whole church full of family and friends was laughing, including the priest himself. No-one could have blamed her if everything she was going through in hospital knocked that out of her and turned her into a withdrawn or wary child, but it never did. Even gravely ill, she remained her bubbly bright self, and that was a big part of helping us stay positive.

Don't get me wrong — both Karina and I had fearful moments when despair beckoned. But they tended to fall on each of us at separate times, so that when one of us was struggling, the other was there to pull them back up. We were both determined to remain optimistic. On the one hand we knew it would be a huge blessing if she made it to her second birthday, but on the other we refused to allow ourselves to be terrorised by thoughts of her death. And we never, ever wanted Mia to pick up on any negative or frightening feelings from us, so we made a point of taking our cues from her uncomplaining sunny nature.

Up until this point she had been getting some feed in liquid form delivered through her nasogastric (NG) tube, but this was only meant to be a supplement. The idea was for her to get 10 per cent of her nutrition this way and the rest from eating her normal food, and drinking bottles of milk. But she had painful chemo-induced mouth ulcers, besides which she was too sick to want to eat much, and when she did she couldn't keep it down. So she was switched to something called total parenteral nutrition (TPN), whereby her full nutritional needs were delivered in the form of fluid straight into her central line. She still had the NG tube in, however, so that her medicines could be administered and the fluid building up in her stomach could be sucked out.

She had tubes running everywhere and there was frequent discussion about whether they were positioned in the correct places deep within her body. Following the first chemo cycle, there were a couple of days where Mia seemed to be in frequent pain despite the drugs, so on April 5 she was given an x-ray of her torso to check the NG placement. The x-ray showed that indeed the tube did need to be repositioned by several centimetres. But it also just happened to catch the fact that she had a broken bone. Specifically it was a fracture of the right humeral head — if you picture where the arm joins the shoulder as a ball and socket, this is the ball part. It was horrible to think she had been in extra pain with a broken bone and we hadn't known.

The medical team said that, even though the cancer had metastasised into Mia's bones and weakened them, this was a very unusual complication to have and they couldn't say precisely what had caused it. (The vast majority of the many people treating her were fantastic, but I couldn't help wondering darkly if someone had been not quite careful enough getting her into position for a procedure. I tried not to dwell on it.) The upshot was that she now came under the care of an orthopaedic team, as well as oncology and surgical teams. They told us that the bone was very unlikely to heal properly while the tumour was present, and that they would need to immobilise it in a sling pressed against her body for four to six weeks. That was a big ask for a toddler, and yet another thing she had to put up with.

It so happened that Mia had the x-ray and we found out about the break when I was at the hospital and Karina was at home with Zac and her mum. She was distraught when I rang with the news. She left Zac with Marg and raced in, bursting into tears again when she saw me. I understood how she felt — as tense and distressing as it often was at the hospital, it was always far worse to not be there. Even when I couldn't do a thing to change the situation, I felt driven to be there as much as humanly possible and Karina felt the same.

So far we'd been splitting the days and nights between the two of us, with one or other of us always with Mia. Karina's mother and mine also spent time with her, particularly when she was in PICU, where they would sit with her for a couple of hours to allow Karina to go down to the ward and take a nap. They also spent a huge amount of time looking after Zac. The support we were getting from our families was fantastic, but by early April it was obvious to everyone that we couldn't keep going as we had been, organising things on the fly just a day or two in advance. Zac needed a predictable routine and we had another baby coming in a matter of weeks. We needed to figure out a new arrangement.

Karina and I didn't have to spend any energy on it; without having to be asked, our parents got together and came up with a system that they felt they could sustain as long as it took to get Mia through treatment. All four of them worked. Mine ran the family building business, with Dad on site and Mum taking care of all the admin. Phil also had his own business, servicing ATMs, while Marg worked Tuesdays and Thursdays as a secretary for a small firm of financial advisors. The four of them figured out a system whereby the mothers would cover half the week each while the fathers picked up as much of the slack as possible. My mum would drive up from Queanbeyan each Sunday and stay until Wednesday afternoon, when Marg would relieve her. Marg would then be on hand until Sunday, when they switched over again. As well as looking after Zac, they cooked and cleaned and washed and did whatever else was needed to keep the house going.

Marg, who had a very understanding boss, changed her work days and Dad got in some extra help to make things easier for Mum. But even so it required an enormous effort from them and they did it unhesitatingly. Dr Luce remarked on it to several of us over the following months, commenting that in all the years he'd been a doctor he had never seen a family pull together the way ours did, keeping it up for the long haul. Mum expressed surprise when he said this to her, replying that she couldn't imagine family members not wanting to help. He explained that most did, at the beginning. There would be an intense period following diagnosis when everyone pitched in, but then they would drift away back to their own normal lives as treatment ground on and on.

Mum just shook her head at this. Not helping simply wasn't an option for her or Dad, just as it wasn't for Marg and Phil. Dad has a saying: 'I have family and I have acquaintances.' It's a jokey exaggeration. Of course, he has friends, but what he means is family is everything in life. Without family there's nothing. (And in fact his close friends become like family to him.) All us Haddins feel the same way and so do Karina's entire family. I realise we were incredibly lucky to have all four parents alive and well and living close enough to step in. I just can't imagine how people who don't have that kind of support cope with one child in hospital and one or more at home.

Having the new system helped Karina feel less anxious about Zac. He still found it very unsettling to be at Westmead and he didn't even like it when people talked too much about Mia's medical details within his earshot at home. With his two loving grandmas on a regular schedule that enabled him to sleep in his own bed every night and go off to kindy and swimming and his other activities as usual, we were hopeful he would soon feel more settled again.

Marg and Mum did their Wednesday 'handover' at the hospital, so they both always saw Mia then and they also came out to Westmead when they could at other times. Their contributions were absolutely essential in helping us to keep going, but both Karina and I sometimes wondered how we were going to get through the day. It was rare for whichever of us stayed by Mia's bedside overnight to get more than a couple of hours' sleep and there were times when we barely had the energy for a simple 'Hello' when the other parent arrived in the morning.

The rest of our family and friends continued to go out of their way to support us, finding presents for Zac to let him know he hadn't been forgotten, or craft or games to help keep Mia occupied when she was feeling well. Mia wasn't too fussed about particular toys or dolls in hospital, she was happy to swap between them, but her beloved blanket was another matter. It was pink and matched a green version Zac had (and still has); they'd each been given them at birth. Zac's had acquired the nickname 'poo blankie', so that became the name for Mia's too. She loved her blankie and got very upset when she couldn't have it. But she was throwing up so much it often had to be taken away to be washed. There were days when I drove home just to wash and dry it, then got it back to her and an hour later was in the car again heading home to do it all again after another vomit. My cousin Michelle took it on herself to find a solution. She spent days driving around Canberra visiting every department store and baby shop until she was able to ring and say excitedly, 'I've found it! And I've bought six of them.' Thoughtful gestures like that made a big difference.

By mid-April Mia was partway through her second chemo cycle and her hair was falling out. She was alternating between drowsiness, the unhappy discomfort of vomiting and rashes, and cheery wide-awakeness. Because she'd lost all connection with normal circadian rhythms, the wakefulness would often be at 2 a.m. The worry, stress and lack of sleep were really taking their toll on us, especially Karina, who was now nearly eight months pregnant. She texted me in the middle of one night, very upset after having given in to the urge to go onto Google and look up information on neuroblastoma survival rates.

In the hope that it would help both Mia and us, on 16 April Mia was allowed outside the hospital for the first time since she had arrived at the Emergency Department 31 days earlier. As excursions go, it wouldn't have even registered before she got sick: being popped in the pram and taken for a walk around the grounds. But after a month of nothing but walls and ceilings and artificial lights, she absolutely loved it, saying, 'More!' when it was time to go back in.

The medical team thought she was going well enough, all things considered, that we might be allowed to bring her home for the night soon. But her bedroom was at the end of a long hall from our room. Even apart from the fact that it had become the grandmothers' room, the location wouldn't work at all: we needed to be able to hear her. So Dad and my cousin Peter came to our house and spent a day putting up a wall to section off part of the living room and create a new bedroom for Mia. We put a cot in there for her as well as a single bed for an adult to rest in while they kept an eye on her.

Before the diagnosis we had been on the point of starting a major building project, tearing down our existing house and rebuilding on the same spot. (While the house wasn't the right size or layout for our needs, we really liked the position and the neighbourhood and had bought with this plan in mind.) But that was all on indefinite hold.

I was fortunate in that even though I wasn't playing, I remained on a Cricket Australia (CA) contract. It followed the usual arrangement of a salary-like base 'retainer', supplemented by match payments. Mine was a two-year contract which ran until June 2013. CA were absolutely great from the moment they learned what was happening. James Sutherland, the CEO, and Pat Howard, the General Manager of Team Performance, reached out to me personally with their kind thoughts and best wishes. They didn't even mention money; the monthly retainer payments just kept coming, even though at that point I didn't know when, or even if, I would be able to play again. In fact, throughout the whole experience they never put any pressure on me about cricket but were only concerned about my family's wellbeing.

The continuation of the retainer took some of the load off my shoulders, but my income dropped enormously without match fees. As well, one of my sponsors triggered a clause in my contract with them whereby they didn't have to honour our agreement because of the length of time since I'd played. We could get by financially for a little while this way, but not indefinitely. Until your life is turned upside down by a life-threatening illness in the family, you just don't realise how the effects can ripple outwards. Before Mia got sick, I pictured childhood cancer in terms of its physical and emotional impacts, not the financial ones. However, for some people being unable to work leads to the loss of their homes and life savings. We were lucky to have a safety cushion, but even if the rebuild had been logistically feasible now — which it obviously wasn't — there was no way we could have committed to it financially. Like pretty much everything else not to do with Mia's fight, it would just have to wait.

A week after our venture into the hospital grounds we were given our first 'gate pass' — approval to go home for a little while, in this case two hours on a Saturday. Karina and Zac were looking forward to it, but I felt very anxious. We all knew how quickly Mia could crash — was this really such a good idea? Dr Santosh and the nurses reassured us we'd be fine and said it was a good way to start preparing for when Mia came home as an outpatient. This was likely to be within days if things went well following the stem-cell extraction she was due to have the following week. Although Mia had started eating again and had been weaned off the TPN, she was still vomiting a lot and so was receiving additional nutrition via her NG tube. For such a short visit, we wouldn't need to know how to do this, but we did have to be trained in administering medication through the tube, and Karina took on this task. It was a delicate and involved procedure, and I was relieved that she seemed so on top of it all.

Mia got very excited when, waiting in her pram out the front of the hospital with Karina, she saw me pull up in the car and realised she really was going home for a visit. She coped fine with the trip and loved looking around her new room and the gifts and toys waiting for her. She also really enjoyed being home with Zac and it was so nice to see them interacting normally — even their bickering over what DVD to watch was quite heart-warming, for a while.

But I was on edge the whole time in case something went wrong. We decided to give her a relaxing bath to get rid of that 'hospital feeling', but it turned out to be a very stressful process. We had to make sure her central line didn't get wet, for fear of infection, so the tubes had to be looped up into a special pouch around her neck and we had to stop her splashing. Two hours at home was definitely long enough. By the end of it she was exhausted and so were we. The stimulation did her a lot of good though — I stayed with her that night at the hospital and for almost the first time she slept through solidly, and as a consequence so did I. The following day we did it all again, only this time the pass was for three hours.

A very important event was scheduled for the following day, 23 April: the extraction of her stem-cell–rich bone marrow. Stem cells are amazing things. They're like molten metal in a foundry: they have the potential to turn into whatever is needed most. They can become brain cells, muscle cells, red blood cells and more. They would be put back into Mia's body during the bone marrow transplant (BMT) stage of her treatment following chemo and surgery. The BMT team had a minimum amount of cells they needed to harvest and if they didn't get it they wouldn't be able to go ahead with the transplant. They'd only know once they had extracted the marrow and analysed it. The machine was hooked up to her central line and she could not move from her cot for well over five hours. There were huge smiles all round when the team told us her marrow had been healthy enough to deliver six times the minimum amount.

The next day, after she had been assessed and we'd been briefed by the oncology, orthopaedic and nutrition teams, and after Karina had proved to their satisfaction that she could handle all aspects of the 'enteral feeds' through the NG tube, we were sent home for five days. With us went a detailed timetable of all the medications that had to be given throughout the day and night, as well as the schedule for the feeds.

Again, it was lovely for Mia to be out of the hospital environment, but caring for her was exhausting and when we finally did get her and Zac into bed, no-one got a decent sleep. Either her alarm buzzer was going off to indicate one of her lines had become blocked, which often happened as she moved around in bed, or Zac was up asking for water at 1 a.m., or Mia was sitting up at 3 a.m. demanding the iPad. We'd been told to call straight away if her temperature rose to 38°C and we didn't even make it to the end of the fifth day before that happened. They told us to come straight into Emergency, where she was put on intravenous fluids and antibiotics, just to be safe. They kept her in for the scheduled week-long stay at the beginning of the next round of chemo, her third, but then sent her home for the three-week recovery period.

I anxiously wondered how we would cope, but it got fractionally easier, or at least we got more used to what it entailed. However, the night-time disruptions continued and it wasn't until mid-May that both Karina and I got three hours' sleep in a row. The reason I know is because it was noteworthy enough for Karina to mention it in her diary. It was also at this point that we got the results from the first scans since chemotherapy began, the first indication of whether it was working. Dr Luce came and found us and said animatedly, 'There has been a significant reduction in the size of the tumour. A significant reduction!' I think he repeated it because he didn't quite see the reaction he was expecting. Of course we were relieved and happy to hear this news, but even after everything that had occurred, after everything we'd been told, we were still thinking, *Well, that's what's supposed to happen, right? Chemo is supposed to do that.* It was only later on when we met and became close to other parents whose children's tumours didn't respond that we fully understood how differently that conversation could have gone.

Dr Luce told us we should celebrate such good news, although he did have a sobering comment for us before we left. He said that with the chemo working the way it was, the neuroblastoma no longer posed such a direct threat to Mia's life. The treatment was another matter. He repeated what he'd told us before: that in order to ensure they completely killed off the cancer and gave it as little chance of recurring as possible, the medical team needed to hit her system so hard that she might die from the cure rather than the disease. In the meantime, though, we'd had a victory, and we'd take any of those we could get.

We'd worked it out so that Mia would receive her fourth round of chemo and be back at home by Monday, 28 May, when the new baby was scheduled to be born by caesarean. On the morning of the big day we got the kids sorted out; then I had just enough time before Karina and I had to leave for the hospital to zip up to the shops for a few last things. I was about to load my basketful onto the checkout conveyer when the lady behind me held out the bottle of water she was buying and said, 'Do you mind if I go first? I have my personal trainer waiting.' I behaved the way I'd been brought up and said, 'Go ahead,' rather than what I was thinking, which was, *I'll see your personal trainer and raise you a three-year-old with an ear infection, a 19-month-old with cancer needing her feed and a pregnant wife who needs to be at hospital in less than 90 minutes to deliver.*

We had planned to hire a specially trained day nurse to focus on Mia for the few days she would be at home while Karina was recovering from the birth, and, after lots of research, we settled on a well-qualified candidate who just happened to be male. When he arrived at the house for a trial run, Karina carefully and patiently explained everything to do with Mia's medications, feeding routine, NG tube care and all the rest of it. She then went out to a medical appointment, at which point the bloke all but stopped paying attention to Mia and started following me around the house asking me cricket questions. His first day with us was his last. Instead, my mother stepped in and her sister Yvonne came from Cowra to help. They would look after Mia while Zac, who was on antibiotics for his ear infection, went to stay with Karina's parents for a few days.

The trip to the Mater Hospital was shorter than to Westmead and we got there a little after noon. Everything went smoothly and at 5.30 p.m. our son was born, a healthy, beautiful boy who looked a lot like Zac did at birth. Despite everything that was going on, we were able to be completely in the moment and his arrival was every bit as special as those of his brother and sister in calmer times. We declined Zac's suggested name — Honda — and went with Hugo Ross instead.

I'd been planning to duck back home to give Mia her medications just after 6 p.m. But, while Karina was generally well, it took a little while for her blood pressure to come down and she remained in the Recovery ward until 7.30 p.m., so instead I had to talk Mum through the process over the phone. At 9.30 p.m., with Karina and Hugo well settled, I started to drive home through pouring rain. I was only about 2 kilometres from the house when I took a call from Mum on the hands-free. Sounding really stressed, she asked if I was far away. Instantly on edge, I said, 'No, why?' She said, 'Mia's turned. She just got sick all of a sudden.' I said, 'I'm coming,' and flew the rest of the way.

I ran in, fearing the worst. Mia was pale and limp, passing in and out of consciousness. Mum and Aunty Vonnie, very upset, explained that they'd done everything just as I had instructed but that Mia had become ill and then had vomited so violently that she had dislodged her NG tube. She looked terrible, and I was truly scared she might die. I picked up Mia and Mum and I raced out to the car and took off for Westmead. I was highly agitated, asking Mum over and over about what had happened. She was in tears as she told me she was sure she'd given the right medication in the right doses and the right order. All the while we were both trying to get Mia to stay awake.

We were rushed through Emergency, Mia was admitted and tests were quickly run, which showed that her haemoglobin level had dropped. While it wasn't as low as it had been when she'd first been diagnosed, it was well below where it needed to be. In this case the cause wasn't internal bleeding; it was the chemo killing off red blood cells. Mum and Aunty Vonnie hadn't done anything wrong; it was just one of those things. The timing was, however, very unfortunate. Karina and I had only been away from Mia for nine hours, but that was by far the longest stretch since her initial admittance during which she hadn't had at least one of us with her. No matter how much I tried to tell myself it was just a coincidence, and the same thing would have happened whether I was there with her or not, I was deeply shaken.

The doctors assured me that she would be much better following a blood transfusion, after which we would be taken down to a bed in the Camperdown ward. Sitting by her bedside in Emergency as that precious liquid went in, I was facing a window that opened onto the corridor. I could see some of the activity happening in a room diagonally across the hall with a lot of staff rushing in, although at first I was too busy focusing on Mia to take in what was happening there. There is so much background noise of beeps and buzzers in hospital that if you spend any time in there at all you automatically tune it out; however, one sound started to cut through, becoming louder by the second. It was a terrible howl that just kept going, and it was coming from the room across the hall.

Doctors and nurses now left the room, much more slowly than they had arrived. One of them was the nurse who was looking after Mia. Soon afterwards she came into our room to check on the transfusion. She looked as though she was holding back emotion. I said, 'Did you just lose someone?' and she nodded. A child had died metres away from us. Mere hours after hearing the lovely cry of my own newborn son for the first time, I was bearing witness to a mother's heart-breaking cry of inconsolable pain. Every detail of that night will remain forever etched in my memory.

The dawn saw Mia restored to a healthy pinkness, sleeping peacefully. She was well enough to go home later that day, though she'd be back the following day for a clinic visit to check that her broken shoulder was continuing to heal. Karina and Hugo stayed in the Mater for five days. I don't know how many women would regard the first days following birth as a relaxing break, but after two and a half months of snatched sleep and endless days in a children's cancer ward, that's exactly how Karina described this time.

The two of them came home on 2 June. Zac had already been in to the Mater to meet Hugo and had received presents from the new addition. ('How did he get to the toy shop while he was still in Mummy's tummy?' He doesn't miss a thing, that kid!) Mia, however, despite all the explanations in the build-up to the birth about what was going to happen, alternated between cuddling and kissing Hugo and clinging to me while looking at him suspiciously.

She had just over a week at home, with clinic visits every second day, then it was time for her next round of chemo — amazingly, we were by now up to the fifth cycle. More scans would be done after this cycle and then the surgery to remove the tumour could finally happen. Having seen her so well it was hard to see her knocked about badly by side-effects again, with one of the chemo drugs making her break out in hives within two minutes of it starting to hit her system and another making her blow up like the Michelin Man. But whatever symptom arose, the doctors continued to have something to counter it.

With Hugo coming along nicely and Mia progressing well, it was time for Karina and me to have a serious conversation about me returning to work. Every family that finds itself in a similar situation to the one we were in reaches the point where at least one parent has to go back to work, and we had reached it. My job, however, made our situation unusual. I couldn't just phone up the HR department and agree on a date for my return. I had to be fit enough and playing well enough to be selected, whether at state or national level, or even in domestic Twenty20 competitions at home or abroad.

I'd continued to train in bits and pieces as best I could over the previous three months and I knew by everyday standards I was still reasonably fit. But the standards required to play elite sport are very, very different and by those I was no longer even on the chart. It was ingrained in me to take care of myself in order to be able to push my body to its limit: the basics were getting enough sleep and making good nutritional choices. But sleep had become a rare and treasured thing and, as for food, at the hospital I'd often go a whole day without eating or just grab a vending machine snack because that was the option that would get me back to Mia's room the quickest.

If you had asked me about my fitness before the day in the West Indies when I got that fateful call from Karina, I'd have told you with absolute certainty that at the age of 34 I still had years of top-level cricket left in me. But now? I wasn't sure. As ever, there was only one way to find out.

Karina and I talked at length about my return to work. Without a doubt, it was going to be challenging, and we could only do it if we were in harmony. I'd still be there as much as I could for her and the children, but a great deal more of the burden would fall on her shoulders. She had to be okay with that, and she was. We also talked it over with both sets of parents. Our mothers were a key part of the plan: without one of them constantly available to be at the hospital with Mia or at home with Zac, we'd never be able to go ahead. Fortunately, they were fully supportive.

Even so, I think those weeks between Hugo's birth and Mia's 12 July surgery were some of the toughest Karina and I had during the whole experience. When Mia was home, we had all of her requirements to take care of plus newbie Hugo and Zac. We worked hard to make sure that Zac, as the one with the fewest demands, never felt neglected. They all woke up at different times throughout the night and our sleep deprivation just got worse and worse, putting a strain on both of us. Having someone else in the house all the time was also taking its toll and we had to have some awkward conversations with family members about boundaries. These discussions were extra painful because everyone involved cared for us deeply and was doing so much to try to help, but we were all living on our nerves 24/7.

The talented and dedicated surgeon who would be operating on Mia, Dr Gordon Thomas, warned us beforehand that he might have to remove one of her kidneys and wouldn't know what else might need to come out until he opened her up. A kind and softly spoken man, he took care to make sure we knew as much as possible about what was going to happen, drawing us a picture of her anatomy in such detail it was like one from a textbook.

The operation took nearly six hours. Afterwards, Dr Thomas explained to us in his calm manner that he'd had to take out her right kidney and adrenal gland. He'd also had to scrape the tumour away from her diaphragm and liver. In all, it came away in 11 pieces. He said he'd taken an 'aggressive' approach to try to make sure no cancer was left to sneak its way into the lymphatic system. As expected, she was left with a large scar running down and across her abdomen. However, she recovered well, only needing two days in PICU, and amazed everyone with how quickly she was kicking her legs in the air and rolling herself around in the cot. Everything seemed to be going perfectly to plan.

That didn't last long. Mia's digestive system had shut down in response to the trauma of the surgery and the medical team warned us that it might take a number of weeks to start working again. In the meantime she was back on TPN feeding (her NG tube was still in and was being used to deliver medicine and remove the fluid that was building up in her stomach). When two weeks had gone by with no sign of things getting back to normal, she underwent a nuclear medicine Gastric Emptying Study, which confirmed that her stomach wasn't processing what went into it and nothing was moving down into the intestines. The doctors said that while her stomach should 'turn back on' in four to six weeks, it wasn't unknown for it to take up to three months for this to happen after such a big operation. But they also said it wouldn't stop them pushing ahead with the sixth cycle of chemo.

Mia battled through the chemo. (I wondered how it was possible for someone who wasn't eating in the normal way to vomit so much, the poor kid.) She then underwent more investigations for her stomach and Dr Thomas revised the time it might take for it to work again out to six months. He said the best tactic was to do nothing, just wait. That sounded unbelievable. Every time she developed a symptom they were immediately onto it, so why was this different? He explained that there was nothing 'mechanically' wrong; the problem was neurological. The nerves that controlled everything in her digestive system had had a major shock and had, in effect, taken the system offline.

What, we asked, would happen if they never came good? He said there were drastic steps that could be taken, including surgically implanting a percutaneous endoscopic gastrostomy (PEG) tube, which carries food directly through the abdominal wall and into the stomach, but that would be a last resort and he felt confident that we wouldn't need to get to that point. His instinct would eventually be proved right, but it's perhaps just as well that we didn't know how long it would take or what the consequences would be.

CHAPTER 8

FROM THE COMETS TO THE BLUES

AS A YOUNG MAN, my plans to move to Sydney after the Cricket Academy year ended were put on hold again thanks to another unexpected but perfectly timed opportunity, one that gave me the chance to make my professional List-A debut.

Australia's domestic one-day series has been running since the end of the 1960s and it's been through a lot of sponsorship name changes over the years. In 1997, the year I turned 20, it was known as the Mercantile Mutual Cup. Previously it had been run along similar lines to the Sheffield Shield four-day games competition where all six states fielded teams but neither of the territories did. However, in the lead-up to the 1997–98 season it was announced that the ACT would be invited to compete in the one-day comp for the first time, with the Canberra Comets going up against heavy-hitting state teams peppered with current World Cup and Test players.

I was selected for the Comets team along with other locals, including Peter Solway; my friend Mark Higgs, with whom I'd grown up; and Stuart Karppinen, then an up-and-coming bowler who had also been through the Academy. Two former international players were lured out of retirement to give the team more depth of experience: larger-than-life bowler Merv Hughes and batsman Mike Veletta. There was no contract, just fairly token match payments (though I also had a paid role with ACT Cricket going out to schools to promote the game). But money was beside the point because the experience itself was priceless. Lots of other young guys around my age were working hard to try to get a shot at a state Second XI team while I was in the right place at the right time to play on the national stage.

Nobody expected the Comets to perform very well. We didn't have the big talent pools the states — even Tasmania — had to call on. But those low expectations were actually a really good thing. First of all, they fired us up — we were intent on making the most of the opportunity and showing everyone that the ACT deserved its place. Second, we were free to really go for it because there was nothing to lose and therefore no need to play conservatively. It was another big step up for me and the anticipation built and built in the lead-up to our first game, which came five weeks into the competition.

I was ultra-nervous as we prepared to walk out onto Manuka Oval the week after my 20th birthday to play a South Australian team that included Test and ODI opening batsman Greg Blewett. But outweighing my nervousness was my intense excitement at finally having the opportunity to pit myself against first-class cricketers.

The South Australian Redbacks batted first. The gap in experience and form revealed itself as Greg Blewett hit our bowlers around the park, reaching 97 before we could get him out. I took one catch in the innings, off the bowling of Higgsy, who was also making his debut at this level. (Tim Neilson was the batsman who nicked the ball and when I made my Test debut, many years later, Tim was coach of the Australian team. We built a close relationship and I joke with him to this day about the fact that he nicked balls way back when and he is still nicking them to me in training 20 years later.) Higgsy also came in handy when I dislocated my finger during the innings, pulling it back into place for me before the physio could get out to the middle.

The Redbacks reached a total of 237. Our top order — Paul Evans, Mike Veletta and Peter Solway — all turned in solid performances but, coming in at number four, I only lasted two overs before getting caught for six. We ended up losing four wickets to run outs, and were all out for 226. So we lost ... but only by 11 runs. It wasn't a fairy-tale start by any means, but it was promising. Just getting out there and playing, instead of repeatedly imagining it, had done a lot to settle my nerves. I'd come out firing at bat, trying to shake things up. It hadn't worked this time, but I knew it was the right strategy and the rest of the team backed me.

Two weeks later we had an away game to Tasmania. Their team was captained by David Boon, and included a promising young batsman, a few years older than me, by the name of Ricky Ponting. Bellerive Oval looks like a jewel box on television, but when you're there it always feels like you've wandered into a giant fridge — those winds seem to come straight from Antarctica no matter how bright the sun's shining. I was too fired up to care, though. This time we went out first and I'd moved down to six in the batting order. I stuck with my plan to go hard and I got 24 off 19 balls, including a six and a four, before I was caught. My strike rate was excellent; I just needed to stay in longer. Tasmania ended up beating us easily, taking the game by four wickets with plenty of play remaining. But every game made us stronger, and the following week it all came together perfectly.

We were away at Bendigo, up against Victoria. In the previous two games Merv had bowled smartly and economically, but before this one he said to me, 'You'll see the real Merv Hughes today and if you young blokes are ever going to fire I want it to be this game.' The Bushrangers' well-seasoned team included big-hitting Brad Hodge; bowler Damien Fleming, halfway through his impressive international career; and dead-set legend Dean Jones, whose aggressive, high-energy approach had pretty much changed the way everyone played the one-day game. Deano, as he was known, was almost four years past the end of his international career, but, as I discovered, he hadn't softened at all.

They won the toss and sent us in to bat. Mike Veletta, captaining the Comets, was still experimenting with the batting order and he'd put me at number five. We were 3 for 28 when I went out to partner Peter Solway. As I approached the wicket, Dean Jones, who was fielding at mid-on, walked up to me. I'd gone into the game determined to watch him closely, wanting to absorb whatever I could of his uncompromising way of playing.

As he got closer, I ran through the possibilities of what he might be about to say to me. This was the bloke who in 1986 (with a bit of sharp encouragement from his captain, AB) had dug so deep to produce a crucial 210 in the killing heat of Madras (Chennai as it's called now) that when it was over he collapsed and had to be taken to hospital and given intravenous fluid. (Funnily enough, Mike Veletta had been the other big contender for the spot Deano got in that Madras game, and they didn't know who was going to be chosen right up until the last minute.) Maybe, knowing I was a young bloke coming up through the ranks, Deano was going to say something to make me feel a bit more at ease. Guess again. What came out of his mouth was, 'You don't deserve to be on the same field as me,' and then he turned on his heel and walked away. *Jeez*, I thought to myself, *that's different.*

I was definitely taken aback, but only for a moment — the game wasn't going to wait for me. I thought about the conversations I'd had with Dad about more senior players' attempts at intimidation and what it signified. Why would Dean Jones, *the* Dean Jones, waste his time coming up and doing that? Were they worried about the result or something? *Righto then*, I said to myself, *let's give them reason to worry. Bring it on.*

The attempts to throw me off my game continued, with bowler Brad Williams spitting and snorting and Damien Fleming giving it his best too. I found it funny. The more relaxed I got, the more annoyed they got, and the more annoyed they got, the more I enjoyed it. Sol and I were having a great time out there. I ended up hitting 89 off 91 balls and he got 73; we learned afterwards that our 174 off 182 balls had set a domestic one-day record for a fourth-wicket partnership.

When it was their turn to bat, I saw what Merv had been talking about: he took the handbrake off and we all got a true look at why he'd been such a class performer for Australia for so long. The Victorian team had thought they'd had us beaten back when our third wicket had fallen. Instead, they fell 15 runs short of our 250 total and we claimed a history-making victory for the Comets. The whole side was ecstatic. We felt like the ACT had really been accepted as a legitimate competitor. For me, being awarded Player of the Match was the icing on the cake.

I didn't say anything to Dean Jones coming off the field. I didn't have to; the results spoke for themselves. And I never held it against him — why would I, when it spurred me to unleash my own competitive edge so effectively? (I do, however, enjoy reminding him of that game, and I get the opportunity to do so because he coaches Islamabad United, the Pakistan Super League Twenty20 team for which I've played in recent years. The first time I mentioned it over a beer I said, 'Do you remember saying that to me?' He replied, 'I don't remember it specifically, but I would have done. Yeah, it's exactly what I would have said. You're probably saying the same things now to young players.' I had to laugh. I said, 'No, Deano, not as harsh as that.' 'Oh well,' he said, 'at least you remembered it.')

Our next match was three weeks later, back home in Canberra, against NSW. It would be nice to be able to report that we were able to continue our winning ways, but with a team that included Australian captain Mark Taylor as well as leg-spinner Stuart 'Magilla' MacGill, keeper Phil Emery and all-rounder Shane Lee and his brother Brett, the Blues had it all over us. There was no chance of Peter Solway and me replicating our previous success: Magilla caught and bowled Peter for 34 and snagged me for just six. It's always better to win than to lose, but losing against a side as powerful as that was a real learning experience, showing me what some of the best in the business looked like up close. I remember thinking I'd never seen a ball turn as much as MacGill's or witnessed such an effective wrong 'un. I itched to have the chance to be on the NSW team keeping for him.

We only had two more games, and we lost both, but again they gave me exposure to a lot of notable players — some established, some on the rise. They included Mike Hussey, Adam Gilchrist, Ryan Campbell, Damien Martyn, Tom Moody and Simon Katich, all part of the talent-packed WA side, and Matthew Hayden, Andrew Symonds and Stuart Law, playing for Queensland, who beat NSW to claim the Cup. We were never in danger of getting into the finals but we'd performed a lot better than anyone expected us to, so much so that we finished sixth overall. And who was below us, at the bottom of the ladder? Victoria. It worked for me.

During that first Cup season with the Comets, in addition to everything I learned about the game, I found out a lot about how to handle things off the field as well, mostly from big Merv. Any cricket fan who'd watched him play knew what a character he was, and he was exactly the same in person: larger than life, the ultimate larrikin. He loved to go out and celebrate a win but was equally happy to go to the Kingston Hotel for steak, beers and a bit of fun after training or any other old time. His passion for the game was incredible and he was terrific company. We had some great, great nights at the Kingo.

Merv was instantly recognisable and would draw attention wherever we went. This was pre-selfies, but strangers were constantly coming up to him asking for his autograph or just wanting to talk to him. Other people might have got irritated with it after a while, but he handled himself amazingly well, keeping everything friendly and good-natured and easy. Of course, now and then there were idiots who wanted to have a go at him; these were often blokes who were worse for wear after too many drinks and thought they'd set him straight on his greatest cricketing mistakes. But Merv never rose to the bait. He didn't let it get to him; he just brushed it off or ignored it. He was a great example in that regard.

He was also a great role model the morning after the night before. He was a thirsty man when he was out, but despite his happy-go-lucky persona and the fact that his serious playing days were behind him, he would always turn up to training ready to go. He didn't make a big deal of it; in fact, just the opposite: he took it for granted that that's what you did. He provided the perfect example of the professionalism required of a top-level athlete.

There was, however, one area where his choices were questionable: post-game attire. He'd been around change rooms all his life and if he ever had any physical modesty it was long gone. He was quite happy to wander around in a towel far too small to cover that great hairy carcass. On one memorable occasion at Manuka Oval, Dad and my cousin Peter came across to the change room for a beer after a game and Merv strolled out looking like Bigfoot in a scrap of material that left little to the imagination. Peter reckons his eyeballs were so badly scarred he's never been the same since.

When I wasn't playing with the Comets, I continued to play for ANU's first-grade team, as did Peter Solway, Stuart Karppinen and Hall O'Meagher. We had a great season, culminating in making it to the three-day 1997–98 Grand Final against a Queanbeyan team that included Higgsy. The ill-feeling between the teams was stronger than ever, making our Premiership victory all the sweeter. It was the perfect way to wrap up what had been an incredibly formative and rewarding five years with ANU — an experience that laid the foundation for everything that followed.

At the end of the Mercantile Mutual Cup tournament, Karpps and I were selected for a notional 'Best of the Competition' team and I was honoured to be chosen as Recruit of the Year against some very stiff competition. (I was also very happy to see Sol named the Comets' Player of the Year.) Cricket ACT officials urged me to stay on for another summer with the Comets. I thanked them but I knew that if I was going to get my shot at the big league it was time to make the move to Sydney so I could be well settled into a new club in time for the 1998–99 season.

I'd attracted plenty of attention from people whose business it was to keep an eye on upcoming talent, putting me in the fortunate position of having my choice of Sydney cricket clubs. Dad and I met with a number of them and they presented some attractive offers, including a university club that offered enrolment to study with a scholarship to cover fees, accommodation on campus and even a part-time job. It was a generous package, but my view remained that I couldn't study and have a full-tilt go at a sporting career at the same time. Among the offers from the other contenders, it wasn't enticements that interested me. My question was always, 'How will you help make me a better cricketer?'

When it came to answering that question, one organisation stood out head and shoulders above the rest: Northern Districts Cricket Club. It had a great tradition, dating back to the 1920s, and had nurtured many good players, including Neil Harvey, Alan Davidson and, most famously, Mark Taylor. The club's home ground was Waitara Oval (since renamed Mark Taylor Oval) and I knew from playing there against the New Zealand Under-19s that it was a good, flat wicket. Other young players heading there included my mates Dominic Thornely and Higgsy. They were both, like me, new to Sydney life and it was another plus that the club's officials understood the kind of guidance we needed.

The officials assured me of the keeper role in first grade and were happy with my request to bat at number four. All of that was important, but the real deciding factor for me was the presence of Neil 'Harpo' Marks, who had been with the club from boyhood, had gone on to play Sheffield Shield, later served as mentor to Tubby Taylor, and, by the time I joined, was a selector for NSW. It's the job of a selector to get around to a wide range of clubs and see a whole lot of different players, and they absolutely do that. But it's only common sense that they're going to be most familiar with the players they see the most often, the ones from their own club. Northern Districts was the place for me.

In theory I had experienced living away from home during my time at the Cricket Academy. In terms of being away from friends and family that was true, but it wasn't really independent living — our meals and accommodation were all provided, we didn't have to pay bills and we were told where to go and what to do. Living in Sydney was going to be very different, but the club put things in place to make the transition as easy as possible. They organised jobs for me on the sales staff of the Wetherill Park Sportscene shop and coaching at an indoor cricket centre on Friday nights, and arranged for me to board for a little while with one of the club's stalwarts, management committee member Rocky Harris, whom I'd known in his role as team manager of the NSW Under-17s when I was playing in that age group.

Playing at Waitara you always knew when Rocky had turned up because you'd smell his distinctive cigar smoke. He had a great love for the club and took huge enjoyment in seeing me and Dom Thornely hitting the ball around the ground. He always had a tip on the races to share, although I used to joke with him that the best way to slow a horse down was for Rocky to back it! He was one of the thousands of largely unsung heroes that keep cricket going in this country. He served on the Northern Districts' committee for a total of 20 years, and whatever needed doing around the club he would do. He also umpired at first-class level and had even officiated in a One Day International. Rocky was 65 when he and his wife Hazel took me in but, far from fading into retirement, he had just the previous year started what turned out to be a 15-year stint as room attendant for visiting interstate and international teams at the SCG. (When he died, at the age of 80 in 2013, Richie Benaud said, 'The Sydney Cricket Ground will never be the same without him.')

From Rocky's I moved into a shared flat with Higgsy and Dom. I didn't seek out Cricket NSW; I just kept my head down and focused on performing well at Northern Districts, aware of the leg-up that my experience with the Comets had given me over many of the other young hopefuls out there. Between my consistently good results and the fact that I was on Neil Marks's radar, it didn't take long for the NSW development team to approach me and offer me a place in the Colts Under-21s development squad. They put me on a rookie contract that paid a token amount, just $2000 a year, but, much more importantly, included the opportunity to train with the state team.

The steps most people took towards playing for NSW were being chosen for the Colts, then moving up to the state's Second

XI, then finally being awarded the Baggy Blue cap that had been worn by everyone from Don Bradman and Bill O'Reilly to Mark and Steve Waugh, Michael Slater and Glenn McGrath, who were then among the stars of the team. My path was much shorter.

The Blues' wicketkeeper was Phil Emery, who had been in the position since 1988 and had captained the team to Sheffield Shield victory. Talented as he was, Phil had played only a single Test match and a single one-dayer for his country, for reasons that were all about timing: his career just happened to overlap almost exactly with Ian Healy's. His chance to play for the national teams had come as a result of Heals injuring his thumb, but then it was over almost before it had begun. It was the classic keepers' situation: with only one pair of gloves to fill, many gifted players miss out. But while Emmers would have loved to have played more, he appreciated the experiences he'd had and he wasn't bitter. He loved the Blues and never, ever saw his spot in the state team as a consolation prize. That made a real impression on me.

His understudy in the squad was a keeper named Craig Glassock, who had been on the scene since 1994 and was considered next in line whenever Phil decided it was time to step down. Respectfully, as the new kid on the block, I approached Craig at my very first training session and asked if I could catch some balls with him. He said, 'No, I'm going to catch over here.' *Ah, right then.* Well I couldn't just stand around like a shag on a rock, so I took myself over to Phil Emery and asked if he needed some catches. He did, and that was the beginning of an invaluable 12 months that basically formed the next stage of my apprenticeship.

I didn't do much catching myself with him — I was there to throw and hit endless balls to help him in his preparation. But by doing that I got an outstanding education. We built a good relationship and he answered countless questions. A lot of it was technical. He would tell me to hit balls to him in certain ways to certain spots. When we took a break I'd ask him why he'd made those choices, what he was working on. I'd also draw on his huge match experience, asking him, 'What happens when it kicks out of the rough, or when it's keeping low? Where do you stand?' He'd come back from playing a Shield game and we'd talk specifics about the wicket: 'Perth bounces a lot these days, so what you need to do is ...' or 'The SCG turns big on the last day so the things to remember are ...' I absorbed it all and stored it away in my mental encyclopedia.

Emmers also taught me a huge amount about the mental side of the game and about earning the right to play. He spoke a lot about what playing for NSW meant, about the proud tradition encapsulated in the Baggy Blue and what it signified to play for the most successful side in the world at the state/province/county level. I understood. The cap demanded success of those who wore it; they were the best in the game and as a kid coming through the ranks you had to earn the right to be around them.

The 1998–99 Colts squad was full of talented guys who had come from all around the state, including Nathan Bracken, Phil Jaques, Dom Thornely and Greg Mail. We were all hungry to succeed and we worked well together. Our coach was Trevor Bayliss. Originally from Goulburn, just up the highway from Queanbeyan, TB was another person with a deep love for NSW. He'd played eight seasons there, including 1989–90 when he hit 992 runs at an average of 55.11 an innings and was voted Player of the Year by his teammates. He and I began building a relationship during my time in the Colts and TB became a key part of my career and is someone whose opinion I still value greatly.

Very early in the season we pulled off a juicy win against the NSW Second XI. These were the guys who were, in theory, all lined up ready to step into the top team. They were meant to be better than us and so people seemed to expect us to feel intimidated going into the game, but we didn't at all. In fact, our view was they were just marking our places for us. As far back as I can remember I've known that if you walk into any kind of sporting contest assuming it's hopeless because you're outclassed, you'll prove yourself right. No-one's going to hand you a victory; you have to take it. And that's just what we did. We went out there and knocked them off and felt good about it.

Frustratingly, the NSW selectors didn't give us much indication that what we were doing was of interest. We certainly didn't expect to just walk into the Shield team, but there were other opportunities they might have considered us for, including the List-A team that played in the Mercantile Mutual Cup. Near the end of 1998, the Comets called me up and asked if I would reconsider my decision not to play a second summer with them. They'd been having a very mixed time of it, including a reasonable loss to NSW, a very solid victory over Tasmania and a nine-wicket thrashing by Queensland. Going into the season, the selectors had hired a big-hitting English batsman with designs on a Test career, Chris Adams, to give them some extra fire power. It hadn't worked out. Adams's heart was never in it — he later admitted that within a few days of landing in Australia he regretted signing the deal. He only played three games before getting back on a plane and going home. The Comets had a hole to fill and the governing body had just changed the rules so that Canberra players who had moved to other states were still eligible to play for the ACT, as long as they hadn't yet represented their new state. I fitted the bill, which is why they were now calling me.

My view was that I was committed to NSW, so the answer would still be no. But then I spoke to the NSW selectors, telling them about the offer. To my surprise, they told me that they weren't going to be picking me anytime soon and that I should say yes. I said, 'But I'm here now; I've chosen the Blues.' They said I didn't need to worry, I was part of the squad and that wouldn't change: I should just go and play for the Comets. So I said I would, for their remaining three games.

The first of these was in Canberra, at Manuka Oval on Sunday, 10 January 1999. I had a point to prove; I went out there determined to show the NSW selectors what they were missing. As it happened, our opponents were Victoria. Dean Jones was no longer with them, but they weren't short of talent, including Brad Hodge, batsman Matthew 'Herb' Elliott and all-rounder Ian Harvey. They won the toss and decided to bat. With the score at 3 for 15, we were on a roll, but then Brad Hodge turned on his magic, getting 118 off 152 balls and contributing over half the Bushrangers' total of 226. Expectations were still almost universally low for the Comets, but I couldn't have cared less about that. Batting at number two, I was on a mission and Hodgey's century only made me more determined to do well. My 133 took just 124 balls and included 14 fours and four sixes before mine became the fifth wicket to fall. We took the match with seven overs and four wickets to spare and I was named Player of the Match. I thought, *Yep, that should get me noticed.*

I was right. I was back at the SCG the following day for training when one of the selectors came up to me and commented on how well I'd done, then asked, 'Why can't you do that for us?' Almost without thinking I answered, 'Well I would, but you haven't picked me,' in a tone that said loud and clear what I thought about that decision. As he walked away, I thought, *Oh crap, what did I go saying that for? It sounded so disrespectful — stupid, stupid.* But either he didn't take offence or my performance was just too good to ignore, because the next day I was named as part of the NSW XI that would take on Canberra in a three-day match to start at Manuka the following Sunday.

Higgsy, who had been having a great season with Northern Districts, had impressed the selectors too and was also chosen for the team. The selection of two of its own was a very proud day for Queanbeyan, and the local paper went with the headline 'NSW dream is realised as Higgs, Haddin face former teammates'. Meanwhile, just in case anyone was tempted to forget the invisible but very real border that separates the two cities, *The Canberra Times* opted for 'From hero to foe ...' While the match wasn't a first-class fixture it was regarded as state level, and in a team that included Shane Lee and all-rounder Brad McNamara, only three of us (me, Higgsy and bowler Trent Johnston) weren't Sheffield Shield players.

It was a bit strange to be playing against Peter Solway and Simon Mann but also good competitive fun. I think those guys felt very proud of me, but no-one was going to give any quarter and under Mike Veletta's captaincy Canberra made us work for a draw. The stats-obsessed might have enjoyed the unintentional symmetry of Manny getting me out lbw for 13 in our first innings and me getting Sol out on 87. I did only marginally better in our second innings, reaching just 19. I would have liked to have shown the NSW selectors that it wasn't just in the limited-overs format that I could perform, particularly because, going into the match, chairman Alan Campbell had been very upfront in a newspaper interview about the fact that the Blues' poor performance in the Sheffield Shield — as opposed to one-dayers, where they were in top spot on the Mercantile Mutual Cup ladder — meant that spots were up for grabs.

In theory, playing for NSW should have ruled me out of going ahead with the other Comets' Mercantile Mutual Cup games, but the administrators decided it was better that I honoured the commitment. Hopes were high in Canberra in the lead-up to the two remaining Comets' matches because winning one would be enough to secure a place in the finals. The Canberra paper got very excited, running a huge story headlined 'Stage set for finals fairytale for Veletta'. But the Comets' happily-ever-afters weren't to be: in the first match WA beat us by 49 runs and in the second SA won with four wickets in hand. My own performances were nothing to write home about, though I did keep up a nice quick run rate. The Comets ended the season coming sixth, above only Tasmania. (In the following season, 1999–2000, they didn't win a match and finished last, after which the Australian Cricket Board announced they would no longer be part of the Mercantile Mutual Cup. The whole experiment had lasted only three years and through pure luck I'd been in exactly the right place at exactly the right time. I'll always be grateful to the guys I played with, who nurtured me at that crucial time in my career.)

Anyway, whatever I did on the field and at training was enough, because by the time the 1999–2000 season started I was officially part of the NSW state squad. The annual contract had a base rate of $10,000, which wasn't enough to live on, but as long as I got selected for the team itself I'd be fine since we also got match fees. If you played right through the season it would add up soon enough — and I planned on doing exactly that. I chucked in my part-time jobs and threw myself into the new, intense full-time training. I loved it. I did everything that was asked of me and more, every single time. I wanted to make a difference. I didn't want to be a guy who'd played a couple of games for NSW and that was the end of it. I'd seen enough high-level performances by now to fully understand the level of work required and I was totally up for it.

Nathan, Dom, Greg and Higgsy were also in the squad: we'd leap-frogged right over the guys who were supposedly next in line. We all trained hard, but we had fun off the field too. We were a bunch of young guys, footloose and fancy-free and making a living from the sport we loved — how could we *not* have fun? We'd all go out together on a Saturday night and have a blast. However, I'd absorbed some good lessons, both from my time at the Academy and from watching how Merv Hughes handled himself, and I never let the out-of-hours fun get in the way of my performance.

In July of 1999, Phil Emery announced his retirement from first-class cricket. His were big shoes to fill; he was second on the all-time list of most games played for the Blues and held the record for most dismissals, with 332 catches and 46 stumpings. I wanted more than anything to have a chance to make that kind of contribution, but I wasn't the only keeper in contention. Craig Glassock was still part of the squad and the name of another Second XI player, Nigel Taylor, was also being bandied about. Coach Steve Small was keeping his options open until the start of the season got closer. There was only one thing for me to do, and it wasn't sitting and fretting, it was working even harder than ever. I knew the selectors would be scrutinising every aspect of my game and of my attitude and I was going to make sure they knew that I was up for the challenge.

The hard work paid off: when the team was announced at the start of the season I was named as keeper for both one-dayers and the Sheffield Shield. It was an incredibly proud moment for me and my whole family. But it was an opening, an opportunity, not a crowning achievement. I was in the hot seat and I wouldn't stay there long if I didn't perform.

I couldn't wait to get out there and give it my all and I got to do just that on 10 October, two weeks before I turned 22. I made my debut as a fully fledged NSW player in the opening game of that year's Mercantile Mutual Cup tournament. We were up against Victoria at North Sydney Oval, a beautiful little ground. My whole family was there to watch, of course, and it turned out to be quite a memorable game one way and another. It was a sunny morning and, when we won the toss, captain Michael Bevan opted to bat. With Mark Taylor having retired the previous summer and Michael Slater away playing for Australia, Rod Davison was chosen to open and I went in to partner him. Unfortunately, we were both out before the sixth over was finished, with my plan to hit big coming unstuck on just eight. Corey Richards dug us out of the hole, but even so we only managed 240 by the end of the innings. Higgsy, who was also making his Blues debut and was not out on 14, had a nice moment when he lofted the ball past the mid-wicket boundary and onto the roof of the grandstand.

Matthew 'Herb' Elliott and Graeme Vimpani opened for the Bushrangers and none of our bowlers — Stuart Clark, Nathan Bracken, Brett Lee, Higgsy or Gavin 'Riddler' Robertson — could stop them as they put on 194 in just over 38 overs. Herb was on 103 when I saw my chance: he unwittingly moved out of his ground as Gavin bowled and I had those bails off in a flash. By this stage, clouds that promised a huge thunderstorm had rolled in and we played the last 30 minutes in an eerie darkness. The final scorecard didn't do anything to lift the gloom, with Victoria cruising to victory by seven wickets with 13 balls remaining. Along with the rest of the team, I just had to shake it off and prepare for the first Sheffield Shield game of the season, nine days later at the Gabba.

The Baggy Blue was incredibly precious to me, but there wasn't a big ceremony for receiving it; I just collected it from the office of Cricket NSW when I picked up the rest of my Shield whites uniform (as opposed to the blue one-day gear). Greg Mail, Don Nash and Greg Hayne also made their debuts and the game started perfectly for us when Matthew Hayden was caught at slip on the first ball. Unfortunately, it all went downhill from there. In fact, thanks to a double-century from Martin Love, Queensland were so far ahead of us that even following on we could only manage to give them an additional target of 81. I didn't take any dismissals but acquitted myself well with the bat, scoring 33 and 54 (with six fours among that half-century) as part of solid partnerships with Greg Mail and Shane Lee. But the Bulls beat us with nine wickets to spare — a result that was so inevitable that the crowd, sparse to begin with, fell to just 500 by Day 4.

(My first innings dismissal was an lbw to a medium pacer from Matthew Hayden. I still think the umpire was intimidated by Haydos into giving me out and I remain dirty about it all these years later. That delights the big bloke, who, when we catch up for a beer, takes great pleasure in first of all reminding me that he got me out in my first game then rubbing in the success Queensland have had in State of Origin rugby league in the past decade. The man is relentless!)

Our one-dayer against the Bulls was a completely different story. Two days after they'd thrashed us in the Shield, we took them on in a Mercantile Mutual Cup game. As well as a catch I got two stumpings — though it would have been preferable if the Haydos one had come *before* he reached 104. Even so, we won comfortably.

A fortnight later, in a Shield game at the SCG against South Australia, I pulled out all the stops, top-scoring with 86 in a line-up that included Michael Slater and Michael Bevan. The game was a draw after rain wiped out most of the final day's play. That was frustrating, but at least we hadn't lost.

As the season unfolded so did our pattern of winning in the limited-overs format and going down on the four-dayers. Our rematch against Queensland, at home this time, was even worse than the first game. Once again we were forced to follow on and this time they beat us by 10 wickets, with Greg Mail's 39 the top score from both our innings. It was painful, as was the following loss to Tasmania. The Blues, once absolutely dominant in the game, hadn't won the Shield since 1993–94 and had actually come bottom the previous year — something that would have been unthinkable to earlier generations.

The idea of bringing on a whole lot of young players was to shake off the malaise and produce a team that was strong enough to do well even when the international players couldn't be there. It was becoming obvious that, if it was going to happen, it wasn't going to happen quickly. We were all just getting used to first-class cricket and, while none of us had been accustomed to losing up to this point in our playing lives, the experience stood us in very good stead later in our careers. The success that lay ahead was all the more enjoyable because of the dark days we had early on.

The very busy schedules of the Test players meant we didn't get to see a lot of them, but it was great for us young blokes when we did get access to them. Their knowledge and experience was invaluable and I soaked it up. Because of their commitments against touring Pakistani and Indian teams, I didn't get to play with the Waugh twins until our fifth Shield match of the season. We were at the WACA having a hit a couple of days before the game when Steve Waugh bowled me a bouncer. I ducked, thinking, *What's going on? Is it some kind of softening-up ritual?* He bowled me another one. Okay, I was getting rattled now. We'd hardly spoken, but had I done something to annoy him somehow? Did he just not like me? Then he sent down another bouncer. I moved from wondering if he was cranky to getting fired up myself. Tugga, as he was known to us, was the captain of the Australian team, an amazing cricketer we all looked up to. But in that moment I thought, *Steve Waugh or not, if he does that again I'm going to hit him out of the net.* Sure enough, the next ball was another bouncer and sure enough I hit it out. He gave me a satisfied nod and said, 'I heard you had a good pull shot; I just wanted to check it.'

The game itself was a well-matched contest, with a solid roster of Test players on both sides. The Warriors' line-up included Mike Hussey, Brad Hogg and Adam Gilchrist, who had made his debut in the Baggy Green a couple of weeks earlier and was their captain for this game as well as wicketkeeper. Our much-needed win was built on second-inning centuries from Tugga and Michael Bevan.

December approached and with it the annual Prime Minister's XI game, this year against India. I was once again invited to be part of the team, not as a gesture of encouragement to a promising youth but, for the first time, as a professional first-class cricketer in my own right. Knowing that Sachin Tendulkar would be playing, we had joked before the game about how we'd better not drop him or he'd bat for a week, so it was a huge relief when I caught him for a duck off Brett Lee.

It had been a pretty great year, but there was one more treat in store for me before it ended: an introduction to Karina Castle. I had no clue at the time, but I had just met the love of my life.

CHAPTER 9

A TASTE OF THE BIG TIME

IT WOULD BE NICE to say that when I first saw Karina in December 1999 I knew instantly she was the one, but I didn't. I was attracted to her and there was chemistry between us, but there were complicating factors, too.

We met at a Northern Districts Cricket Club Christmas party at the Orient Hotel in The Rocks. She had a friend in the club who had invited her along. He introduced us, telling me that Karina was an athlete too, a world champion in fact. She was beautiful, with a warm manner that made her easy to talk to. We'd both recently turned 22 and I got a buzz out of discovering that her birthday was the day before mine. I learned that her sport was touch football. She was too modest to tell me all of this at the time, but she'd played throughout high school, been chosen for the NSW state side in Year 12 and a year later she was picked to play for Australia in the national mixed team. She then received the ultimate accolade of being picked for the national women's team.

Eight months earlier she had played in the sport's World Cup held in Sydney. Australia had won the trophy and become world champions. That was a noteworthy achievement but I didn't recall hearing anything much about it at the time. Karina wasn't surprised. Unlike cricket or other footy codes, touch football was a strictly amateur sport, even at the highest level. She and her teammates covered their own costs on training camps and paid their own way when they travelled around Australia or across to New Zealand to compete. In addition to their training and playing schedule, they were required to find time for fundraising to help cover costs.

To get all that done you had to be very focused, as she clearly was. I later learned that as soon as she was allowed to, at age 14 and nine months, she had found herself a weekend job in a fish and chip shop near her family home at Terrigal on the NSW Central Coast. And even though she'd gone to Newcastle Uni, two train rides and more than an hour and a half away, she'd commuted for the first two years of her Radiography degree so that she could continue to meet the obligations of her job and touch footy. Now fully qualified and working and living in Sydney, she had to fit training and competing around her full-time job. That kind of drive and work ethic was very impressive. We had a great night together and more fun going to the movies and to dinner in the following weeks, but the timing just wasn't right for either of us to start a new relationship.

It was a bit of a shame, but I was preoccupied, having been unexpectedly selected to play for Australia A (Australia's second team) in two one-dayers against the visiting Pakistan team. My goal for the season had been to build up Sheffield Shield experience, so getting the call that I'd been selected was a real thrill.

The first game took place on 2 January 2000 at Perth's WACA. There was some strong talent on the Pakistan side, but it was skewed towards players near the end of their international careers, such as Wasim Akram and Saeed Anwar (both former Pakistan Test captains), rather than younger names like Shoaib Malik. Our side, on the other hand, consisted of half younger players the selectors wanted to see in action, including Andrew Symonds, Brad Hodge and Brad Williams (yes, we were a three-Brad team), and half experienced hands including Matthew Hayden, Shane Lee and Stuart MacGill. I didn't make the impression I was hoping for when

I was stumped for a duck in the first innings, but helped make up for it with three catches. We won that game and the following one, two days later at the Adelaide Oval.

I stayed down in Adelaide for NSW's next Shield match. Unfortunately, our Shield losing streak continued there and in the remaining four games, leaving the Blues stone, motherless last for the second season in a row. But although we couldn't take a trick in the long format we continued our winning ways in the Mercantile Mutual Cup (MMC), including in a match against the Canberra Comets at Manuka where Mark Higgs and I led the charge against our old team. My score of 70 included a half-century off just 38 balls, a season record for the tournament. That delivered a cash bonus of $1000 for the team kitty.

This was dwarfed by the windfall the following week at the WACA when, batting with Corey Richards against the Western Warriors, I hit the Mercantile Mutual sponsor sign on the full, something that had only been done twice before (by Steve Waugh and Shane Lee) in the eight seasons the promotion had been running. The prize was $150,000, which, like match-winners' prize money and Player of the Match payments, went into the central kitty to be distributed throughout the squad on a pro-rata basis at the end of the season.

NSW were in a strong position heading into the MMC semi-final but the Queensland Bulls were that bit too good for us on the day (they fell, in turn, to the Western Warriors in the final). I finished the season as NSW Rookie of the Year, which meant a lot to me. It had been a huge learning period, a mix of team and individual challenges, disappointments and victories that really pushed me along as a cricketer.

I hoped to continue my development over the Australian winter with my first experience of playing in England. I joined the Wallasey club, on the west coast just across the Mersey River from Liverpool. My intention had been to experience different playing conditions and I did that. I had success with the bat and by round 10 we had won the club league. I enjoyed my time there and met a lot of nice people but ended up coming home a bit earlier than planned in order to return to the environment of professional cricket.

Back in Australia, we learned that Steve 'Stumper' Rixon would be taking over as coach of the Blues in an effort to lift us from the slump of the previous seasons. That was good news. He had spent five seasons coaching NSW at the start of the 1990s with excellent results: the Blues made the Sheffield Shield final in every one of those years, claiming the championship three times, including two years when they'd also taken out the one-day cup. As a player he had been a wicketkeeper (hence the nickname). He'd been good enough to fill the position left vacant in the Australian Test team when Rod Marsh joined Kerry Packer's World Series Cricket in 1977, but lost the spot the following year when the Australian Cricket Board (the precursor to Cricket Australia) reached a truce with Marsh and the other players who had departed for the lucrative 'pyjama game'. Six and a half years passed before Stumper came back into the Test side in 1984, when he played the last three of his 13 Tests, but during the entire time he had played for NSW with class. I had high hopes he might be able to help me move to the next level, and that's exactly what happened.

I asked Stumper recently what he remembered of those early days. He said, 'I'd been aware of you for a while through the Comets, as a promising player but one of a number of keepers around at the time. Coming up through the ranks before you got to NSW, it was obvious you were good, although like most kids coming out of the country your keeping was really raw. [Stumper, coming from Albury himself, was in a fair position to make this comment.] Did you need work? Yes, but you had the talent. I liked your tenacity and the bit of cheek you had, which I think works really well for a keeper. That "poking the chest out" sort of stuff. The very good keepers have a presence and I thought you had it. By the time you started with the Blues you'd developed as a cricketer and as a person. It didn't take a Rhodes scholar to work out you were going to be a talent in cricket, but whether you were going to get your opportunity was the question.'

Stumper had a well-earned reputation for being hard-nosed and demanding a lot of his players. He had a huge work ethic and he expected the same of us. He and I got on well from the start, and formed a very close relationship over the years. He became a crucial force in my development and is someone whose opinions I continue to seek out. I always attributed the strength of our connection to the fact that I was a keeper, like him. That was a big part of it, for sure, but when I asked him about it he said there was another factor too: 'You wanted to learn. Of course you could play, but there are people who can play who don't want to learn. Give me someone who wants to learn and you'll get my full attention every time.'

He spent countless hours honing my technique. Because there's only one of you, a wicketkeeper can sometimes get lost in training. You're sent off to do your stuff by yourself and you can get stuck in a rut. Stumper made sure that didn't happen. He grabbed me and we worked together and if I wasn't doing something right he'd tell me about it. That straight-shooting approach was perfect for me. I was able to figure out what needed to change and work on it. I'd been wicketkeeping for more than a decade by this point, man and boy, but with Stumper I really started to understand the craft and hone my skills and technique.

We had a lot of conversations, sitting down during a break in training or over a beer or dinner. I asked him hundreds of questions about why we were doing things, or how come we were doing them in this way and not that. It's no secret that patience is not one of his virtues, but he was happy to talk things over in minute detail and, as our relationship developed, debate different approaches until we found a middle ground. All the pieces really started to click for me. I could now look back on techniques Ian Healy had demonstrated during the wicketkeepers' week at the Cricket Academy with a whole new understanding of what he was doing and why.

Just before our first Sheffield Shield match of the 2000–2001 season, Michael Slater gave a big newspaper interview in which he talked about the changes that had to happen to lift us above the dismal results of the previous couple of years. He singled out the young guys on the team as the area that required the most change — we needed to step up and deliver. He said that while we had the confidence to do well in the one-day game, in the Shield, 'our younger guys haven't believed in themselves as much ... They have to believe they're in the team on their own merits and not because a few guys are away on Australian duty'. He was spot on. We had six senior players who might be called away for international games; we couldn't just sit back in awe when they were around or we'd have no answer for the opposition when they were gone.

We certainly came out with a bang, winning the first Shield game, away to Victoria, by 117 runs in a rain-shortened match. My contributions were stronger with the gloves than the bat, leading to one of the defining moments in my relationship with Stumper. I got five dismissals in their second innings — four catches and a stumping — and at the end of the game the congratulations were coming in thick and fast from my teammates. But even hugely experienced bowlers and batsmen can't truly assess a keeper: only another keeper can see what passes everyone else by. When things had quietened down a bit, Stumper sat down next to me and said, 'How did you go today?' I said, 'You bloody well know how I went. I didn't keep very well. I was untidy and I missed chances.' He said, 'Good, I'm glad you recognise that. We'll work on it.'

Knowing that he picked up every nuance of what I was doing made it all the sweeter when I did do well and he saw it — even if no-one else did. Many times over the years I've had days when no chances came my way and I didn't take a catch, even whole games like that. I might have moved perfectly and not made a single mistake the entire time, but to the non-keeper's eye it looked like a dud job. Only another keeper understands. You'd never succeed as a keeper if you were needy for praise, that's for sure. During the course of my career there were untold times when I got a perfect take, maybe a leg-side stumping where the batsman crossed his feet going forward off a medium pacer, or a low nick taken on a textbook dive, or a big edge off a spinner judged to the millisecond. I'd think to myself,

Oh yeah, how good was that! I'd look around and my teammates would be going, 'Well bowled, let's go,' gesturing for the ball. I'd think, *Don't you guys realise what just happened there?* But they didn't, because great wicketkeeping makes the hardest things look easy. Stumper always knew though, and an appreciative nod from him meant more than volumes of unearned praise from others.

Like our Shield tournament, our one-day campaign also got off to a really strong start, with an eight-wicket victory in our first MMC game of the season, at North Sydney Oval against Victoria in mid-October 2000. I was put in the opening partnership with Slats and I went for it, smashing 69 off 52 balls. Shane Warne was coming back from minor knee surgery and wasn't in top form, although I didn't know that at the time. I still enjoyed the two sixes I got off him in a single over, including one that went right onto the grandstand roof.

People were noticing, that's for sure: I got a fantastic 23rd birthday present when I was told I'd been chosen to go to the week-long Queensland training camp the Australian Cricket Board held for its 25 contracted players plus a few rising talents. Two other wicketkeepers had also been invited — Ryan Campbell from Western Australia and Wade Seccombe from Queensland. John Buchanan, who was then the Australian coach, was explicit about the fact that we were there as potential future replacements for Adam Gilchrist, both as short-term fill-ins and perhaps to follow him into the team long term. It was a great experience that left me hungry for more.

We won two of our next three MMC games with not much help from me, out for two, seven and two. Test cricketer turned commentator Simon O'Donnell took me to task for it on national television, suggesting that I was playing arrogantly by not giving due respect to bowlers of the calibre of Andy Bichel. Newspaper sports reporters also had their say. It was my first real taste of that kind of public criticism. People were entitled to their opinions, and I had to take the good with the bad.

I was moved down the batting order for the next one-dayer, but that didn't signify anything since the line-up was always game-dependent and chopped and changed at the drop of a hat. Coming in at number eight at home against South Australia I managed to find a balance, maintaining a nice quick strike rate without taking unnecessary chances, and I top-scored with 63 off 58 balls. Both Stumper and Steve Waugh, our captain, were pleased with my effort but neither was thrilled with the big picture. We lost the game and, even though it was only by six runs, Tugga's view was that as a team we just weren't hungry enough; there was still too much leaving it to other blokes to do the work. Stumper agreed wholeheartedly.

It was turning out to be a very wet summer, with games rain-shortened or, in one case, abandoned without a ball bowled. I was still having trouble turning in consistent results when we went into a Shield game against WA. Our big guns were all away playing in a Test. We batted first and everything Tugga and Stumper had said about the team falling apart under pressure seemed to be coming true: when I went in to partner Mark Higgs we were 5 for 49. If ever there was a time to dig deep, this was it. Higgsy and I delivered a 114-run partnership that put us right back in the game. On 87, I was caught by Damien Martyn just inside the boundary. Stumper, who spent the game doing his trademark superstitious walk-and-sit routine around the oval, was relieved we'd won, although he felt I'd missed an opportunity and could have got to 150. Even so, he praised the extent to which I'd successfully changed the tempo and pattern of the game — a critical ability for anyone who wanted to make it all the way to the top.

Unfortunately, a badly timed broken finger ruled me out of the next Australia A match. The break happened in the first week of 2001 in a Shield game against South Australia. As I dived for a wide ball, my finger got stuck in the ground and I heard a snap from the top joint on the middle finger of my left hand. I knew straight away the bone had broken. Broken fingers hurt like hell. It's generally not a big enough injury to make your body go into shock, which gives you temporary protection from pain. Instead, you feel every sharp, stomach-turning bit of it. But — and this is a very significant but — as a wicketkeeper you come up in the game knowing that pain is part and parcel of the role.

I grew up hearing the stories about how Ian Healy played with two broken fingers because he didn't want to give anyone else the chance to claim his position. He knew how easily that could happen because that's exactly how he got his shot. He was in Queensland, where a very talented keeper called Peter Anderson looked unassailable in the position for the state side — until he broke his finger and stood aside temporarily. Heals was brought in as the replacement. He stayed in the job for five Shield games and impressed the national selectors so much they moved Greg Dyer out of the Australian team and brought Heals in to tour Pakistan. The rest is history.

In his 12 years as Australian keeper, Heals missed a grand total of one Test, when he broke his thumb on tour in Pakistan. This gave Phil Emery his opening. Emmers kept without incident for Pakistan's first innings then went in as night watchman, but his second run came off a Mohsin Kamal fast ball that broke his thumb and ripped the nail off. He sat out the next day but went back out after lunch on Day 4. His thumb was so swollen he'd had to cut his glove up to get it on, pouring Dettol over the lot before he went out in the hope of avoiding infection. He did whatever it took to get out there. He wasn't going to let the team down and he wasn't going to miss the experience of playing Test cricket for anything. It was the right choice: Heals took the plaster off his own thumb a week early, reclaimed his spot and never again gave another keeper a look-in.

Heals had spoken to me and the other young keepers at the Cricket Academy about dealing with injuries. He said wicketkeepers are a different breed because we have to be. He also said that a broken finger hurts a lot more at training than it does in a game, and even as a young bloke with just a couple of first-class seasons under my belt I'd found that he was completely right. The adrenaline buzz you get when you walk out onto the pitch on match day goes a long way to helping you deal with pain. It's not that you don't know it's there, more that you're able to push it to the back of your mind to deal with later.

Top: Our first family photo after Hugo's birth was taken in the Camperdown ward of the Children's Hospital, Westmead, on 8 August 2012. Hugo was three and a half months, Mia 22 months and Zachary nearly four years old.

Above: Zac, Hugo and Mia on the front lawn at home, enjoying Easter Show bags, March 2013

Right: The kids awaiting my return from a World Cup game, March 2015

Top left: Dad with two-year-old me in the Cowra Magpies' shed in the winter of 1980

Top right: My brother Michael and me on the bar at the Criterion Hotel in Gundagai, not long after we moved there in 1982

Above: I was seven, Michael five and Christopher just six months old when we fronted up to Pixie Photos in Gundagai for this family shot.

Left: We moved to this house in Greenback Avenue,

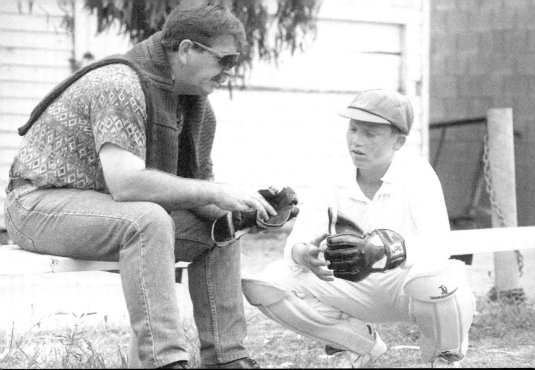

Above: In his role as Director of the Australian Cricket Academy, Rod Marsh encouraged up-and-coming players, including me at 15, as seen here in Hobart in January 1992. *(Kim Eiszele/ Newspix)*

Right: Celebrating the Canberra Comets' win over Victoria during the 1997–98 Mercantile Mutual Cup season, with Mark Higgs (on my left), Peter Solway (above me) and big Merv Hughes (top left).

Left: In my first season with the Eastern Suburbs Cricket Club, 2003–04, we won the first-grade Belvedere Cup final, the One Day competition and the State Challenge.

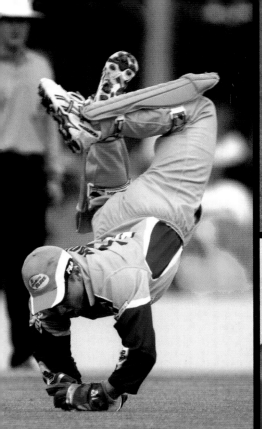

Above: Diving for the ball during an ING cup match against Victoria at the SCG, 1 December 2002. *(Phil Hillyard/Newspix)*

Below: With the Blues, celebrating victory in the 2001–02 Mercantile Mutual Cup final. *(Robert Cianfione/Getty Images)*

Top: Taking a catch to dismiss Shane Watson of the Tasmanian Tigers, in a Sheffield Shield match in Hobart, 25 November 2002. *(Robert Cianfione/Getty Images)*

Above: Talking tactics with Blues coach turned mentor and friend Steve Rixon. *(Matt King/Getty Images)*

FEBRUARY, 2001

PAY 2000-2001 MERCANTILE MUTUAL CUP CHAMPIONS

THE SUM OF SEVENTY FIVE THOUSAND DOLLARS $75,000

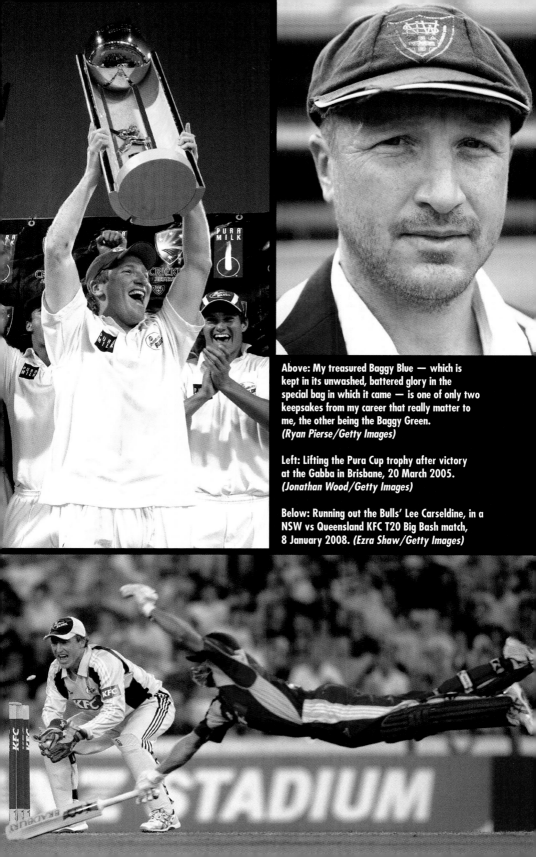

Above: My treasured Baggy Blue — which is kept in its unwashed, battered glory in the special bag in which it came — is one of only two keepsakes from my career that really matter to me, the other being the Baggy Green. *(Ryan Pierse/Getty Images)*

Left: Lifting the Pura Cup trophy after victory at the Gabba in Brisbane, 20 March 2005. *(Jonathan Wood/Getty Images)*

Below: Running out the Bulls' Lee Carseldine, in a NSW vs Queensland KFC T20 Big Bash match, 8 January 2008. *(Ezra Shaw/Getty Images)*

Above: After being selected as Australia's 400th player, I was presented with my Baggy Green on 22 May 2008, prior to the First Test match against the West Indies at Sabina Park, Kingston. *(Ryan Pierse/Getty Images)*

Left: Hitting a four in my debut One Day International, against Zimbabwe at Bellerive Oval, Hobart, 30 January 2001. *(Hamish Blair/Getty Images)*

Below: Being congratulated by my teammates after running out Shanth Sreesanth, in a One Day International against India at the Gabba, 3 February 2008. *(Cameron Spencer/Getty Images)*

A quick single on day four of my debut Test match, against the West Indies, 25 May 2008. *(Harry How/Getty Images)*

After suffering numerous injuries to my fingers, I've learned to play through the pain. *(Ryan Pierse/Getty Images)*

Keeping a close eye on Sachin Tendulkar, in the second Test against India, at Mohali, 17 October 2008. *(Michael Steele/Getty Images)*

Above: At home in Elliott Street, Queanbeyan, for Michael's 21st birthday, August 2000

Right: With Karina at our first Allan Border Medal dinner, Melbourne, 6 February 2006. *(Hamish Blair/Getty Images)*

Above left: The bridal party at our wedding, on 2 August 2007 — my brothers Michael and Christopher, Karina's sister Danielle and her best friend, Jaimie Hoy (at right) — assembled at Balmoral Beach for photos.

Above: The presence of our families and close friends made our wedding a magical occasion.

Left: My teammates Stuart Clark, Dom Thornely, Ed Cowan and Michael Clarke shared the special

Above: Sightseeing atop Table Mountain, Cape Town, with Karina and six-month-old Zac, March 2009

Above right: Gear ready to go in our garage storeroom, 2010

Right: Zac meets his new sister soon after Mia's birth on 21 October 2010

Below left: Mia watching me play against New Zealand at the Gabba, 5 December 2011

Below right: In the SCG change rooms after our 4–0 series win against India, 6 January 2012

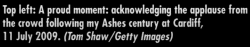

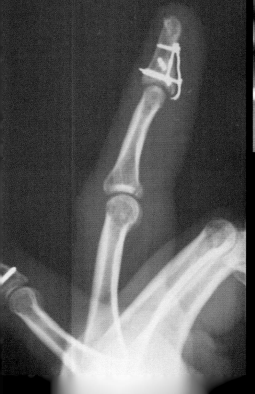

Top left: A proud moment: acknowledging the applause from the crowd following my Ashes century at Cardiff, 11 July 2009. *(Tom Shaw/Getty Images)*

Top right: Getting one away in our KFC T20 International against the West Indies in Hobart, 21 February 2010. *(Quinn Rooney/Getty Images)*

Above: Taking a catch to dismiss England's Alastair Cook in the second Test at Adelaide Oval, 5 December 2010. *(Hamish Blair/Getty Images)*

Left: An x-ray of my finger following surgery to insert two plates and five screws after it shattered like a Violet Crumble during the 2009 Ashes campaign.

Zac, aged two, visiting me in the nets at
Blacktown Oval, in November 2010
(Phil Hillyard/Newspix)

Ryan Harris, Mike Hussey, me and Nathan Lyon at
Kirribilli House, Sydney 1 December 2012

Watching the ball in a match against New Zealand at the ICC Cricket World Cup in Nagpur, India, 25 February
2011. (Matthew Lewis/Getty Images)

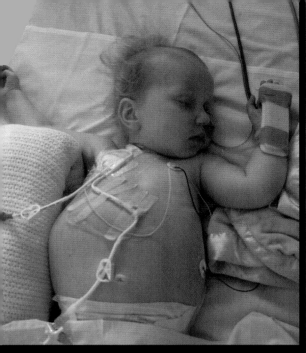

Above: I couldn't believe how unwell Mia looked when I arrived home from the West Indies on 20 March 2012.

Above right: A rare moment when Mia was free of nasal tubes. I loved every minute of that cuddle.

Right: Mia on her way back to the ward after radiation therapy at the adult hospital, November 2012

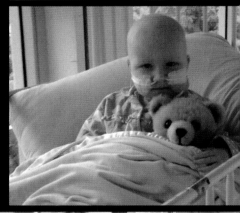

Below: Oncology Fellow Dr Santosh Valdi, Clinical Nurse Consultant Erin Sheehan and Oncologist Dr Luciano Dalla-Pozza reviewing Mia's progress during immunotherapy, 7 May 2013

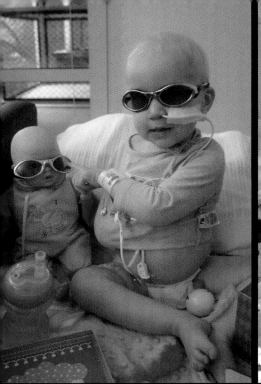

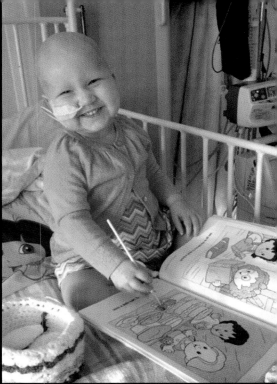

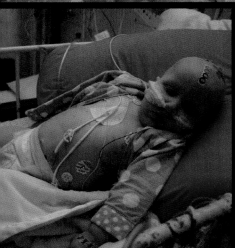

Above left: Even with a broken shoulder, Mia still managed to have some fun.

Above: Mia's bright smiles helped us all stay positive.

Left: During the bone marrow transplant in September 2012, Mia gained 3 kilograms of fluid, which affected her liver, her remaining kidney and her lungs.

Below left: The grandparents played a critical role in my ability to return to the cricket field. My mum and dad were there to share Mia's second birthday with her while I was away, on 21 October 2012.

Below: Karina's parents, Marg and Phil, celebrated their milestones in the ward so that Mia didn't miss out. On 25 July 2012 it was Phil's birthday.

Celebrating with the Sydney Sixers after winning the final of the Champions League T20 in Johannesburg, South Africa, 28 October 2012. *(Stephane de Sakutin/Getty Images)*

Rejoicing after taking the wicket of Stuart Broad during the First Ashes Test of the Commonwealth Bank Ashes Series at the Gabba, 24 November 2013. *(Ryan Pierse/Getty Images)*

Everyone except the English team enjoyed this one-handed catch, which dismissed Joe Root in the Third Ashes Test at the WACA, 16 December 2013. *(Quinn Rooney/Getty Images)*

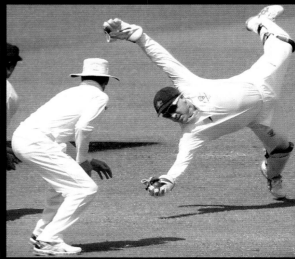

Wicketkeepers have to be perfectly positioned to take a bottom edge, like the one Ben Stokes got on a Nathan Lyon ball, on the fifth day of the Ashes' Third Test, 17 December 2013. *(Gareth Copley/Getty Images)*

Above: Enjoying Sydney's 2013 New Year's Eve fireworks as a family

Left: Zac celebrates his first ton, in the MCG nets, Christmas Day 2013. *(Scott Barbour/Getty Images)*

Above left: At 2.15 a.m., in the middle of the MCG, I lead the team song for the last time, following our 2015 World Cup victory over New Zealand. *(Ryan Pierse/Getty Images)*

Above right: My parents with the World Cup. *Rob Lindblade/ICC*

Left: Throwing a golf ball against a wall during a nets session at Windsor Park, Dominica, 31 May 2015. *(Ryan Pierse/Getty Images)*

Above: Announcing my retirement from all forms of cricket except T20, September 2015. *(Mark Metcalfe/Getty Images)*

Right: With my family at the SCG for a career lap of honour, 21 January 2016. *(Hamilton Lund)*

Below: Team Mia supporting research into neuroblastoma in the annual Run2Cure, 22 June 2014

Above: Our amazingly brave and gorgeous Mia on her first day at school, 29 January 2016

Left: A family portrait, 16 February 2015. Back row, left to right: Karina, me, my parents, my grandmother Mar, Christopher and Jenna, and Amy and Michael and daughter Georgia. Front row: Zachary, Hugo, Mia and their cousin Molly.

A lot of athletes have a high pain threshold and keepers aren't the only tough ones out on a cricket pitch by any means. What fast bowlers put their bodies through is horrendous. Towards the end of my career I played a Test match in South Africa in which Ryan Harris had such fluid build-up on his knee it locked in the last session just before tea. We all thought he was gone, but in the break he had a hypodermic needle put in to drain it, giving him back a little bit of movement. He came out and bowled the last session, even though he could barely run. He got through it on sheer will, muscling the ball on the last two steps of his delivery and taking the final wicket that won us the whole series.

If you're not extra stoic, you won't get far in my line of work. I always found it a bit funny when doctors told me to rate my pain on a scale of one to ten. I wanted to ask if that was a normal 10 or a wicketkeeper's 10. If I answered according to the normal scale, I'd say 10 and the doctor would say, 'Well, you obviously can't play with that,' to which my response was, 'Yeah, it hurts, but I can still do what I have to do.' (I should probably note that according to my brother Chris my stoicism is reserved for the sporting arena. He would have you believe that I react to a dose of 'man flu' as if it were Ebola. I'll maintain a dignified silence on that allegation.)

So, when I broke my finger in the game against South Australia and the doctor suggested I have surgery to insert a metal pin in it, my first question was, 'How long would that put me out for?' When he said three to four weeks, my decision was easy. No way was I having surgery in the middle of the season when so many opportunities were coming my way. Instead I'd just grit my teeth and play with the finger strapped. It wouldn't pass the medical check needed to play in the Australia A game — there was no way around that, and Wade Seccombe was chosen instead — but I hoped I would be fine to play again the following week, for our MMC game against South Australia. Indeed, the finger healed enough by then for me to bat, but Greg Mail stood in for me as keeper in that match and the following one a few days later. After that, I was fine to resume my normal duties.

There were some nice things being said about me, including Steve Waugh describing me as 'a cross between Ian Healy and Adam Gilchrist' and adding, 'He looks like one of those players destined for the next level.' That was a huge compliment but I knew I had a lot to learn and I didn't want to get too far ahead of myself, which is why I reacted the way I did when my phone rang one Sunday evening when I was at the Blue Gum Hotel celebrating after a game with my Northern Districts teammates in January 2001.

The caller introduced himself as Steve Bernard. Well, obviously I knew the name: he was the manager of the Australian cricket team. He said, 'You're going to need to go home and pack a bag. You're in the Australian one-day team for the game in Hobart against Zimbabwe on Tuesday. You'll be flying down there in the morning.' I could only reply, 'Sorry, what?' 'Yep,' the voice said, 'Gilly's having a rest and you're in.' It had to be one of my mates pulling a prank. 'Oh yeah,' I said. 'And who is this?' 'It's Steve Bernard, Brad.' 'Yeah, yeah, but who is it really?' He didn't seem surprised at my reaction; I think he'd heard something like it a few times before. It finally got through to me that he was for real.

He briefly told me about the arrangements and then rang off. I excitedly phoned my parents and said, 'Guess what, I've just been chosen for Australia!' They understood just how much it meant to me and immediately said they would fly down for the game, as did my good mate Jason Swift. I found it pretty hard to get to sleep that night. On the one hand, this was exactly what I'd dreamed about, but on the other there was the daunting realisation that it represented another huge step. Sure, I'd already played against international teams, and during the domestic competitions I'd gained a fair bit of game time with and against several members of the Australian team — guys like Glenn McGrath, Shane Warne, the Waugh twins and rising star Ricky Ponting. But I knew enough to realise how much I didn't know. So far I'd really only dipped my toe in the water. Now it was time to dive in head-first.

A couple of the senior players heading down from Sydney were at the airport. I was proud but self-conscious as I travelled alongside them, wearing the Australian Cricket team polo. Picking up the official kitbag off the carousel at the airport in Hobart, I felt like people were looking at me, wondering, *Who's this kid with the dyed blond hair and the earring? What's he up to?* I headed for the hotel as I'd been told to do. The media manager called, introduced himself and said he needed me across the road in half an hour for an interview and photo. 'Wear your media polo,' he said. 'Yep, no worries,' I replied. How hard could it be? Then I opened the gear bag that had been put in my room and saw four polos, all with the team logo and all different. I eenie-meenie-miney-mo'd one and went downstairs to be interviewed in my capacity as Australia's newest recruit, if only for one game. (Steve Bernard had explained this was a long-planned rest for Gilly. He didn't have to spell out that it was also a pressure test for me.)

I'd definitely be wicketkeeping, but there was no certainty I'd get to bat. Sports commentators were saying I was unlikely to be placed above number seven on the sheet, and Australia hadn't lost more than six wickets the entire tri-series (the West Indies was the third competitor). However the game went, I hoped to perform well, but my entire thinking focused on the team, not me as an individual. I was walking into arguably one of the best cricket teams ever to play. They did not expect to lose, and no matter what, I couldn't let them down.

My nerves were high as I got on the team bus to go to Bellerive Oval. I didn't feel any better when we reached the ground. I found excuses to dilly dally on the way into the change room to allow everyone else to get ahead so I didn't accidentally claim anyone's spot. Secretly I hoped we would lose the toss and have to field first — that way I wouldn't have to sit around for a couple of hours getting even more nervous. My heart sank a bit when the coin fell our way, but it rose again when Steve Waugh decided to send Zimbabwe in to bat. There's no better way to settle nerves, for me anyway, than getting out there amongst it.

And so on 30 January 2001, I made my One Day International (ODI) debut. Ian Healy was at the game in his role as a commentator for the Nine Network and he presented me with my one-day cap in a ritual introduced under Steve Waugh's captaincy. The team formed a circle on the field and Heals said ... Well, I can't remember exactly what he said: I was so keyed up, it went by in a blur. I know he welcomed me to 'the unique family' of people who've played for their country, and I'm pretty sure he ended with, 'You deserve this opportunity. Go out and fulfil your childhood dream.' One by one the team filed past to shake my hand; then it was game on.

Zimbabwe came out strong. Opener Alistair Campbell took a little while to get going against the bowling of Glenn McGrath and Damien Fleming, but once he hit his stride he piled on runs without offering up any real chances. I didn't get flustered; I just kept my eyes open, ready to make the most of any little slip. By the 23rd over, Campbell and Guy Whittall had reached 94 (an opening partnership record for Zimbabwe in one-dayers against Australia) when Whittall tapped the ball off to the side and started for a single. I saw my opening and instantly seized it, jumping out from behind my wicket, scooping up the ball, flicking my glove off and landing a direct hit on the stumps at the non-striker's end. The team was very happy with that effort, although since run outs are not classed as personal dismissals I still had not yet officially claimed my first international scalp.

Andrew Symonds got Zimbabwe's number three, Stuart Carlisle, with a very nice running catch at long-on, but we had no luck taking Campbell's wicket until Warnie's bowling spell. I had a real 'wow' moment, sitting in my crouch thinking, *I'm about to keep to Shane Warne* and I thanked my lucky stars for the experience I'd gained keeping up to the stumps for Stuart MacGill's spin bowling. Finally, at the start of the 48th over, with Campbell on 124, a slider came off his bat past the outside edge. I had it, then I didn't. Sweeping it back over towards the stumps, I fumbled, before regaining control and making the stumping. I knew it was good, but the fumble made it hard for the umpire to be sure, so he sent it upstairs. I stayed calm, although I did think, *Jeez, I hope I haven't fluffed one off Shane Warne; I'll never hear the end of it.* The wait seemed to go on forever, but finally the third umpire signalled 'Out'. *Yes!* There was a brief celebration — everyone in the team understood what a moment like that represented for a young player — then we were back into it.

Zimbabwe finished on 279, exciting the statisticians because it was their highest total of the series, an ODI record at Hobart and a bigger score than Australia had ever bettered in a one-dayer at home. We made good ground against them, however, thanks to Andrew 'Symo' Symonds and Steve Waugh, and a dogged Mark Waugh (known as Junior because he is a few minutes younger than his twin), who was on 90 when I went out following Steve's dismissal halfway through the 35th over. (I'd been listed to bat at number seven but, when it looked like we were going to win, Steve said, 'Put your pads on and go out and have a hit.') We needed 46 to win and we had 14 overs and six wickets in hand. I'd played alongside Mark in the Blues a fair bit by this point, and walking out to him I was keen to hear the advice he would have for me.

What he actually said, in classic Junior fashion, was, 'Mate, make sure I get 100. Don't get too many runs before I do.' That immediately became my focus: *Make sure Junior gets his ton.* But, dammit, if I didn't get a four early on and then another. I was nicely warmed up by my 11th ball in, a full toss from a leg-spinner called Brian Murphy. It was right there, begging to be popped straight to the stand, but my only thought was *Don't hit it for six, 'cos then he mightn't get his numbers.* I attempted to roll it, but it went straight up and I was out for 13. Walking back off, I was thinking, *Well, we still look set to win the game and at least I didn't get in Junior's way.* It all came back to the importance of knowing your place. The respect was real — those senior guys had earned it with what they'd done for the game. I hoped one day I'd be seen in a similar light, but that was a long way off.

Junior finished on 102 not out, and we won the game with six overs to spare. I caught up briefly with my family then went out for beers with some of my cricketing heroes — as a fellow member of the Australian team. How about that? It was a really great end to a memorable day (it would even be worth how bad I felt flying out in turbulence at 6 a.m. the next morning after too little sleep and too many celebratory drinks). Back home, the selectors let me know they were happy with the way I had played, and that was that. Their unstated but clearly understood message was, 'Get your mind back on state cricket and continue to perform there so that if the opportunity comes again you're ready.'

Before my international debut game I thought I knew what it was to want a place in the Australian side. Now I *really* knew and I was even more determined to do whatever it took to get that opportunity again. It was going to take a lot. The difference between what I'd been used to and what I'd just been part of was unmistakable. Everything about it — up to and including the banter that fielders used in an attempt to get into a batsman's head — all of it had a completely different intensity.

Prior to that game I thought I was working hard, but now I could clearly see that the preparation I'd been doing was never going to earn me any more than a cameo in the Australian team. I had to work even harder. It was going to be tough, but now I knew the pay-off would be worth it. The feeling I'd had being part of the game at that level was addictive. I wanted more it, all of it — even the anxiety and that sick feeling in the stomach when you know how much is at stake and how much scrutiny you're under. I talked it over with Steve Rixon and asked him to help me get to a whole other level. He was happy to oblige, coming up with extra training for me on top of what the rest of the team was doing.

The rest of the season's MMC one-dayers didn't all go our way, but we won more than we lost and in late February we went up against the Western Warriors in the final at the WACA. They batted first and, led by some big hitting from Tom Moody and Mike Hussey, reached 272. Michael Clarke and I opened the batting for the Blues. Pup, as Michael is known, got 57, but I was caught for eight. Fortunately, Michael Bevan stayed the course and his quick 135 secured the win for us with 10 balls remaining. The Blues had won the domestic one-day championship for the first time in six years! We were thrilled and celebrated in true NSW fashion. At one point, batsman Graeme Rummans did a great re-enactment of the catch he'd dropped that he'd thought was going to cost us the final. It seemed a lot funnier after a few beers in the change rooms than it had several hours earlier.

I was having a fantastic summer already, but it got even better one night when I was out with the Northern Districts boys and Karina turned up. We started talking, catching up on what we'd each been doing over the past year or so. I enjoyed her company, but the guys I was out with were talking about moving on to another pub. I'd had enough of the night. I got up to go home and was halfway out the door when Karina caught me and asked if I'd come back and dance with her. She told me later she thought she'd better be bold and let me know she liked me, or we'd miss our chance. I wasn't big on dancing, I'm more of a stand-at-the-bar kind of guy, but I liked her too, so back I went. We danced and talked and talked some more and by the time she dropped me home we knew we wanted to see a lot more of each other. We've never been apart since.

At the beginning of March 2001, I was playing in a Shield game against the Queensland Bulls at the SCG. We were without Michael Slater and the Waugh brothers, who were touring India. The First Test, at Mumbai, had finished the day before. It was riveting stuff. India's first innings were a pure battle of will between Sachin Tendulkar and Australia's skipper, Steve Waugh, who deployed Glenn McGrath and Shane Warne to great effect before the Little Master fought back. The following day, Australia were in trouble at 5 for 99 before Adam Gilchrist came to the rescue. Like millions of other Aussies, I was looking forward to seeing what happened 10 days later in the Second Test, in Kolkata (formerly Calcutta).

Meanwhile, the Blues had stepped up under Stumper's coaching. We were starting to develop our ability to maintain momentum as a team even when the senior players were away on international duty. We won the toss and went in to bat, feeling confident. Personally, I've had better days at the office, but fortunately my duck was not a problem, thanks to massive stands by Michael Bevan, Shane Lee and Mark Higgs. Queensland had no answer and were struggling by lunchtime on Day 3, when Trevor Hohns, the chairman of selectors, pulled me aside and asked for a word.

He told me that Gilly had pulled up okay from his big 122 in Mumbai, but had strained his hip at training. While everyone was fairly confident he would be right for the Second Test there was no back-up keeper on the tour and they wanted to rest him for the three-day Board President's XI tour match starting the following day in Cochin. I had to get home and pack quick-smart: I was flying out that afternoon to serve as his stand-in. It was amazing news. The whole thing was head-spinning, including the TV cameras and journalists who were waiting for me when I arrived at Sydney airport.

In fact it all happened so fast I really didn't have time to get myself worked up about the possibility that I might be making my Test debut. I reminded myself that I was there for the tour match and that was almost certainly all, so there was no point projecting beyond that. I touched down in India at midnight, local time, on 5 March, and the game was underway by 9.30 the following morning. With everything happening so fast, I didn't have time to take in anything about India itself. It was all I could do to get my head in the game. Fortunately, we won the toss and Steve Waugh chose to bat, which gave me time to settle.

This time it was Tugga and Ricky 'Punter' Ponting who got centuries (Junior was stopped in his tracks at 62). I contributed a quick 24 to our total of 451. It was interesting to see the Indian bowling line-up in action, but my real education came when I got behind the wicket. I'd had a previous taste of subcontinental conditions on my Under-19s tour of Pakistan, but that was a long way from this level of the game. The conditions were unlike anything in Australia. Forget about the ball coming up to waist-height; it doesn't bounce above knee level on that hard and dusty ground and you have to stand so much closer to the stumps. Then there's the fact that, as the ball ages, it reverse-swings in an unexpected way. None of it was bad; it was simply very, very different from anything

I knew — making it a great experience for me. On that wicket we were unlikely to bowl the opposition out, so we played for and got a draw.

I was asked to stay on until the Second Test was underway, to make certain Gilly was going to be fit to play. The squad travelled to Kolkata, getting there two days before the start of the game. The city is home to the Udayan Care centre, where children of leprosy patients are cared for and educated. Steve Waugh had already been a supporter of Udayan for a few years at that point, after having what he described as a life-changing encounter with Mother Teresa. Following training on the first day, he and Justin Langer were heading there for a visit and I asked if I could join them. It was an eye-opening experience. Even the bit I'd seen of Pakistan didn't prepare me for the level of poverty I witnessed driving through the streets of Kolkata. The mothers with famished babies and the tiny children begging alone got to me the most. Because of the way cricketers are idolised and mobbed in India, we had high security, making us and our privileged existence even more visible. I could understand why Steve had been moved to do what he could to help. Feeling way out of my depth, I really admired his easy way with the Udayan kids. He was (and still is) a great ambassador for his country.

Gilly looked good in training and was cleared to play, which I'll admit came as a huge relief to me. Of course, if I'd been asked to go out there in his place, I would have gone willingly and given it my very best. But 'baptism of fire' would be an understatement for what that experience would have been like. Eden Gardens is the world's second-largest cricket ground behind the MCG. It has an official capacity of 66,000, but you often get crowds of nearly 100,000 crammed into that cauldron. Nothing I'd seen on television or heard from people who'd been there prepared me for what the noise was like when you were there. On the sideline, running drinks, I couldn't hear the words of someone standing six inches away from me. As Indian cricket writer Anand Vasu has put it, it's more like being at a bullring than a cricket ground.

That kind of atmosphere is just one of the reasons why visiting Australian teams often have trouble vanquishing India in Test cricket. The likelihood of getting 'Delhi belly' was another for many years, and even in 2001 you still couldn't just grab a sandwich or a piece of fruit in the lunch break without wondering how it had been prepared. Also, the humidity is a killer, even for Aussies used to heat, and having a crowd of thousands of people outside your hotel and everywhere else you go feels pretty strange. And then there are those unfamiliar wickets. All these factors add up, which is why Tugga called India 'the final frontier' for the Australian team.

So, much as I dreamed of making my debut in the Baggy Green, I didn't mind at all sitting this one out. I felt incredibly grateful just to be there, with a sideline view of what turned out to be one of the most remarkable Test matches of all time. With India forced to follow on after producing just 171 in answer to Australia's first innings total of 445 (110 of those runs from Tugga; his first Test century in India), they looked set to go down in under three days as they had in the First Test. But then VVS Laxman and Rahul Dravid delivered one of the greatest batting partnerships of all time, adding 376 before Laxman finally fell to a Glenn McGrath delivery on 281 and Dravid was run out five overs later on 180. Going into the final day, Australia needed 384 to win, but Harbhajan Singh was unbeatable on the fifth-day wicket, claiming six scalps to give India the Test. The atmosphere really was indescribable. The passion that the Indian crowds have for cricket is impossible to explain to anyone who hasn't experienced it for themselves.

I was home in time for the NSW vs Queensland Sheffield Shield match at the Gabba, but the Bulls were too good for us, winning by nine wickets and knocking us out of the comp. We finished the season third on the ladder. It was a significant improvement on our bottom place in the previous season, when we'd only managed to win a single game. We still had quite a way to go, but we were on the right path.

CHAPTER 10

DOING THE BLUES PROUD

BY THE EARLY PART of 2001, numerous sports commentators were routinely referring to me as the most likely successor to Adam Gilchrist whenever he eventually retired. Respecting Gilly and the Baggy Green as I did, I never encouraged that kind of talk. But it did seem to fit with the positive message the national selectors had sent in picking me for the ODI against Zimbabwe and with the feedback Steve Rixon was giving me about the development in my game. All signs indicated I was progressing very nicely towards the aspiration I'd had since I was a little kid: playing for my country.

In May, the selectors announced the back-up keeper they were sending to England for that year's three-month Ashes tour of England (plus a triangular one-day series with Pakistan). It wasn't me; it was 28-year-old Wade Seccombe, an integral part of the Queensland team that had recently won the Sheffield Shield for the second year in a row. Stumper, who'd dealt with the uncertainty of not knowing if he was ever going to get to play a Test and then with long years of not knowing if he'd ever get to play another, was a great person to talk to about all of this. I also spoke to Dad, of course, who had excellent advice as usual: keep your head down and work harder than ever; don't waste time worrying about things you can't control (including selection panel decision-making); don't think about players who are supposedly ahead of or behind you. Instead, put every bit of energy into being the best wicketkeeper you can possibly be, and be accountable for your own performances. So that's what I did.

Over the winter of 2001, Stumper ramped up the NSW team's training even further. He felt that there were critical games at the pointy end of the previous season's Sheffield Shield tournament that we'd lost through lack of fitness. He wasn't going to let that happen again and he had a new six-day-a-week training schedule for us. He brought in fitness specialists who had us running up and down sandhills at first light and swimming off Bondi on bitingly cold mornings (I had flashbacks to Rod Marsh's steely approach at the Cricket Academy). Given my views on training, it's no surprise I was one of the players who supported the new approach. But it was a big change and it didn't please everyone, particularly the older players, as some of them made clear. However, Stumper held his ground and nearing the start of the 2001–02 season almost everyone was prepared to admit how much difference the new regime had made — you had only to look around the change room to see it.

I was raring to go, and warmed up by scoring 191 for Northern Districts in a grade game. A week later, playing Tasmania in what had become the ING (rather than Mercantile Mutual) Cup, Mark Waugh and I forged a 228-run opening partnership for the Blues, during which I reached a ton off 74 balls, equalling the record for the fastest domestic one-day century. It wasn't the only record in that game, played at Bankstown Oval on a perfect batting wicket. Our winning total of 4 for 397 was the highest first-class one-day score ever in Australia (and the third highest in the world). Stumper's new approach was off to a good start.

I copped the first of the season's broken bones not too long after, when I chipped my left thumb, and then had to miss a Shield game because the Blues' manager and physio were concerned about my ability to bat. But I pushed through and was back in the team 10 days later when we were away to Victoria. We lost the toss and batted on a wet wicket and damned if the second ball I faced didn't smash into my right hand. I could feel the forefinger sticking out at a strange angle in my glove. I figured it was just dislocated, so I grabbed it and rolled it back over. I heard it click and thought I'd fixed it, but it just got more and more painful. Of course it was broken, and I went into the next innings wicketkeeping with breaks in both hands. I could manage one without an anaesthetic block, but not both. I had the needle and went out and did the job, feeling every slam of the ball into the gloves.

The problem with blocks is that they wear off all of a sudden, hours later. That night at the hotel I was in bed when sensation in the newest break returned with a vengeance. The throbbing was so bad I couldn't sleep. Eventually I gave up trying, got up and dressed and went downstairs to the bar. It's a given that you just don't drink during a match, but I had to do something to take the edge off, so I had a beer. I was halfway through a second when Stumper walked past, looked in and saw me sitting there. He came in and said with a shake of his head, 'What are you doing?' I thought, *This isn't going to end well*, but I told him the truth. 'Mate, my hands are cooked. I can't get to sleep for the pain.' I don't know how many coaches would have understood, but he was a fellow wicketkeeper. 'Good point,' he said, 'I'm buying.' Then, turning to the barman: 'Two more, thanks.' We sat there for an hour and a half talking, until I was ready to turn in.

The Blues' momentum in the ING Cup continued and we powered through the season with only three losses to seven wins, getting us into the final against Queensland on 24 February 2002. They won the toss and sent us in to bat. Corey Richards and I opened, and at 0 for 82 we were feeling pretty good, but Stuart Law got me out with a huge diving catch and Corey was gone in the following over with no runs added. We got to a scrappy 204, which seemed well within the Bulls' grasp, especially when Martin Love got his half-century. But we regrouped. With the game on the line I took one of my best catches, off Shawn Bradstreet to dismiss

James Hopes. It was one of those catches you train hard for, the kind I'd visualised ever since I'd first picked up keeper's gloves: a full-stretch one-hander just like the ones I was imagining when I hurled myself horizontally into the pool as a kid. We had no slip fielder in place to stop it, and if I'd missed it would have gone for four and changed the momentum of the game. But I didn't miss. I had it, safe as houses. Shawn and Dom Thornely then tore through their middle and lower order, and we got their last five wickets for 36 runs, keeping them to a total of just 185. For the second year in a row, we claimed victory in the Cup.

That win felt great but the one-dayers weren't the problem. It was in the four-day Shield games that the cracks showed, and unfortunately that was exactly what happened yet again. We started the campaign fairly well, with a draw against Tasmania followed by strong wins against South Australia and Victoria, but it was all downhill from there. Those victories were the only ones we had in the whole series; the other eight games were evenly split between draws and losses and we finished right at the bottom of the ladder.

I was still following Dad's advice not to worry about what the selectors were up to. But Stumper became worked up when the selectors chose WA's Ryan Campbell as Gilly's replacement for a one-dayer against New Zealand at the SCG early in 2002. He told a journalist that he was so shocked about the decision that he'd called the selectors to find out what they were thinking. He was a lot more worked up about it than I was — I really wasn't fussed about Ryan's selection or anyone else's for these one-off opportunities. My entire focus in that regard was getting myself ready to step up when the real opportunity came.

The thing I found most difficult whenever there was public speculation about what the selectors had done or were likely to do was having people around me talk about it. Not my family, who took the same view as I did, but acquaintances who probably thought they were being supportive when they said, 'Oh you should have been picked instead of so and so …' What on earth are you supposed to say to that? It just made me uncomfortable. The chairman of selectors, Trevor Hohns, on the other hand, made a comment I found helpful. He took me aside at one point and said, 'You're going well; we can see that. You're getting some runs and you're keeping well. But we want you to win more games with the bat. We want to see more of you scoring those tough runs under pressure.' Specific feedback given in a direct, straightforward manner: perfect.

The following season, 2002–03, turned out to be an amazing one for the Blues. Simon Katich had come over to us during the winter, leaving WA after five years during which they'd twice won the Sheffield Shield. He had made his Test debut a year before he came to NSW but hadn't been selected for the national side since. With Michael Slater still struggling with the bat and not certain of a call-up, and Steve Waugh on international duty, Kat came into the Blues in the very strange position of captaining a side he'd never played for.

In our first six Shield games, we claimed three wins (plus a draw and two losses), which was more than we'd achieved in the whole previous season. Based on recent form, our campaign still could have gone either way, but our next game, in which we took on WA in Newcastle in late January 2003, changed everything. Despite some solid work by openers Greg Mail and Slats, we were 4 for 131 after lunch on the first day, with Kat out for a duck (the first of what would be seven dismissals by Ryan Campbell) and Steve Waugh gone for 20. We got back on track thanks to the steady hand of Mark Waugh, whose satisfying 73 included partnerships with Michael Clarke (69) and me (39).

WA went in on Day 2 chasing 370 and, despite strong bowling by Stuart Clark, Doug Bollinger and Stuart MacGill, got to 388, mostly thanks to a 194 fourth-wicket partnership from Michael Hussey and Geoff Marsh's son Shaun. Our second innings saw Kat get 50, Junior 83 and Pup 116 (I contributed 20) for a total of just 316. WA came out strongly in reply, hitting a ton before they lost their first wicket. At 4 for 272, they only needed 27 runs for victory. It was obvious to everyone there was no way they could lose — everyone but us. Instead of yielding, we dug deep.

Kat was up against his old Warriors teammates, but on the field there was absolutely no doubt where his loyalties lay. First he set up a Stuart MacGill catch on Justin Langer, then he got Callum Thorp out lbw for a duck. WA's next three wickets, including Huss, went for just 20 runs. At this point, with three runs needed to win and just five balls remaining, the atmosphere was electric. Beau Casson tried for a big six off a MacGill ball — and sent it straight into Michael Clarke's hands. It was an incredible win for us against all the odds. In fact, Steve Waugh, who at this point had 73 Sheffield Shield games and 150 Test matches under his belt, said afterwards it was one of the best wins he'd been part of, domestic or otherwise.

The entire side came out of that game with a whole new self-belief, which was put to the test when we went in to bat against Victoria on a difficult MCG wicket. Opening as usual, Greg Mail found runs steadily but Slats and Kat each went for a duck. Fortunately, Tugga pulled out one of his trademark innings-saving performances, striding out to the pitch in the fourth over and ending the day there on 125 not out. His final 211 included partnerships with Pup (78) and me; inspired, I reached my first century of the season in a 117 knock that included 10 fours and four sixes.

Our 544 first innings total was looking pretty decent until the Bushrangers started whacking us all around the MCG. Jason Arnberger got his century and his opening partner, Matthew Mott, got a double. Peter Roach, batting down at number eight, decided to chuck one in for good measure. Then, on Day 3, as we headed for the draw, our side accidentally did what the other side hadn't been able to — nobbled Steve Waugh. We were coming up to the third new ball, which would normally go to Stuart Clark, nicknamed Sarfraz or Sarf because his bowling reminded people of Pakistani player Sarfraz Nawaz. Stuart and I were good mates and had played together in the Blues long enough to be confident of our positions — confident, mind you, not cocky. We were both still very respectful of the senior players, Steve Waugh most of all. Steve was the very last person we would ever want to annoy.

Sarf was fielding on the boundary when he grabbed the ball and threw it back to Tugga in covers. Unfortunately, his throw was off and the ball hit our revered skipper fair in the temple. Sarf naturally rushed in to see if Tugga was hurt. He was physically okay (although he got taken to hospital for a scan as a precaution), but he was not a happy camper. He left some instructions before departing the field and, pointedly, the ball didn't go to Sarf as expected, it went to Greg Mail, an opening batsman no less. I felt for my mate but, you know, never let a chance go by. Walking past Sarf shortly afterwards, I said, 'I don't think you're ever going to play again.' 'Me neither,' he said with a nervous laugh. Of course he did, but it was a long time before we let him forget that chuck.

The dominance we'd exerted over the one-day competition for the previous two seasons continued, and we went into the 2002–03 ING Cup final with seven wins and a tie under our belts, against just three losses. I contributed a quick 34 to our win and it felt terrific to be tournament champions for the third year in a row.

On paper, it looked as though I'd had a poor season in the one-dayers, with 70 my highest score and all the others below 20. But numbers don't always tell the full story. With players from the national team coming in and out, I hadn't had a consistent position on the batting order but instead had moved up and down according to need, being sent in to 'pinch hit' and chase bonus points. That's what the team required of me and I was happy to do it. Yes, it affected my personal statistics, but I have never been one to dwell on stats. It's true to say I was craving more responsibility and accountability, particularly in the short-form games. However, I was cemented in the team, performing the role I'd been given, and there was no chance I would be left out the following season.

We followed the ING Cup victory with wins in our remaining two Sheffield Shield matches, one of them a 241-run thrashing of the Queensland Bulls. We were through to the final, playing at the Gabba against Queensland, who had won it for the past three years. The Blues hadn't made a Sheffield Shield final since 1993–94, when Phil Emery guided a team including Michael

Bevan and Shane Lee to victory over Tasmania. But it was an even earlier finals game that was on the minds of Steve Rixon and Steve Waugh. In March 1985, precisely 18 years earlier, the two had been part of a NSW team that took on a Queensland line-up led by Allan Border and featuring bowler Trevor Hohns well before his selector days. Stumper was already a veteran by then, but it was Tugga's debut season in the state side. They'd fought hard right to the end to claim the win in that game.

The two Steves talked a lot to us young blokes about the importance of backing ourselves and never letting up. Too often we'd seen Queensland as unbeatable at home, but what we'd achieved over the season showed us that nothing was out of our reach if we wanted it enough. Heritage and tradition were honoured when Tugga took the field in the Baggy Blue cap he'd worn in his first season.

Queensland won the toss and sent us in to bat. We were fired up all right, but if it hadn't been for our senior players we would have been in all sorts of trouble. Michael Slater and Greg Mail opened. The second over wasn't even done before Greg was sent back to the pavilion on two. But Simon Katich, who took his place, crafted a 191 partnership with Slats. Joe Dawes claimed Tugga for nine and Pup for a duck, both lbws. Michael Kasprowicz got Junior for one then I went down to Dawes, another lbw, for just one, putting us on 6 for 215. Don Nash and Stuart Clark added some much needed runs, giving us a first innings total of 282 — a good total on that 'sporty' (in other words, bowler-friendly) Gabba wicket.

Our bowlers were on fire and the endless hours of fielding drills Stumper had put the team through paid off. Don Nash's 2 for 4 was a sight to see, but Stuart MacGill was the man of the hour with an incredible 5 for 16, including three ducks, in a mere 32 balls. Just 122 minutes after their first innings had begun, Queensland were all out for 84. Our second innings total of 263 was more evenly spread across the team and we benefited from some sloppy fielding on their behalf, although to my shock I was caught by Wade Seccombe for a duck off an Ashley Noffke ball — I'd been attempting to leave the ball, only to have it hit the toe-end of my bat. Queensland tried to fight back in their second innings but they didn't have much chance against Stuart MacGill and Simon Katich, who each took 3 for 43, keeping the Bulls to a total of 215. We'd won: the coveted Sheffield Shield was ours!

Every one of us was thrilled with the victory, even the old hands who'd been in numerous winning teams at the World Cup and Test level. Yes, this was a purely domestic competition but delivering a win for their beloved NSW meant a huge amount to them. It brought home to me more forcefully than ever what an immense privilege it was to play for the Blues. It was especially sweet to have claimed victory in both domestic competitions.

The reasons to celebrate kept coming outside cricket too. Things were going really well with Karina. Over the summer we'd started living together — the first of the many 'house moves' she took care of because I was off playing. It was time to take the plunge and ask her to marry me. I did the traditional thing and spoke to her dad, Phil, about it and he gave the idea the thumbs up. Buying the right ring took me less than five minutes. But then I had to get up the courage to pop the question. The ring in its box was like a time bomb hidden away in the flat and I worried the whole time she was going to find it before I came up with some kind of plan. Finally it just had to be done. I booked a table for the Saturday of the Easter long weekend at a lovely restaurant overlooking Sydney Harbour Bridge. I had the whole thing planned: dinner, then a walk along the foreshore under the bridge, where I would propose.

Walking into the restaurant with the box in the pocket of my pants, I was more nervous than I've ever been on a cricket pitch. We happened to be seated so that I was on a bench running along a wall, facing the view over Karina's shoulder. At the end of the meal she decided to come and sit next to me to enjoy the sights for a few minutes — a perfectly reasonable thing to do, except unknowingly she came and sat right next to my loaded pocket and rested her hand on my leg. I was sure she was about to discover my little surprise, inadvertently creating a situation where I had to do the deed in front of a restaurant full of people. Just the thought of that made me break out in a sweat. I blurted out the first thing that came into my head, 'Move. I've got a cramp.' Romantic, I know, but what can I say, I was in a state of panic.

The rain that had been threatening when we set out had arrived while we were eating, but I was a man with a plan. 'Let's go for a walk,' I said. 'Let's not. It's pouring,' came the sensible reply. *Fine,* I thought, *we'll get a cab home but before we get there the rain will have stopped and I'll divert us down to a favourite beachside promenade.* Not only did it not stop, it became torrential. But I was fixated. 'C'mon,' I said, 'let's go to Balmoral and get an ice cream.' Karina looked at me like I was crazy, so we went home. I'd worked myself up so much that I couldn't stand not to do it, even if the harbour lights had to be replaced by the lounge-room light. Frankly, if Karina had said she was so tired she was heading straight to bed, I'd have thrust the ring into her hand and said, 'Take this with you,' though fortunately it didn't come to that. I went down on one knee, managed to get the words out and she cried with happiness as she said yes. My relief at having it all over was indescribable. Give me a big, fearsome West Indian fast bowler any day!

Two months later, at the end of May 2003 I went to Kumagaya, Japan, to watch Karina and her team attempt to defend their Touch Football World Champions title (the tournaments are held every four years). There were 10 nations participating overall and five in the women's division, with New Zealand being Australia's greatest threat. Karina had trained really hard, fitting in the sessions around her full-time job as a radiographer. She played in the middle, having a significant effect on the flow of the game. She loved playing and enjoyed winning, but we had almost diametrically opposed attitudes to competition. I felt the nerves when I was about to play on a big stage but I relished the feeling of going up against an opposition knowing no quarter would be given and none asked. Karina would genuinely have been happier playing in a local Sydney comp with her good friends, rather than being in a national team who were drawn from around the country and didn't know each other very well.

Even as a defending world champion, she had to convince herself she could get through the game and that she was just as good as the opposition. On the other hand, she thrived having loved ones around when she was competing. Her parents had also come to watch and she was much more relaxed having the three of us around, whereas I discovered over the next few years that I usually preferred to give single-minded attention to the job at hand. Anyway, it was really nice to be there for her and watch as in a hard-fought final against the Kiwis the Aussies held on to the title. (Karina was such a talented touch player that only a broken collarbone copped at a training camp prevented her from making a third World Cup appearance four years later in South Africa.)

In the lead-up to the 2003–04 season, I moved clubs from Northern Districts to Eastern Suburbs. I was still young, just 26, but many on the team were even younger and Northern Districts wanted me to take on the captaincy. However, that meant also becoming a selector for the first-grade team and I didn't want that pressure taking my focus away from the continuation of my own progress. Easts, on the other hand, had older players, including Mark Patterson, Adrian Tucker and Jason Swift (as well as rising young talents including 15-year-old David Warner). The running of the team was in capable hands and all they required of me was that I play, which suited me down to the ground. (Northern Districts had been so good to me I always knew I would go back there eventually, and I did so after 10 enjoyable and successful years with Easts.)

I missed a couple of Blues games in the first half of the season, first after straining my quad in one of the first grade games of the year with my new side, then in December when I had surgery to clear an infection out of the nail bed of one of my fingers (something keepers have to deal with from time to time). It was the last season before retirement for Steve and Mark Waugh. It would have been perfect if we'd been able to ride the wave of our previous triumphs and send them out on another set of victories in the domestic competition, but our ING Cup performance was not good enough to get us to the finals, with five wins against four losses and a tie. Our Sheffield

Shield results were even worse. We started with a win against WA then couldn't replicate that result for the next seven games.

Even so, the selectors appreciated the work I was putting in and called me back to the international arena, first of all in the Australia A team against Zimbabwe on New Year's Day 2004 in Perth, where the Zimbabweans squeaked home by eight runs, then six days later in Adelaide where we smashed out 327 (including my 45) to beat them by 119 runs. Following this I was selected for the Australian ODI team for two games to give Adam Gilchrist a chance to rest his sore knees. Those games were also against Zimbabwe, in Adelaide on Australia Day and Melbourne three days later. We edged them out by 13 runs in Adelaide and reached a reasonable 263 in Melbourne, although unfortunately the match was rained out. My contributions had been noticed and in February I got a call telling me I was in the Australian one-day squad for the upcoming six-week-long one-day and Test tour of Sri Lanka (Wade Seccombe went as the back-up keeper for the Test squad).

A game in Colombo was the only one I played on the tour. Gilly was serving as acting captain as well as keeping and brought me in to give me some batting experience in these unfamiliar conditions. He and I opened but, unfortunately, less than seven overs later, I was out for nine after I mistimed a straight drive off seam bowler Nuwan Zoysa. Gilly became his second scalp, going lbw for 34 in a game that the home team won by three wickets. But the tour was a great experience and I relished the chance to work and train with Gilly, which we did throughout the whole tour.

I was back home for the final Sheffield Shield game of the season, against Queensland at the SCG, the site of so many unforgettable stands by the Waughs. We went into Day 4 chasing 277 — not out of the question by any means. But we got off to a very shaky start when Greg Mail and Phil Jaques went for a combined 11. Bevo and Pup brought things back on track with a 50-run partnership, but they were also out not long afterwards, as was our captain, Tugga, gone for just nine in the final innings of his career. (He'd had a more fitting farewell eight weeks earlier in his final Test match, also at the SCG, with an impressive second innings 80 against India.)

At 5 for 92, things were a bit grim, but Junior and I dug in and produced a game-changing 115 runs in just 12 overs. Junior went for 72, caught and bowled by Andy Bichel. I stayed out there as our last four batsmen came and went and reached 62 not out. In the end we fell just 37 runs short — not the send-off we would like to have given our departing legends but a gritty effort considering the way things had looked for a while there.

We would go into the following summer without some of our most experienced figures: Steve and Mark Waugh; Michael Bevan, who had joined Tasmania; Michael Slater, who had retired after developing a very painful form of inflammatory arthritis in the spine; and Steve Rixon, who had gone to coach the English county side Surrey. We didn't capitalise on our previous Shield victory. In fact, we only managed two wins in the whole tournament, against six losses and two draws, leaving us second-last on the ladder. We needed to shake things up, big time. It had been wonderful to play with cricketers as talented as the Waughs and those other big names, but it was time for a group of us still with the team to take on some of the responsibility we craved and carve out our own chapters within NSW cricket. As it turned out, being thrown into the deep end was exactly what the Blues needed and it proved the making of many of us, including me.

In the off-season, with Adam Gilchrist home for the birth of one of his children, I travelled to Europe with the Australian one-day team for a couple of games against India and Pakistan intended to serve as preparation for an upcoming Champions Trophy tournament. Back at home, Trevor Bayliss, who had been assistant to Steve Rixon, took over the NSW coaching role. I'd known TB since he had coached the Colts squad I'd been part of in 1998–99. He had been pretty handy as a player back in his day, but as a coach he proved to be exceptional. He came in at just the right time — we had a clean slate and his style was perfect for the group.

It was also the beginning of a new era for me. I probably wouldn't have been ready to learn from TB the way I did any earlier in my career, but a decade after I'd made my first-grade debut I was primed to make a quantum leap, and he recognised that even when others couldn't. One of his first decisions was to appoint me to serve as captain of the team when Simon Katich was away on international duty, which was a lot at that point. The board of Cricket NSW disagreed with his choice, feeling I was too inexperienced. But TB lobbied hard, saying that I was the one who would get the best out of the young squad. Eventually the board approved the appointment, though some of them remained deeply sceptical.

TB really understood potential. In the same way that he'd seen something inside me and knew how to help me bring it out, he could see where the team needed to be and how we could get there. His expectations for us were high, but he knew that in order to meet them we needed to develop as individuals and as a group. The crucial word was accountability. A lot of us thought we understood accountability by this point. Over the previous couple of years, Steve Rixon and Steve Waugh had emphasised its importance countless times. Superficially we got it, but the inconsistency of our results revealed the truth: despite everything, we had still looked to our Test players to carry the load. When they'd been playing with us the mentality was, 'Oh Bevo or the Waughs will get the runs,' and by overly relying on them when they were on the scene we'd left ourselves with nothing to fall back on when they weren't.

There was a group of us young blokes, including Stuart Clark, Phil Jaques, Dom Thornely, Nathan Bracken, Michael Clarke and myself, who regarded ourselves as professionals but were in fact still playing with a carefree approach that we couldn't afford now there was no senior group to lean on. I'd started out so strongly in my first year with NSW, but, if I was truthful, five years in I was selling myself short. I had the skills and I regarded myself as mentally tough. In many ways I was, but something was missing.

True mental toughness gives you clarity under pressure, so that when the squeeze is put on in a game you don't second-guess what you're doing, you just continue to perform. Trevor's message about accountability really hit home to me: it's not about the runs you score or the wickets you take, it's about the ability to get them under pressure and make them count. It should never be about getting a pretty 40 that you think looks good for a selector and will get you picked for the next game. It should be about turning that 40 into 80 and winning the game for your team. You can only really do that if you're secure in your position, not looking over your shoulder the whole time worrying you're going to be dropped, and TB gave us that security. He took the long view and his support didn't waver, which gave us the opportunity to make mistakes and learn from them.

Our first Shield match of the 2004–05 season was against Queensland at the Gabba, where the wicket was completely different to the spin-friendly SCG. We'd lost there so often we expected to do so, putting us at a psychological disadvantage before play even started. We couldn't operate that way anymore.

As part of our preparation for the game, I talked to the team about paying respect to the past while taking responsibility for the future. We had the huge honour of representing a team that had included some of the all-time greats (including Keith Miller, who had died days earlier) but we couldn't rest on that history. It was time to write our own story. That would begin with a new attitude to playing the Bulls. I said, 'We've got to find a way to win here. Traditionally, we fluff around for a couple of days; they intimidate us a bit and get the best of us on the green wicket. But we've got to find a way to combat that. We've got to move the game forward and play the attacking brand of cricket NSW is known for.'

We got off to a good start. But 1 for 89 turned into 2 for 89, then 3 for 89, then 4 for 89 as Andy Bichel tore through us, with Joe Dawes hot on his heels. I dug in for 66 and we were all out for 203. Then it was our bowlers' turn to go to town, led by Matthew Nicholson and Nathan Bracken. Queensland went into their second innings chasing 240 for the win and we got them to 7 for 197 before their tail-enders, Bichel and Ashley Noffke, secured the win with two wickets and 22 balls to spare.

Cricket NSW had originally arranged it so that we would fly home immediately after the game, but Trevor and I had been insistent about changing that and allowing the team to stay over. We had a plan in mind. At the end of the match I said to our young bowlers, 'Well done. That was a really good effort.' They looked a bit confused, replying, 'But we lost.' I said, 'Yeah, we did. They were better than us today. Now we're going to grab a beer and take it over to their rooms and talk to them.' They said, 'We can't do that. We lost!' I said, 'Of course we can. I want you to talk to Andy Bichel and Jimmy Maher and spend a bit of time with them off the field.' We went over and had a drink and a laugh and everyone relaxed.

At our first training session back at the SCG we talked about what had happened after the game, how when you spend time with opposition players and have a beer with them you get to see they're exactly the same as your side. They have their insecurities, they have good days and bad days, and the only way they can intimidate you is if you let them. It was a real revelation to the younger players, just as TB and I had hoped, and it marked a turning point for NSW. We didn't take a backward step after that, losing only one more Shield game the entire season and winning six. Even when we drew, it was because we'd made a strategic decision to do so in order not to lose, after a win moved out of our reach.

The ING Cup was a different story: we lost more than we won and finished last on the table. But those losses didn't affect the incredible team dynamic we built over the course of that season. Seemingly small changes made a huge difference. One of the things I did straight away was encourage everyone to recognise and enjoy good performances in their teammates. Not by making a song and dance about it in team meetings, but in the natural way that happens when you relax together. Instead of picking up the kitbag and walking out at the end of a game, we started sitting down together just enjoying what we'd done.

We were all going to have days when everything came together perfectly and days when nothing did. But if we could genuinely celebrate each other's good days, my view was that our own bad days wouldn't bog us down. I wanted the guy who'd got a ton or a five-for to leave feeling, 'I did do something special today and my teammates recognised it.' The following week if he got two ducks and someone else got 100, he'd be able to genuinely celebrate that. By the end of that season we would sit there for hours after a game, revelling in the camaraderie.

With TB as a valuable sounding board, I found I had a knack for leadership. I'd always responded well to receiving feedback and I could take emotion out of the situation when it came to giving it. Trevor gave me an invaluable tip when he said, 'When considering your message you have to realise that not everyone will be thinking like you. You might understand what you mean, but unless you put it in a way that's clear to that person they can take something completely different from it.' I found I really enjoyed finding the most effective way to communicate with each individual. Some needed a sympathetic ear, others needed tough love. You could only figure out the right approach by getting to know them as people, spending time with them over a meal or a coffee and figuring out what made them tick.

Clear expectations were an absolute must. You had to set the standard at the start and not compromise; only then could everyone work for the same goal. Taking the emotion out of it helped enormously when I had to tell someone they weren't performing well enough, but there were still times when it felt awkward. Even so, it had to be done and if it was done right everyone benefited. Dom Thornely was one of my best friends, but I had to take him aside early in the season and say, 'Mate, I think you need to aim it up a bit. You're going okay, but you're missing those tough moments. You're getting out at crucial times. You need to find a way to get through. It doesn't mean you've got to get 150. It might mean getting a 60 to win a game or finishing the job off with a tail-end batter.'

It was an uncomfortable conversation, but for the good of the team it needed to be said. In our next game Dom had some trouble with the short ball and got hit a bit, but he struggled through it for 90 and put us in a position where we could win. The following game we got into trouble against South Australia. At 4 for 1, we were gone, until Dom came out and hit 60 not out, winning us the match. Back at the hotel there was a knock on my door. It was Dom, standing there with a six-pack. We sat down and had a beer. In that typically blokey way, he said simply, 'Thanks,' and I replied, 'No worries,' and a full conversation's worth of meaning passed between us. Dom went on to have a thousand-run year and get picked for his first Australian A series.

There were definitely some characters on the team, including bowler Doug Bollinger, known as Bald Eagle. Energetic is an understatement. His class-clown nature could make him a pain in the change room, but he put in when he was on the field. Another part of captaincy was learning how to deal with umpires, and I found Doug's personality could be quite a useful tool in that regard. He'd sometimes go a bit too close to the line in attempting to intimidate a batsman, and in one game the umpire said to me, 'Make sure you calm Doug down, mate, or he'll get reported.' If what Doug was saying had come out of the mouth of a more mature player like Stuart Clark, he'd already have been reported, but Bald Eagle's reputation preceded him and I could use it to my advantage. I said to the umpire, 'Come on, it's Doug. We all know what he's like.' He said, 'Yeah, okay, just keep an eye on him.' I nodded and kept walking. As I passed Doug, I said out of the corner of my mouth, 'Keep going, mate, you're doing good.' You use the weapons you have available.

By mid-March 2005, heading into the Sheffield Shield final against Queensland, we were a very different team than we had been a year earlier. I was a wiser, tougher, more highly disciplined player, accountable for all my actions and ready to take on any challenge that could be thrown at me. I'd started to understand what made teams great and I knew the mark I wanted to leave.

The final was at the Gabba and we walked out there feeling the Shield was ours to claim. We won the toss and I sent the Bulls in to bat. Our bowlers were unstoppable, with Nathan Bracken in sensational form, taking 6 for 27 as we kept Queensland to a first-innings total of 102. We had a lot of wickets fall cheaply too, but I was in the groove, reaching an undefeated 68 as part of our 188 total. The Bulls' second innings total of 268, built around a Martin Love century, left us with an achievable target of 183, but they fought back hard. We were 7 for 158 in our second innings when my wicket fell, and 8 for 161 after keeper Wade Seccombe caught Matthew Nicholson off a Joe Dawes delivery.

I went from feeling that the game was in safe hands to taking my pads off deep in the Gabba change rooms sure that our collapse was going to cost us the win. I quickly made my way to the viewing room so I was at least there to share the pain of the loss. Queensland were also sure at that point that they had it won, but in one of the most exciting finishes I've ever been part of, our tail-enders Bracks and Stuart MacGill found 20 of the 22 runs we needed. Then in near darkness Nathan sent an Andy Bichel ball off to the right of the keeper. Wade had his glove to the ball and it was all over for us … except he dropped it and suddenly we were back in with a chance. The tension was almost unbearable. I found myself dry retching over a bucket, my nerves were so bad. But Magilla kept his cool and swatted a Joe Dawes ball off his hip to take the final two runs needed to claim the match and the Shield. Trevor Bayliss very rarely showed emotion — it was one of his strengths as a coach — but even he jumped up and embraced everyone around him.

It was the perfect end to a perfect season, which still ranks right up there as one of the most enjoyable and rewarding I have ever played. Sometimes lightning strikes and you come across a group of players who just click, working together with the same level of passion for the same cause. That's how it was with the Blues that year. There's a saying that a champion team beats a team of champions, and we were living proof.

I finished the summer with an average of almost 70 in Shield games and 45 in the domestic one-dayers. I not only played again for Australia A, I captained the team as we won one game against Pakistan and lost another by just 13 runs (though I was satisfied

I'd given it everything, reaching 129 off 124 balls). That led to the opportunity to return to Australia's one-day team for three games over a 10-day period, when Adam Gilchrist had to withdraw because of a knee injury. All three were wins for Australia — two over Pakistan and one over the West Indies. I'd taken the field for my country before, but now I could see that I hadn't understood the difference between playing for Australia and being an Australian cricketer in the deepest sense. After that incredible summer I really got it. When the selectors named me as part of the squad for the upcoming Ashes tour of England, I was ready.

CHAPTER 11

LEARNING FROM THE BEST

PEOPLE WHO ARE OUTSIDE the sport have asked me if being part of the squad for the 2005 Ashes was frustrating since, as expected, I didn't play in the series. I know where they were coming from ... sort of. They were imagining it was like being a kid with your face pressed up against the window of a closed lolly shop. But it wasn't like that at all. It was the most exciting thing that had happened to me in cricket up to that point, and I'd been capped 10 times for Australia's one-day team.

As a kid growing up in the sport, your dreams follow a hierarchy — playing for your state, then above that being selected for your country, and above that earning the Baggy Green cap of a Test cricketer, and above that the holy grail: playing in an Ashes series. It's the pinnacle in cricket and I would argue it is up there with the best any sport has to offer. The rivalry between Australia and England has such a rich history, full of stories of heroes and villains, great courage and larger-than-life characters, wins against the odds and devastating losses. Coming up through the game you hang on stories about Don Bradman's 1948 Invincibles; Ian Chappell's so-called 'Ugly Australians' changing the game in 1974–75; Allan Border leading what the British media dubbed 'the worst side to ever tour England' in 1989 and showing the Poms how it was done 4–0; Michael Slater in 1993 getting a half-century on debut and a brilliant century in the following Test; and Mark Taylor turning his career around in the 1997 series.

The theatre behind the Ashes is like nothing else — everything is heightened to the nth degree. It feels like everyone in both countries is glued to the action and has an opinion to share. The scrutiny is unbelievable. Where you might get five or 10 journalists at a media conference after some Test matches, you'll get 50 at the end of a day of Ashes competition. As for the players, you can see how much it means to each and every one to go into an Ashes campaign. Now I was part of that tradition, having earned my place fair and square with big performances over a massive summer. I was part of the squad alongside Ricky Ponting, Justin Langer, Matthew Hayden, Shane Warne and Glenn McGrath. What a buzz!

Karina and I talked about whether she should come over to England to meet up with me, but we decided against it. We had bought our first home together, in the inner-west suburb of Cabarita, and had invited a good friend of ours, Nick Berry, to come and stay for a while. Nick, a few years younger than me, had moved from Cowra to play cricket at the Eastern Suburbs club and we wanted to help him settle into Sydney life. Besides which, Karina had her work and her own sporting commitments, and I didn't want anything to distract me. It was important for me to be able to show everyone involved how much it meant to me to be there, how much I appreciated what a special experience this was.

The tour ran from July to September and despite later media chatter, in my experience there was no 'us and them' between the Ashes players and those who were there as back-ups. I felt fully accepted by the team. I knew my place and was respectful of the service the senior players had already given their country, but I had a voice like everyone else. Everyone was encouraged to have a say, in the most constructive way. If I saw something that I thought could help the team I had the confidence to say to Ricky Ponting or his vice-captain, Gilly, or coach John Buchanan, 'What do you reckon about this?'

In Australia, you get from game to game in a plane, but the great thing about travelling around England is that you travel together by bus up and down the country. It's a relaxed time when you build good friendships and enjoy each other's company. I had a lot of great conversations on those rides, shooting the breeze about life in general but also talking in detail about how to approach certain playing conditions or how key moments had changed the outcome of specific games.

I was a sponge, soaking it all up: the top players' work ethic; the way they prepared for a match; how they dealt with pressure within the game and coped with the constant commentary about their performance; and how they handled the big occasions on field and off (including meeting the Queen, as we did on that tour). What struck me was how players of the calibre of Haydos never stopped learning about the game. You'd think they might rest on their laurels, but the greats stayed hungry and welcomed the chance to do things better.

That tour was also where I got one of the only imaginative nicknames I've ever been given. Australian cricket is renowned for some of the best nicknames around. Tugga Waugh is an all-time classic (just say it out loud). Dizzy Gillespie isn't bad, nor is Bacchus Marsh. Mine were much less interesting: I was always just Hadds or BJ, except to Haydos and the aforementioned Jason/Dizzy who had a liking for a radio comedy character called Guido Hatzis. Somehow 'Haddin' reminded them of 'Hatzis' and to this day I'm 'Guido' to them. But other than that I was plain vanilla all the way, until on that Ashes tour Warnie decided my hairdo resembled Rod Stewart's and dubbed me Rockin' Rod. (That nickname didn't stick beyond the tour, but a decade later I helped give Nathan Lyon one that's still with him. It came about when he set a new record for most wickets taken by an Australian off-spinner. We knew from the commentators that the record was coming up. When he got it I called out, 'Well done, Goat!' — a cry that was promptly taken up by some of the other blokes. Now, Nathan's one of my best mates but he's a nervous sort of character. He said, 'What? Goat?' I said, 'Mate, Greatest Of All Time. GOAT.' It might have died at this point, but young Nathan made a tactical error. 'I don't like it,' he said. Well, it was on then. A bunch of us started using the nickname at every opportunity. It was quickly picked up on the stump mic and from there it was only a matter of time before a columnist with space to fill followed up on it. Sure enough, Nathan fronted a press conference all ready to talk about the day's play only to be asked, 'Where does the name "Goat" come from?' You're welcome, mate.)

Going into the Ashes series, Punter predicted it would be the closest since 1989, when Australia's most recent winning streak had started, and he was right. England had climbed back from the terrible state they'd been in for so long and developed talented players, including Kevin Pietersen and Andrew 'Freddie' Flintoff. They were in for the fight, although we dominated the opening Test at Lord's. That match gave me a couple of firsts. One was my first taste of the famed Lord's lunches. Forget the usual ham salad sandwiches; it's like a restaurant up there, with steak, prawns, an array of desserts and anything else you might desire. No wonder the bowlers love it when it's a batting day at Lord's — all the dieticians' work went out the window during that stop.

Much more significantly, after we won the match I got my first experience of our revered victory song, 'Under the Southern Cross I Stand'. The singing was led by Justin Langer, who made it plain just how much it meant. Being part of that song, which the team sings after winning a Test match or claiming an ODI series, is one of the most special moments you have as an Australian cricketer. The emotions are intense and I found the desire to repeat the experience positively addictive.

I played in the tour game against Worcestershire that followed the First Test and felt even more reassured that I had earned my place on the tour after I top-scored with 94. The Second Test started three days later and in the pre-match warm-up at Edgbaston, Glenn McGrath went down hard after stepping on a stray cricket ball, resulting in torn ankle ligaments that prevented him from playing. The match turned into an unbelievably hard-fought contest, with England winning by just two runs. Then it was my turn to cop an injury, on my knee.

Unsurprisingly, given the stance in which we spend so many hours, wicketkeepers are well known for knee problems. They've plagued many of the best, including Gilly. I've had them too; however, they've never been the direct result of keeping. By the time I went to England I'd already had two previous injuries, each requiring surgery. The first one happened in training with the Blues. We were playing soccer and I was trying to stop the ball and turn the motion into a scissor-kick when my knee went from under me and I was carried off the field to the ironic applause of my amused teammates. The second was also a Blues incident, this time at a team-bonding paintball day. Put 20 ultra-competitive athletes together in that environment and things are bound to get a bit hectic. I came up over a rise to find four of the 'enemy' coming at me. In the heat of the moment, I took a flying leap sideways, rolling out of range. A couple of days later in a trial match I felt something locking in my knee. The physio took a look and told me I'd torn my meniscus — the cartilage 'shock absorber' that sits between the bones. He asked what I could have done to hurt it. I sheepishly mentioned paintball and he just shook his head.

This time, in Birmingham, I was with a couple of the guys getting dropped back at the hotel in a taxi after a team dinner. I got out and walked behind the car, but the driver accidentally put it into reverse and came back into me just on the side of the knee. I fell down but was able to get back up again. He was extremely apologetic. I said, 'I'm right,' and I thought I was when I went up to my room and lay down on the bed to watch a movie. About an hour later when I tried to stand, however, the knee had seized up. I was sent to London to get a scan, which revealed it wasn't as bad as the paintball tear, though it eventually also needed surgery. (I ended up being too busy playing to get it done for a year. In the meantime I managed with a combination of short-term pain relief and physio followed by intensive conditioning work with trainer

Stuart Karppinen, which further built up the supporting muscles in the leg and took the load off the knee.)

Stakes were high for the Third Test at Old Trafford. It wasn't looking good for us by Day 3, but Ricky Ponting put in a huge Man of the Match effort to claw back a draw. It was my turn to run drinks at that incredibly suspenseful point in the game but the call went out that none of us were to move, for fear of putting the mockers on. I'm not one for sporting superstitions myself, but quite a few players are and I wasn't about to upset the apple cart, so I stayed put until Punter's 156 was done.

Partway through the tour I became concerned about my match readiness. I'd got on the plane in peak form but I wasn't getting the catching practice I felt I needed. So I got permission from John Buchanan to go down to Surrey and spend three days working intensively on my keeping with Steve Rixon. That did me a world of good, although it might have left me a bit too relaxed since, for the first and last time in my career, I missed the team bus on the first day of the Fifth Test. That is of course an absolute no-no, but fortunately everyone was so pre-occupied with their preparation that no-one noticed my absence. With a hefty financial inducement my cab driver was able to get me to The Oval players' entrance just as my teammates were filing in, and I wove myself into the line as if I'd been there all along.

Still, the work I did with Stumper set me up perfectly for my next challenge — captaining an Australia A team to Pakistan for a mix of longer-form games and one-dayers. Stuart Clark, Brad Hodge and I had to depart London on the second day of that final Test, so we didn't see the finale of the game, which ended in a draw, giving England the overall Ashes victory 2–1. But we'd seen enough to agree with the fans and sportswriters who declared it an enthralling series that reinvigorated the whole Ashes competition.

The first Australia A game, a four-dayer in the northern Pakistani city of Rawalpindi, started on the fourth anniversary of the 9/11 attacks. It was a fairly hairy time to be in that part of the world, with the Americans hunting for Osama Bin Laden, and plenty of local unrest. The tour was a chance for the selectors to assess how far off players were from being able to step up to the national side. Despite big efforts from Phil Jaques, Nathan Bracken and Shane Watson, Pakistan A were just too good for us in the conditions of the first game and we lost by seven wickets. Next up was another four-day match in Rawalpindi; then we were to move to Lahore for three one-dayers. Unfortunately, I broke a finger on the third day of the Rawalpindi game (which ended in a draw).

I'd stopped counting broken bones by this point; they were just an inconvenient cost of doing business. I spoke to selector Trevor Hohns about it and offered to stay on the trip, telling him I could play with the injury. But he said, 'It's fine, you're not on this tour to prove anything; we already know what you can do. If Gilly gets busted, you'll play, so just go home and get yourself ready.' I can't say I was sorry to leave Pakistan, particularly after my final night with the team, in Lahore, when there were two bomb blasts, one in a spot our bus had just passed.

Back in Australia, the Blues, as defending Sheffield Shield champions, got off to a good start in the 2005–06 season. We won our first game, in October, and the two that followed, but we couldn't maintain the momentum. After that came three draws and four consecutive losses, meaning we finished at the bottom of the table. A large part of the problem was that the team wasn't coping well with the disruption of players coming and going as a number of us were called out to international duty; without consistency from game to game it was too easy for the team to lose its way within a game.

Yet again it was a very different story in the one-day domestic tournament (its last year under the ING Cup name), which we won for the fourth time in six seasons. The February final against SA was a real nail-biter. We looked to have it all our way after keeping the Redbacks to just 154, but then Shaun Tait cut loose, taking six of our wickets for just 41. Suddenly we were shaky on 9 for 149, with five needed to win. But our tail-enders, Moises Henriques and Stuart MacGill, saved the day, with the winning run coming from Stuart — a leg glance off Darren Lehmann — just as it had the previous year in the Sheffield Shield. It was one of the most memorable games I've ever played because there was such a great sense of pride in the fact that such an inexperienced team had been able to come together so effectively. We felt that here, at least, we'd done the Blues proud.

I was very conscious that the next World Cup was only a year away, in March 2007, and I wanted to put myself in the best possible shape to be considered for inclusion in the squad. I was determined not to lose fitness during the off-season; in fact, I decided to increase my already intensive workout routine. I sought out fitness trainer and boxing specialist Christian Marchegiani and told him I wanted to be pushed to the edge. He was the right bloke for the job. I did endless hours of boxing, skipping, medicine balls and weights. It was hard and it hurt and I loved it. I was so fit I felt like I was made of iron.

In July 2006, I led an Australian A team that included Shaun Tait, Phil Jaques, Brad Hodge and Shane Watson against India A and Pakistan A in a 'Top End' series, in Cairns and Darwin, of four-day matches, one-dayers and the relatively new Twenty20 format — although Australia was far still behind countries like India in understanding what the new format had to offer and how popular it could become.

Another wonderful opportunity came my way when I was selected for an ODI tour. The previous summer I had filled in for Gilly in a couple of ODIs against Sri Lanka and South Africa. I was always made welcome and it was terrific to get the experience — I certainly never took the privilege of playing for Australia for granted — but at the same time I was very conscious that it was a stand-in arrangement. I'd typically get a call on, say, a Wednesday telling me I was needed in Melbourne on the Friday. I'd fly down, play, and be on an 8 o'clock flight back the next morning to get ready for a state game. However, this time I'd been selected in my own right.

There had been unhappy rumblings from a number of quarters about how heavily international players' schedules were being loaded. Gilly was one of those who felt that teams weren't being given enough rest time and that performances would inevitably suffer, so he was happy to sit out the tri-series against the West Indies and India, which was to be held in Malaysia in an attempt by cricket bodies to create new markets for the game. That gave me the opportunity to be an integral part of the team for the entire tour, and knowing that I had time to prepare properly and would have the whole tour to demonstrate I was good enough to play at the international level meant that I went into it in a much more relaxed state than I had for previous ODIs.

The tour was serving as a warm-up for the ICC Champions Trophy being held the following month and the 2007 World Cup four months after that, so a larger squad than usual was sent and we trained more than you normally would on that kind of tour. It was really enjoyable, pushing one another to do our best, knowing that we all had our eye on the prize of a spot in the World Cup squad.

We were in Kuala Lumpur for a good chunk of September 2006 and it felt great to be part of it all, be able to have in-depth conversations about game strategy based on what I observed, and interact with the other players in an informal way, just as I had on the Ashes tour. The senior members of the team had some sage advice about what not to do on the field. Going into the games against the West Indies, we were specifically warned not to try any gamesmanship on Brian Lara: 'Whatever you do, don't engage him. Don't say anything to him. Do not switch him on or you'll regret it.' I'd already seen him close up, including playing against him in an Australian A game where he had scored a double century. I took the advice to heart.

We played five games, two against India (who were being coached by Greg Chappell) and three against the West Indies, including the final. Our second Windies game was our only loss. Despite Matthew Hayden's strong opening effort, we were 4 for 64 and things weren't looking good, but Michael Hussey and I worked hard to save the game. We found a great rhythm out there together and our 165-run stand was a new Australian one-day record for a sixth-wicket partnership, a record that still stands. Huss, taking over captaining duties from Ricky Ponting, got his first ODI century, finishing on 109 not out, while I went for 70, which was my highest ODI score to that point.

Unfortunately, the West Indies got past our 272 total with three wickets to spare, thanks in large part to Brian Lara getting fired up. We had a young spinner called Dan Cullen who was trying to make his name. He bowled to Lara, who blocked the shot. Dan picked the ball up and said something I couldn't catch. I saw the response it got though. Lara turned around to glare at me. I immediately found a fascinating bit of dirt to stare at, thinking to myself, *I'm not looking him in the eye. He can talk to the top of my head. Do not engage, do not engage.* He turned back to Dan and said loudly enough for my benefit, 'I'm going to teach this kid a lesson.' The sleeping giant had awoken and it was on: *whack, whack, whack, whack, whack,* all over the ground, until Huss finally caught him off a Brett Lee ball for 87.

I was pleased with my performance in Malaysia with both bat and gloves, and came home fired up for the domestic season ahead. It started well. November was an especially productive time for the Blues, with a win in the Sheffield Shield and three in the Ford Ranger Cup (as the domestic limited-overs comp previously called the ING Cup was now known). One of the latter was in a match at the SCG against WA in which I scored 115 off just 102 balls. My knock, which included nine fours and three sixes, was part of a 146-run partnership with Dom Thornely; and we needed every single one of those runs in a game that was definitely not for the faint-hearted. Warriors' tail-ender Brett Dorey managed to drag victory back within reach, needing two runs off the last ball. He skied it to deep square leg and Daniel Christian, in his first season with NSW, grabbed it and hung on to win us the game. You don't see a finish like that every day.

My parents continued to give me incredible support, coming to every Blues one-day home game. They would drive up from

Queanbeyan early enough to be there in time for the warm-ups so Dad could walk around the ground and get a feel for how each team was looking before play began. Karina and I enjoyed attending the 2007 Allan Border Medal presentation in early February feeling very much the interested onlookers as paparazzi snapped shots of the big names. Then in February I went to New Zealand as part of the Australian one-day team to play the three-game Chappell–Hadlee Trophy series. This was another one Gilly was sitting out, as was Ricky Ponting, with Michael Hussey again taking on captaincy duties. There'd been a lot of talk in the lead-up to the series about how much the team's senior players had left to give. Their playing schedule was one concern, but so was the intensive training regime instituted by John Buchanan, with recently retired Warnie being particularly outspoken on the issue. Unfortunately, our performance in New Zealand did nothing to answer the critics, as the Kiwis beat us 3–0.

I returned home for the end of the 2006–07 season. NSW had been leading the Ford Ranger Cup league in the first part of the summer but, unfortunately, we had lost every game after that thriller against WA (including one against Victoria at Canberra's Manuka Oval, despite the enthusiastic support of family and friends) and we finished right at the bottom of the domestic one-day ladder.

In a marked change from the previous season, this time it was in the Shield that we did our best, pulling ourselves up from a mid-season slump to make it into the final against Tasmania at Bellerive Oval. However, the Devils dominated the game from the start, winning by 421 runs. There wasn't any single reason that explained the Blues' up-and-down performances in the two domestic competitions — it was frustrating that we rarely had a season where we did well in both. Consistency was certainly one big factor though, both in terms of the team line-up and in terms of different captaincy styles. Because NSW traditionally has so many players in the national teams across the various formats, these are challenges that have affected the side for a long time. It's not unknown for the Blues to have three captains across the course of a season as players come and go on international duty. That's not conducive to building a cohesive culture.

I couldn't be in Hobart to play. It's a tough call to miss a Sheffield Shield final — there'd better be a pretty good reason not to be there helping out your team. There was. I'd been named as part of the Australian squad for the World Cup and I was in the West Indies, along with Tassie Devils' captain, Punter. There's always good banter on tour about which state is better (for cricket, footy and in general) and when you're up against each other in a final like this it's taken to the next level. The game was being played overnight our time, and we were getting regular updates. I came to breakfast the morning after things had turned Tassie's way to find Punter had arranged it so that the only vacant seat was next to him, allowing him to rub in the result at his leisure.

Karina and I had been engaged for almost four years by now. We hadn't intended to have a long engagement; we both wanted to get married and start a family. We just hadn't been able to find a clear space in 2005 or 2006 to hold the wedding. First, I'd gone off to England in the Ashes squad, then there had been Malaysia and my Australia A duties — there always seemed to be something. Finally we set a date in May 2007 and booked the reception venue. But then my World Cup call-up scuppered that plan, since I'd be in the West Indies from February to the beginning of May, assuming Australia made the finals, which we had every expectation of doing. In fact, we were going into the tournament aiming to do something no team had ever done before: win it three times running.

Being chosen for the squad was fantastic in its own right but it was even more special because I wasn't just there as a back-up wicketkeeper. As a leading scorer in the Ford Ranger Cup, with an average of 67.66, I'd been selected on the strength of my batting abilities. As it turned out, I played only a couple of practice games in the preparation period, not in any of the games in the tournament itself. But just as I had 18 months earlier on the Ashes tour, I enjoyed every second.

Sportswriters had started saying that if there wasn't such an extraordinary once-in-a-generation cricketer as Gilly already doing the job, I'd have been in the national team a year earlier, although there was always talk about other sharp batsman-keepers, including Queenslander Chris Hartley. I tried to tune it all out. I understood that journalists had space to fill and everyone was looking for an angle they could work, but I didn't have to buy into it. If I spent time worrying about what other people said, good or bad, I wouldn't have my head in the game. And if I expended a whole lot of nervous energy worrying about if or when the spot was going to open up and who else would be vying for it, I'd be selling myself short as a cricketer and, frankly, as a person.

My mindset was never that Adam Gilchrist was an obstacle to my career. He was an inspiration. His giftedness as a batsman as well as a keeper raised the bar for all who followed. But there is a big difference between being inspired and trying to become a Gilly clone. I think a lot of spinners fell into that trap with Shane Warne — instead of developing their own style they tried to mimic his. That approach never works. All I could do was keep challenging myself to be the best I could possibly be. If in the end that wasn't good enough, I'd be able to look anyone in the eye and know I'd done everything I was capable of. If it was, I'd get my chance.

So I didn't get frustrated not playing in the World Cup. Just the opposite: I thought it was a brilliant opportunity to learn and to contribute to the team's success. It was great being able to watch other wicketkeepers in action and chew the fat with Gilly about the craft when we met down by the pool at lunchtime or at training. And it wasn't just me as the younger bloke who felt that way. Gilly had the hunger to keep on learning that marks out the best in any field. As he wrote in his memoir *True Colours*, 'There is a mentality in cricket that only wicketkeepers share and knowledge that nobody else possesses ... I loved having another gloveman around, and we helped each other become better keepers.'

The conversations I enjoyed most were the ones when we talked about how to get out of 'quicksand'. Everyone has a bad day at the office from time to time; quicksand is my name for a bad day on the cricket pitch. It happens to every player, be they a bowler, batsman or keeper, and it generally comes out of the blue. The day starts fine. You wake up in the hotel, you have breakfast, everything's normal. You go to the ground, you warm up; it's just like any other day. Then the game starts and one or two things you try don't quite go to plan. You start feeling the worm of doubt deep inside yourself. You try harder, but the harder you try the more you tense up and the worse it gets. Your hands feel stiff, your legs stop working, your feet don't go where you need them to go.

It's a horrible feeling whenever it happens, but for me it's a thousand times worse when I'm keeping than when I'm batting. I'd rather get 10 ducks in a row than drop a catch. When you're in quicksand behind the stumps you dread the ball coming to you, and that's a very bad place for a wicketkeeper to be. Because it all starts in the mind, the way you're playing sometimes doesn't look anywhere near as bad to an observer as it feels to you. Your whole team is out there with you, but you feel so alone and exposed. If you can't arrest it, you go into a kind of self-perpetuating death spiral, where everything you try just makes you sink further.

It's easy when you're looking up admiringly at the greats of the game to assume they turn up every week and perform without being troubled by insecurities and doubts — that they never experience the feeling of being in quicksand. So it was a real revelation for me to gain access to that inner sanctum and find out that every single one of those top players experienced those feelings from time to time; every one of them had days when they were vulnerable. What made them greats is the way they dealt with that. I already had the skills I needed with gloves and bat but my time as a member of those squads gave me knowledge that made all the difference and allowed me to become an Australian cricketer with longevity. The camaraderie was fantastic. Going into a match, everyone in the squad who wasn't playing would do any little thing they could to make life as easy as possible for the 11 guys on the sheet so they could focus purely on the game. Whether it was running gloves out to them, making sure their drink bottle was topped up or just paying attention in case they called for something, everyone knew their place and worked hard for each other. And everyone was part of celebrating the individual successes and team wins.

There were a lot of wins to celebrate. The 16 teams in the tournament were split into four initial pools; the top two teams went into a 'super 8' round robin, from which came the four semi-finalists. Weariness and doubts were shaken off, the team galvanised, and Australia did not lose a game all the way through to the finals, where we went up against Sri Lanka.

That game was memorable for its highs and lows. The highest of the highs was Gilly's flowing 149 off 104 balls. The farcical lowest of the lows was the way the rain-affected final ended. Sri Lanka had batted for 33 overs when the revised total left them needing to score 61 off 18 balls. But then the umpires decided it was too dark to continue and suspended play, which meant that because Sri Lanka had completed their required 20 overs the game was finished. Australia had won the World Cup! We were all jumping around celebrating when the umpires told Ricky Ponting that no, it wasn't over yet — the remaining three overs would need to be bowled the following day (even though Sri Lanka had no hope of getting the required runs).

Sri Lankan captain Mahela Jayawardene said this was not necessary, but the umpires insisted the remaining three overs had to be played and so they sent the teams out in pitch darkness, after first calling a halt to the crew who had already started erecting the podium up on the field for the following day's presentation ceremony. Not wanting anyone to get hurt playing under these ridiculous conditions, Punter and Jayawardene agreed to have spinners Andrew Symonds and Michael Clarke bowl the last balls and keep them gentle. (The umpires' decision, which was a major embarrassment for West Indies Cricket and the International Cricket Council, was based on a complete misunderstanding of the rules; ICC boss Malcolm Speed later formally apologised for it.)

When it was finally over — this time for real — the celebrations were mighty.

The tournament was Glenn McGrath's last. He'd retired from Test cricket after the Sydney New Year game and announced then that he would bow out completely after the World Cup. He was a real genius of the game as I'd seen for myself during the tournament, with his contribution to the team meeting before Australia played South Africa providing a great example. He said, 'I've watched Ashwell Prince and when he first gets out there he likes to hook even though he doesn't yet have a feel for it. He hits it high and the ball drops a metre behind the square umpire. I'm going to give him a bouncer early; he won't be able to resist it and if we've got someone there he'll be gone.' Not everyone was persuaded, but he knew what he was talking about. Sure enough, Prince hooked it, Matthew Hayden was where Pigeon said he needed to be and the South African was out for one. It felt beautifully appropriate that Glenn's record 26 wickets in the campaign saw him named World Cup Player of the Tournament — one more brilliant moment in what had been an extraordinary couple of months in the Caribbean.

That trip had also given Karina her first taste of touring life when she flew over for the two-week visitor period organised by Cricket Australia. These periods helped partners understand the demands put on players by the long distances travelled, the official functions and other commitments, but also allowed them to enjoy being fêted guests, watching the game from a corporate box, and get to know the other partners on day-trips or over meals.

Home in Sydney again, it was time for me to get the procedure done to fix the knee injury I'd received in 2005. It was day surgery, in and out, but it did stop me playing or even training properly for more than a month. Karina, who had been patient for a long time, seized the moment and organised our wedding. With so little notice, the only available spot at the reception venue was a Thursday evening, 2 August. Among her other qualities, Karina is a very good organiser. So she took care of everything. I had to do only two things: be there on the day and front up to dreaded dance lessons beforehand so we could get through the traditional bridal waltz without tripping over. I'd rather have taken ice baths — and I *hate* ice baths — but I did it. I still took the precaution of saying to my brothers, 'As soon as I get up on that dance floor, make sure you get out there as quick as you can.'

Both Karina and I love to entertain people and make sure they're having a good time. We didn't want to have the ceremony then leave the guests hanging about while we went off for photos, so we took care of that first. We met in our finest down at Balmoral, where I'd tried to persuade her to go on the night of our engagement. This time we got lucky with the weather; it was a stunning winter afternoon — almost as stunning as my about-to-be bride. We had the photos taken then went separately to the historic Gunners Barracks nearby, were married in the courtyard outside and then went straight inside and got the party started. It wasn't at all how we'd imagined it when we had first talked about it years earlier, but it was perfect in every way and our guests kept telling us it was one of the best weddings they'd ever been to. We had a four-day honeymoon on Lizard Island, where amid all the relaxing I was able to do some running to help get my knee back into shape for the coming season.

My duties with the Blues were, however, going to have to wait, since I'd had the brilliant news that I was going to be touring India in late September and October as part of the Australian one-day side — not as a back-up for Adam Gilchrist or in his place, but in addition to him, as a batsman. The tour covered seven ODIs and a T20I. Australia had come a long, long way in terms of success on Indian soil by this point, having won the 2006 Champions Trophy and only losing two of the last 15 one-dayers on the subcontinent.

Conditions for travelling teams had improved enormously, although 'Delhi belly' was still a risk. (And, indeed, Michael Clarke needed to call on the team doctor to make it through the first game of our tour. He was lucky; it was the first time in 20 years the team had travelled with a doctor.) We had it all to play for and when Ricky Ponting injured his hamstring I was put into the batting line-up at number six for the opening encounter, in Bangalore.

There were some absolute class players on the Indian side — Sachin Tendulkar, Sourav Ganguly and Rahul Dravid among them — but there were also a couple of guys with big mouths and hot heads who ended up drawing attention to that tour for all the wrong reasons. They were the bowlers Shanth Sreesanth, a newcomer, and Harbhajan Singh, who I'd watched help India win at Eden Park in 2001. We won the toss in that first game and chose to bat and when I walked out to the wicket Sreesanth was having a good day, having already dispatched Matthew Hayden, Brad Hodge and Andrew Symonds for a combined total of 41 (Gilly had also gone, for 12). He greeted me by bowling a beamer, though he did apologise for it. Michael Clarke and I turned things around with a 144-run partnership, with Pup's 130 and my 69 helping our side to a 307 total. Indian captain MS Dhoni blamed a batting-friendly pitch for his team's inability to pull us back, although the rain that washed the match out meant he didn't have to put that to the test.

The second game, three days later, was in Kochi, which just happened to be Sreesanth's hometown. He went all out to be noticed and he succeeded. India won the toss and decided to field. Once again we found ourselves on the back foot early, at 3 for 66, but once again we fought back and this time there was no poor weather to leave any room for doubt. Haydos dug in for 75 and Andrew Symonds and I both reached a score of 87 (mine not out) to contribute to a total of 306. They had no answer to our bowlers, with Brad Hogg and Pup leading the charge, and were all out for 222. I had the interesting experience of fielding on the boundary and getting to interact with the passionate Indian fans, which was fun. At game's end I was thrilled to be named Player of the Match.

But unfortunately, if understandably, it wasn't determination or achievement that everyone was interested in talking about at the end of the game, it was the rancour and aggro that had run through it, centring on a particularly stupid piece of behaviour from Sreesanth. At one point during my partnership with Symo I'd gone for one of Sreesanth's deliveries and missed. He'd been doing his best to get under our skins the whole time but I'd heard it all before and from better than him. Symo, however, wanted to give me an encouraging word, so as Sreesanth picked up the ball he started to walk down to my end, at which point Sreesanth pulled the bails off his stump and yelled out, 'Howzat, run out!' Now, I have happily claimed the wicket of batsmen who were out of their ground during play, but that's not what this was. Even Dhoni initially thought Sreesanth's ridiculous move was just a poor attempt at a joke. It was downright embarrassing, but Sreesanth didn't pull his head in; if anything, he got worse.

The tension kept building and Harbhajan had already got himself in a lather when he came out to bat. He kept saying to Gilly, 'Do you want a fight? Do you want a fight?' Gilly, who, with Punter still out of action, was acting captain, just kept his cool. But, after being stumped for four off a Michael Clarke ball, Harbhajan made a show of standing out in the middle pointing his bat around the place. Then he complained afterwards that he was the one who had been hard done by, having been subjected to 'vulgar' abuse. What he and the more sensible members of the Indian team had been subjected to was an 84-run loss.

Punter was back in the team for the third game, in Hyderabad, and either Brad Hodge or I had to go to make room. This time it was me who sat it out, and I was totally comfortable with that. I understood that I was on the tour as a spare batsman. My time would come. We won by 47 runs, in a game where the umpire kept a tight lid on things to prevent any more on-field blow-ups. I sat out game four as well, as did Sreesanth, although even as 12th man he still managed to make trouble, getting in Symo's face as he went out to bat and again when he returned to the pavilion. India scraped out an eight-run win, their first of the series.

In the next match, in Vadodara in the northwestern state of Gujarat, the problem wasn't on the field, it was with the crowd. As Mitchell Johnson and Adam Gilchrist tore through India, with Johnno getting his first international five-for and Gilly notching up a record fifth instance of six dismissals in a one-day innings, Symo, who is of Afro–Caribbean descent, was fielding on the boundary. A section of the crowd started making monkey noises. It seemed like a clear-cut instance of racism, but the local authorities claimed that the spectators hadn't been making monkey sounds: they'd been doing a religious chant in response to their team's heavy loss.

I played again in the sixth game, in Nagpur, and was out in the middle with Symo as he channelled his feelings about everything that had happened on the tour so far into a match- and series-winning stand. Our 75-run partnership was a crucial part of Australia's 18-run win. There was extra satisfaction in the knowledge that Symo's eventual 107 not out came after Sreesanth was unable to hold the ball he top-edged off Harbhajan when he was on just two. Moments like that are great little victories within the wider game.

In Mumbai for the final game I got my own second chance when I was dropped at deep midwicket, but moments later Murali Kartik got me lbw with an arm ball. Kartik claimed five other wickets and then was half of a tail-end partnership that won India the game. But once again there were 'monkey' taunts from the crowd and, even worse, Harbhajan said it directly to Symo on the field, as Symo told us after the game. As a team, we discussed what to do about it. Symo's choice was to go and see Harbhajan in India's change room, where Harbhajan apologised and said it wouldn't happen again and offered a handshake — although he later denied the conversation had ever taken place and famously resorted to vile name-calling again on India's tour of Australia just a few months later.

The tour finished with a T20I. India had won the World Twenty20 comp in South Africa the previous month after knocking us out in the semi-final; both the team and their home crowds regarded as a huge deal, whereas to us Twenty20 was the hit-and-giggle format. They thrashed us in the tour-ending T20I in Mumbai on 20 October, three days before my 30th birthday. To our bemusement they seemed to feel that it made up for losing the ODI series. Our attitude was, 'Whatever you say, fellas.' In fact, the Indian players were keenly aware of the new Indian Premier League (IPL), which offered huge contracts to players for the

Twenty20 format. Australian players would eventually realise the opportunities there too, but at the time we still viewed Twenty20 as a novelty.

The tour was a big experience for me and the intensity really was a shock to the system. Senior players talked about coming back from India completely wiped out, mentally drained, and that's exactly how I found myself. I could do little other than sleep for a week until the batteries recharged.

I'd missed the first game of the 2007–08 Sheffield Shield tournament, but I was back for the second, in late October. At the end of the previous season I'd told the NSW board that I wanted to step down from the captaincy role in order to be able to concentrate fully on my game. Captaincy is a privileged position, not something you should ever put your hand up or lobby for. I'd been honoured to have been asked to do it for NSW and I was pleased to have had success in the role, but it wasn't something I'd ever wanted to do long term. In my view it's too hard for a wicketkeeper to captain over an extended period. While we keepers have (literally) the best view of the game, we have too much else going on. I think keepers make good vice-captains. To last in the role of keeper, fundamentally you need to be a good bloke. There's only one of us in the team; we have to get along with everyone. The parts of captaincy I enjoyed most were related to that: knowing how to get the best out of people and bring a team together. But those are things you can contribute as vice-captain without having to deal with the other demands of captaincy, including selection.

So, going up against Queensland at the SCG, I could leave all the captaincy issues to Simon Katich and pour everything into my performance. It was a batsman's paradise out there. The Bulls won the toss and, to no-one's surprise, chose to bat. Matthew Hayden hit a massive 179 and we were 316 behind by stumps on the second day, but the game was a long, long way from over. Kat was already on 88 when I went out at number six. We proceeded to put on a 62-over 334 partnership, before Ashley Noffke got me lbw on 123. Kat amassed 306 before Noffke eventually got him too. We'd answered Queensland's 467 with 601 of our own. Jimmy Maher declared at 7 for 398 in their second innings, and we batted for eight overs to make the draw official.

We had two more Shield draws and didn't lose a match the entire season (unlike the Ford Ranger Cup, where we finished last), with scorecards reading, 'NSW won by an innings and 35 runs', 'NSW won by 9 wickets', 'NSW won by an innings and 162 runs' and so on. We won the final against Victoria in equally emphatic style, taking it by 258 runs, and I finished the season with three centuries and one half-century in the seven games I'd played.

I'd missed the other games because of being called away to four ODIs where, in recognition of the performances I was now consistently delivering, I'd been selected as a batsman, playing alongside Adam Gilchrist as I'd done in India. I did, however, end up wicketkeeping in his stead when he was rested in the final Chappell–Hadlee Trophy game, which it was our turn to host. (One of the games was washed out, but we won both the others, reclaiming the trophy after the previous year's drubbing.) Another of the ODIs was a loss to Sri Lanka (I was out for seven) and the remaining two were against India (one was washed out and in the other I was stumped by Dhoni off a ball from Harbhajan Singh on five).

But in much of the coverage the results in the Australia vs India games in both Test and ODI formats took second place to the tensions on the field. As has been well documented elsewhere, Harbhajan Singh in particular triggered some ugly moments, bringing back the spectre of racial abuse that Andrew Symonds had faced in India. Commentators, including Peter Roebuck, reacted by heaping criticism on the Australian team and painting the Indian side as innocent victims. The Australian cricket authorities had the chance to step in and make things right but seemed to be more concerned about the business implications. It was sickening to watch all this unfold from a distance, knowing these guys personally. Symo was as good a team man as I'd ever played with. He lived and breathed the team and always put it first. That made it all the harder to see him and Ricky Ponting left hanging. Ricky has said

Symo was never the same player after that summer, and it's hard to argue with him.

As the season unfolded, speculation about Adam Gilchrist's retirement reached fever pitch. It seemed to be all anyone other than those closest to me wanted to talk to me about or, more accurately, talk *at* me about. Out at the pub, at a barbecue, at a grade match, people kept on offering their opinions and I kept closing the conversations down as politely as possible (despite my desire just to tell them to shut the hell up). I'd try to palm them off with generic statements like, 'Well, who knows what will happen.' If that didn't work I'd attempt to change the subject. If they just kept on, as many did, I'd lie and say, 'Look, I'm too old now anyway.' That usually did it.

Only Gilly himself had the right to say when it was time to go, and during the Adelaide Test against India at the end of January 2008 he came to his decision. When I reached for my ringing phone on the Test's third day and saw Gilly's name displayed, I knew my world was about to change.

CHAPTER 12

A CHARACTER-BUILDING YEAR

ADAM GILCHRIST HAD BEEN going back and forth in his mind about retiring for a long period, as he revealed later. When the Adelaide Test started on Thursday, 24 January 2008, he was expecting to play for at least another 10 months and said so publicly. But by the end of the second day he had decided it was time to go. He broke the news to Ricky Ponting that night, and the following day, after telling his teammates and other key people, he made the thoughtful gesture of phoning me to let me know of his decision before going public. I congratulated him on a wonderful career and said, 'You've changed the way wicketkeepers are perceived around the world. You should be very proud of that. He replied, 'Well, it's your turn now. Get ready to be the next Australian wicketkeeper.'

It was true that the consistency of my performance had put me in the box seat. All the effort I'd put in over the past five years to make myself the obvious choice to succeed Gilly had come to fruition. But the selectors would make up their own minds and they were bound to weigh up all the possible options, including Ryan Campbell, Wade Seccombe and Darren Berry. I just needed to hang tight and not get ahead of myself.

It had been unfolding as a huge week even before Gilly's call, with Karina confirming two days earlier that she was pregnant with our first child. There was another cause for celebration in the family, with my brother Michael's engagement party set to start just a couple of hours after Gilly's call. Walking into the party, only Karina and I, my parents, my brothers and their partners knew what had happened; Gilly had not yet started his media conference in Adelaide. I had my phone switched off and most of the guests had muted theirs, but we knew as soon as the news broke: people all around the room were checking the phones that had been vibrating in their pockets or bags, then looking over at me. I didn't respond. This was Michael and Amy's night.

It took a few weeks for the selectors to make their decision, but finally Cricket Australia General Manager Michael Brown called to say yes, they were handing the gloves to me. I was going to become only the 400th person to play for Australia in more than 130 years of Test cricket history. It's a nice round number, 400, but I wouldn't have minded if it wasn't — it's what those numerals represent that counts. Gilly decided that while Adelaide, his 96th Test, would be his last, he would play out the rest of the summer's one-dayers in the triangular series featuring India and Sri Lanka. I made the most of the opportunity to talk shop with him as I played alongside him in three of those games and he was generous with his advice and help, as always.

I would have made my Test debut in Pakistan had the tour gone ahead as planned in March, but it was cancelled amid mounting security concerns that had led the Department of Foreign Affairs to warn Australians against unnecessary travel to the region. But everything was fine for the May tour to the West Indies. Dad had always said that if and when I made my Test debut he would take the whole family to see it. He jokingly grumbled about why I couldn't debut in Sydney or even Perth ... no, it had to be all the way over on the other side of the world. In fact, they wouldn't have missed it for anything.

I flew over with the team, of course, following our pre-tour camp. Karina, who was 25 weeks' pregnant, her sister and their parents and my parents and brothers and Amy all came. They made a holiday of it, with stops in the US along the way to Kingston, Jamaica, where the first match would be played.

The tour consisted of the three Tests in the Frank Worrell Trophy, a T20I, then five ODIs, with a four-day warm-up game against a local 'Select XI' the week before our first Test. On the morning of this game it became apparent that everyone was expecting me to wear the Baggy Green cap that had been brought along for me, just as they would be wearing theirs. I didn't want to be a troublemaker, but no way could I go along with that. The Baggy Green belongs to Test cricketers. I would not be a Test cricketer until I made my Test debut the following week. It was going to be a very special moment and one I had waited a long time for. I couldn't just chuck on the cap now like it meant nothing, and I said so to Ricky Ponting.

Punter discussed it with team manager Steve Bernard and, not wanting the team to take the field in an assortment of headgear, decided we'd wear our blue training caps for the first day's play. The caps carried the logo of the sponsor, VB, which really didn't register too much with anyone present. But back home some people couldn't wait to grab the wrong end of the stick and wave it around, fuming in the media about how we'd supposedly disgraced Australia by giving in to the sponsor's demands to wear their gear. So what if that wasn't the truth? It was particularly disappointing that some of these commentators were former Test players who should have well understood what it meant to earn the right to wear the Baggy Green. (Wisely, Cricket Australia decided to come up with a solution that would avoid the situation in future, and ever since then players who are awaiting their debut have travelled with the Australia A Baggy Green, which has a different emblem to the real thing.)

After all that kerfuffle, you'd hope the experience of having the Baggy Green bestowed on me a week later was pretty special — and it was. The first game was at Sabina Park on 22 May 2008.

Before the warm-up the team gathered in a circle on the field and Ricky Ponting said a few brief but meaningful words welcoming me to this very special club. It was a profound moment for me, the culmination of all the hard work and sacrifices not just from me but from everyone around me over the past 20 years: every time Dad didn't collapse on the sofa exhausted at the end of a long day but came out to throw the ball to me instead; every time Mum got up early to drive me to some distant carnival; every time Karina went to family celebrations alone because I was interstate or overseas; every time a teammate or a coach or a trainer went the extra mile for me; and every time I fooled my exhausted body into giving just a little bit more — it all came to fruition then and there.

That's why players and ex-players still reminisce about the day they got their Baggy Green cap. For nearly all of us, it's one of the most treasured possessions we could ever have. It certainly is for me. I'm not big on memorabilia, not one of those guys who want to take stumps or swap shirts at the end of a game. There are only two keepsakes from my career that really matter to me — my Baggy Green and my Baggy Blue, kept in all their unwashed and battered glory in the special bags in which they came, on the outside of which are embroidered the player's name and number, inextricably linked.

I hadn't had a lot of sleep the few nights before the big day and I was riding a huge wave of emotion by the time the game got underway. We won the toss and Punter opted to bat. I was on the sheet at number eight, so I just sat there vibrating with tension. Simon Katich was making his return to the side two and a half years after his last Test. He and Phil Jaques opened and unfortunately Fidel Edwards got them both before the seventh over was done. But Punter hit his stride and had notched up 158 by the time he was caught just before stumps. Even though I hadn't caught or hit a ball I was exhausted at the end of my first day as a Test cricketer, so worn out with nervous energy I actually got some sleep that night. With Mike Hussey, Brad Hodge and Andrew Symonds all getting over the half-century mark, we were 6 for 350 when I went in late morning on Day 2. I spent the first few overs getting a feel for the wicket and the bowling of Dwayne Bravo and Darren Sammy. Nine overs in, having picked up ones and twos and survived a couple of appeals, I felt like I was getting the measure of things as I pulled a Bravo ball over wide mid-on for four. But, unfortunately, in the following over, sitting on 11, I was caught by my rival wicketkeeper Denesh Ramdin when I went for the pull again, this time on a ball from Sammy that I should really have left alone.

We finished our first innings after lunch on 431 and Brett Lee and Mitchell Johnson opened the bowling for us. I was excited to be finally getting to work as a Test keeper. I was moving well, jumping around, feeling good. In the 11th over, Johnno was bowling to Devon Smith. It was great keeping to Johnno because of the pace and the fear he put into batsmen, but the flip side was that sometimes there were days when you could not tell where the ball was going. He sprayed it wide down the leg side and I dived to get it. It wasn't a catch; I was just trying to stop the ball. If it had been later in the game I wouldn't have dived for it, but I was full of beans and away I went. The ball hit the tip of my right ring finger and I knew instantly I'd broken it.

I wouldn't have minded a few minutes to feel sorry for myself and kick some cans around, but that wasn't going to happen. I straightened up and took a couple of breaths, trying to get on top of the pain and the fact that I'd broken my bloody finger in my debut Test. In the grandstand, Dad was watching closely, slightly apart from the rest of the group as usual. He turned to them and said, 'Brad's just broken his finger.' He says he can always tell from my posture. Apparently I have a 'tell' that appears to everyone else as though I'm simply stretching: I bend my head a bit and push my hands into my hips. When I didn't leave the field, Karina's folks and our friends said, 'No, surely not. If he had he'd be coming off.' Dad said, 'No, he'll keep going; he won't say a thing.'

He was right. Well, almost right. I did turn to Mike Hussey, fielding at gully, and say quietly, 'You wouldn't believe it, I've just broken my finger.' In most workplaces your colleague might ask if you were okay or see how they could help you. A cricket field full of players competing at the elite level is not most workplaces. Huss was just as aware as I was that there was no back-up wicketkeeper on the tour. The cleaned-up version of what he said is, 'Don't even think about going off; I'll have to wicketkeep.' I said, 'Don't worry, I'm not going anywhere.' There was nothing for it but to grit my teeth and get on with it. Seven overs later, I got my first Test dismissal, when Ramnaresh Sarwan attempted a cut on a ball from Stuart Clark and instead got an edge, sending it up high to my right. I jumped for it and got it. Broken finger or not, I wasn't letting that one slip. It was the first of four catches I took that innings, as we got the Windies out for 312.

I didn't say anything to anyone, just played through the pain and did better in our second innings than I had in the first, contributing 23 before falling to an impressive catch from Runako Morton off a Bravo ball. The Windies kept us to 167 and seemed to have it all over us — a surprise to some since Australia were world number one at that point, while the West Indies had sunk to number eight. But the two Stuarts, Clark and MacGill, were on fire and we ended up winning the match by 95 runs.

Stuart Clark was a very deserving Player of the Match, with a brilliant second innings 5 for 32. But Shivnarine Chanderpaul would have been the local fans' choice. He'd been on 86 in the first innings when he tried to duck from a Brett Lee bouncer but copped the ball hard on the back of his helmet. He crashed to the ground and didn't move for several long, sickening moments. Brett and I and his batting partner, Fidel Edwards, rushed to him, closely followed by the rest of the Australian team. The West Indies team doctor and physio raced out with a stretcher. Even though he was responding to our questions and was able to have a drink of water, everyone expected Chanderpaul to be carried off. But to the enormous relief of every single person present, none more so than our shaken bowler, he gathered himself, got to his feet, reassured the medical staff he was fit to continue, and batted on to 118, almost single-handedly dragging his team back into the game. (Precautionary scans after the game confirmed he was fine, thankfully.)

At the end of the match I got the debutant's privilege of having my family come to the terrace outside our change rooms for a celebratory drink. It's great to share very special moments with the loved ones who have helped you get there, although in recent years it's become common to have families around the team at all sorts of times, which I think can be distracting.

The second Test was in Antigua. While a doctor had travelled with the team in India the previous year, we didn't have one with us on this tour; we only had a team physiotherapist, Alex Kountouris. Following the flight from Jamaica to Antigua, Alex didn't feel right. It turned out he was suffering from deep vein thrombosis, which is of course a potentially very dangerous condition and required his hospitalisation. With Alex out of the picture, any medical matters, including the injection of anaesthetic blocks, had to be treated by local doctors. Cricket Australia found someone they thought suitable to needle my finger and take care of the various other things that players needed.

Sometimes I had to go to this doctor's house overlooking the Caribbean; sometimes he came to the ground. The finger looked pretty gruesome by this point, nicely purple and swollen — unsurprising, since the bone had actually been broken in four places. One morning we were at the ground in the small room assigned to medical procedures. I had my finger out on the table as the doctor prepared the hypodermic when I heard Andrew Symonds yelling, 'Someone find my camera, quick.' I thought, *I know where this is going*, and sure enough, next minute Symo's in the room calling out for the other players to join him: 'C'mon, you've gotta get a load of this!' The doctor was saying to me, 'Now I'm about to inject it, so make sure your hand is stable there,' while Symo jostled around trying to get the best angle for his shot. If you were ever in any kind of real trouble, your teammates would be there like a shot, doing anything they possibly could to help. But if they knew you were suffering but basically fine, they seized on the humour of the situation and made the most of it. I was exactly the same.

Unfortunately, the finger got worse. I guess for some reason it didn't like being stuffed in a sweaty glove for eight hours a day and slammed by 140kph balls. A day or two later I was at the doctor's house, waiting for him to do the injection, when he suddenly leaned forward with a pair of surgical scissors and pulled my nail off. I couldn't believe it. Not only did it hurt like hell, the whole top of the finger dropped down as soon as I lifted my hand. The nail had been the only thing holding it all in place. He said, 'Oh, it's broken.' *What?! How could he have been treating me for days and only be saying that now? He'd been sent the x-rays; he'd been briefed, hadn't he?* I said, 'What the ...' He said, 'I thought it would relieve the pressure. I should have left it.'

Up to this point, the swelling had come from the impact, but within 24 hours of the nail bed being exposed it had developed an infection. If you think having an unprotected nail bed is agonising, you should try having an infected one, though I hope you never do. But I had waited so long for this chance to play Test cricket I simply could not give it up now.

Punter was hoping for a win from the match, but failing that would play for a draw, since he was determined not to lose the Frank Worrell Trophy. We won the toss and went in to bat. Kat was in brilliant form, getting his century on the first day, with Pup emulating him on Day 2. Punter and Binga both got their half-centuries and I got to 33 as part of our 479 total — the Windies feeling the lack of a spinner on the slow wicket after Chris Gayle had dropped out injured.

Binga had an even better time with the ball, using the reverse swing to devastating effect and taking 5 for 59, including an amazing 19-ball sequence where he gave away only five runs. Chanderpaul was again the hero for the Windies, with help from Sarwan (who I'd been sure we had out on 92 — Stuart MacGill had found his rhythm and bowled a leg break that drew the batsman out of his crease; I had the bails off before he could blink, but the umpires sent it upstairs for review and it eventually came back as not out). The game ended in a draw.

Those two Tests would be the only ones I played with Magilla, to my disappointment. The fact that I was in the Australian team was in no small part due to the experience I'd had keeping to him at NSW. He was a world-class spinner, but he was in a similar situation to the one I was in, spending a long time behind a game-dominating great — in his case, Shane Warne. Guys at state level outside NSW had okay spinners to work with, but I was lucky enough to have someone of his rare talent from the get-go. Keepers can be defined by how well they keep up to the stumps to spinners in general. Having to keep to such a quality spinner on a last-day SCG wicket, where the bounce is so inconsistent, is as hard a task as a glove-man can face anywhere. In addition, there is nothing better for a keeper than getting a leg-side stumping, where you can't see the ball for half its passage and you have to trust that all the work you've put in will ensure you're in the right position, and I had a lot of those off Magilla. What I learned keeping to him gave me the edge on every other aspiring wicketkeeper around the country. I would have liked to have had him around longer for that reason.

Of course, he could be a very difficult and testy character; there's no secret about that. He didn't just challenge me as a keeper; he challenged me as his Blues captain too. I remember one game when we had to take six wickets in the last session to win against Tasmania, and we needed that win to get through to the Sheffield Shield final. Michael Bevan, an ex-NSW man who was now playing for Tasmania, was batting. Approaching a break in play I told a fielder to move in on the batsman's off side. Magilla said, 'I don't want him there.' I said, 'We'll leave him there for this over and try to get the bloke to do something different so we can get a wicket.' He colourfully expressed the view that he would tell me where *he* wanted the field. We stepped to one side and had a few words on the field, and then some even more heated ones walking back to the change room at the break. He didn't say a thing to me after we went back on the field (set the way I wanted), but I wasn't worried about that even slightly, as long as he took those last six wickets — and he did.

So he might not be someone I'd want to be trapped with on a desert island, but I've always been able to separate the game from my personal feelings. I've kept for some very talented bowlers over the years, from Glenn McGrath and Brett Lee to Mitchell Johnson and Ryan Harris, but Stuart MacGill is the one I enjoyed keeping for the most. However, by the time that West Indies tour rolled around he was 37, he'd been struggling with a knee injury and he'd lost his taste for pushing himself the way you have to in order to play at that level.

I'd heard many players over the years say, 'You'll know when you know as far as retirement goes.' We young blokes would ask, 'What does that mean?' They'd say, 'You just stop wanting to do all those little things you have to do to get better. You lose the taste for it.' I'd be thinking, *That's ridiculous. I'm never going to feel like that. As long as I can bend my knees to crouch behind the stumps, or curl my hands around a bat, I'm going to want to play.* I would eventually find out they were right, of course, but in 2008 I was still as hungry as I could be — in the ways that mattered most, my career had only just started — and I wasn't about to let a broken finger get in the way of that.

The final Test was in Barbados. I bound the finger and continued to get the anaesthetic blocks and played on, working hard to compartmentalise the pain. Anaesthetic blocks don't always work as well as you would hope and they pose their own challenges. At least when you're wicketkeeping the glove helps the numbed fingers move as one (because the block also affects the fingers on either side of the broken one). However, when you're batting, trying to put pressure on your grip hand without being able to feel your position is an interesting challenge. You have to continually flick glances down at the bat handle to make sure you're where you need to be. Even so, I got 32 and 45 not out and took seven catches in all, an effort I would have been happy with whether I was injured or not, and we won the match by 87 runs.

Unsure if I was going to be able to keep playing, Cricket Australia had dispatched New Zealand-born West Australian Luke Ronchi as a back-up keeper. Luke (who would go on to the unusual feat of representing two countries in international cricket after he moved back to New Zealand) stood in for me in the T20I, but I was back for the first ODI game in St Vincent on 24 June, hitting my half-century and taking three catches as well as a run out as part of our 84-run win.

There were four ODIs to go and I tried to kid myself I could get through them, but the infection had become so bad that I couldn't close my hand and the pain was excruciating. I had to make myself go to Ricky Ponting and tell him that I was out for the rest of the tour. It certainly wasn't the way I'd pictured my first Test tour ending, but Punter reassured me that my 16 dismissals and 151 runs in the three Test matches showed that I was the right man for the job and he looked forward to having me back as soon as I was fit to play again.

At home in Sydney my hand specialist, Dr Doug Wheen, confirmed that it would have been much, much better to have left the nail on; however, as it was now almost six weeks after the original break there was no point in surgery. We just needed to clear out the infection and let the bone finish healing.

Regardless of the injury I was always going to be back from the Caribbean in plenty of time for our baby's birth, although I was going to have to leave again very soon after. The enforced lay-off gave me a bit more time with Karina before he arrived, which was nice. I knew the baby was a boy because I'd been with Karina at one of her ultrasound check-ups before I'd left for the West Indies, and when she popped out to use the bathroom I asked the sonographer. I didn't have a preference either way; I just wanted to know. I've never been big on surprises. I'm happy to know what my Christmas presents are in advance; I'll still be just as pleased on the day. Karina initially said she didn't want to know the sex, and I had fun joking as she and her friends and family speculated on what she was having, saying one minute it was a boy and the next it was a girl. As the birth approached, Karina decided she wanted to know after all, and we decided on the name Zachary, giving him my middle name, James.

I thought my finger was healed in time for three ODIs against Bangladesh in Darwin over the course of a week at the beginning of September, although in retrospect I should have left it longer. It was still angry-looking and painful but now that I'd finally made it into the team I wanted to play as much as possible. There wasn't much of note about the games themselves, all of which we won easily. However, during our time in Darwin, Symo skipped a team meeting to go fishing and in response the leadership group and selectors left him off the tour to India for a four-match Test series due to start on 9 October. His absence would be felt.

We were to fly out for India in the third week of September. Karina did what so many partners do and rearranged things around the tour schedule, opting to have a scheduled caesarean in order to give me seven days with the baby before I had to go. I was present for Zac's 12 September birth, which was joyous and thrilling on a level that cricket couldn't possibly ever match. It's been said many times before, but there is no greater privilege than to be part of bringing a new life into the world. I'd never felt prouder than I did holding him for the first time.

He was a small baby and is still little for his age — just like I was. He's always had a lovely temperament, but for the first two and a half years that child did not sleep for more than a few hours at a time and he never really wanted to eat. It was very hard on Karina, who was to all intents and purposes a single parent to a brand new baby, although both her mother and mine helped as much as possible.

In fact, it was often a lot harder than Karina let on, as she tried to shield me from the emotional ups and downs in order to let me focus on performing at the highest level so that I could have a genuine Test cricket career. We knew it wasn't forever. In most other careers longevity means decades; in professional sport it means years — if you're lucky. It is a time when a lot has to go by the wayside in single-minded pursuit of a goal. However, all going well, what can be a few very tough years allow you to set up your family for everything that follows.

There were sacrifices all round, as there are in any professional athlete's life. My brother Michael and his fiancée, Amy, had set their wedding date for November, before their relocation to the UAE, and wanted me to be a groomsman. After my call-up into the Australian team, Michael talked to me about changing the date to ensure that I could be there. But as Karina and I knew first-hand from trying to organise our own wedding, there isn't a 'good time' — it's always cricket season somewhere. I told Michael that they had to pick the date that worked best for them, not think about me. If I was at home I wouldn't miss it for the world, but if I couldn't be there physically I would be in spirit. Being as close and family-oriented as we are, it was hard not to be there for that wonderful moment in my brother's life, no question, but that same closeness meant he understood perfectly that I couldn't be.

I was away in India for almost three months. The tour was not a great one for Australia. With two losses and two draws, India claimed the Border–Gavaskar Trophy. Over the previous couple of years, the once invincible Australian side had said goodbye to Shane Warne, Glenn McGrath, Justin Langer, Damien Martyn and Adam Gilchrist. Ricky Ponting is the best captain I ever played under, a wonderful leader of men who inspired the people around him to want to be better. But, although for the most part he did an excellent job of hiding it, he was struggling on that tour, coming under relentless criticism from Indian and Australian commentators alike, which I thought was unwarranted.

The mood on the field was often tense. In the second innings of the First Test in Bangalore Shane Watson and I fought hard to bring the game back our way with a batting partnership in which I got 35 not out. But much more attention was given to my run-in with Zaheer Khan, who decided to wave his bat at my head after we had a difference of opinion about the level of precipitation and whether it required stopping play. Harbhajan Singh was once again pushing far over the line from gamesmanship to provocation. It felt to me as though the previous summer had shown him the power India's financial impact on cricket gave it and he was taking full advantage. The Indian players often seemed to be a law unto themselves, and we just had to cop it. In the Second Test at Mohali, India beat us by 320 runs, their largest victory margin ever. My 37 runs in that game was my highest score in all four matches, but in the circumstances it represented a stubborn fight as the wickets fell around me.

I kept wicket pretty well throughout the tour, standing up to the stumps on unpredictable pitches. I got criticised in the newspapers at home, including in a column by Dean Jones, for the number of byes I let through (23 in the first innings at Bangalore and 16 in the second — a record in Australia–India Tests that I could have done without). But there are good byes and bad byes. If you're missing balls you should be taking, then yes, you're falling down on the job. But in India, in particular, you can be doing everything right and a ball will kick out of the rough and go square a metre and you can't do a thing about it. Ian Healy said a keeper should never worry about byes in those circumstances, because when you're working the way you should, the ones that get through don't mean too much and if you're not careful they can mess with your head.

There were only two weeks between the fourth and final Test in India and the first of the two Tests against New Zealand in the Trans-Tasman Trophy, at the Gabba. Even though Karina had been fantastic about texting me lots of photos and keeping me up to date with Zac's development, it was a strange experience to leave a seven-day-old newborn and come home to a two-and-a-half-month-old boy. All cricketers' wives know the exasperation of having someone come home from tour and take a couple of days to remember they're not living in a hotel anymore, but it's much sharper once you have children. It's great to be home and it's lovely for your partner and kids to have you there, but you have to be mindful of the fact that you're lobbing into an environment where everyone has their routines and that's what's kept it all going while you've been away. As with any first-time parents, there was a lot of figuring out how the pieces fitted together.

The rumblings of criticism about my performance in India became full-throated shouts after the first game against the Kiwis, despite the fact that we won it handily. I had a bit of a shocker, it's true. In our first innings I was caught by Jamie How on just six after being tempted by a Jesse Ryder delivery that bounced a bit more than I was expecting. Then in New Zealand's first innings I only took one catch — Jesse Ryder for 30 off a Shane Watson ball. The problem was that I had already dropped Ryder when he was on 11, diving to get a ball that every man and his dog said afterwards was obviously headed straight for Haydos at first slip. I could have left it, except as a wicketkeeper it's your responsibility to catch any ball you can. If you think you can get it you have to go for it. They don't all stick but you have to try, and then you have to live with the consequences.

When I went out to bat for the second time, Daniel Vettori got the most out of the Gabba wicket, bowling me for 19 with a straight ball. I'd made the mistake of trying to play cautiously rather than trying to change the game. I walked off thinking, *I don't get out like that: I played the bowler not the ball.* The newspapers were full of reports about how I was struggling, was under serious threat of losing my position and was 'running out of chances'. Steve Rixon, Ian Healy and Adam Gilchrist were all approached for comment and all said much the same thing: that I had the goods but was yet to find my feet. Heals said that the mental pressure of being in the Test side had led to some technical flaws getting into my game and that I wasn't clearing my mind to concentrate on my technique.

My fitness wasn't an issue; I'd continued to work with Christian Marchegiani and was confident I was as fit as, or fitter than, anyone in the team. Nor was willingness: I was hungry for success. Part of it was the trap of falling into mental quicksand. The solution was to simplify. You could arrest a slide that started during a game by putting absolute concentration on the most fundamental elements of the game: foot position and watching the ball. If you've done all the training and drills you can focus on those basics and trust your reactions when it counts. It sounds easy, but it takes a lot of mental strength. It works, though, and it was among the useful feedback I got from Heals and Stumper, whose opinions I respected.

I did, however, think there was also something else going on in the way people were reacting to me: I was being judged in comparison to Adam Gilchrist. In a very literal sense people were criticising me for not being Gilly — and specifically for not being him at the height of his Test career, despite the fact that I was just at the start of mine. The same thing happened with perfectly capable spinners after Shane Warne retired.

Mike Hussey and I had to do an appearance together around this time and it turned out to be a very helpful thing for me. Huss had made his debut a couple of years before me and we were able to have a really good conversation about the kind of pressure you find yourself under when you first join the team and how you can find your way through it and free your mind.

I'd walked across the Gabba on my way back to the pavilion thinking, *I'm not doing this again. I'm going to get out there and play my natural game.* And that's just what I did in the Second Test at Adelaide Oval, where it all came together for me. New Zealand won the toss and chose to bat. No chances were escaping my gloves this time round, and I took three solid catches as we kept them to 270 on the fairly flat wicket. It was Matthew Hayden's 100th Test and it would have been great to see him get a ton, but it wasn't to be — he went for 24 and his opening partner Simon Katich for one less than that. Punter and Huss both got half-centuries and kept going into the 70s. Pup was on 48 when I came out, at 5 for 247. He and I had batted together a lot and understood each other's games so well that I felt relaxed and comfortable out there. I could see the gaps; I knew exactly where I wanted the ball to go and how to get it there. It was one of those rare days in life when everything you touch turns to gold. I reached 70 quickly, putting the partnership on 100, but I wasn't done yet, not by a long shot. My ton came with a Tim Southee ball I sent sailing past midwicket for four.

It was an incredibly emotional moment for me. Here was vindication that I deserved to be there and a demonstration of exactly what I had to give for my team and my country. I got a standing ovation from the crowd. Thirty-three overs later, I was inches away from yet another boundary when Peter Fulton scooped the catch. My score of 169 included 24 fours and two sixes. Not only was it my first Test century, it was the highest Test score by an Australian in two years and the highest score by an Australian keeper on home soil ever. I was walking on air.

I'd helped the team to a 535 total, which the Kiwis showed no chance of catching, and we won by an innings and 62 runs. The score was big enough and the stand gutsy enough to silence even the most negative critics. Wayne Phillips, a South Australian wicketkeeper who'd played 27 Tests in the 1980s, was one of those who had said publicly I wasn't up to the job; he thought another South Australian, Graham Manou, should be in the side instead. He was entitled to his opinion, although I wondered if he still held it as I passed him in the stand on my way to be awarded Player of the Match.

On 17 December, the three Test series against South Africa began, to be followed by a couple of T20I games and five ODIs. The Proteas, coached by Mickey Arthur, were talking a big game before they arrived. They had some justification: having started 2007 ranked number eight in the world, they were approaching the end of 2008 having risen to number two. Their batsmen had hit a purple patch, with captain Graeme Smith, Hashim Amla and Neil McKenzie already having passed 1000 Test runs for the year, and Ashwell Prince and AB de Villiers rapidly closing in on that marker. But we were still number one and we had not lost a Test series at home since ceding a hard-fought five-game series to Richie Richardson's West Indies team in 1992–93. No-one expected us to lose, but lose we did.

We won the toss in the first game at the WACA and chose to bat. Thirty minutes into the game we were 3 for 15, with Huss and Punter both gone for a duck, Punter on his first ball. That was a shock to the system all right. But Simon Katich, back on his original home ground, and Michael Clarke turned the game around with a 149 partnership, with Kat finally falling for 83. Symo and I put together another 93, and we finished our first innings on a respectable 375. Mitchell Johnson had a blinder in the Proteas' first innings, taking 8 for 61, and with South Africa all out for 281 we were looking great.

Our second innings could have gone quickly south when we were 6 for 157 (one of those wickets was Haydos', given out caught and bowled off his pad in a decision for which umpire Aleem Dar later apologised), but I had an enjoyable time at the crease. I got 94 off 136 balls. I was flying, controlling the game; I felt bulletproof. I could almost taste my next century and I knew just how I would get the six that I needed — I'd pop one into the stands. But it was a classic case of getting caught up in the emotion. I missed and Boucher stumped me. Damn.

With 319 that innings, we should have been out of reach, leaving them chasing 414 in under 120 overs. But impossible turned into unlikely and then likely and then certain, with de Villiers contributing 106 after we missed chances to run him out on 18 and catch him on 67. South Africa claimed the game by succeeding in the second-biggest run chase in the entire history of Test cricket. I was glad to have batted well and taken six dismissals in the match, but it was a hard loss for us to swallow.

The Melbourne Boxing Day Test was next. Because the team has to be there on Christmas Day, preparing for the match, this is always a real family time. Wives and children are put up in the team hotel and, after training on Christmas morning, the players quickly come back, get dressed and walk with their families down to a big lunch, which includes a visit from Santa for the kids. Karina flew down with three-month-old Zac and, while we wouldn't have wanted to be apart, it wasn't exactly a relaxing time for either of us. My parents were also there and they got to see the game, but I think Karina spent most of those days wheeling Zac around the ground in his pram, trying to get him to sleep. Meanwhile, like the rest of the team, I was feeling the intense pressure from our first loss.

The MCG pitch was slower than usual and once again we should have had the game. But South Africa rampaged through us, despite Punter's 101 in the first innings and 99 in the second and good support from Pup and Kat. They took the match by nine wickets and claimed the series with a game still to go. Punter came under relentless attack from all quarters and to read the papers you'd have thought the loss was a national disaster. One tabloid newspaper's front page was a gravestone reading 'RIP Australian Cricket', with contributing causes of death listed as 'incompetent selectors, inept batting, impotent bowling, dreadful catching, poor captaincy'. It was rough stuff, but, if you want the ticker-tape parades when you win, you have to bear that kind of no-holds-barred attack when you lose. It goes with the territory and we all understood that, but even so it was sometimes hard to take.

The 2009 New Year's Test in Sydney was a dead rubber, but neither side treated it that way. South Africa needed the win to propel them to world number one and we needed it to restore some semblance of pride. We fought all the way to the end and won with five minutes and 10 balls left to play. Peter Siddle, playing in just his fourth Test, claimed eight wickets and constantly lifted the energy of the team and was a well-deserved Player of the Match.

That game was Matthew Hayden's last Test and he took the opportunity to teach Sidds and I a great insiders' SCG tradition. We were sitting in the change room drinking beers when he told us to stomp on the floor. He's a legend of the game and we weren't about to say no. Nothing happened and we asked why we were doing it. He told us to wait and see. A bit later we did it again and this time there was an answering whack from below: it was the staff down in the cellar signalling that they were ready for players to come down and celebrate the finish of the Test series with some fine wine or whisky.

It was definitely better to have won than lost in that final Test, but it was poor consolation for the loss of the series. And things became worse when the one-dayers got underway. We could only claim one win to South Africa's four, which meant they took the ICC number-one ranking from us after all. The first couple of weeks of

February brought five Chappell–Hadlee Trophy ODIs against New Zealand. The first game, at the WACA, triggered a blow-up in the media that was the perfect example of how what happens within the game can get distorted outside of it — which is why any public figure who wants to keep their sanity needs to be able to ignore the white noise of constant chatter and uninformed opinion.

What happened was that Neil Broom was on 29 when he was beaten by a Michael Clarke ball that hit the top of off-stump then came up into my gloves. To me it was clearly out and I whipped off the bails. Broom thought otherwise, but he was given out. The controversy came because it was unclear in the video replay whether I was right about the ball, but on close examination it was clear that I'd unintentionally had my gloves slightly forward of the stumps at the time — something that should have resulted in a 'no ball' ruling. Broom didn't look very happy as he walked off, but dismissed batsmen rarely do.

We thought no more about it until after the game (which New Zealand won), when Daniel Vettori said to a journalist that surely I must have known *something* was wrong at the time and should have said so. He did not accuse me of cheating, but suddenly — boom! — that word was being used next to my name all over the place. Ricky Ponting spoke up strongly in my defence at a media conference. Ignoring the advice of the team's media liaison officer, I had a comment to make about it too, which was that I'd played a lot against Daniel and he was a great competitor, but if he had a problem with me he should have come and had a conversation about it, not aired it in the media. Dan sent me a text message clarifying that while we would have to agree to disagree about what happened between ball and bail, he never thought I was cheating and that he looked forward to our next game.

Despite that, you'd only have to spend about 10 seconds searching online to find endless blog posts and opinion pieces from people who don't like the way I played, citing my supposed cheating in that game as prime evidence. That kind of thing is sometimes hard on family and friends, although I think mine have all become pretty good at understanding that it's not worth engaging with. People aren't always going to like you in life, and in professional sport that's amplified. You're a hero in some people's eyes, a villain in others', and rarely anything in between. In the end the only people's opinions worth paying attention to, in my view, are those of your teammates and those who were there on the spot.

It was a storm in a teacup in the context of the whole five-game series, of which we won two, two went to New Zealand and one was washed out. I worked hard and performed well, with 109 at the SCG and 88 not out at the Gabba. I also had my first experience of captaining a national side when I led the Twenty20 team to a one-run win against New Zealand at the SCG, a ground I knew as well as anyone after the one-dayers were over.

I couldn't say my first 12 months as a Test cricketer had been easy, but if it was easy everyone would do it. I reminded myself that wins build confidence, losses build character. Karina and I had brought a child into the world this year. Did we want him to grow up afraid to try for fear he might not succeed, or willing to give up after setbacks? No, of course not. We were going to raise him the way we'd been raised: to try hard every time and keep on trying no matter what. That's what I was about to do in a few weeks' time when the Australian team travelled to play South Africa in a return Test series on their home ground. Commentators were prepared to call the results before a ball had been played — clearly, we stood no chance. *Oh yeah?* I thought, *just you wait and see.*

CHAPTER 13

PAIN ON AND OFF THE FIELD

I'M GLAD I DIDN'T know in early 2009 the extent to which injury would affect me and keep me off the field over the next three years. I might not have believed it anyway, since I was as fit as a Mallee bull as we headed to South Africa for a three-Test series, two T20I games and five ODIs.

It would have been easy for the team, and Ricky Ponting in particular, to be crushed by the mountain of criticism and condemnation that had been piled on us over the past year. Instead, Punter and coach Tim Nielsen worked out a detailed plan to pull us together and set us on a winning path. It centred on a six-day camp in a place called Potchefstroom, an hour or two's drive away from Johannesburg, where we would play our first Test starting on 26 February.

The squad included four new faces: all-rounder Marcus North, fast bowler Ben Hilfenhaus, leg-spinner Bryce McGain and opening batsman Phillip Hughes. I'd encountered all the new blokes through either Sheffield Shield or ODI games but Phil, who was the only NSW player, was the one I knew best. He'd made an impressive debut with the Blues the previous season, particularly in our finals win over Victoria, where he recovered from a first-innings six to score 116 in the second innings. Like a lot of players before him, he'd come to the Big Smoke as a country teenager hoping to make his mark. He was a very unworldly 19-year-old and his culture shock was bigger than most because the town where he grew up, Macksville, was so tiny, with a population under 3000. He had a car but wasn't comfortable behind the wheel in Sydney traffic, so he often came to training with me.

Various other members of the group had also trained and played together, but the bonds between us weren't yet strong. As far as experience went, only Punter and Mike Hussey had been on Australia's previous tour of South Africa in 2006. Tim and Punter had a plan to build us into a cohesive force and mapped out all the training sessions ahead of time. In nets sessions Punter stood behind the stumps at the non-striker's end and watched over everything. We formed groups in which we put into words what we wanted to achieve individually and as a group on the tour, and we developed 'mission statements'. And we had a night session where Punter led the more senior players in telling yarns from previous tours. At the end of the story-telling session he said that it marked the end of talk about senior or junior players — we all had to be equally accountable to ourselves and each other.

The plan worked brilliantly. We got to know and trust one another over those six days and came together as a tight unit, ready to shake off the hoodoo and not be intimidated by the fact that the Proteas had won 18 of their previous 25 Tests, including the ones they'd claimed from us in Australia. Ricky won the toss and we were all expecting him to say we'd field first but instead he chose to bat, reasoning that there would be more nicks to be had as the ground hardened up on the second day (which proved to be the case). Phil Hughes was out for a duck and Huss and Simon Katich didn't fare much better. At 3 for 38, a change of direction was needed to arrest our decline and it came in the form of a 113-run partnership from Punter and Pup, followed by another 113-run double-hander from Marcus North and me (I'd played a lot of cricket with Marcus and it was terrific to be there to see him get a brilliant 117 in his Test debut), plus a big 96 from Mitchell Johnson, who then went to work on their batsmen, giving them no hope of matching our 466 total. Ricky chose not to enforce the follow on, and we won by 162 runs.

The feeling of shared pride in what we'd achieved was immense. We all knew we'd been part of something special. It was a wonderful moment when Huss led us in 'Under the Southern Cross I Stand', out there in the middle of the New Wanderers Stadium. He finished by bringing the circle in and reminding us that while this was a victory to savour, we couldn't get carried away with ourselves. We still had a series to win.

We did so with our victory in the Second Test four days later in Durban. Once again we batted first. Phil Hughes and Simon Katich came out firing on all cylinders, each passing 100, contributing the bulk of our 352 total. Unfortunately, in contrast to my 63 and 37 from the previous game, I was out for just five in the first innings of this one. However, I had a good time behind the stumps, beginning with a big stretching catch to get South African opener Neil McKenzie out for a duck off Johnno's third ball.

Peter Siddle took it upon himself to get out the Proteas' tail, including Dale Steyn. His attitude was, 'We're here to play and it's a contest all the way to the end.' He knew he'd cop it in the second innings from Steyn, who was one of the most feared fast bowlers around, but he didn't care. It was a great instance of putting the team first. Again, Punter had the option of enforcing the follow on. By not doing so he allowed Phil Hughes to make history and become Player of the Match after his second innings 160 made him the youngest man ever to score a century in both innings of a Test. Our fifth wicket declaration meant I didn't bat a second time, but I was very happy with my six catches and a stumping in the match.

Ricky said in the media conference afterwards that our series win with a game to go was his proudest moment as captain. He'd thoroughly earned that feeling, having shown great leadership in steering us from underdogs to champions in such a short time. It really felt like we had turned a corner. We celebrated with another memorable singing of the team song and a wonderful party, creating indelible, treasured memories.

There was a sanctioned visitor period during the tour. Some players' family members had already arrived, but Karina and I had arranged that she and Zac would fly straight into Cape Town, site of the Third Test. We were looking forward to seeing each other but an 18-hour flight with a six-month-old baby is no picnic and when they landed Karina found the luggage had been sent to the wrong destination. She arrived at the hotel exhausted, wanting nothing more than to hand Zac over to me and fall into bed.

There was more than a week until the game started and we had a few days' break before training recommenced, giving us time to splash around in the pool with Zac, go for ice creams on the waterfront and make the excursion to the top of Table Mountain with the other couples. It was very nice for those of us who had visitors but for various reasons not everyone did. Life on the road gets tough for everyone at some point — we've all been there — and after Karina and Zac had gone home I spent some time having a few beers and chewing the fat with Mitchell Johnson, Stuart Karppinen and bowling coach Troy Cooley (it's easy for people to forget that the support staff go through the same things in terms of missing family and home as the players).

The team went into the Third Test feeling strong. Once again we won the toss and went into bat. But we'd somehow lost our mojo and the Proteas had found theirs. My 42 was the second-highest score of the first innings, in which they kept us to 209; they then easily eluded our bowlers, amassing 651 in their own first innings. It was all over on Day 4, when South Africa won by an innings and 20 runs. They also took the two T20I games. No-one was overly bothered about that but we would have liked to have taken out the one-day series. We had a good win in the first game, but they took the next three to clinch it. Dead rubber or not, we played to win in the final game and the victory lifted us to world number two in the one-day rankings. Pup and I opened the batting for the one-dayers and I was satisfied that I'd made a good contribution, scoring above a half-century in three of the five games.

Our major focus now was the Ashes series that would start in July, but first up we had a series of ODIs (and a T20I) against Pakistan. The subcontinent was going through a period of instability. Six months earlier, just after our tour of India had wrapped up, the world had been rocked by the Mumbai attacks, and Pakistan continued to be in turmoil. With the Australian Government, Cricket Australia and the Australian Cricketers' Association deciding the situation was still too unstable for us to play the Pakistanis in their own country, the decision was taken to move the games to the UAE.

The move had been announced shortly after we left Australia in February, and the wisdom of it was confirmed in the most awful way just a few weeks later. Following the events in Mumbai, the Indian Government had barred its team from touring its northwestern neighbour. Sri Lanka stepped in to fill the hole in the schedule, and the team was on its way to a game at Gaddafi Stadium in Lahore in early March when a dozen terrorists ambushed the bus in a targeted attack. Six police officers, one of the drivers and another civilian were killed and six members of the Sri Lankan team and a member of the coaching staff were injured. The news reached us in South Africa and our thoughts were with all concerned, including Trevor Bayliss, who had left NSW the previous year and taken up the position of Sri Lankan coach. TB was on the bus when it came under fire, but narrowly escaped being hit.

We claimed the one-day series in UAE, but it was a good tussle, with us winning three of the games and Pakistan two. It's always a bit strange playing in the UAE in terms of atmosphere. The Emiratis themselves don't have a huge interest in cricket. The migrant workers, who make up almost 90 per cent of the population, often do, since the vast majority come from South Asian countries. However, they frequently can't afford the ticket prices or can't attend games because they are working, leaving the stadiums largely empty. Despite that I really enjoyed the actual cricket, because keeping in those conditions, which mimic those of the subcontinent itself with their low bounce and lack of carry through, is so challenging. It's hard work but it keeps you on your toes, which I appreciate. There was also enjoyment to be had with the bat, including a zippy opening partnership with Shane Watson in the fifth game, when we got to 51 in just eight overs. As a bonus, Karina and Zac (now six months old) flew over for a quick visit and we all got to spend time with Michael and Amy and their growing family, who hadn't seen Zac since he was eight weeks old.

I got back to Sydney on 10 May but only had two weeks at home before it was time to head to Queensland for the pre-Ashes camp. This was all about taking care of the promotion and media side of the tour: having photos taken in all the different shirts, filing TV commercials and having briefings on Cricket Australia's strategy — all part of the life of a professional athlete.

We arrived in England full of determination, bolstered by what we'd achieved in South Africa. Recent history had seen a win for each side: England had claimed the coveted trophy in the 2005 series then lost it 5–0 in the summer of 2006–07. But there'd been a changing of the guard in both teams since then. There was everything to play for.

At the beginning of June, a month before the First Test, we played against Sri Lanka and the West Indies in the first round of the World Twenty20 tournament. We lost both games and were knocked out of the competition. It wasn't ideal, but it wasn't Test cricket either. It didn't affect our confidence as we headed into the opening match of the Ashes campaign, which was held at Cardiff in a Test first. I'd thought my previous experience of the Ashes was intense but, knowing I was going to play, everything was heightened to an incredible degree — the anxiety, the tension and the excitement. Even the tour match we played at Hove in the lead-up to the First Test was something else, with the ground sold out every day.

England won the toss and went in to bat on an excellent pitch. They produced a reasonable first innings score of 435. (I only took one catch, but it was a beauty, getting Paul Collingwood off a Ben

Hilfenhaus ball.) However, we delivered a massive response. Simon Katich worked away until he had 122, Punter hung in there for a valuable 150 (having passed 11,000 Test runs on the way), and the scoreboard read 5 for 474 when I went out to bat just before stumps on Day 3. It wasn't actually supposed to be me going out. Ricky was sorting out a nightwatchman and told Peter Siddle to get his gear on. I had too much nervous energy to just sit there. I saw my chance, flew into my own gear while Sidds was still only half ready, and ran out the door. I've never been a fan of the nightwatchman concept; my view is any batsman should be out there trying to score runs. I added four before the end of play. When I walked back into the change room I said to Ricky, 'Mate, I just could not wait any more.' If I'd got out he would have strangled me, but as it was he just shook his head with a laugh.

Resuming play the following morning, I was on four and Marcus North on 54. It was another one of those perfect days. I was so in tune that I almost felt I could control the approach of the ball. Three hours later I had reached 121 off 151 balls. To have made a century in my first Ashes game meant the world to me, and it was even more special that my parents were there to see it. I was going for my fourth six when Ravi Bopara caught me at deep mid-wicket off a Collingwood ball. With Marcus on 125 not out, Punter declared at 674.

We had this. We'd totally outplayed England. We had a 232 lead and more than a day's play to go. All we had to do now was bowl them out and add a few more runs of our own and the game was ours. At 7 for 159 we were looking great, and at 9 for 233 with 40 minutes to go it should have been all but a formality. But their tail-enders, Jimmy Anderson and Monty Panesar, hung on ferociously. Peter Siddle, Nathan Hauritz and Marcus North all gave it their best but could not break through.

With the tension ratcheting up with every passing minute, we were very unimpressed by what seemed like blatant stalling, as their 12th man ran out with a change of gloves two overs in a row and their physio took a leisurely stroll out to the middle, despite not having been called for. There were also frequent confabs between the two batsmen, slowing things down. After the game, England captain Andrew Strauss flatly rejected the idea that his side had been deliberately wasting time — but a few years later Jimmy Anderson confirmed what was obvious to everyone: they had used 'all the tactics we could' to chew up minutes and avoid the loss.

Ultimately, though, as irritating as this gamesmanship was, it should not have been enough to cost us the match. We'd driven the game, controlled the tempo. It should have been ours but we failed to win the big moment by getting that final wicket. And so the match ended in a draw. In retrospect, I think having had a win in Cardiff would have made a huge difference to the way the series unfolded. It would have given us the mental armour we needed to push forward in every part of every game. Instead, the draw got the England side 'out of jail' and gave them the impetus to push and keep pushing.

Four days later, the Second Test started at Lord's. Zac, Karina, and her sister, Danielle, had timed a holiday in England around the game and experienced some of the intensity of the Ashes passing through a cordon of paparazzi as they left the hotel each morning.

Australia had lost to England here precisely once in the twentieth century, way back in 1934. The day before the match, England's Freddie Flintoff announced that as a result of ongoing knee problems that had flared up again at Cardiff, he would retire after the final Test in the series. There were also a couple of changes in the English line-up, including the fact that, despite his match-saving effort in the previous game, Monty Panesar was out to make room for Graham Onions. But far from being unsettled by all this, the Poms seemed to be inspired, with openers Strauss and Alastair Cook reaching 196 before we could make a breakthrough. Johnno got Cook lbw for 95 (his 100th Test wicket) and we started to fight back. By close of play we'd claimed half a dozen wickets, but England finished the day on 364, including Strauss's 161 not out.

It wasn't one of my best days on the field, that's for sure. I slipped into the quicksand and Johnno was struggling too, spraying them left and right. Lord's can be tricky for keepers at the best of times, with the ball moving in mysterious ways, wobbling and dropping. The byes started building up. Some of them were ones I just couldn't reach, but others bobbled up and I missed them because I was second-guessing myself and Johnno. Wides were being called and the pressure was building up from the huge crowd. I didn't miss any catches, but I started having trouble with Peter Siddle too, as we racked up 10 extras in two overs. I walked off the ground thinking, *Thank god that's over.* As a team we had not performed well. Someone had to front the media conference but no-one wanted to, knowing what it would be like. I said, 'Bugger it, I'll do it. They're going to get stuck into me either way.'

I walked into the packed media room and the first thing I said when I sat down was, 'We didn't have a great day today. I was partly to blame. I had one of those days when things didn't go my way and I didn't play the way I wanted to.' Instantly all the tension went out of the room. It was fascinating. Five minutes before, the press had had the taste of blood and if I'd been defensive or tried to bluster my way through it would have been a mauling. Instead, I went straight onto the front foot and it took all the anxiety out of the situation. A few of the journos even clapped when we wrapped up. All my life I've had trouble sleeping properly when I'm worried. That night I slept perfectly. The experience reinforced the fact that it's always better to deal with an issue head-on rather than trying to duck it or leaving your mess for someone else to fix.

The following day's play started beautifully, with Ben Hilfenhaus bowling Strauss on just the second delivery of the morning. We had them all out before lunch for 425, but we didn't bat the way we needed to. In this case, the numbers did tell the story: Huss was the only one who got over 50 and we were all out for 215. Our 406 second innings was a hell of a lot better, including Michael Clarke's 136 and my 80, but it wasn't good enough, and England won the Lord's clash for the first time in 75 years. It was a big blow to our confidence, although we reminded ourselves that the series was far from over.

I didn't even make it into the game in the Third Test at Edgbaston. We'd already done the toss and were in the pre-game warm-up. Peter Siddle was bowling. I would normally never catch balls off the bowlers in a warm-up, but there had been some criticism of Sidds for running on the wicket. Troy Cooley had asked me to take a look at a few deliveries — no batsman, just watching how the balls came through. The ball wobbled, as it does in England. I caught it but it smashed down onto my left ring finger. I knew instantly there was real damage. I ran to the change room to see Alex, the physio, who asked me to move the finger. It bent in completely the wrong direction. He asked if I could play and I said, 'I have movement.' Alex put his hand on the finger as I moved it again and felt fragments of bone shifting inside. He couldn't understand how I was able to move it at all, but the break had been bad enough to send me into shock, even though I didn't realise it at the time. He told me I needed a scan and delivered the obvious verdict: 'You're out of the match.'

Punter went to see Andrew Strauss just as they were about to go out to bat and told him what had happened. The teams had been picked, the team sheets handed in. It would have been within the rules for Strauss to force me to play injured. But in a piece of good sportsmanship he said, 'Send in your back-up keeper, that's fine.' Graham Manou was the man on the spot. As had been the case for me in 2005, he hadn't really been expecting to play during the whole series, and he knew he wasn't playing today because the team had been set. So it was no wonder the blood drained from his face when Punter and Tim Nielsen told him he was about to make his Test debut after all, in the most dramatic circumstances. (As it turned out, that was his only appearance in the Baggy Green.)

I went off to get a scan, which revealed the bone had more or less exploded. (When my hand surgeon, Doug Wheen, eventually got a look at it, he described it as having shattered the way a Violet Crumble does.) The Edgbaston game was a draw, meaning England were just one game away from winning the series. Knowing what I know now, I have to admit I should probably have gone back to Australia and had surgery as soon as possible. But it was an

Ashes campaign with everything at stake. I just couldn't leave. Even before the game wrapped up, I was trying to ease my glove on. From across the change room, Punter caught me doing it. We exchanged a look and he nodded. We didn't have to say anything. He understood completely.

The pendulum swung our way — and how! — in the Fourth Test, at Headingley. I had to get needled every day at training, and in the game, with an anaesthetic block on either side of the finger, but it didn't stop me from taking six catches, including a useful one-hander on Matt Prior in the second innings. Johnno and Sidds had both found their form and we bowled England out on the first day for a mere 102, their lowest Ashes innings in more than 30 years. We won the game by an innings and 80 runs.

Heading into the final match, at The Oval, we were jubilant. The bookies had us as favourites to win it and retain the Ashes. England won the toss and batted first. They did okay, with a first innings 332. It should have been no problem for us to better that, but our batting effort was, as Punter rightly put it, woeful. We had no answer to Stuart Broad, who took five wickets (one of them mine) for just 37 runs. Johnno and Marcus North had successes in England's second innings, but it wasn't enough, not with Strauss's 75, Jonathan Trott's maiden century and a tail-end that just wouldn't quit. They declared on 373, leaving us chasing 546 in the final two days.

Shane Watson and Simon Katich opened and were both still in at 80 at the end of Day 4, but both went lbw within the first five overs the following morning. Punter and Huss dug in and it felt like there was still hope when their partnership reached 127, but momentary hesitation saw Punter run out on 66. Huss tried hard to arrest the decline and he and I together added 91 before I went for 34.

My usual routine in any game when we were batting was to watch the first bit from up in the stand. I'd stay there for five overs or so, having a look at where the ball was going, then head down, often with Sidds or Johnno, and watch the rest on television in the change rooms. There I could really focus on what was happening and not miss a ball. If there was a milestone, like someone's century, I'd go back up to the balcony for it, but otherwise I'd be in the bunker. That's where I was at The Oval, sick to the stomach watching as Huss ran out of batting partners and finally, having put in a heroic effort to get to 121, fell himself. England won by 197 runs and, at 2–1 for the series, reclaimed the Ashes.

Losing that campaign, when we'd had everything we needed to win it, hurt more than any cricketing loss before or since. We had three of the leading four wicket-takers in the series and six of the top seven leading run scorers (with 278 runs, I was at number six on the list). But we simply hadn't pounced on the big moments and won them the way we'd been able to do in South Africa. England won the big moments — it was as simple and as heartbreaking as that.

Along with Simon Katich and Stuart Clark, I came back to Australia in late August while Punter and the boys stayed on and won six of the seven games in the ODI series against England. They then travelled back to South Africa for the ICC Champions Trophy one-dayers tournament, beating New Zealand in the final, then going on to India where they were victors in the ODI series there. Twenty-four-year-old Tim Paine was the man behind the stumps for all these games, as I was forced to sit out for almost three months following surgery to insert two plates and five screws and reattach tendon to bone in the finger that had shattered at Edgbaston. I could never be anything other than pleased by Australia winning, but it was very hard to have to watch it from a distance instead of being out there in the middle of the action.

There was a silver lining in that I was able to be present for Zac's first birthday. As an international cricketer you have to miss so many key moments that being able to do something as simple as put my son's birthday cake in front of him and see his reaction was priceless. I continued to train with Christian and with the NSW squad. I couldn't box but I could do just about everything else and prior to the start of the season I was given the go-ahead to return to playing cricket. While it had felt frustrating to have the enforced time off it was actually a good thing for me as a player.

With the international schedule so busy, there is never a pre-season to regroup and rebuild; injuries that lead to significant time out can actually help with career longevity.

The summer's first visitors were to be the West Indies, here for the three-match Frank Worrell Trophy Test series, plus five ODIs and two T20Is. I was in the squads for all three formats. I got my match fitness back by playing in a couple of Sheffield Shield Games and domestic one-dayers as well as a grade game or two, and I was positively champing at the bit by the time the first Test started at the Gabba on 26 November. The whole team was firing and we won easily after forcing the Windies into the follow on. They performed much better in the Second Test, and set a target of 330 runs from 81 overs. We had a choice to make: charge ahead and hope for the best or play for a strategic draw. With the series at risk, a draw was by far the better option this time around.

Both sides went into the Third Test at the WACA hungry to win. The competitiveness went a bit too far for a couple of players, including yours truly. It was a perfect batting wicket and we made the most of it, with five of us going over the half-century (I got 88), although Punter had to retire hurt for the first time in his career after catching a bumper from Kemar Roach on the arm. When Mitchell Johnson joined me at the crease we were 5 for 444. Coming back after lunch, Sulieman Benn was getting frustrated at not being able to take a wicket, and what started as an accidental bump between him and Johnno at the non-striker's end kicked off aggro all around.

I objected to the way Benn handled the situation and let him know it, pointing my bat at him. The two-metre-tall Barbadian got even angrier and at the end of the over there was shoving and chest-bumping between him and Johnno. Benn was definitely out of line and I don't apologise for sticking up for my teammates. However, I shouldn't have pointed my bat at him; it's not a good example for younger players. Mitchell and I pleaded guilty to a conduct charge and match referee Chris Broad fined us (I lost 25 per cent of my match fee) but suspended Benn, who'd pleaded not guilty, for two games. Two days later, Shane Watson was fined for yelling at mouthy Windies captain Chris Gayle after getting him for 21 when Gayle played an inside edge and I took the catch. This was the culmination of tensions that had built up during 10 overs, as Gayle talked himself up and bragged that Shane would never be able to get him out. When it was Shane's turn to bowl he took Gayle's wicket with his first ball, leading to that triumphant yell. It was an edgy match, but we stayed on track and won it by 35 runs to claim the trophy.

Next up was a three-match Test series against Pakistan, beginning on Boxing Day in Melbourne. This series attracted retrospective controversy months later when a British bookmaker claimed that one of the games had been secretly fixed to benefit people gambling against Pakistan. Pakistani players Mohammad Amir, Mohammad Asif and Salman Butt were eventually jailed after they were found to have corruptly engaged in 'spot-fixing' (bowling no-balls at prearranged times, for instance) but this happened on their tour of England months after they'd left Australia and an investigation by the ICC's Anti-Corruption and Security Unit found no evidence that claims about the Australian series were anything more than attempts by the bookmaker (also later jailed on corruption charges) to big-note himself. Unfortunately, the taint still lingers in the minds of many, who heard the original allegations but missed the enquiry findings. That's a shame, because we fought hard for our wins in that series and from the Australian team's perspective Pakistan's dropped catches and other missteps seemed to be the result of dissension within their side.

I did all right with the gloves in the First Test but was out for a duck in my only turn at bat. Fortunately, Shane Watson, Simon Katich, Mike Hussey and even Nathan 'Horrie' Hauritz (with a career-best 75) were in form and we won by 170 runs. At the Second Test, in Sydney, I didn't do a lot better with the bat, but Horrie and I played key roles in what the media dubbed 'a miracle win' after we were all out for 127 on the first day and were left 200 behind after first innings. Horrie's 5 for 53 was a thing of beauty and the nine catches I took in the match were just two behind the world record held by English wicketkeeper Robert Charles 'Jack' Russell (established in a Test match against South Africa in Johannesburg in 1995 and since equalled by AB de Villers). They included one of those takes that's a real crowd-pleaser — a full-stretch dive off to the leg side to get Butt out on 21 off a ball from Johnno. We won the game by 36 runs and made the series a clean sweep in Hobart a couple of weeks later.

It was a great start to 2010. Our successful run continued as we won the ODI series against both Pakistan and the West Indies in clean sweeps, as well as the T20I games against both countries. By doing so, we achieved an unbeaten summer — something that, at that point, had only been done once since ODIs became a regular part of the Australian season in the wake of the World Series Cricket shake-up in 1979.

Although Karina and I didn't know it when I left Sydney towards the end of February for a six-week tour of New Zealand, she was pregnant with our second child. We had always talked about having two children, or maybe even three, and we wanted to have them close together, so I was thrilled to hear the news in New Zealand, when she and Zac came over for a visit during the tour. This time we were both happy to know the sex right away and learned early on we were having a little sister for Zac.

Karina had got through the first, difficult 12 months of parenthood and come out the other side. She'd returned to work, as an MRI radiographer, part-time, and had the support of both sets of parents and her mothers' group during my frequent absences. Zac still wasn't sleeping well, but he was moving from the baby stage into being a toddler and was a delight to be around. The new baby was due in late October and, while it was clearly going to be challenging to have two children under 25 months old, I knew that Karina was a wonderful mother and would do a great job.

The team's winning streak continued in New Zealand, although we didn't have it all our own way. We split the warm-up T20I games one apiece before starting on the five-game ODI series. The Kiwis took the first game by two wickets and we claimed the second by 12 runs. We weren't playing badly by any means, but we hadn't pulled it out of the box either, with our top order failing to capitalise on good starts. Going into the third game at Hamilton's Seddon Park, Ricky Ponting challenged me, Shane Watson, Michael Hussey and himself to get out there and be more accountable, to turn our starts into hundreds. Well, I do love a challenge. Ricky won the toss and chose to send New Zealand in first; this surprised many observers, but it was the right call. We bowled them out for 245, with three wickets each to Mitchell Johnson and Ryan Harris, who followed a great summer in Australia with his Test debut in New Zealand. Shane Watson and I opened. Unfortunately, Shane was run out for 15. Punter was next up. I was in the zone and so was he as we racked up 151 in a match-winning partnership. My 110 (from 121 balls) was my second ODI century and brought me the Player of the Match accolade. Each side won one of the remaining two games, giving us the Chappell–Hadlee Trophy 3–2. We went on to win both Tests, giving us the Trans-Tasman Trophy as well.

It was surprising to stop and think that by the end of March, when the New Zealand tour wrapped up, I'd played 65 ODIs over a six-year period and 27 Tests in less than two years. Playing those two formats alone allowed very little downtime or chance to recuperate from injuries. When you added the increasingly popular Twenty20 games, things were even more hectic. The packed schedule was behind Punter's decision to pull out of Twenty20 competition the previous year, so he wasn't among the squad heading over to the Caribbean after an all-too-brief visit home. The World Twenty20 tournament had begun in 2007 and was supposed to be held every second year, but the calendar was rejigged because the Champions Trophy ODI tournament that should have taken place in Pakistan hadn't gone ahead due to the aforementioned security concerns.

With the last game in New Zealand finishing on 31 March and the tournament starting in the West Indies on 1 May, I really did feel as though I had barely walked in and put my bags down before it was time to kiss Zac and Karina goodbye and get on a plane again. While getting that century in Hamilton had felt great, it marked the beginning of real problems with my elbow, which I realised had been troubling me for months. From the way it blew up after the Hamilton game I knew deep down I probably shouldn't be pushing it by going on to the West Indies, but the drive to be part of the team was just too strong.

After the Caribbean, I was supposed to be moving on to an ODI series against England on their home turf, followed by a two-game Test series against Pakistan also in England (security reasons, again), then two Tests in India, then the Ashes over the following Australian summer. But the best-laid plans have a habit of going astray. We went through the qualifying rounds and semi-final of the World Twenty20 undefeated. It was an enjoyable tournament and interest was building at home, where the format was starting to be taken more seriously. We made it to the final, where we disappointingly lost to England. I got through all seven of our games, but by the end of the tournament the elbow just stopped working. I couldn't even move my arm to pick up a glass of water.

The condition is called tennis elbow, but in my case, as in many others, it had nothing to do with tennis. It's an over-use injury caused by repetitive movements putting pressure on the tendons that hold muscle to bone. There was no way of knowing how it had started, but in all likelihood the roots lay in playing with the badly broken finger from the 2009 Ashes. It had caused me to adjust my grip on the bat and, as I learned later, when you do that you alter the load points on the tendon. Theoretically, having the reconstructive surgery on the finger should have put things back to the way they were, but the subtle alteration in my grip remained. Then I'd been hit on the elbow in the nets before the Boxing Day Test and the further adjustments I'd made to compensate for that injury had exacerbated the problem. I'd had a couple of cortisone injections to keep me going, but that had just masked the problem rather than fixing it, and by mid-May my elbow was telling me in no uncertain terms it had had enough.

Scans showed that tendon had partially come away from the bone, but I was not ready to admit that I needed significant time out — not with the start of the Ashes only six months away.

The medical team came up with a physio rehab program, which I completed, but the very first time I picked up the bat again the elbow gave way. I felt there was too much at risk in terms of my career for me to rely solely on a physio who was caring for the whole team, so, in conjunction with Cricket Australia, I secured the services of a second physio, Danny Redrup, who could put extra time into looking after my elbow. We tried various approaches to treatment, including plasma injections, where blood is removed, separated and reinjected in an attempt to speed healing. But it didn't respond the way I needed it to, and the Ashes loomed ever closer.

In the end, the approach that worked best was consulting specialist physios in other sports at the AIS in Canberra. It might seem counter-intuitive to consult people experienced in treating tennis and golf issues, but I wanted them to treat the symptoms in a way that would really last, rather than treat me as a cricketer they were trying to get right for a particular match. Danny and I travelled there every four weeks for ongoing assessments on how the elbow was responding to the treatment plan. As it came good, I began a regime of special stretches and worked on my grip to make sure the problem didn't recur.

I was partway through the process when Karina and I sold our house and bought a family home at Tennyson Point on the Parramatta River. The idea was to live there for a year or two then tear the house down and rebuild, making room for our growing brood. By the beginning of October, a few weeks after we celebrated Zac's second birthday, I was ready to see if my rehabilitated elbow would hold up under playing conditions. Australia had lost the ODI series to England 3–2, drawn the Test series against Pakistan, lost the Test series to India and lost the ODI series to India and Sri Lanka. However, Tim Paine had performed well enough while I was out that some thought he should stay in the team for the Ashes; Rod Marsh was one who said it was going to be hard for me to get back in. But I wanted to be playing again at that level so badly I could taste it. There's only one trick to getting selected: perform so well you can't be ignored. So that's what I did, delivering noteworthy start-of-the-season efforts for my grade team, Eastern Suburbs; the NSW Second XI; and then for the Blues in the Sheffield Shield and the domestic one-day competition.

On 21 October, one day before Karina's 32nd birthday and two days before mine, our little girl was born. We had decided on a name we both liked, Mia, and Karina's middle name, Kay. Mia was healthy and beautiful and, as parents tend to be second time around, we were much more relaxed about everything. Having grown up in a house of boys, it felt very exciting to have a little daughter. But as I was cradling our gorgeous new girl at the hospital, I was suddenly taken out of the moment when I felt something click in my elbow. I had to play the next day for NSW in a one-dayer against Tasmania at the SCG. The Test team announcement was only weeks away; it was imperative that I had the capacity to play to my best. So I called Danny and told him what had happened. He understood immediately and was as concerned as I was — like me, he had believed the problem was fixed. I left the hospital and drove straight to meet him at the SCG. I got there about 10 p.m. and he worked on me until after 2 a.m., making sure it was right. He then sat nervously up in the top corner of the grandstand the next day with his eyes glued on my every move as I hit 56 from 63 balls. To our mutual relief, the elbow was fine, and I was subsequently named in the Ashes squad.

If it was possible, there was even more pressure than usual on the national team going into the 2010 series. Not since 1988 had Australia lost three Tests in a row, as we had just done. Then again, England hadn't won the Ashes in Australia since 1986–87. Going into the First Test at the Gabba, there was a huge amount at stake for the whole team: for Ricky Ponting, whose captaincy was once again under the microscope; for me wanting to prove I was back better than ever; and for Mike Hussey, who had been struggling for a year to perform the way he wanted to (in the lead-up to the game Dean Jones, at it again, said publicly he would rather wash his car than watch Huss bat).

England won the toss and went in to bat but soon wished they hadn't as Peter Siddle gave himself a birthday present in the form of the first Ashes hat-trick by an Australian bowler since Shane Warne had achieved the feat 16 years earlier, and he went on to a remarkable 6 for 54. We had them all out for 260. Our openers, Shane Watson and Simon Katich, started well, but England fought back and when I went in to partner Huss, on 32, we were in trouble, on 5 for 143. We both had a huge amount to prove and we were ready to go. We played strategically and with restraint until the scores were level, then I let loose. Richie Benaud called it the most valuable innings I'd played for Australia to date. It was a fierce contest — the Poms didn't give an inch — but Huss and I were in charge. There was pure electricity in hitting Graeme Swann for six to bring up my century. When I finally got out for 136 (after being dropped by Cook on 63) we'd put on 307 runs — a Gabba partnership record and the 15th highest stand in Australia's Test history. (Huss went three overs later for an absolutely massive 195.)

The six hours we spent out there together were so enjoyable — neither of us would have been anywhere else for quids. There's nowhere to hide in an arena like that and if you allow any sign of weakness it will be exploited mercilessly. We didn't crack as we stood up to some of the best bowling I've ever faced. The banter was fierce on both sides, which only added to the fun, although I had to break it to Jimmy Anderson that whatever niggles he was trying to get in were totally lost on me because I couldn't understand a thing he said in his thick Lancashire accent.

It's worth making a note here about banter on the field. Some people refer to it as sledging, but that's not what was happening between the England players and us. It was gamesmanship, pure and simple. Gamesmanship involves trying to switch your opponent's focus to put them off their game. Sledging is personal abuse. If my early years in cricket had been spent playing on a vicarage lawn between rounds of cucumber sandwiches, I might not have been comfortable engaging in gamesmanship, but it's how I was taught to play and it's part of the uncompromising style of the game that is the hallmark of the Australian team. You respect the opposition, you respect the officials and you play within the rules, but you're out there to win and you use whatever you can within the rules to do that.

One of the things you can use to your advantage is a break in your opponent's concentration. Sometimes you can achieve that without even saying a word directly to him. As a keeper, you might be having a chat to first slip between deliveries, talking about something completely unrelated to the game, cracking funny lines. You're seemingly talking between yourselves but really it's for the batsman's benefit. You're wanting to see him smile or even laugh: if he does, you know you've got him. He has tuned in to your conversation, which means he's lost his own focus, however briefly. The chances of him making a mistake have just shot up.

Other times you do talk directly to your opponent. But there's always a very clear line you don't cross. You can talk about their performance all you like but you never, ever say anything personal or bring family into it. If you ever heard one of your teammates doing that you'd pull them up straight away, saying, 'Mate, that's not on; it's not how we play the game.' And part and parcel of gamesmanship is that you've got to be able to cop it right back. That's only fair. Personally, when those tactics were directed against me I recognised them for what they were and they didn't bother or distract me.

Nothing the Poms could say pulled Huss or me out of the moment and our effort lifted Australia to a first innings total of 481, putting England 221 runs behind. Talk about a turnaround in perception. He and I were all over the media in headlines like 'Whipping Boys to Pom Bashers', 'Bats out of Hell' and 'Tons of Respect'. The commentators were so sure the match was ours they practically had their wrap-ups written, but sport doesn't work that way. That's the reason it's endlessly fascinating, because you never *really* know what's going to happen. It turned out we weren't the only ones who could set records. We were absolutely sure Andrew Strauss was gone lbw to Ben Hilfenhaus in the very first ball, but

Aleem Dar ruled no and Strauss and Alistair Cook went on to a 188-run partnership. We finally got Strauss out for 110, only to have Jonathan Trott come out and make a 329-run partnership with Cook. England declared at 1 for 517. With 41 overs to play, Shane Watson and Ricky Ponting reduced the 297 deficit to 170 before we declared, resulting in a draw. We'd bowled so well in the first innings and fought back so effectively with the bat that not being able to claim the win was very frustrating, especially because of how important the first-match win is in setting the tone for the series.

As disappointing as that was, the Second Test in Adelaide was worse — much worse. We chose to bat first and proceeded to make the worst start to a Test innings in 60 years, at 3 for 2. Shane Watson and I dug in for half-centuries and Huss almost got another century, but we couldn't do it on our own and England answered our first innings 245 with 625, helped by too many dropped catches from us. England outplayed us, winning the game by an innings and 71 runs. Rain started just half an hour after we lost our final wicket; if we'd been able to hang in there for that time we would at least have had a draw. Again, the frustration level was high, as was the disappointment at playing so far below our best, but we had to leave it behind us and get ready for the next game.

England are traditionally very uncomfortable playing on the WACA pitch, so the Third Test in Perth should have been ours for the taking. But here too our top order collapsed after England sent us in to bat. Once again Michael Hussey and I dug in, getting 61 and 53 respectively — though it was Mitchell Johnson who top-scored, nudging one run over Huss, with his fellow fast-bowler Pete Siddle adding a valuable 35 not out. Once bowling, Johnno was unstoppable, taking 6 for 38 to finish England off before tea on the second day. Huss and Shane Watson's efforts in the second innings and Ryan Harris's 6 for 47 put us out of the Poms' reach and our 267-run win levelled the series. We were all too aware that if we'd managed to get that draw in Adelaide we'd have had a 1–0 lead, but even so we emerged with our positive energy recharged, determined to win at the MCG.

But the Boxing Day Test turned out to be one of those games you wish had been a bad dream. The Christmas celebrations for the families were lovely and it was special to have Karina and our two little ones there, but it was all downhill after that in Melbourne. Ryan Harris fractured his ankle in a run-up; frustration about umpires' decision-making and the way they were using the video technology saw Punter fined 40 per cent of his match fee; and we went into the second innings 415 runs behind. Sidds and I refused to go down without a fight, building an 86-run partnership on the fourth day, but after he went for 40 and Ben Hilfenhaus got a duck, I'd run out of partners on 55. It was all over. Not just the match, but our campaign. England's win meant they retained the trophy. The whole team felt sick about losing another Ashes campaign.

We had the chance to claw back a bit of pride in Sydney; however, the New Year's Eve fireworks, enjoyed with all our families, was the only bright spot. Punter was out with an injured finger (I'd heard the noise when it broke in Perth as he went for a catch alongside me in the slips cordon; he'd damaged it further in Melbourne), so Michael Clarke took over captain duties and I was vice-captain. The harder the team tried, the worse we played and England thrashed us again, winning by an innings and 83 runs, leaving us drained and disheartened.

Yet the one-day series against England that ran from mid-January 2011 into February was a different story. Here we could barely put a foot wrong, winning six of the seven games. That boded well for the ICC Cricket World Cup, which started just two weeks later in India, with games also played in Bangladesh and Sri Lanka, where Karina, Zac and Mia visited me. While Zac was racking up stamps in his passport, it was Mia's first flight, at four months old.

After Australia's all-conquering triple-title win in the previous World Cup, in the West Indies, expectations were high. But we were knocked out in the quarter-finals by India. The fact that they went on to win the tournament wasn't much consolation; we were all very disappointed with the result. Ricky Ponting decided it was time to step down as captain and Michael Clarke was appointed as his successor, with Shane Watson as vice-captain. It was a real blow to lose Ricky as captain, considering the standing he had in the game and his passion for the team; none of us wanted to see him leave the captaincy that way. I thought I had a good skill-set to be considered as vice-captain; however, believing as I do that you should never lobby for leadership roles, I was comfortable with the decision the board made.

Our last World Cup game was on 24 March. By 7 April, we were in Bangladesh playing a tour match as a warm-up for a three-game ODI series. No-one wanted to be there, not really. Like the rest of the team I was longing to get home and freshen myself up to prepare for the following season, which would start with a Test, ODI and T20I tour in Sri Lanka starting in August, followed by the same in South Africa before we even got to the Australian summer tours by New Zealand and India. Instead, here we were in a country that had its challenges for visitors, exhausted and mentally fatigued, playing more or less on autopilot.

In the opening ODI I went forward for a low catch. The tip of my left middle finger hooked into the ground and I felt it break. I finished that game and played the next but then I talked to Tim Nielsen and decided to sit out the third game, since we had the option of using Tim Paine, who'd been sent as back-up for the World Cup and had travelled on with us.

The finger was stable, which meant that it didn't need surgery; it just needed time to heal over the Australian winter. But while it was healing I had to change my grip on the bat, turning my bottom hand further to take more of the weight in order to relieve the discomfort. And by the time the bone had knit, the new, slightly altered grip felt natural to me and the correct technique I'd previously used felt completely foreign. The problem with my new normal was that it constricted me as a batsman by reducing the range within which I could hit the ball. Restricting my shot choice made me vulnerable to certain balls I hadn't been vulnerable to before and hindered the rhythm of my game. The result was inconsistency at the crease: I couldn't get the runs I needed to as often as I needed to get them.

It's easy to look back now and pinpoint the problem but, even though it was clear to me quite early on that there was some kind of blockage, it took quite a while to isolate the cause. After all, we're talking about a very subtle shift in the balance of my grip. The selectors sent a confusing message when they praised my contributions but then dropped me from the Twenty20I squad, reinstating me before the tour to Sri Lanka. We won the Test series (in which Nathan Lyon made his debut) and the ODI series but lost the T20Is. Again Karina popped over for a visit with Zac, which resulted in the appearance of baby number three, Hugo, nine months later.

I'd been frustrated by my performance at bat in Sri Lanka and it got worse when we went to South Africa. The two-match Test series against the Proteas was a draw and we won the ODI series, but all anyone wanted to talk about was our second innings score in the First Test. We'd scored 284 first up, and bowled the Proteas out for just 96, which should have put us in the box seat. But the wicket had flattened out and we had had a shocker, not even reaching 20 by the time I came on at number six. My mindset was that we had to change the momentum of the game. I had to take a risk in an effort to move the game forward. If I could get a four they might change the field; then maybe we could scramble to 150 and then we'd have a game on our hands. I was trying to change the length of the ball when I stepped down the wicket towards a ball from Vernon Philander (who took 5 for 15 in this innings), got a flashing one and was out for a duck, one of four ducks in a total score of 47.

Commentators described my shot as 'reckless' and 'irresponsible', which, again, just highlights the vast crevasse between what happens inside the game and how people interpret it. Of course I'd rather have succeeded and of course it stung to get out in that manner, but 'irresponsible' would have been if I hadn't tried to make a breakthrough. However, part of playing at that level is living with the consequences of your choices. You have to be accountable and I didn't shy away from that. My average over the nine Test innings we played in the Ashes had been 45; in the seven innings since then it had dropped to less than 14. The target was well and truly on my back and every mention of me in the press was linked with speculation about me being dropped (the same was true of Ricky Ponting, Mitchell Johnson and Phil Hughes).

We were shattered after that game and had a big soul-searching team debrief. Meetings like that one were an invaluable part of our team culture. They were open forums where everyone had the opportunity to speak up. You could talk honestly about your own struggles, knowing that we were all there for one another. If someone had an observation about your playing they thought could help you, they were comfortable making it, knowing it would be taken in the right spirit. All of us were working together to make the team better. By getting everything out in the open we were able to move on, individually and as a group, and turn things around in time for the next game. In this case it was clear to us all we were selling ourselves short, not claiming those big moments, and that we needed to aim up and go into the Second Test knowing we could win it. We did exactly that, chasing down 300 for a big win, including 55 from me.

By the time we played New Zealand in the Trans-Tasman Trophy, Cricket Australia had replaced Tim Nielsen as the national coach with South African Mickey Arthur, and John Inverarity had become chairman of selectors. I got 80 at the Gabba against the Kiwis (the series was a tie), but, frustratingly, even though I was keeping perfectly well, the fact that I wasn't getting runs the way I wanted to meant people started looking at my keeping in a different light. Instead of the five catches I took in the Boxing Day Test against India and the three in the following game at the SCG, it was the one that got away, a missed chance on Gautam Gambhir off a James Pattinson ball, that everyone focused on. We won the series 4–0, but the pressure on me didn't lessen and as 2011 ended and the new year began, the level of chatter about who I might be replaced with rose, with Matthew Wade's name coming up most often.

I simply ignored it all, just as I'd ignored the constant speculation before Gilly retired. I focused on enjoying the wins and the wonderful opportunities that came my way. One of these was being given the honour of captaining the Prime Minister's XI game scheduled for the beginning of February 2012. It was special having 19-year-old Dean Solway, the son of my ANUCC mentor Peter Solway, as the junior player in the team. Unfortunately, the game was washed out before a ball could be bowled, but it did allow for some lovely family catch-up time, with Zac, at nearly three and a half, running round madly, and 15-month-old Mia seemingly so well and happy, toddling from one big cuddle to another.

Right around this time I was taken out of the Australian one-day team for a tri-series against India and Sri Lanka and Matthew Wade put in. Initially, John Inverarity insisted I was just being rested because of my 'heavy workload'. But I knew I'd been dropped, and said so when I was asked about it on radio. It took almost three weeks for Cricket Australia to admit it. If you're not performing, you get dropped; it's simple. It happens to everyone at some point and there shouldn't be any nonsense or drama about it. Everyone just needs to be upfront. They tell you you're out and you set about fighting your way back in. Life goes on.

I was still firmly part of the Test team for the upcoming tour of the West Indies. I was working intensively with my batting coach Mark O'Neill. We'd figured out where things had gone wrong with my grip and I'd put a huge effort into changing it. The six weeks or so I spent not playing ODI games was, in fact, a great help in that it gave me extra time to work on it. As our departure for the Caribbean approached, it all came together. I saw the improvement in a couple of grade games early in the season and then came a game where everything fell into place and I had my full range of shots back, both sides of the wicket, smooth and powerful. The problem was completely fixed, my rhythm had returned. I was confident and focused, certain that I had returned to a form with the bat that would silence the critics and see me back in the one-day team as well as the Test squad.

Karina and the kids and I made the most of our time together before I departed. I was going to miss them, as I was scheduled to be away for almost three months before returning at the beginning of May in time for Hugo's birth. But they'd have some pleasant distractions while I was gone, including a summer holiday at Nelson Bay with Karina's family. Mia seemed a bit out of sorts at this point, but it didn't appear to be anything to worry about. Karina said she'd take her along to the doctor if she didn't pick up soon.

CHAPTER 14

COMING BACK AND COMING HOME

BY THE END OF July 2012, it felt as if years, not months, had passed since I'd picked up the phone in that Caribbean hotel room and learned Mia had cancer. For decades I'd focused intensely on cricket, but during that call its importance faded away and it continued to mean little in the chaotic period after her diagnosis.

However, by late July our little girl had come a long way. She'd made it through five of her six chemo cycles and she'd survived the complicated and dangerous six-hour surgery to remove her tumour and one of her kidneys. By most measures, Mia was recovering brilliantly from the operation, looking well and happy and moving around freely despite the huge scar on her abdomen. The one thing troubling us and her doctors was that her digestive system had still shown no signs of getting back into gear.

Mia's surgeon, Dr Thomas, continued to reassure us, saying he was confident things would return to normal ... eventually. The analogy that made the most sense to me was that Mia's stomach was reacting similarly to a person who'd been punched. He said, 'You know how if you've been hit you tense up and stay tensed up waiting for the next blow to land, and it's only when you're finally convinced it's not coming that you start relaxing? Well, it's like that. We had to be so aggressive to make sure we got every tiny bit of the tumour that the stomach has tensed up. Eventually it will realise that the attack is over and start working again. We just have to wait.'

The stomach issue wasn't a problem in terms of nutrition; the total parenteral nutrition (TPN) ensured that Mia was getting a precise balance of everything she needed in fluid form, delivered directly into her veins through her central line. (The NG tube, which still ran in through her nose and down the back of her throat to her stomach, was used both to deliver medications and to aspirate the stomach, removing the fluid that continued to build up there.) It's true that long-term TPN use can cause complications, including liver damage, but Mia was being monitored carefully to guard against that. No, the real problem was that if she wasn't eating she couldn't be discharged and could only be away from the hospital on a gate pass.

The next scheduled stage of treatment was the final chemo cycle, followed by the bone marrow transplant, or BMT. The medical team delayed starting on this, waiting to see some progress in her digestion. We often ate in front of her, hoping it would spark her interest, and always offered her food too. Everyone got seriously excited the day she gave a little lick at the icing on a cupcake, but it didn't lead anywhere. A week or two later she nibbled at a couple of hot chips and once again we were briefly thrilled. But there was no progress beyond these occasional flickers.

With the six cycles of chemo completed and treatment not going anywhere fast due to the feeding issues, Karina and I talked in depth about the need for me to return to work, whether it was cricket or something else. There was no question in my mind that I still had the skills to play the game at the highest level. But did I really want to do everything it would take to get back to the top?

Even after months away from the game I was extremely fit compared to the average bloke. But, having played professionally for 15 years, I knew how far off I was. Bowlers love to joke that wicketkeepers are the short, fat fellows who are put behind the stumps because they can't do anything else. The reality is that skin-fold tests, databases of reaction times, minute-by-minute training records and detailed daily health diaries are a given for every member of the Australian cricket team, as they are for elite athletes in most sports. I knew what it would take to get myself back into the required shape — and how much it would hurt. With Mia's life still hanging in the balance, what I didn't know was whether I had the will to put myself through that.

My first step was to talk to Christian, who'd come to know me very well over the years I'd been training with him. I told him what was on my mind, including the fact that because I was still doing overnights at the hospital and spending many daytime hours there, my availability to train would be erratic. He was totally supportive, offering to work around me. True to his word, he met me whenever I could fit in a session, whether it was 9.30 at night or 4.30 in the morning.

He worked me hard and offered endless encouragement, but he also recognised when I needed to talk more than I needed to box. Like Dad, Christian was a great sounding board. There were times when I would turn up after an especially rough night or at the end of a bad day. I'd be hitting walls, full of fear and anxiety that I didn't want to lay on Karina, who already had so much to deal with. I'd say to Christian I was ready to train and he'd look at me and say, 'Uh-huh. How about we get a coffee instead?' Initially I'd say, 'No, I'm right.' But he would see I wasn't, so he'd sit me down for coffee and listen while I got it all off my chest, then send me back into the fray in a much better frame of mind. It wasn't long before I felt the old familiar feelings of wanting to push myself and be pushed even harder.

The previous summer, in addition to my commitments to the national team and the Blues, I'd played in the inaugural season of the Big Bash League, signing on as founding captain of the Sydney Sixers. Among the other players were Mitchell Starc, Steve Smith, Brett Lee, Stuart MacGill, Moises Henriques and a couple of overseas signings, including West Indian Dwayne Bravo. Trevor

Bayliss, newly back from Sri Lanka, was coach. The Twenty20 season is short and sharp, just six weeks from mid-December to the finals in late January, and it's a lot of fun. It's definitely still very competitive, but without the pressure of the other forms of the game. The Sixers had a great first season, topped off with a win in the final against the Perth Scorchers. As national winners we'd qualified for the Champions League Twenty20 competition to be held in South Africa in October. With Karina's encouragement, I accepted the Sixers' offer of a contract for the coming season; however, I was upfront about the fact that I didn't know whether I'd be able to go to South Africa and wouldn't be able to make that call until close to the departure date in October.

I also told the Blues I'd be available for the upcoming season. It was going to be a try-it-and-see situation: Karina and I didn't know how Mia's treatment would go or how we'd all handle the fact that I'd have to travel interstate, but we felt that we could make it work. Cricket Australia continued to be supportive. I stayed in touch with team performance general manager Pat Howard, being completely upfront with him concerning my uncertainty about if and when I'd be available for the national team again, and my plan to test the waters by playing with NSW. He reinforced the fact that everyone at CA was behind me and whatever decision I made.

I wish I could say my experience with Cricket NSW was the same. Despite my deep roots with the Blues, no-one from management got in touch after Mia's diagnosis to check in on me or wish us well. Plenty of individual players and support staff did, but from the organisation as a whole there was nothing. I wasn't surprised; it coincided with the views I'd formed of a couple of the key people. (No-one who had anything to do with the Blues was surprised when it all came to a head 18 months later, leading to a long-overdue regime change.) When I let the Blues management know I was ready to play again, I wasn't counting on much help from them. I didn't need it; all I wanted was to get out there on the pitch and perform. The first step would be the pre-season training camp, followed by a couple of trial games leading into the season proper. There'd be nothing half-hearted about it. If I was going back, I was going to do everything needed and more. So as well as continuing to work with Christian, I called on Tom Carter.

Tom happens to be one of my closest mates, but he's also one of the country's best and toughest high-performance trainers. I told him that I didn't want to return to playing in anything less than my best possible condition. I asked him to strip me down and help rebuild me as an athlete. Before he became an exercise scientist and elite trainer, Tom spent 10 years playing professional rugby union with the Waratahs and was capped 85 times. So he knows about pushing human biology to its very limits, he knows about pain and he knows what can be achieved if the mind refuses to listen when the body cries out that it has nothing left to give. I trusted him completely.

He wrote a training program that started out at incredibly demanding and ramped up from there. A lot of what we focused on was getting power through the legs, which is essential for a wicketkeeper. We did a lot of working the legs separately to ensure I could take a catch pushing off one-legged and land without straining a knee. He had me doing everything from gymnastics to strength work. He's based at Sydney University, which, despite being in the heart of Sydney, has beautifully lush ovals — all the better for torturing people. One of his favourite drills was getting me to put a stretch-band around my legs and then walk round the entire oval in a crouch position. My reward for finishing was to do it again backwards. The aim was to build up all the power I could possibly need in my glutes and legs.

I was feeling strong, but just days before I was due to return to training with the Blues I came down with a gastro bug, one of those crook-at-both-ends viruses. I couldn't take the chance of passing it on to Karina or the boys, who might then pass it on to Mia, so I took myself off to a nearby motel for a couple of nights, where I wore a track between the bed and the bathroom. I was still as sick as a dog on the morning of my first training session. I had a choice. I could turn up, explain the state I was in and excuse myself from the on-field work, or I could dig deep and get through it. In deciding to come back to the game I'd vowed to myself I was never, ever going to use what Mia was going through as an excuse for anything. By the same token, I wasn't going to use this. No excuses, now or in the future. I might have had a small mental groan at the news that we were starting with six fast one-kilometre runs but I didn't let my reaction show. I told myself it was 50 minutes of pain that I needed to push through, and I did.

It was interesting coming back to the Blues and seeing parallels with the way things had been when I was with them earlier, except this time from the other side of the fence. In the absence of the international players (including Michael Clarke), they were a young group with inexperienced leadership, and struggling a bit. A lot of them didn't realise how big a gap there was between the effort they were putting in and the level they'd have to reach to even be considered to play for Australia. I've always been pretty good at cutting out the stuff that didn't matter, but what we were going through with Mia distilled things to their essence and left me with no tolerance for crap. I was there to work and I didn't have time to waste.

It was a point of pride for me that no matter how bad things were in the hospital or how little sleep I got, I was never late for a NSW training session and always gave it everything I had. However, there were some rules I couldn't follow. We had a phone app into which we were required to enter our stats each day: how much sleep we'd had, what training we'd done and how we'd performed. The aim was to allow the trainers and coaches to tailor our programs to get the best out of us. I knew there was no way I could put in my real figures or I wouldn't be passed to play. I told the Blues' trainer Paul Chapman that I couldn't do it and explained why, saying, 'My situation is that I can't always get eight hours' sleep, or even six. If you read my numbers and see that I've only had one or two hours the night before a game, you're going to judge me on that; you won't be able to help it. But I only want to be judged on how I play.' He could have made things difficult, but he totally understood and had faith in the fact that if I wasn't fit to play I'd say so. He said,

'That's fine. I know you. I'll watch you when you train and make my decisions on that.'

There were a few comments from other Blues players about how much training had ramped up since my return but, even so, I didn't feel that it was pushing me anywhere near as hard as I needed, so I continued to work with Tom and Christian. My goal was to be in top form by mid-August when Cricket Australia's annual pre-season camp was to take place in Darwin. It would be the first time most of my teammates and the coaches and selectors would have seen me since Mia got sick. I was determined to perform at the highest level so no-one could look at me, see something sub-par and 'make an allowance' because of what my family was going through. I couldn't stomach that idea.

All the hard work paid off. By the time the camp started, I was as fit as I'd ever been — among other feats, I could jump 1.5 metres in the air from a standing start. There was no awkwardness about being back in that environment, just the opposite: it felt really good to be with guys like Ricky Ponting, Mitchell Johnson and Peter Siddle again. But I was on a mission to show that I was still one of the best players in the country. I didn't talk about it; I let my actions speak for me. On the second day, after we'd been through a battery of different tests, Justin Langer, who was the team's batting coach, looked at me and said, 'You're back, aren't you?' Justin is one of the proudest guys ever to wear the Baggy Green. He understood what it had taken to get to that moment. We exchanged nods and got back to it. My next goal was to make sure I was peaking by the start of the Blues' season.

Back in Sydney, Mia's stomach still wasn't working. Her medical team decided they'd waited long enough; it was time to go ahead with the treatment. On 20 August, Karina and I met with the BMT team to talk through the process in detail. The doctors were kind and compassionate, but a lot of what they had to say was very hard to listen to. They had the results from scans done after Mia's surgery which bore the magical letters 'NED' — No Evidence of Disease. That was exactly the result they'd been hoping for (and it was testament to Dr Thomas's surgical skills). But, they told us gently, the form of neuroblastoma Mia had was so aggressive that if the threat it posed was an iceberg, all the treatment so far had only dealt with the tip.

They now had to do everything possible to try to make sure it had no way to come back. The BMT would help by putting healthy stem cells — taken from Mia in April — back into her body to form new, strong bone marrow. But before she could have the transplant she had to be given an extremely high-dose chemo cycle that would 'make room' for the new marrow by killing off all her existing bone marrow and — with it — any lurking cancer cells. This would make her vulnerable to any infection with which she came into contact: she would have literally no immunity. In order to save her life, they had to all but kill her first.

They explained that Mia would be at very, very high risk for four to six weeks after the procedure, during which time she would remain in isolation in a specially prepared room on the Camperdown ward. She would then continue to be at a degree of risk for a whole year while her immune system built back up to full capacity. During that time she couldn't go to shopping centres or anywhere else where there were large groups of people. She couldn't go to friends' birthday parties or mothers'-group get-togethers. We couldn't have anyone over to visit who had any sign of illness. And everyone in contact with her had to carefully guard their hygiene.

As well as the infection risk, for two to three weeks after the transplant she would feel extremely nauseated and unwell. She was at risk of complications that can be fatal for BMT recipients, including respiratory failure and something called veno-occlusive disease, or VOD, whereby the liver stops functioning properly because of blockages in the tiny blood vessels. If one organ failed there was a chance others might follow, leading to fatal multisystem organ failure. It was horrible to think about what could go wrong. All we could do was hope she got lucky. As risky as the procedure was, it was an even greater risk to do nothing.

Because chemo can cause hearing loss and sight difficulties, Mia had been tested in these areas before treatment began. Re-testing her now showed that while her sight was fine, she had been left with mild to moderate hearing loss and there was the chance this might be made worse by the high-dose chemo. The tumours had gone from her arms and legs but had left behind weakened, aching bones. She was nauseated a lot of the time. For the first time, she had now started to dislike hospital, and she hated having to go back to her room after a visit outside to the playground. As well, the Clown Doctors now made her cry and we had to quickly wave them away if they came to the door. She'd also begun to get cranky with nurses she didn't like.

The chemo was scheduled to be delivered over the course of a week that coincided with the NSW Blues' pre-season training camp. I really wasn't sure about going away, but Karina assured me that she would be fine, and had both our mothers, her sister Danielle and her aunts Robyn and Judy lined up to help. Our sister-in-law Amy would also be arriving, bringing her young daughter Molly on a visit from Dubai. Even so, I found it hard to go. I stayed with Mia at hospital the night before the flight and when it was time to leave I didn't want to stop cuddling her. Compared to the worst times during the five months since diagnosis, she was doing well. When her pain was under control, she was lively and cheeky and happy; her cheeks were pink and her eyes sparkled. I knew she wouldn't look like that when I got back a week later.

Mia was never out of my mind when I was at camp, but I forced myself to focus on what I needed to do. If I was going to be away from my little girl, every minute had to count, so I'd paid for Christian to travel to the camp and stay in the same hotel as us. Before breakfast and at the end of a day of training or playing in a trial game, when the younger guys were relaxing, I worked with him, boxing or doing some other preparation for my first real game back. Despite that, one of the people charged with overseeing the team said to Michael Clarke, 'Do you reckon Brad's in the right headspace to play?' To his credit, Michael said something to the effect of, 'Don't go behind his back; ask him yourself. He's a professional and he knows where he's at. He's never been anything but a straight shooter. If he doesn't want to be here he'll tell you.' That speculation about my readiness to play was completely unhelpful and unnecessary. Unfortunately, though, this bloke wasn't alone in trying to second-guess how I was feeling or what was best for my family. It would happen far too often over the next few years and I hated it.

I spoke to Karina at least once a day while I was away to find out how Mia was coping with the chemo. It was rough. Even with nothing in her stomach, she was vomiting frequently. It got so bad that she had an abdominal x-ray to check for a bowel obstruction. Nothing showed up; it seemed to be purely a chemo reaction.

The first thing I wanted to do when I arrived back in Sydney on 1 September was go out to Westmead. But I'd picked up a cold while I was away and that made me too much of a risk. It was great to be home with Zac, but very hard to not be out at the hospital to help. Karina prepared for the move to the isolation room by culling a lot of things that had accumulated in Mia's room. Everything else — from toys to the small storage drawers to the cot in which 13-week-old baby Hugo slept every night next to Mia's larger cot — had to be cleaned and sterilised before the move.

Mia was sicker by the day and the doctors were trying various combinations of medication to try to relieve her constant nausea. The transplant took place on 4 September. I still had cold symptoms and so couldn't be there, but Karina described it all to me. She said the process of delivering the stem cells was strangely anticlimactic. So much was riding on these cells and they had such a big job to do that Karina said she'd been thinking about them in terms of liquid gold surrounded by glitter and stars! In reality, they took the form of a 45ml bag of generic-looking fluid, which took 10 minutes to go in intravenously, followed by two hours of hydration fluids.

Almost immediately, Mia's body reacted to the transplant. Her heart rate and blood pressure jumped and her liver function was affected. By the end of the day she had developed the beginning of chemo-triggered mucositis, an incredibly painful condition that affects the mucous membranes lining the digestive tract all the way from the mouth on down. The affected tissue swells up and forms ulcers that get covered in a thick discharge. It becomes hard to swallow or speak. It not only feels horrible but can also be dangerous, bringing the chance of infection.

By the next morning, Karina reported that Mia was puffy from fluid build-up. She was on a lot of different drugs to manage the symptoms, including antibiotics and an anti-fungal, and she'd had a chest x-ray to check her lungs and an ECG to monitor her heart. I had to go play cricket, which was the last thing I felt like doing. Normally I would at least have been able to spend time with Mia beforehand, but my cold symptoms meant I had to stay away.

It was clear that Karina couldn't go on trying to care for Hugo full-time while also looking after Mia. She called her parents, who came to pick up Hugo. He was still being breast-fed, so handing him over to her mother meant coping with the physical discomfort of weaning him so suddenly, as well as the emotional roller-coaster that came with it.

Only a day and a half after the stem cells had gone in, Mia developed an infection, although the doctors didn't yet know what kind it was. She had a blood transfusion but continued to deteriorate so quickly that by 4.30 p.m. she was in PICU.

The game I was playing was a squad trial at Blacktown, as a warm-up for the City vs Country pre-season trial two days later. When I checked my phone at the end of play there was a message from Karina asking me to call. I could tell from the tension in her voice that something was wrong. I called back. She was in PICU and put the doctor there on the phone. I said, 'Are things under control? I would come in but I have a cold.' He said, 'You should come anyway.' My stomach dropped. This time round I understood the significance: they were gravely concerned about Mia making it through the night.

When I arrived I was fitted with a special, very tight mask before I went to Mia's bedside. It was shocking how swollen she looked. Her eyes were like slits in her puffy face, she couldn't swallow, and she had lines of different kinds going everywhere.

And yet she smiled when she saw me and wouldn't let go of my finger. I would have given anything to change places with her and save her from all this suffering.

Zac and Hugo were being well cared for by their grandparents, so I didn't have to go home. It was just as well, because although I couldn't stay in PICU I couldn't bear to leave the hospital. I spent the night in the parked car, dreading the possibility of the phone ringing. I didn't even want to think about the fact that in a week I was supposed to be going away to Perth for the first games of the domestic season.

The following day the doctors were still trying to get Mia's heart rate and blood pressure down. She cried every time she had to be moved and was too sick to even watch a DVD. But she slowly improved as time passed and 24 hours later was well enough to go back down to her isolation room. The following day I had the City–Country game and I breathed a huge sigh of relief on hearing that all was well when I checked my messages after the game.

A couple of days later, Mia had improved so much she decided she wanted to eat hot chips and a sausage roll. Karina raced down to the cafeteria, but when she got back with them Mia just licked a couple of chips. Well, at least she was thinking about food. That was really important because the dietician told us that all the time she'd had to spend being fed by tube meant that she'd skipped some important stages kids go through at her age, such as getting a feel for food textures and tastes and learning about chewing enough to swallow without choking. She warned us that even when Mia's stomach did get back to normal we'd have to help her train herself to eat.

The twelfth of September was Zac's fourth birthday and we wanted to make it really special for him. My mum stayed with Mia while we took Zac to a favourite spot in Sydney Olympic Park and held a birthday party with his friends. I have no idea where she found the time or energy, but somehow Karina had managed to be at home long enough to make Zac an amazing pirate-themed cake, complete with an ocean and a filled treasure-chest, and organise games for the kids to play. It was great to see him so happy and carefree.

The next morning I had to leave for Perth to play against WA in the Blues' 2012–13 season openers, a one-dayer followed by a Shield game. I was going to be gone for a week, which would have seemed like nothing at all a year ago. Now, with Mia only just out of PICU and still so unwell, it seemed like forever. And why did the first games have to be right across the country, rather than an hour or so away in Melbourne or Brisbane?

The whole time I was away I felt anxious, worried that I would get a call telling me Mia was critical and I needed to come home urgently, or something even worse. There was good reason to be concerned. I'd only been in Perth for a day when Karina rang to tell me that Mia was in the first stages of VOD. The blood vessels in the liver had become inflamed. Blood couldn't pass through, which made the liver swell up and stopped it doing its job of removing toxins and residue from the blood. This in turn caused fluid to build up in Mia's tummy and prevented her remaining kidney from working properly.

VOD was uncommon and we had hoped she might dodge this particular bullet, but as the nurses remarked, the poor girl could not take a trick. Karina had agonised about how much she should tell me, but correctly decided I had a right to know what was going on and could handle it. She filled me in, adding that while the condition was definitely serious, the medical team was on top of it and Mia was going to be fine. I wanted to believe that, but I remembered Dr Luce's words about hospitals being places where things don't always go right. I asked if I should come home. She said no, I should stay on and play.

Back in Sydney, my cricket had been just where it needed to be, but I found it really hard to get in the right mindset to perform for the one-dayer. In the end we won, although I scored only seven and took a single catch. In addition to our phone calls, Karina was sending me photos of Mia each day. Her swollen abdomen was painful to look at. In fact, I found it hard to look at the photos at all, she was so clearly unwell. But I had to find a way to separate my feelings from what I needed to do on the field, and I managed it more effectively in the Shield game than I had in the one-dayer, taking three good catches early on the first day's play.

There was a big scare with Mia the following day when her vital signs dropped so suddenly and severely that the rapid-response-team alarm was triggered. Soon afterwards she was moved back to PICU because fluid was building up in her lungs, making it hard for her to breathe. When Karina called to tell me, I thought immediately of the multisystem organ failure we'd been warned about. 'Is Mia going to die?' I asked her — the same question I'd asked when she had called me in the West Indies, but this time more urgent. I knew now how quickly things could go wrong. Karina told me that Mia was a fighter and so far her liver and lungs were still functioning. The treatment team was constantly monitoring her and dealing with each problem as it arose. I tried to stay positive, but I was incredibly relieved when we won the match on Day 3 and I could go home early.

I went straight from the airport to the hospital. While I was in transit, Mia had bounced back enough to be moved out of PICU again, although she was still very puffed up, having gained 3kg of fluid in a couple of days, and was on oxygen to help her breathe. But she was continuing to improve. As we cuddled and played together, something shifted in my thinking. I knew I was at a fork in the road. To continue with cricket, I had to find a different way of dealing with things when I was out there on the field. I needed to compartmentalise my feelings and thoughts so that I could fully focus and deal with one thing at a time: cricket when it needed to be cricket; family the rest of the time. I'd gone away and although Mia had suffered setbacks, the terrible scenarios I'd imagined hadn't happened. From that moment on, everything changed. I didn't stop worrying about Mia or thinking about her, but I found a way to corral those thoughts and fears and hold them to one side to deal with later.

On 27 September, five days after my return, we had our next Shield game, up against Tasmania. This time it was in Sydney, at Bankstown Oval. I went into the game in a very different frame of mind than I'd had in Perth. It was time to perform. We won the toss and Michael Clarke sent us in to bat. At my accustomed number six on the batting order, I watched in concern as our top order collapsed at 3 for 7. Pup and Steve Smith went some way to rectifying things, but things were still very dicey at 4 for 64 when I went in. I knew that my mother had gone to stay with Mia, enabling Karina, Zac and Hugo to be at the ground for the match, and I spotted them by the sightscreen.

Steve and I put on 60 together at a reasonably slow rate before he went for 64. Then Moises Henriques came out and we just opened up. My century approached and everything felt right. Hitting 100 brought a wave of emotion. I sank to my knees for a moment, thinking of Mia and everything we had been through. Punter walked past, tapped me on the back and said, 'Well done.' Resuming play, I added another 14 before being caught, with Moises and I contributing a much-needed 275 of our total of 442. I was back — better than ever. The rest of the game felt just as good, and I kept well across the entire match. It really was a turning point for me, and from that game onwards I played the best cricket of my career in all forms of the game.

By the beginning of October 2012, Mia had been in hospital for 80 days straight following her surgery, and the doctors estimated it would be at least another four to six weeks before she'd be going anywhere. Radiation was the next stage of treatment, and if all had gone to plan it would have started at this point. But until her liver was back to its normal size — probably in a month or so — nothing could happen. Not surprisingly, Karina, who was with Mia most of the time, had periods when she struggled with the continual setbacks and she fiercely missed Zac and Hugo, sometimes having to go without seeing them for days at a time. But the positivity and strength of character that had drawn me to her saw her bounce back quickly, and she encouraged me to stay the course and keep on playing cricket.

Mia had more ups and downs over the next couple of days, but overall she improved so much that on 5 October she was allowed out of her isolation room into the hospital grounds, which she absolutely loved. It went so well that the following day she got a four-hour gate pass to come home. Everything had to be thoroughly cleaned before her arrival and she was encumbered by an oxygen tank and pain-relief pump, adding an extra level of complication to the challenge posed by her central line. It was beautiful to see her at home, although we were all ready to drop when it was time to go back to the hospital.

After coming through her BMT successfully, Mia was doing so well that Karina and I had decided I should go to South Africa with the Sydney Sixers for the Champions League Twenty20 Trophy. It was to be a three-week trip starting on 9 October, which meant I'd be away for Mia's second birthday. When the day came I got to the airport just fine, but despite the shift that had happened in my thinking after the Perth game, I found that after I'd checked in I had to go for a walk through the terminal on my own so I could convince myself to get on the plane.

I didn't have much time to brood once we arrived: our first warm-up game was on 11 October. We won that one and every one of the next four in our group. They were great games, with the team working really well together. I relished the feeling of playing at my best, and it was nice to be recognised with a Player of the Match award in our defeat of Yorkshire. I also enjoyed the tactical challenges of captaincy — those game-changing decisions like deploying spinners instead of quicks in attack. The semi-final was an edge-of-the-seat thriller that came right down to the final over, but we won it, securing us a berth in the final against the South African Highveld Lions. I took a ball to the thumb in that game, which left the bone with a small crack and damaged the nail bed, but I played on anyway and had an anaesthetic block for the final game. It too was thrilling stuff and we absolutely nailed it, winning by 10 wickets to claim the trophy on our very first appearance in the tournament.

Before I'd left, Karina and I had made a pact that she would tell me exactly was happening with Mia rather than keep things from me for fear it would affect my playing. If I'd been worried there was bad news I didn't know about, it wouldn't have been possible to concentrate on the field and I wouldn't have been able to do justice to my teammates or myself. As long as I knew exactly what was going on, I could compartmentalise my mind the way I needed to. When I was playing, I was fully present. When we'd finished, I could check my phone and deal with things as they were.

The news wasn't all good, that's for sure, but at least Mia didn't end up back in PICU. In trying to make some progress on Mia's stomach issues, gastroenterologist Dr Annabel Magoffin assessed her and warned Karina that the condition may never get better and that she might need surgery to put in place a bypass from her stomach to her intestines. This was very upsetting news for Karina, the latest in a long list of possible long-term complications, including heart problems, diabetes and a higher risk of certain other cancers. Unable to sleep, she texted me in the middle of the night, early evening my time. I wrote back, 'She will be fine. Our job is to give her the best life she can have. Also love her like no other person has been loved.'

Karina said afterwards that she found a lot of comfort in that message, reminding herself of it the following day when an x-ray revealed the horrible news that the head of Mia's left femur, the long bone in her thigh, was fractured — possibly months earlier, when the chemo got rid of the tumour. The doctors were amazed that Mia was able to move her leg freely let alone stand on it, but it certainly explained a lot of her pain. There was more. Out of its correct position, the bone wasn't getting the blood supply it needed. As a result, Mia was at best likely to have a permanent limp and at worst be confined to a wheelchair and need a hip replacement in her teens. The orthopaedic specialist, Dr David Little, looked at her MRI and said he'd never seen anything like it before.

I arrived back in Sydney to learn that further scans had revealed she also had fractures above her right knee. However, endocrinologist Dr Craig Munns said a newly developed drug designed to boost blood supply in the bones offered hope. She now had a second nasal tube, a transpyloric tube (TPT), which went through her nostril and past her stomach and dripped liquid food right into her intestine. During the course of several weeks her tolerance built from 5ml, to 10ml then 14ml of fluid per hour, which when you think about it is not much, but it was progress and by 6 November she was well enough to undergo two weeks of daily radiation. This was delivered in the adult hospital and the looks of shock and pity on the faces of the other people in the waiting room when an orderly pushed in tiny bald Mia in her cot brought Karina to tears every day. The procedure itself took less than an hour but required Mia to have a general anaesthetic to ensure she didn't move, which meant by the end of the radiation she'd had 25 general anaesthetics in six months. She was back in her room by 11 a.m. each day, wide awake and wanting to play, but had to be confined to lying in her cot because of her hip. Somehow she just accepted this and didn't try to fight it, which was pretty amazing for a two-year-old.

With all that going on, I wasn't ready to re-enter the Australian team yet and it was no surprise when John Inverarity called to tell me they were going with Matthew Wade for the summer's Tests against South Africa. He made sure I knew the door wasn't shut to me, though, which I appreciated. I continued to play strongly in the domestic competitions, including a Player of the Match performance in a Blues victory over Queensland in a Sheffield Shield game at Manuka Oval at the end of November. A couple of days later we had an even bigger win on the family front when Mia was allowed home overnight for the first time in almost five months. That visit went so well that four days later, on 6 December, she got her longed-for discharge. It was true that she would be readmitted a mere three days later to begin the final stage of treatment. But after 148 days straight as an inpatient that discharge felt like the most precious piece of paper in the world. There were a lot of miles still to travel but finally things were looking up.

CHAPTER 15

RENEWAL IN THE AIR

WE SAW OUT 2012 on a roller-coaster of emotions. Having Mia home after five continuous months in hospital was a huge high, even though the number of things that could go wrong was still nerve-racking. We knew that she'd barely be home before she had to go in again, but the release was enormous, particularly for Karina. That made the crash all the worse when it was time to take her back, on 9 December. Karina tried to stay strong for Mia but she told me that just walking back into the Camperdown ward made her feel sick. She shed a lot of tears that day.

Mia was back in hospital to undergo immunotherapy, a new technique designed to 'train' her immune system to recognise and destroy neuroblastoma cells. It relies on some pretty amazing medical science. First, researchers isolate a particular substance that appears on the surface of many neuroblastoma cells; they then artificially create an antibody (the protein the immune system sends out to seek and destroy harmful invaders) that specifically targets this substance. As an extra boost, the patient also gets immune-system hormones. It's the medical equivalent of putting up a wanted poster, offering a reward, creating a posse and then supplying them each with a weapon custom-made to eliminate that particular bad guy.

The process wasn't quick, though. She would receive it in five courses, each part of a month-long cycle. If everything went right (we weren't holding our breath on that one) she would be able to come home between cycles, and her treatment would finish in early May. There were a lot of potential side-effects and, true to form, Mia got them all at one time or another: nerve pain so severe she had to go back on heavy-duty pain relief; fluid build-up; allergic reactions; fever; raised heart rate; low blood pressure; vomiting; diarrhoea; low platelets; fatigue; flu-like achiness; and constipation.

Feeding continued to be an issue, but there was progress. Mia was still on tube feeding, which was an involved, time-consuming procedure, and fluid still had to be manually removed from her stomach. Karina continued to look after all of this as well as caring for the boys and even with the family's help it was a very challenging time. But Mia's digestion had finally started working again — at one-quarter the speed it should have been. She was getting her feeds in three single lots, called boluses, spread across the waking hours to help her system get back to a three-meals-a-day routine. The idea was to get the body back to a normal wake/sleep eating cycle, rather than the round-the-clock one she had been on. So, as her tolerance of the day feeds very gradually built up, the 12-hourly TPN night feeds were decreased accordingly. She was often moody and irritable during this time, which we thought was a fairly natural response to everything she'd been through and simply being a two-year-old. But, looking back, we think perhaps we hadn't got the feeding balance right. Perhaps she was simply hungry.

She started nibbling on real food, and developed fixations on certain foods, one at a time. The first was devon. The dieticians had talked a lot about getting her to try a broad spectrum of healthy food, so we were a bit concerned when she started craving sandwich meat, of all things. But as usual Dr Luce had the most helpful perspective. He said, 'If she's interested in food, let's encourage her. We can fix up her diet along the track; the most important thing is to get her actually eating.' So if she wanted devon, she got devon. Once or twice she asked for it at 10 at night (her sleeping habits were still all over the place) when we were due to go shopping the next day and had run out. But I got in the car and went and found an all-night supermarket. When she moved on to a strawberry craze, we didn't go anywhere without taking carefully washed strawberries.

Even in the periods during the immunotherapy cycle when Mia was an outpatient, many days were spent at the hospital in clinic and if she had a temperature above 38°C she was admitted on the spot. We did get to have her home for the night on Christmas Eve, although she had to return to Westmead as scheduled the following day. It was lovely to see the effort the staff made to try to give the kids in there a special day. It was also surprising how many thoughtful strangers brought presents to be distributed in the ward. Some of them were just kind people with no connection to the hospital, but some knew first-hand what it was like to be in there at Christmas, including a 17-year-old boy we met who was delivering presents to the ward where he'd been treated as a pre-schooler.

It was the first time in five years we hadn't been in Melbourne with the other cricketing families ahead of the Boxing Day Test. But between the Sheffield Shield, the Ryobi Cup (as the domestic one-day comp was called after another sponsorship change) and the Big Bash League, there was plenty of other cricket for me and I continued to bat and wicketkeep with confidence and purpose. My results were noticed and 2013 started with the news that I was in the Australian ODI team to play two games against Sri Lanka in place of Matthew Wade, who was being rested. Going into the first game, at the MCG on 11 January, there was plenty of talk in the media about how we were a 'B-team' because Michael Clarke, Shane Watson and Michael Hussey were all out, and four players, including Phillip Hughes, were making their one-day debuts. Talk is cheap, results count; and the result was we won by 107 runs in a cracker of a game. Phil made his mark with a century and among my three catches was a one-handed blinder when Dinesh Chandimal got a thick outside edge on a Clint McKay ball.

I was really comfortable with my game and it felt fantastic to be back out there on the international arena, both in Melbourne and going into the next game two days later in Adelaide. We batted first and were struggling at 6 for 83, but I was able to change the momentum of the game with a nice quick half-century. Unfortunately, I felt pain in my hamstring running between the wickets towards the end of it. By the 19th over of Sri Lanka's innings, I had to do something I'd never done before and retire injured, handing the gloves to Phil Hughes. Sri Lanka won the match this time round.

There was a strange encounter with Mickey Arthur after the game. He'd come in as coach such a short time before Mia got sick that I hadn't worked with him long enough to form too strong an opinion of him — although he had made a bit of an odd first impression. The team happened to be in South Africa in November 2011 when his appointment was announced. We'd just finished the Jo'burg Test and were at the bar in the hotel having a drink with the Proteas when the news came through. Naturally enough, since he'd coached the South African team from 2005 to 2010, we asked what they thought of the choice. The general response was, 'Well, he's a lovely person. It'll be interesting to see what you think of him in the job.'

We had our first team meeting with him a few weeks later. He was the first non-Australian coach to ever hold the position and he made the unusual choice of starting the meeting by talking about what Australia should be doing better and what he wanted to change about the way we played. Any new coach is going to come into a side with ideas about the direction they want the team to go in; however, it created an uncomfortable feeling in the room when he chose to lead with that instead of getting to know us and working up to it. For all I knew, however, that had been an initial bump and everything had gone really smoothly for him from then on.

Ian Healy had come out in the media around the time of the Adelaide one-dayer criticising the standard of Matthew Wade's wicketkeeping. Going through the airport on the way home after the game Mickey said to me, 'Did you see Heals's comments about Wadey?' I nodded and left it at that. He said, 'I wish he wouldn't do it.' I started to make a general comment about how all the players realised that kind of scrutiny was part of the deal and we learned to handle it and so on, but Mickey broke in with, 'We all know, Brad, you're the best wicketkeeper-batsman in the country.' That was a pretty weird thing for a person on the selection panel to say to someone who wasn't in the team, but I did not have the time or mental energy to figure out where he was going with it. I wasn't going to touch it. I said, 'I'm just here to do my best for the team,' and continued on my way.

What I thought was a hamstring injury turned out to be a nerve problem, which physio Patrick Farhart (Danny Redrup's clinic partner) treated quickly and effectively. So I was all set to play a week later when I was included in the team for the ODI against the West Indies at the MCG on 10 February, in place of Matthew Wade who was in India preparing for a four-Test series that was about to start. The Windies, who had everything to prove after losing the previous four one-dayers in the series, made a strong start against us (our openers went in the first two overs) and looked like having it all their way until Adam Voges and I put on a 111-run fifth-wicket partnership that turned things around. (Adam went on to make his first international century.)

I was firing on all fronts: in March, with the domestic season wrapping up, I had an average of 42 in the Ryobi Cup, was one of the top run-scorers in the Sheffield Shield with an average of 52, had made three centuries across the two formats, and had kept well all summer. As I was about to fly back to Sydney from Melbourne early on a Sunday morning after a Blues' victory in our second-last Shield game of the season, I got a call from John Inverarity to say that I was on standby to go to India. Matthew Wade had rolled his ankle playing a bit of muck-around basketball a few days before the Third Test. I was to pack a bag as soon as I got home because if scans showed that his injury was serious, I'd be on a plane to India the following morning — and that's exactly what happened. By 1 p.m. on Monday, 11 March, I was in the air on my way to Delhi.

It was a great opportunity and I welcomed the chance to help the Australian team in its hour of need, but having to leave so suddenly was tough on the family. With Mia still spending significant periods in hospital, my mother and Karina's were continuing, between them, to provide full-time support. (Karina's sister, Danielle, was also helping out a lot.) They'd been doing it for an entire year — an incredible effort but one that couldn't continue indefinitely, even though they never complained. I was already travelling a lot again within Australia and I'd signed up for two months playing Twenty20 in the Indian Premier League season, in April and May. (It was, in theory, my third season with the Kolkata Knight Riders. I first joined them in 2011 but was out for the rest of the season after only one game thanks to the finger injury I'd got in Bangladesh. Then 12 months later, with Trevor Bayliss newly installed as KKR coach, I'd signed on for the 2012 season, but obviously Mia's diagnosis meant that didn't happen.) Karina and I had decided to employ a nanny, but she'd only just begun to look for suitable candidates when I got on the plane for India. I didn't want to leave her in the lurch, but she assured me everything would be fine.

Things were definitely not fine with the Australian team. Despite winning the toss both times, they'd lost the first two Tests. The eight-wicket loss in the First Test in Chennai stung, but it was the Second Test thrashing in Hyderabad that really hurt. It was the first time in Test history a side had declared in the first innings then gone on to lose by an innings (and 135 runs). While I was in the air between Sydney and Delhi, the consequences of this loss were unfolding in a way that would have a dramatic effect on the team for months to come.

With the support of captain Michael Clarke, Mickey Arthur had asked each player in the squad to reflect on the result and hand in a sheet identifying three areas where there was room for improvement. Apparently it was the kind of thing that had worked well for him during his time coaching South Africa, but at best it left most of the Australian players scratching their heads. Four of them — vice-captain Shane Watson and James Pattinson, who had played in the match, and Mitchell Johnson and Usman Khawaja, who hadn't — didn't hand in their sheets by the deadline. I think all of Australia, and most of the rest of the cricketing world, knows what happened next: Mickey Arthur punished them by suspending them from the Third Test. It was huge news, with the media quickly dubbing the incident 'Homeworkgate' and everyone from Mark Waugh to Freddie Flintoff commenting on what a bizarre move it was. As Mark put it in his typically blunt way, 'I've never heard anything so stupid in all my life. It's not Under-6s; this is Test cricket.'

Michael Clarke held the line, maintaining that the missing forms weren't the whole story, just 'the straw that broke the camel's back', but that didn't really change any minds about what had taken place. Shane Watson was due to go home a bit later in the tour to be there for the birth of his first child, but after being suspended he headed back early, saying that what had happened was 'very harsh' and made him question his future in the game.

I got on the plane before the story broke. Landing early in the morning in Delhi, where I was to catch a flight on to Mohali, I turned on my phone to find a bunch of messages letting me know what had gone down and warning me there might be media in the airport. I took a discreet look ahead as we came through the terminal and, indeed, there were media everywhere. I succeeded in getting to my gate unnoticed, then sat there waiting for my connecting flight wondering what on earth I was walking into.

I arrived at the hotel in Mohali, put my things in my room, got changed, picked up my bag and went to join the rest of the team at training. I walked in and exchanged greetings with the guys, then sat down for a pre-training talk from staff. Team manager Gavin Dovey said a few things about what we needed to do going up against this strong Indian team two days later, then he called everyone's attention to me, saying, 'And another thing: this is what playing for Australia is all about. Did you see what Brad did? He got here, checked in, got himself ready and he's here, ready to go.' I was thinking to myself, *Riiight, and this is worth mentioning why?*

There was definitely a weird vibe among the team. I'd toured India before, I'd played Test cricket there; I knew how much it could wear down players and teams and expose any weaknesses. But that's not what this was. They'd only been there a month and played two tour games and two Test matches. Yet they seemed a bit ... lost. Not only the younger guys, either; experienced cricketers like Johnno and Peter Siddle too. It just did not feel like an Australian cricket team change room.

The first day of the Test was rained out, so we spent it sitting in a room with a leadership coach Mickey Arthur had brought in. We had started a similar process just before I'd left the West Indies when Mia got sick and apparently it was still going on 12 months later. The leadership coach started going round the room asking people to say one by one what they stood for. It wasn't just a bit like what had been happening a year earlier — it was exactly the same! She got round to me and I answered the question by saying I was there to make a difference by doing whatever would help the team.

Then she asked me what I thought of the process itself. I didn't have time to waste and I didn't have any interest in dancing around things. I said, 'Well, I've been out of the team for 12 months but the changes you're talking about now are exactly the ones that were being talked about back then. I don't think the message is coming across. I don't think it's working.' She continued round the group and everyone was on eggshells, afraid to come out and say what they thought in a straightforward, positive manner. I recalled the openness and honesty and trust that the team had been built on previously and I couldn't believe how much things had changed.

When play finally got underway, I performed well with both gloves and bat and, with Watto absent, served as acting captain on the field when Pup had to go off to get treatment for his sore back. Unfortunately, however, the game had got too far away from us for my partnership with Phillip Hughes and that of tail-enders Mitchell Starc and Xavier Doherty to be able to pull it back within our reach. Steve Rixon was on the tour as senior assistant coach and when it was all over I said to him, 'Let's go get a beer at the hotel bar.' Pretty normal stuff, I'd have thought, but a couple of the boys saw us heading down and asked what we were doing. We told them, adding that they were welcome to join us. Stumper and I went down and had a catch-up about where Mia was at, then relaxed into our usual post-game wind-down. Matt Hayden, who was there as a commentator, arrived, then a couple of the other guys appeared and joined us, then a couple more and a couple more. At one point one of them leaned over to me and said, 'I miss this.' I said, 'What do you mean?' He said, 'Sitting here like this with the guys, having a chat, talking about the game, talking about life, taking the piss out of each other. I really miss it.' All I could do was shake my head.

We went on to Delhi for the final Test. Shane Watson was back and he served as captain when Pup's back injury prevented him playing. Matthew Wade's ankle was looking like it would be fine for him to play, but I was there just in case. The day before the game started I was walking out onto the field for training when Mickey Arthur said to me, 'Oh, you're not playing in this Test match.' I said, 'I know, I'm going out to hit some balls with Wadey.' He said, 'You know what I mean.' I said, 'I was just here as a replacement, I understand.' He looked at me and said, significantly, 'But the Ashes will be different.' I didn't have the patience for head games. Looking back on it now, I think he was perhaps feeling insecure, having come under attack from pretty much everyone for the past 10 days. I said, 'Mate, what are you talking about?' He said, 'The Ashes, they'll be different. You'll be there. Everyone knows you're the best wicketkeeper-batsman in Australia.'

I'd let it go when he said that in Adelaide but this time it was hard to cop. For a start, it sounded to me as though he was suggesting the game coming up, a Test match, didn't matter. Second, no-one understood the way things were better than me. I'd walked away from the game to be with my family; now I had to earn my way back in. Matthew Wade, who had been named vice-captain for the game, would be doing the very best he could in an effort to retain his spot. It was up to the selectors to decide who had the most to offer, but him talking about it in this way seemed to me to be disrespectful to both of us. Third, nothing in the sport was more important to me, and to every Australian cricket fan, than the Ashes. You don't play games with that stuff. I said, 'Mate, you're kidding. I've had enough of this. You've just told me again that I'm the best player in my position and you're not picking me for a Test match. You've got this all wrong. I'm out. Leave me alone.' I walked away from him past Nathan Lyon, who'd been within earshot of the whole exchange. He said a quiet, 'Good work, Hadds,' as I went by.

Mickey is not a bad person by any means; in my view it was simply that the job had got away from him. He'd lost the change room. At every level of the game, the coach has a huge influence on the players. Go down to your local park on a Saturday morning where kids play a team sport — watching their faces for five minutes will tell you everything you need to know about what their coach is like, whether calm and encouraging, well-meaning but disorganised, an overbearing loudmouth or anything in between. You might think that at the elite level all that falls away, and athletes at the very top are so highly trained and motivated they don't need external guidance or reinforcement, but that's not true at all. Whether it's the Gundagai Tigers' Under-7s or the Australian Test cricket team, the influence of the coach in bringing out the best in each person and binding the whole team together is huge.

India won that Delhi Test, just as they'd won the previous three matches. The statisticians had to go back to 1979 after the destabilisation caused by the World Series departures to find the last time Australia had lost so many matches in a Test series. The nervy, uncomfortable atmosphere in the change room was shackling the team on the field and the poor performances in the game were making players further doubt themselves and each other, creating even more tension off the field. It was a snowball that didn't look like stopping anytime soon.

Michael Clarke was heading home to get treatment for his back, and he and I were on a flight together. We talked for many hours about how things stood and how far away they were from the Australian cricket team spirit we both knew and loved. Michael had a very good relationship with Mickey and backed him all the way. (Even when he looked back much later, after Mickey said he regretted the way things unfolded during the 'Homeworkgate' period and would do it differently given the chance, Michael stood by Mickey's choices.) But he too was feeling the pressure and with the Ashes less than three months away he was determined to find a way to change the team mentality. It was clear he appreciated the chance to talk things through freely and constructively with someone who'd been away long enough to have a fresh perspective and didn't have a particular barrow to push.

Back in Australia, I didn't have time to think much more about cricket. Mia was still in and out of hospital. Karina had found a supposedly professional nanny, only to have her walk out without notice a week later saying it was all too hard — even though, unlike Karina or our mothers, she was being paid to do the job. I had only a week at home to help out before I had to depart for India again, on 31 March, this time for Kolkata for the IPL.

Karina and I spoke daily and I'd only been away three or four days when Mia started having some very worrying symptoms. The Westmead team monitored her, but she worsened to the point where she was producing black vomit and screaming in pain. She was admitted through the Emergency Department with gastritis, a painful inflammation of the lining of the stomach. The boys stayed down in Queanbeyan and Karina split shifts with her mother at the hospital over the next few days until Mia was well enough to come home.

Life didn't slow down waiting for us to catch up. On 20 April, Shane Watson announced he was standing down as vice-captain of the Australian cricket team in order to concentrate on playing and four days later I got a call from Pat Howard to tell me that I was in the team for the Ashes campaign in England and that I was the new vice-captain. He said, 'We need to get back to where we used to be: playing tough cricket and starting to win games again.'

I was thrilled to be back in the team that I was so passionate about and tremendously honoured to be asked to play a leadership role, in conjunction with Michael Clarke. I wanted to be accountable for making the team better. My parents, who'd been there every step of the way over the past 13 months, were so proud when I called to share the news. But things still felt very unsettled on the home front and, even though Karina and I had talked a lot about my return to cricket, this was completely different. I could not pull out of another tour the way I had previously: I couldn't do it to the team. If I had to leave again there would be no going back; it would mean retiring on the spot. I told Trevor Bayliss that I wouldn't be able to play out the remaining month in the IPL. He understood completely and gave me his blessing to head back to Sydney.

I'd been home hardly any time at all when we had a terrifying incident that saw Mia once again hovering between life and death. Even though she was now eating some solid food, it was nowhere near enough to sustain her, so she still needed TPN through her central line. To allow for freedom of movement during the day, the nutritionists had put us on an overnight schedule, whereby the liquid feed was slowly going into her digestive system over a 12-hour period from 7 p.m. to 7 a.m.

Karina took care of all of this. It was a very demanding process that took half an hour to set up and get started and another half an hour to remove and pack up. Mia's room, the one Dad and Peter had built for us, was set up like a home version of her hospital room, with a special table for the syringes, gloves, wipes, covers and all the other equipment needed. Karina followed strict hand-washing and sterile handling techniques to connect the feed tube to Mia's central line. She then entered the details into the machine that controlled the flow and sent warning beeps if the line became blocked.

On this particular day, Mia had attended clinic, as she did many days, and the nurses had taken a blood sample via her central line — a totally standard procedure. In the middle of the night, Mia was unsettled, which she was very often for one reason or another. Karina went in and, unable to settle her, moved her from the cot into the bed in the room and lay down with her. Mia's temperature was up, but she eventually settled and the two of them fell back asleep. At 5.30 a.m. Karina was woken by Mia's entire body shaking. She had rigors, which is when a fever makes the sufferer feel freezing cold, rather than hot, and they shiver violently. Her temperature reading was only 38°C, but she looked unbelievably sick. Within five minutes we had her bundled up and in the car. Karina drove her to hospital and her mother rushed over to mind the boys so I could follow. By the time Mia reached the Emergency Department at Westmead her temperature was up to 41°C. It was purely the speed with which the admissions team recognised that she had sepsis and started pumping antibiotics into her that saved her life.

Sepsis (also known as blood poisoning or septicaemia) is what happens when an infection rages out of control. From the original site where the bacteria attacked, it spreads throughout the entire body, and there is a very narrow window to treat it before septic shock sets in, leading to multisystem organ failure and death. We'd got Mia to the hospital just in the nick of time. Even so, it was touch and go for the first two of the four days she spent in PICU, and she needed another six days in the Camperdown ward after that before she was well enough to come home on 13 May 2013.

I'd been supposed to go to Queensland for the pre-Ashes camp, but there was no way I could leave until Mia was home safely again. Karina gave herself a terribly hard time, fearing that it was her handling of the tube for the evening feed that had allowed the infection in, even though she'd done everything exactly the same as every other time and the line had been accessed hours before that at the hospital. The medical staff assured her it wasn't her fault and pointed out that it could and did happen to the best of them and that Mia had experienced several infections in the line during her many months as an inpatient. The only difference was that in the hospital she was being monitored so closely that immediate antibiotics had prevented sepsis developing.

We were so thankful for the work of the doctors and nurses who had saved Mia yet again that we were happy to agree to the hospital PR department's request that we do some media interviews to increase awareness of sepsis and the importance of urgent treatment. (In a similar vein, Karina had been delighted to take up Dr Lord's suggestion that she write a letter to the Sargents Pies company, whose charitable arm had funded the multi-million-dollar equipment he'd used to save Mia's life.)

Once Mia was safely out of the woods, Karina and I had a very intense discussion about whether we could really make things work with me rejoining the Australian team, leaving so much weight on her shoulders. The conversation started very tensely, as they often did when we were under so much strain. However, we stuck with it and listened to each other and found a resolution. What we'd been through, and were still going through, would test any couple, but we had a bedrock of love and respect that kept us tightly bonded. I was in awe of Karina's ability to cope with so much and be such a wonderful mother to all three children. And I was deeply touched by her encouragement and belief in me.

Together we decided that we could handle anything that was thrown at us, and so at the end of May I said goodbye to her and the kids, knowing I wouldn't see them again in person for more than three months. Soon after I left, Karina found a really wonderful nanny called Natalie Dekker, who stayed with us for the next two years and was a brilliant help. Then in mid-June she phoned to tell me that Mia's first regular post-treatment scan had come back absolutely clear. The relief was indescribable and afterwards I was able to really focus my mind on the Ashes campaign.

Meanwhile, I took every opportunity I could to sound out cricketers like Matthew Hayden and Ricky Ponting as well as younger players like Steve Smith, Nathan Lyon, Ryan Harris, Peter Siddle and Mitchell Johnson about where things stood and the way they should be, and spoke in depth with Michael Clarke about how I could support him in turning things around and bringing the best out of the players. Mickey Arthur's coaching contract ran until 2015, and the changes we were hoping to bring about were in the context of working closely with him.

As a warm-up for the Ashes, I went on a short Australia A tour of Scotland, Northern Ireland and England in a team that included Moises Henriques, Peter Siddle, James Pattinson, Steve

Smith and Ashton Agar and was coached by Darren Lehmann (known to us as Boof). I played my natural game, starting with a first-day 113 against Scotland in Edinburgh, part of a 118 sixth-wicket partnership with Sidds, who got his first first-class century. The whole team was having a good time; we were really enjoying our cricket, and it showed in our unbeaten results. Unfortunately, the Australian team wasn't having the same experience, making headlines for a nightclub altercation between David Warner and Joe Root rather than their achievements on the field, after being knocked out in the first stage of the ICC Champions Trophy. The word we were hearing was that there was a lot of uncertainty about things, such as who was actually going to play in the Ashes. It was hard to know exactly how things stood without being in the same room, but it didn't sound very good.

The two teams met up in Gloucester, where I had my third and final memorable-for-all-the-wrong-reasons conversation with Mickey Arthur within six months. We sat down together and he asked me what I thought the best line-up was for the First Test, a very common conversation for a coach to have with a vice-captain. I'd opened my mouth to answer when he spoke again, saying, 'And just assume that you're in the team.' It's true that Matthew Wade was on the tour and was keeping for the one-dayers and T20Is that would follow the Test series, but that was a completely bizarre thing to say when everyone from John Inverarity down had repeatedly made it plain in public and in private that I was the Australian team's Test wicketkeeper. Not to mention the fact that I was vice-captain! I had no idea what he was trying to get at, but once again I didn't have the time or interest to figure it out. I said, 'Mate, I can't deal with this,' and left him to it.

The following day Pat Howard took a number of players aside and asked them for their assessment of where the team was, with the Ashes almost upon us. The day after that we were informed that Mickey had been sacked and was to be replaced by Darren Lehmann. It was as much a shock to us as it was to the public, but it wasn't a surprise. It's a bold move — to replace a coach less than three weeks before the start of such an important tournament — but I thought it was the right choice, one that had to be made. Boof was exactly the right bloke to oversee the rebuilding of a team that had lost its way. He was great to talk cricket with because he understood the game so well. But he was also gifted at bringing out the best in people. He'd been involved in a lot of successful Australian teams and he played cricket the right way. By this I mean he trained the squad hard and he played to win, but he also recognised and celebrated achievements and gave players time away from the game to relax and regroup.

There was a feeling of relief in the team at the idea that someone was there to pull everyone out of the quicksand. It could have been a difficult time for Michael, who'd worked on making his relationship with Mickey a good one, but Darren helped take the pressure off him and you could feel the anxiety level drop across the whole change room. Players for whom cricket at the top level had become a chore, rather than an incredible privilege and joy, started to feel they could enjoy it again. There was no uncertainty because everyone knew where they stood with Darren. Following the nightclub incident, David Warner had been barred from training with the team for a certain amount of time. Boof put an immediate end to that, saying, 'If you're here, you're a part of us. But, mate, if you stuff up again, you're out, sacked, and you won't play for Australia again.'

I cherished the opportunity to play my part in changing the team culture. Michael (who at his own request had stepped down as a selector) had his strengths and I had mine. I had no desire to be Australian captain, but one of the things I could do effectively was bring a team together and get them working for the same goal while really enjoying each other's company. With me there, Michael didn't have to worry about his message being misunderstood; I could communicate equally well with him and with the other guys.

Very quickly we could all feel the change as the respect for the Baggy Green returned and the team started to enjoy the game again in the way I'd learned to do from the likes of Justin Langer, Glenn McGrath, Ricky Ponting and the Waughs. The simplest things made a big difference. Our first tour game was against Somerset. Tour games are about getting used to the local conditions, finding your feet. We wanted to win it and we did. Afterwards, when we jumped on the bus for the trip to the next spot, there were cold beers waiting for us. The mood was relaxed, no-one was looking over their shoulders; we had a laugh and we started to feel we were regaining our purpose.

The approach to training changed. Previously it had often felt like going through the motions, with overly long sessions just for the sake of it. Boof made sure everything had a point and he upped the intensity so sessions could be both shorter and much more effective. The changes took time to consistently show up on the field, but gradually we started to once again play the way Australia is famous for playing. Guys stopped being scared to make mistakes and began to bounce back from losses.

If you made the same mistake twice Darren was going to tell you pretty bluntly. But the emphasis was on learning your game and moving forward. It was an important part of my role as vice-captain to say to the young guys, 'Okay, today we lost this situation and this is the reason. Mistakes are going to happen but don't go back into your shell because of it; learn from it. The next time you get into this situation, don't get scared, hold your nerve and play the way you want to play.' I made sure to tell them my door was always open. There were lots of coffees and lots of conversations about great memories of playing for Australia.

Even when things weren't going our way on the field, I cherished every moment of that tour. I felt so incredibly grateful that everything had come together to allow me to play again and I didn't take a second of it for granted.

The First Test, starting at Trent Bridge on 10 July, was my 45th, and it turned out to be a huge trial of my ability to keep my head in the game no matter what. Mum and Dad had come over to travel around and watch the series and it was really nice to have them there and see them relaxing after the massive effort they'd put in to help us over the past 15 months. The match started well. England won the toss and went in to bat and we were effective in keeping their score low, getting them all out for 215. Unfortunately, they also kept our first innings total down, and by the time we started our second innings, before lunch on the fourth day, we were chasing 311 runs. When I came in near the end of the day we were 5 for 161, then Phil Hughes went lbw for a duck.

That night Karina phoned me. Mia had been a bit miserable with a cold for a couple of days and when it had got worse and her temperature had gone up over 38°C Karina had followed the protocol and taken her to the Emergency Department at Westmead. There Mia had been given a dose of medication to help her and been admitted overnight just for observation, no drama. Except, as Karina was now ringing to tell me, the following day the doctors had found that she had been given a massive overdose of the medication. Instead of getting 30mg she had been given 30mg per kilo of body weight — 10 times the correct dose. It was simple human error; someone had misread the chart. They thought she'd be fine. And if she wasn't? The worst case scenario was that her single kidney would not be able to clear the extra toxins from her body, which would lead to kidney failure, dialysis and perhaps even death. The only way they would know which outcome it was going to be was to sit back and watch and wait over the next 48 hours.

I told my parents and we swapped disbelief, anxiety and reassurances back and forth. But I knew that to get out there and play the next day I was going to have to put all of those feelings in a box to deal with when my innings was over. Mia was in good hands (this frustratingly avoidable mistake notwithstanding) and there was nothing I could do to help her. I had to find a way to clear my head and do my job. Mum and Dad were the only ones who knew what was going on. I didn't breathe a word to anyone else because I didn't want anyone to lose concentration on their own task because they were worrying about me, and I didn't want anyone feeling sorry for us, as kindly as that might have been intended.

At the start of the day's play we needed 137 to win. We started strong but, although I dug in, wickets kept falling at the other end. When our number 11, James Pattinson, came out, we still needed 70. A more colourful way of putting it is that we needed a miracle. The pair of us did our very best to deliver it, hitting hard and fast, and getting lucky at one point to avoid a run-out. Our deficit was down to 24 when I was dropped on 64 at deep square leg. England did a bit of time-wasting and then it was the lunch break. James and I came back out full of fight, but on 71 my luck ran out. England wicketkeeper Matt Prior thought I'd got an inside edge. Umpire Aleem Dar hadn't seen it, but they used one of their remaining DRS (Decision Review System) referrals. While we were waiting on the decision, Matt Prior looked me in the eye and asked me if I'd hit it and I answered honestly, 'Yes.' Our run was over but against all odds we had pulled the game back, coming within 14 runs of victory, which was a huge achievement.

It would have meant nothing if things had been going badly at home, but, to my immense relief, when I spoke to Karina after the game she told me Mia had pulled through yet another close call, and was doing just fine.

England punished us all the way through the four days of the Second Test at Lord's, beating us by 347 runs. Our draw in the rain-shortened Third Test at Old Trafford meant that England retained the Ashes, but we were starting to have more good days than bad and there was the justified feeling in the change room that if it wasn't for the horrible British weather we'd have had a very good shot at winning. The Fourth Test, at Durham, showed that we still weren't recognising key moments in the game quickly enough, or doing enough to swing the momentum back to us. England won it, but we probably should have done. Stuart Broad bowled a spell that threw us much more than it should have: the team as a whole still didn't have the game awareness to recognise that we simply needed to push through that spell and come out the back end of it.

Before training in the lead-up to the Fifth Test at The Oval, Darren pulled a group of senior players aside — me, Michael Clarke,

Ryan Harris and Peter Siddle — and said that while there had been definite progress, England were getting away with standing over our young blokes too much. We needed to aim up and make sure we were sticking up for the junior players; if England tried to make things uncomfortable we'd do the same. We were a better team by then than the results showed. We'd lost the series and that was never good, but we all had our eyes on the prize of the return bout in Australia in four months' time. We went into the final game ready to push ourselves and lift to a new level, and while the risk we took to make a game of it ultimately didn't come off, so that we walked away with a draw, there was a feeling of renewal in the air.

The match brought me a personal milestone: a world record for the most dismissals in a Test series. Going into the game, one of the sportswriters had noted that if I got four dismissals I'd pass the record of 28, which had stood since Rod Marsh set it 30 years earlier. I took three in the first innings. Our second innings declaration brought the Poms back out and in the fifth over Joe Root feathered one and there it was — I'd done it. When I got back to my room I found that Rod had left me a bottle of champagne and a very nice note, which was a classy gesture. Even so, I think he'd understand better than anyone when I say that while it felt good to have set a new record I'd have traded it in a heartbeat for overall Ashes victory for the team. Ah well, we'd have our chance to try to claim back the urn soon enough. And it would mean everything to be able to do that on Australian soil in front of the family who made it all worthwhile.

CHAPTER 16

THE GREATEST VICTORY

SKYPE IS A TERRIFIC invention, but there is nothing in the world to beat picking up your kids and hugging them tight, especially when you've been away for months. There were lots of changes to take in when I got back from England at the beginning of September 2013. Being the youngest, Hugo had changed the most. I'd left an 11-month-old baby; now he was a curious toddler getting ready to talk. Zac was full of beans, mad for cricket, with endless news from preschool to share. And cheeky, gorgeous Mia was doing well enough that Dr Luce thought she might be able to have her central line out in a month or so. Karina had done a wonderful job in my absence and, with a nanny providing hands-on help, our mothers had been able to ease back into being beloved grandmas rather than carers. Spring was in the air. The underlying knowledge that things could change without warning was always there, but I felt cautiously hopeful that perhaps the worst was behind us.

Soon after I returned we got the terribly sad news that Mia's closest friend in hospital, Katie Tarpey, had died. It was a stark and painful reminder that, no matter how hard they tried, the doctors couldn't save everyone. There's a very real sense of understanding and support between almost all the parents in a children's cancer ward. When other people learn what your child is going through they make more or less the same remarks in more or less the same order; it's a conversation you have over and over and over during the long months of treatment. But in the ward everyone is way past that. Instead of, 'Oh dear, a two-year-old undergoing chemotherapy, how awful!', you ask what cycle each child is up to and swap tips about what helps with the mouth ulcers. Even the briefest conversations by the microwave come from a place of shared experience far removed from the 'outside world'. But every now and then you make an extra special connection, and Katie and her family were in that category.

Katie was almost the exact same age as Mia and she, too, had neuroblastoma, although hers had made its presence felt not long after she turned two. Soon after Katie started treatment, Karina met her mother, Serina, and other members of their close and loving family — her twin, Elyse, another sister, Georgia, who was Zac's age, and her Nana. When they were well enough, Katie and Mia loved to spend time together in the Camperdown playroom and the girls' friendship had drawn the two families close together. But, while Mia responded well to her treatment, the therapy for Katie sadly failed to produce a response, despite 10 rounds of chemo and surgery.

Her funeral would have been terribly sad under any circumstances, but seeing Mia and Katie so happy together in the photo montage and knowing that Karina and I could so easily have been in Serina and her husband Troy's places, and they in ours, made it absolutely heartbreaking. (The connection between our families remains strong: Serina is overjoyed each time we get a clear scan result and Mia often talks about Katie 'up in the clouds'.)

By the beginning of October, 18 months after Mia first had a central line inserted, she was doing well enough to have it surgically removed — a huge milestone. Eating was still an issue and she had a nasal tube delivering nutritional supplements and medicine. She also started weekly 'occupational therapy' sessions to encourage her interest in more types of food and build up her confidence tackling different textures. But having the central line out greatly reduced her chance of infection, so when I left for a six-week ODI tour of India, it was on that very positive note. However, there was no chance of becoming complacent, as Mia was admitted to hospital just a week later with a temperature-raising virus. Fortunately, after treatment, she was back home again in time to celebrate her third birthday, though of course I wasn't able to be there to celebrate with the family.

There were seven games in the series and India won 3–2 (rain accounted for the other two). The wickets were paradise for batsmen and a bunch of records were set although, the way games went, I didn't have many opportunities to bat for long periods. This made me concerned I wasn't getting the preparation I needed leading up to the coming Ashes so I sat down with batting coach Michael Di Venuto and we came up with a plan of things for me to work on.

I was feeling strong and ready for the summer ahead. Cricket NSW had made the smart move of reappointing Trevor Bayliss as coach. He asked me to take on the captaincy again. With so much on my plate, both at home and as vice-captain of the national team, I wouldn't have done it for anyone else, but for TB I said yes. We knew that my having to be away with the Australian team would limit the number of games I could play, but I was there for a lot of the pre-season and that enabled TB and I to work on the changes in the team's standards and approach needed after the disappointing previous year.

I've commented previously about the intense scrutiny surrounding every Ashes campaign. But after the events of the previous 10 months, from the failures on the field and the dramas off it in India, to the replacement of Mickey Arthur and the changes that the team had subsequently made, the external pressure surrounding the 2013–14 Ashes was multiplied by a factor of 10. And yet, because the team had put in the work and rediscovered the way we wanted to play, we were settled and ready. Darren had talked a lot to us about creating our own story. We'd had great Australian teams in the past; now it was our turn to take our place. We were primed for the challenge.

Personally, I was as comfortable going into that series as I've ever been. I was still extremely competitive; more so, in a way, because I felt I had a point to prove to those who thought that at 36 I was too old, the wrong choice for the role. But I had a different perspective now. I'd seen life and death and this wasn't it. This was a game. A great game, yes. The greatest game of all, in my opinion. But just a game. So I went into it feeling both sharp and loose: keenly focused but not tense, just clear and ready.

The Brisbane game, which started on 21 November, was a huge occasion for me. Not only was it my first Test match back on home soil since I'd rejoined the national team, it was my 50th Test, a milestone that seemed so unlikely 18 months earlier. So many people who mattered to me were there to cheer us on, including my parents, my brother Chris and his partner, Jenna, and a contingent of my old ANUCC teammates — Peter Solway, Greg Irvine, Simon Mann and Colin Smart — which meant a huge amount to me. My manager and friend, Peter Lovitt, was there with another dear friend and Mia's godfather, Paul Byrom. Most wonderfully of all, Karina, Zac, Mia and Hugo were all there, with our friend Kim Starkey lending a hand. Mia was in great form, bossing everyone around and sending Dad out to buy her chicken nuggets with sweet and sour sauce, her latest obsession.

We won the toss and went in to bat on a good Gabba wicket. But Stuart Broad was in form and 30 overs in we were 4 for 83 and, not long after, when I went in to partner Steve Smith, 5 for 100. It was one of those true tests of character. The game was not yet lost, but it would be if we couldn't change the momentum right away. Nine overs later, Steve was caught and Mitchell Johnson came out. The bowling was alternating between Broad and Graeme Swann. We'd planned for this, but when you're in the crucible in front of 42,000 people and commentators have already started writing off the entire match with comments like 'Australia are the same flawed team with a penchant for self-sabotage we saw a few months ago', panic can set in. We couldn't let that happen.

Johnno said, 'We've just got to get through Swann.' But that wasn't the strategy we'd agreed on. With the fielders at mid-off and mid-on up close, the plan was to hit Swann to get him out of the attack. We thought if we milked the strike and hit Swann for singles, there was a very strong chance that after a couple of overs England captain Alistair Cook would be tempted to bring his fast bowlers back; then we could go for it. It was a good plan; now all we needed to do was follow it. I reminded Mitchell of what we'd agreed. It was a big moment between us, with things hanging in the balance. I said, 'We have to trust ourselves and our plan, otherwise we're reverting to those bad habits we've worked so hard to change.' He looked at me, nodded, and we got down to it.

If the plan hadn't worked we'd have looked like idiots and copped it from all sides. But it did work and Johnno and I put on 114 runs before Broad bowled him for 64, not long before the end of play on the first day. I was on 78 at stumps and I wasn't done yet. I made it to 94 the next day before I got run out trying to protect Nathan Lyon from the strike, so he didn't cop one on the head. The questions I got afterwards from the media showed that some people expected me to feel disappointed about not having reached a century, but if I had to pick a single innings from my entire career as the most special to me and the most important to my team it would be that one. As I walked to the pavilion and compared the position we were in to where we'd been when I went out to bat, I felt just as good as after a win. I told the journos truthfully that I was actually glad I hadn't reached my ton, because doing so knowing my children — all three children — were there to see it would have been too emotionally overwhelming. Friends and family in the grandstand didn't have to hold back, however, and they wept openly, including Paul, not caring what anyone around him made of a bloke in RM Williams boots and checked shirt with a TAB ticket poking out of the top pocket and a schooner of beer in his hand having tears run down his cheeks.

On the field, England had no answer to the searing form of Johnno and Ryan Harris; then David Warner and Michael Clarke both got centuries in our second innings and I got 53 as we went on to win by 381 runs. That game was a real turning point for the team. It's where we started to genuinely trust in our own abilities, to see that the changes we'd made were working, to wholeheartedly enjoy each other's successes and to be accountable to ourselves and each other. It gave us a self-belief that we carried right throughout that incredible, memorable summer.

Our luck with the coin toss continued in Adelaide, enabling us to bat first. We started better than in Brisbane, reaching 155 before the second wicket fell. But then we faltered, losing the next three for only 19 runs. It was, once again, a pivot point when the game could go either way. Michael Clarke started to accumulate much-needed runs, but Monty Panesar got Steve Smith cheaply. George Bailey put on 53 but, even so, when I came out in the 85th over, at 5 for 257, we were a long way from where we wanted to be.

In a leadership role, what you say is important, but it's what you do that really counts. Michael and I wanted the team to remember the lessons of the Gabba and put them into action. It was time to lead by example, which we did with a 200-run game-changing partnership. This time around I got my century and as I pulled the ball through mid-wicket for a four I felt the energy in the crowd surging towards me. It literally took my breath away. I felt an enormous sense of achievement and I was so proud to be Australian.

By the time I nicked a Stuart Broad ball after tea on Day 2, I was on 118 and we had reached 9 for 529. We declared eight overs later for 570. Both Michael and I batted powerfully and extremely well that day, but we also benefited from England's sloppy fielding, with my near misses including a dropped catch when I was on five. There was an even closer shave when I seemed to have been caught on 51 off a ball from Ben Stokes, who was making his debut in the game. I nicked it and it was caught, no argument about that. I was walking off when the umpire called me back, saying he thought it was a no ball. I looked up at the big screen as we awaited the decision and, sure enough, Stokes's foot had been over the line.

Stokes had already shown a couple of signs that he might slot in at the 'fiery' end if anyone was classifying redheads. (And sure enough, a few weeks later he performed well enough in an ODI against Australia to get Player of the Match, but chucked enough abuse around to get fined 15 per cent of his match fee.) I knew how much hard work it took to get to your Test debut and how emotional that day was, how badly you wanted that first wicket. I also knew those things made Stokes vulnerable to attempts to get under his skin. He was making his unhappiness about the decision known when I walked past him back into position and said quietly, 'Congratulations on your first Test wicket. I know how hard that is to get.' He instantly blew up at me but I'd already passed him and I just kept walking. Down at the non-striker's end he was fielding next to me and whenever the umpire turned away I did it again: 'Psst, well done on that first wicket.' I was using gamesmanship, trying to play on Stokes's emotions and get a reaction out of him because the more his mind was on me the less it would be on the game, and up he went, every time.

The more the Adelaide Test went on, the more England got rattled as they fell further behind. Our bowlers bamboozled them and we didn't miss the chances when they came. We won by 218 runs and went into the Third Test in Perth knowing the Ashes were ours for the taking. All we had to do was stay the course.

The big contributions to our WACA first innings 385 were David Warner's 60, Steve Smith's rock-sold 111 and my 55. Again, England had no real comeback and they went into their second innings chasing 504. I was so in the zone with the bat and the gloves that it all felt almost effortless. I took four catches in the first innings and another four in the second, including a couple that went straight into my top 10 list. The first was a diving one-hander in front of first slip to get Joe Root's wicket. That was definitely the one that drew the attention. But my favourite was the one that got Ben Stokes out.

Stokes was one of the few members of the England team who had any fight left in him by the time we got to the fourth day. At stumps he was on 75 and looked ready to come back with more of the same the following day. Darren Lehmann's spray let the team know he wasn't about to let anyone turn up on the last day offering any less than they had on the first. Stokes got his century on the fifth morning and added another 20, but then we had him. Nathan Lyon was bowling and I was keeping up to the stumps when Stokes tried to sweep a delivery, only to connect on the bat's bottom edge. In that situation the keeper is blind. Your natural reaction is to stand up, which is why a catch like that is such a pure test of keeping skills. You have to hold your position perfectly and know that this is the microsecond all your training has prepared you for — nailing that kind of catch is one of the greatest sensations a wicketkeeper can have.

For such a talented cricketer, Nathan had faced frustrations maintaining his place in the side, having been selected then left off the sheet for the first two Tests in the previous Ashes. But now everyone was in agreement about his contribution. It's been said that the way I was able to stand up to the stumps for him in these Ashes helped people really recognise how good he was. If that's the case, it's something I'm very proud of, and not just because we're such good mates. The wicketkeeper–spinner relationship is one of the most important in the team. The communication between the two of you needs to be spot on and the trust needs to be absolute: if he knows you'll take all the half chances he offers, it gives him the confidence to try different things.

The emotion out there on the WACA at the end of the fifth day when we got that final wicket, leaving England 150 runs behind, was immense. There were still two games to go in the series but we'd already done it! We'd won the Ashes back! No-one was ashamed to shed a tear when Nathan led us in 'Under the Southern Cross I Stand'. (Nathan was song-leader for the Test team and I had the privilege of doing it for the ODI team.) Other than Michael Clarke, none of us had been part of a victorious Ashes side before. Everyone was riding a huge wave of joy and relief and camaraderie and pride. For me there was even more meaning because of what it had taken to be there after everything that had happened with Mia. The reason I had wanted to come back was because I'd believed the team had this win in them and that I could contribute to making it happen. We did, and I had.

The celebrations continued in Melbourne. It was wonderful to have Karina, the children and my parents there for the Christmas luncheon attended by all the families. England, who batted first, looked like they might stutter back into life on the third day, but Nathan and I delivered a 40-run 10th-wicket partnership that changed the course of the game (my overall 65 came from 68 balls), and in the end we claimed victory without having to go past number four on the batting order in our second innings.

Four down, one to go: the New Year's Test in Sydney. I'd be walking out onto my home ground in my first Test appearance there since Mia's diagnosis. I thought that in honour of the occasion it would be very special for Mia and Zac to come out for the singing of the national anthem. (Hugo was still too little.) Singing those words as a representative of your country is one of the most special things you can ever get to do. No matter how many times I'd sung it over the years, it never failed to touch my heart and that was never more true than on this occasion.

I walked out holding Mia, but Zac, who fancies himself as a fast bowler, went out with Ryan Harris. Karina, Hugo, my parents, Chris and Jenna and my cousins Peter and Michelle were in the stands along with many friends. (Michael's business commitments meant he was unable to make the trip from Dubai, where he'd been based for a few years.) Mum is even more affected by the national anthem than me — overcast day or not, she makes sure she has her sunnies on before the first note starts — but she certainly wasn't the only one shedding a tear that day among those who knew how miraculous it was that Mia was there. (To the delight of the girl of the hour, a photo of her in my arms wearing her green and gold top and matching hat ran on the front page of the newspaper the following day.)

There were strong rumours even before the game that I was going to announce my retirement, and some people saw the fact that I had the kids on the field as confirmation. The chatter had gathered so much steam by the start of the match that the journos demanded a definitive answer from Peter Lovitt, even after he assured them I'd had no such conversation with him. When they kept pushing, he said, 'Look, there's one bloke here who will know: Brad's father. I'll go ask him.' He went and found Dad and put the question to him: 'Is Bradley retiring?' Dad said, 'That one's easily answered. Is Michael here?' Peter knew immediately what that meant: there's no way something so momentous would happen without the entire family present. He laughed and went away to hose everyone down.

The game only lasted three days and everything about it was meaningful, starting with the fact that for the first time in Australia's history the team remained unchanged throughout the five-Test series. We batted first and, not for the first time, got into trouble early on. When I came in to partner Steve Smith in the 28th over, we were 5 for 97. The crowd's energy can affect a game, no question. Forty-five thousand people can make a hell of a noise and if they're behind you it's like getting a surge of adrenaline. When I walked out onto the SCG, the cheer was massive, and at every four and every big drive another huge roar went up. I really felt as though the whole of Australia was behind me and I played as well as I've ever played that day. By the time I was out, caught for 75, Steve and I had added 128 at a run rate of 4.68, including 20 boundaries in 20 overs.

England wilted in front of our eyes after that. Only Ben Stokes and Stuart Broad had any fight left in them, and that wasn't enough. When Boyd Rankin got a thick outside edge off a Ryan Harris ball after tea on the third day and Michael Clarke caught him for a duck to finish the game, the feeling was unbelievable. Not only had we won the Ashes, we'd done it in a 5–0 clean sweep, something Australia had achieved only twice before, first in 1920–21 and not again until the legendary team led by Ricky Ponting in 2006–07. Now we were in that hallowed company: we were Ashes heroes to kids all around the country, just as champions like Ian Healy and Mark Taylor had been to me as a young player. No matter how long I live, I'll never forget what it was like to stand in the middle of the SCG locked in a circle with those guys as we raised our voices to the sky singing our victory song.

All the people closest to us came back to the change room afterwards. Dad was almost speechless, brimming over with emotion as he shook my hand; it's one of the few times in my life I've seen him shed a tear. It was going around. Simon Woolford is a good friend who played more than 260 NRL games and captained the Canberra Raiders for six years. He understood exactly what had gone into that achievement and what it meant. He too had a tear in his eye when he hugged me.

Going into the Ashes, there had been plenty of criticism of the advanced age of the side overall and in particular of my ability to do my job. The phrase 'defying Father Time' made its way into at least one story. Five games later, I'd accumulated 493 runs at an average of 61.62, more than any other wicketkeeper or number seven batsman had ever scored in an Ashes series; I'd scored a half-century or more in every first innings of the series, becoming the first to do so in an Ashes since Keith Stackpole in 1972; and at the Gabba I'd taken my 200th dismissal and become the second-fastest keeper to do so after Adam Gilchrist. As with other personal stats, I didn't place any importance on these numbers myself, but they did provide objective proof that age was irrelevant as long as you could perform. No way was I going to retire yet: I still had too much cricket left in me. The World Cup was coming up in just over 12 months; I wanted to be part of claiming it for Australia.

Over the next couple of weeks I played in three ODIs against England (we won them all), but, like a number of the Test players, I was rested from the remaining couple in preparation for our upcoming tour of South Africa. That meant I could be around as we got ready for a couple of very significant milestones with the children: Zac starting school and Mia, her immune system having built back up, starting preschool. With Darren Lehmann's blessing, I flew out a day later than the rest of the team so I could see our little man walk proudly through the school gates. Karina sent me lots of photos of Mia's big day later that week. (She'd been fitted with hearing aids and humoured us by wearing them even though she was convinced she didn't need them.)

In South Africa we played a three-Test series plus a couple of T20Is. I couldn't reproduce the batting results I'd got in the Ashes, and Dale Steyn bowled me twice in the Second Test with a couple of crackers when he got the ball to reverse. There was some kind of kerfuffle in the media about him supposedly celebrating a bit too boisterously, but there was no problem about that at all between us on the field — one more example of the gap between the perception and the reality.

We claimed victory in the final Test in Cape Town in the last over of the fifth day. To win that match in the style we did gave the team as good a feeling as I have ever experienced in a change room. Ryan Harris, James Pattinson and Michael Clarke had all fought through significant injuries, pushing so hard and putting the team above themselves to get us that result. It was a wonderful feeling and clinched us the series 2–1. That was a fantastic achievement considering the Proteas were the number-one team in the world at that point and we were on their turf. It showed how far we had come and how tight our bonds had grown.

Thing were going well enough with the kids that Karina and I decided she should come over for a week-long visit during the tour. I was pretty nervous about the possibility that something might go wrong with Mia when we were both out of the country. However, nothing did, and after everything that we had gone through, having those few days together meant a lot to both of us.

I got home from South Africa in mid-April and didn't have to leave again until August, so we were able to participate as a whole family in the Run2Cure Neuroblastoma fundraiser in June. All the money raised goes specifically to research into treating and preventing the disease. Karina had originally hoped she might be able to raise $10,000 for the cause, but in the end she tripled that to an amazing $30,000, with $220,000 being raised overall. It was a beautiful day, with thoughts of Katie Tarpey and the other children who hadn't survived fuelling the determination of all involved to try to stop neuroblastoma in its tracks.

In late August I was back in Africa, Zimbabwe this time, for a one-dayer tri-series with South Africa. We won two of the qualifying games and lost two, getting through to the final against the Proteas, where they were just too good for us, thanks in large part to Steyn.

The following month we played Pakistan in both ODIs and Tests, with the matches again held in the UAE for security reasons. We won the ODI series 3–0, but the Tests got away from us in a pretty big way, as Pakistan used their spinners to excellent effect and we couldn't change the momentum of the game. They beat us in the first Test by 221 runs, a record win for them over Australia. The record stood for less than two weeks, until they thrashed us by 356 runs in the Second Test. Unfortunately, I damaged my shoulder early on the second day of that game, diving for a short catch. All my weight went down onto my right shoulder and I felt something pop, bringing with it a ton of pain. I got back to my feet and felt a click. I thought I'd dislocated the shoulder but I didn't realise I had also torn the deltoid muscle away from the bone, which was why I couldn't lift my hand up to my face.

The physio came out and took a look, but I said I'd stay there for a few balls to try to get the movement back. I had to admit to myself it wasn't coming good, and reluctantly went off. David Warner kept in my place and when he came off at the break I thought he looked pretty cooked (all batsmen think wicketkeeping is easy until they have to do it). I was very conscious that we needed him fresh to open the batting later in the day so I chose to go back out, which probably wasn't the smartest thing I could have done since it most likely exacerbated the injury. I stuck it out for as long as I could but eventually I had to come off again.

Being in the UAE gave me the chance to catch up with Michael and Amy and spend time with my nieces. And since Karina and I would turn 37 while I was there, we'd decided she would bring Zac over for a short holiday while Mia and Hugo got some grandparent time. My injury put a bit of a crimp in the family time we had planned, but it was still so good to be together.

CHAPTER 17

PULLING UP STUMPS

MY SHOULDER INJURY RESPONDED well to treatment, but I was sitting out our five-game ODI home series against South Africa to get it completely right for the upcoming Test series against India. Michael Clarke had struggled with injury himself in South Africa, including hamstring problems. When he reinjured his hammy in the subsequent tri-series against South Africa and Zimbabwe, it seemed certain he would miss at least the first of those Tests, in Brisbane on 4 December; Rod Marsh had told me to get ready to captain in his absence.

By NSW's fourth game of the Sheffield Shield season, I was fit to play again and was looking forward to getting in some match time against South Australia at the SCG. The game started on Tuesday, 25 November. The Blues line-up included Doug Bollinger, Mitchell Starc, Shane Watson, David Warner and Sean Abbott, who had made his ODI debut in the UAE against Pakistan the previous month. The morning's play unfolded just like any other day.

The Redbacks won the toss and went in to bat. Phillip Hughes, who had joined the team two years earlier, opened with Mark Cosgrove. We got Mark out, then Callum Ferguson after him, but Phil was in good form and had reached 63 when he attempted to hook a Sean Abbott ball. He was a fraction too quick through the shot and instinctively turned his head away. The ball came up and hit him on his helmet, or at least that's how it looked. Pretty much every batsman who has played for any length of time has copped a ball like that. Sometimes it takes you a few moments to gather yourself and that's what I thought Phil was doing as he stood unmoving. But a second or two later his eyes rolled back and he let out a groan, a noise the like of which I have never heard before or since. His whole body went limp and he fell face-first to the ground.

I got to him first to check that he was okay, with other players close behind me. I'd seen Shivnarine Chanderpaul knocked out with a blow to the helmet in my Test debut then come round again, but Phil wasn't coming round. We called out for urgent medical help. NSW team doctor John Orchard raced out and performed CPR. He continued this as Phil was taken off the ground by medi-cab and was assisted by intensive-care specialist Dr Tim Stanley, who happened to be in the stands watching the game and leapt over the fence to help. Phil was taken to hospital but unfortunately there was no possibility of saving him. In an absolute freak accident, the ball had hit just below the helmet, on the neck, causing the vertebral artery to split, leading to massive non-survivable bleeding on the brain. In the whole history of medicine, there had only ever been 100 previous cases. There was nothing special about that ball — tens of thousands like it are bowled around the world every year. It was something no-one would ever have believed possible.

Phil should have turned 26 later that week, but he died after two days in an induced coma, during which time family and friends, including those of us who were at the game, got the chance to go to the hospital and say goodbye. People close to him were grieving, players were in shock; people throughout the nation and the cricketing world were distressed.

Something changed forever as a result of that terrible accident. Generation after generation of Aussie kids had grown up loving cricket, playing it in the backyard, on the beach, down the side of Nan's house. It represented fun and joy. No parent dropped their child off at a Saturday morning game thinking cricket might cost their life. But now that shadow crept in. On the day of Phillip's death I took Zac to his regular cricket game. At the start of the season I had given the kids in his team a cap with my Test number, 400, on it. In a poignant gesture they had all altered the final zero to make it Phillip's number, 408, and they held the caps close during a minute's silence. Looking at their faces and those of their parents, I felt so sad to think that these families would never be able to recapture the carefree pleasure in the game I'd grown up with. Some of cricket's sunny innocence had been lost forever.

The First Test in the Border–Gavaskar Trophy series against the touring Indian side was supposed to start a week later in Brisbane but was postponed by five days (and moved to Adelaide) to allow for the funeral. No-one knew what would happen when the game did finally take place, whether players would even be able to take the field and, if they did, whether they'd be overcome during the game. Our coaches and the Cricket Australia staff did an extraordinary job of supporting us. Counselling was offered to anyone who might want it and the sports psychologists spent a lot of time with players, but there was no pressure put on anyone to play that Test match; it was purely a personal decision. There was none of the usual strategising or planning. Darren Lehmann said it might be that some players couldn't take the field and, if so, that would be okay. Once the game started, people might feel they couldn't continue to play, and that would also be okay.

For myself, I felt trying to resume the game was the thing that would help me the most. It was an incredibly emotional time for me but my main thoughts were with Phillip's family and what they must be going through. Tributes had taken off through social media, particularly 'put your bats out', and we players honoured him by listing him as 13th man in that opening Test and having his Test cap number, 408, sewn under the coat of arms on our playing shirts.

No-one was unable to take the field or continue to play but the psychological scars of what had happened remained. I don't think I've ever been in a game where a player didn't get hit by a ball at some point, somewhere on their body. But now, whenever it happened, time seemed to stand still for a moment. Everyone there felt a split second of dread, as awful memories and fears surged up then subsided. That lessened slightly as time went on, but it never completely went away — it was another way in which things had irrevocably changed.

The few extra days before the game meant that Michael Clarke did take the field after all, although the injuries he was carrying saw him retire hurt on the first day and out of the game completely on the fifth and final day, when we claimed the match by 48 runs. The mood in the change room afterwards was very different to how it usually would be after a win. We had a beer but no-one was sure how to feel. The person who got us through it was Barry 'Nugget' Rees, a legendary figure in Australian cricket. There is literally no-one like him. He has been a loved and treasured honorary member of the team/assistant coach since the 1960s. He never misses a match at Adelaide Oval and in his younger years often accompanied touring teams, even overseas. His warmth and huge heart and pure love for cricket, his country and the teams who play for it mean that he is the only non-player or member of the support staff who is allowed in the change room before a game. There could not have been a more welcome presence in that strange time.

I had captained during Michael's absence in the Adelaide Test and I knew from the discussions that had been going on earlier in the month that, with Michael out for the rest of the series and maybe longer, Cricket Australia were looking at me as a good option to take over the captaincy. But while it would have been an honour for me, I felt it wouldn't be the best choice for the team over the longer term. Following the game, a lot of the ex-players doing TV commentary came to spend time with the team, wanting to come together after the events of the previous few weeks. Ian Healy, Geoff Marsh, Michael Slater and Mark Taylor were all there, and I took the opportunity to have a quiet word with Mark, who was on the Cricket Australia board that was about to decide the captaincy. I said, 'I know you're making the decision in the next day, but don't make it me. I'm not going anywhere yet, but the team will be better off with someone who has more playing years in them. Steve Smith would be a great choice and I'll be there to give him whatever help and support he needs while he settles into the job.'

The board obviously felt the same way I did about Steve, and he was announced as captain shortly afterwards. He debuted as captain in the Second Test, at the Gabba, which we also won, this time by four wickets. Runs were still a bit elusive for me, but I was sharper than I'd ever been with the gloves, taking nine dismissals in that game — six in the first innings alone, equalling Wally Grout, Rod Marsh and Ian Healy for most in a Test innings. In the Boxing Day Test at the MCG, we were 5 for 216 when I came out to partner Steve after tea on the first day. By the time I was caught at 55 on Day 2, we'd put on 110 and Steve was on his way to 192. A draw in the game meant we reclaimed the Border–Gavaskar Trophy. We also drew the following game, at the SCG, where I was feeling in great touch with the bat, hitting a six off my first ball, although I wasn't there long in either innings before we declared.

There was some criticism of the timing of the tri-series we won against England and India, specifically the fact that it ran in the last half of January 2015 and finished just two weeks before the six-week-long 2015 World Cup. But I thought the schedule was good for the Australian team. Being forced to focus on the game really helped us through the emotional intensity of this period. During the World Cup campaign we had one game a week, which gave us some downtime, but not too much. Australia and New Zealand co-hosted the tournament, with games split between the two countries. World Cups are always huge, colourful, festive events and this was no exception, with squads and fans from 14 countries, including Afghanistan, Scotland, Ireland and the UAE alongside the traditional cricket powerhouses.

The day before the first game I thought I was out before we had even begun, after I stepped on a ball at training and snapped ligaments in my ankle. I spent the night icing it, and in the morning I thought to myself, *I'm in trouble here.* But I was the only keeper in the squad so I had to get out there no matter what. The physio strapped the ankle to within an inch of its life and I got an anaesthetic block. I played through the first game that way and continued with it for the rest of the tournament. (I made the mistake of leaving the uncomfortable strapping off for the semi-final, but it went straight back on after I rolled the ankle again.)

We played some fantastic cricket. In fact, the only game we lost leading up to the finals was a group-stage match against New Zealand at Eden Park. For me this was another big test of my ability to compartmentalise. Back home in Sydney the day before the game, Karina had taken a pale and unwell Mia to an outpatient clinic visit that turned into an emergency admission when the doctors discovered she was bleeding internally. The symptoms fit a lot of things, including the return of the neuroblastoma. Mia was given a blood transfusion and Karina rang to fill me in. 'Is it a tumour? Is the cancer back?' I asked. She told me we would know in a day or two when further tests and scans were run.

Somehow I had to clear my mind enough to prepare for the game against New Zealand. There was already something strange going on there. From the moment we'd arrived in the country, the Kiwi players had been really nice to us. Too nice. They were calling up guys on our team asking if they needed anything organised for them while they were in the country. They spoke nicely about us in the media. On game day when both sides walked out for the anthem they greeted us like old friends, chatting away and asking us what we'd been up to during our stay. They were even nice to us as we went out to bat. The whole thing felt very odd. We had a shocker batting (I top-scored with 43) and were really slow to get on the attack. By the time we did, it was too late and they claimed victory by a wicket with 161 balls remaining.

Thinking it over afterwards, it occurred to me that perhaps their behaviour was a deliberate tactic to throw us off our naturally up-tempo and uncompromising style of play. I went for a coffee with our team sports psychologist, Michael Lloyd, and asked him if he thought there was anything to my theory. Lloydy felt it was spot on, agreeing that they'd done it to get under our guard and put us off our game … and it had worked brilliantly for them. Leading into the final, where the two sides would face off again, I brought it up with the team and asked if anyone else had felt uncomfortable in the earlier match. It turned out everyone had. They had got us to change the brand of cricket we played and as a result they'd beaten us. None of us wanted that to happen again.

The final was at the MCG on 29 March and both teams were in the same hotel. Following the plan we'd made, we didn't chat to the Kiwi players, didn't engage in any way. On the field we tried to break their focus. New Zealand is a wonderful cricketing nation but deep down they never really believe they can beat Australia. Despite their previous victory, we thought this was still the case and early on in the game when one of their batsmen said, 'You don't think I'm good enough to be out here,' we knew the game was ours. We targeted the doubts that made them vulnerable and didn't let up. But we also didn't stray outside the rules (as is obvious from the fact that no-one was fined or sanctioned).

We played hard but fair and we reaped the reward, getting them all out for 183 and beating that target with seven wickets in hand. There was a bit of carry on about a light-hearted interview I gave the next day when we were still riding high on the win. I joked around and said some tongue-in-cheek things about the tactics the Kiwis had used and how we'd countered them. I certainly didn't mean to offend anyone and I'm happy to apologise if the humour didn't come across, but I think that if people want to blow things out of proportion they will, no matter what.

All of that storm-in-a-teacup stuff blew away, but what will stay with me forever is what it felt like to win the World Cup and not just that, but to do it at home. Our celebrations were mighty and they had the added depth for me of knowing this was my farewell to the one-day format, the perfect way to go out. It is tradition that no-one leaves the change room until the songmaster has sung the song, and when you're the holder of that honour it is your right to say how long celebrations will continue. This was a massive achievement and I made sure we gave it its due. It was 2 a.m. before I led the team and our support staff out to the middle of the MCG and, 14 years and 126 games after I'd made my ODI debut, said a few words about how well everyone had done and how proud they should be, and led them for a final time in 'Under the Southern Cross I Stand'. Meeting the eyes of everyone as they sang their hearts out was an incredibly special experience.

By now we had received a diagnosis that explained Mia's bleeding — portal hypertension. The portal vein is what gives the liver most of the blood it needs. If the vein becomes blocked, the body tries to create new blood vessels (varices) to relieve the building pressure. But they often fail, hence the internal bleeding. It's an extremely rare condition in children and we still don't know which part of the treatment caused it. Karina filled me in as the situation became clear: while the bleeding was low level at the moment, left uncontrolled it could lead to catastrophic, life-threatening blood loss.

There were a couple of options. The most effective was an operation to create a shunt to bypass the damaged section. But that was more major surgery, to be avoided if at all possible. A better short-term solution, the doctors advised, was 'variceal banding' — putting special rubber bands around the bulging vessels to decompress them. This could be done during an endoscopy, where a thin camera-equipped tube is inserted through the digestive system under general anaesthetic. We went ahead with it and the procedure worked, but we were warned it would probably need to be redone as other varices formed, and indeed that proved to be the case just three months later.

Excluding medical emergencies, Mia's post-treatment scans were three-monthly during this period. Scan weeks were always horrible. Everyone in our inner circle at home was aware when they were coming up. We'd start getting texts a day or two before saying, 'What's the news? When will you know?' And on the day the results were due, Dad would find one reason after another to pop back home to 'get something from the office' and while he was there he'd just happen to ask Mum if she'd heard anything. If I was away playing, I preferred not to tell anyone it was coming up, just keep it to myself and handle it my own way. Occasionally, if I felt too much tension building, I might quietly let Darren Lehmann know, and when a clear result came through I'd share it with close friends Peter Siddle or Ryan Harris.

In April, a scan showed lesions on Mia's liver. Was this the cancer returning or something benign? Further tests didn't reveal an answer and, while Dr Luce said his instinct was that it wasn't cancer, we would only know for sure after waiting five weeks and then running more scans to see if the lesions had grown. Unfortunately, I had to leave on tour during this stressful time. I tried very hard not to read anything into the fact that my destination was the West Indies, but I could hardly breathe when Karina called me to give me the results of the second scan. When she said the lesions hadn't changed and therefore were almost certainly benign and not cancer, the sense of relief was indescribable.

The West Indies tour was only three weeks or so long, taking in a warm-up tour match and two Tests (which we won). Back in Sydney, 100 family and friends joined Team Mia in the annual Run2Cure Neuroblastoma, with Karina raising another $15,500 for the cause. I cheered them on from across the world before heading with the team to England to prepare for our Ashes campaign.

I hadn't made a decision about whether I would retire after the Ashes or at the end of the following Australian summer. Either way, this would be the last time I toured and because of that Karina and I had decided that if Mia's health allowed, she and the kids would come over to join the other families on the tour. In truth, I was very apprehensive about the idea, both at the thought of something going wrong with Mia's health and at the thought of the knock-on effect of that. Previously, through all the medical crises we'd had since I'd returned to the game, I'd been able to keep it private and make my own decisions about whether I was mentally all right to play. But if my family was travelling with the other families and something went wrong, everyone would have an opinion on what I should and shouldn't be doing. I really hated that idea. However,

Karina's parents and sister, Danielle, would be along for the trip and all of them, especially Mia and Karina, deserved a chance to unwind and forget for a little while what the inside of Westmead Hospital looked like.

Dr Luce and the rest of the team were okay with the idea. They told us there was a chance Mia might have another bleed while she was away, but that the risk was no greater than it would be if she was at home. Just in case something went wrong, they prepared a detailed summary of Mia's medical history, including disk copies of her scans, which Karina brought with her. She and the kids and her parents and Danielle left at the beginning of July, with a four-day stopover in Singapore on the way. They had a ball and Mia was running around, swimming and playing just like her brothers. They flew into London then met me in Cardiff, where I got to see how much the kids had grown in just a couple of months. Play was to start there on 8 July in the First Test of the series, my 66th overall.

Trevor Bayliss had been appointed coach of the England team six weeks earlier. I saw him with his squad not long after we arrived. Walking past, I said a cheeky, 'G'day, coach.' Mike Atherton, standing nearby, looked a bit taken aback, but TB laughed as I knew he would.

The memories of losing in 2009 at Cardiff in a game we should have won were still raw. This time round we were determined to claim the victory and we had the goods to do it. We were ranked number two in the world versus England's number six, and they hadn't been able to take a single game from us the last time we'd met. Unfortunately, though, we didn't deliver. They batted first and we started reasonably, taking their first three wickets for 43, but it went downhill for us from there and the truth is that over the course of the four days they outplayed us.

There were a few key factors: we definitely missed having Ryan Harris in our attack (he had been forced to announce his retirement before the first Test started because of his knee problems); TB was a crucial weapon for England despite having been there such a short time, because, knowing us so well, he knew exactly the brand of cricket they needed against us, a new aggressive style of play that worked well for them; and then, of course, there was that famous dropped catch on the first day.

The five catches I took in that match faded into obscurity next to the one I dropped off Joe Root on his second ball when he was yet to score. The reason it lives on is because he went on to get 134 in that innings, changing his team's fortune. We finally got him on an lbw appeal that went our way after being referred to the Hawkeye system. Despite his impressive total, his was the opposite of a controlled innings, but that doesn't stick in the memory of commentators and fans and I totally get why. No-one felt worse about that dropped catch than me. As a keeper, you know how hard the bowlers work and you know the plan. There isn't a worse feeling in the game than feeling you've let your teammates down by dropping one you should have taken. It makes you want to crawl under a rock. But the unavoidable reality is that keepers are going to drop catches; it's a horrible feeling that every keeper has to live with. In fact the hardest thing about being a wicketkeeper is finding the mental strength to bring yourself back up after a dropped catch. You have to find a way to do it because the game doesn't stop, no matter how bad you feel.

But it's still a game and as long as everything was okay with my family the world kept spinning. Unfortunately, however, on the fourth (and, as it turned out, final) day, when I was at the ground warming up and Karina was at the hotel having breakfast with the kids and her family, she realised something was wrong with our little girl. Mia looked pale and clung to her mum, only wanting to be in her lap, after having happily chosen for herself at the buffet on previous days. While Karina's parents looked after the boys, she and Danielle took Mia to the Emergency Department of the nearby Cardiff University Hospital. There a blood test showed her haemoglobin level had halved. She was given a blood transfusion, which made her feel brighter, and the doctors started discussing arrangements to move her to a hospital that could carry out a specialist children's endoscopy to confirm that it was another varices bleed and band it.

Because Mia was stable and there was nothing I could do by being at the hospital, Karina made the decision to wait until the end of the day's play to phone and fill me in; then we'd be able to decide the next step together. Unfortunately, operating on a thought process I can't even guess at, another player's partner took it upon herself to phone team manager Gavin Dovey and say, 'Mia's in hospital. You have to tell Brad,' and so that's how I heard. Word then passed around the entire group. This was exactly the situation I'd wanted to avoid: other people wanting to make decisions for us. They had good intentions, but in the end how much difference does that make? The reality was that Karina and I had things under control, just as we had done for more than two years, and what happened next should have been purely up to us as a family. But as soon as other people got involved I knew my playing future was in the balance.

Mia was looking reasonably well when I got to the hospital, although they were giving her an extra transfusion as a boost. There were hospitals in both Birmingham and London that could do the endoscopy. Together Karina and I decided that, with the team about to travel to the Second Test at Lord's, we would take the London option and, if Mia remained stable, I would go ahead and play as planned.

I briefed Michael Lloyd and Darren Lehmann, saying I'd be able to let them know more when they arrived in London in a day or two. Then Mia and Karina went in an overnight ambulance to London and I followed by train. The endoscopy results were worrying: there had definitely been internal bleeding but the London team couldn't find any varices. Were they hidden in an inaccessible spot, or was it something more sinister? Mia was going to have to return to Westmead to find those answers, but the British doctors could give her medication to restrict the blood flow and keep her safe on the flight home.

All this happened on a Sunday, four days before the start of the Second Test. On the Tuesday I spoke to Michael Lloyd and updated him on Mia's status and we discussed the fact that, just as I'd feared, the rest of the players were talking and worrying about her and me. I had performed under much more pressure than this many times before, with Mia in PICU in serious danger, but I'd been able to do it because no-one around me knew. I hadn't had to worry about how my situation was affecting the other players' game; I'd only had to get myself right. But now, I told him, everyone, and not just the players, had an opinion about whether I should play or not. By the end of the conversation I knew that I was going to have to make myself unavailable for the game. I couldn't risk my situation distracting the team.

Peter Nevill was the back-up keeper on the tour. I'd played with him at NSW and we had formed a close relationship. On the bus heading to Lord's for a training session, I gave him a quick heads-up so he could start mentally preparing for the fact that he would be playing in the match. At the ground I went to talk to Darren Lehmann and selector Rod Marsh. I told them I had to make myself unavailable for the Second Test and explained why. Rod said immediately, 'I fully understand,' but Darren's reaction was a bit odd, I think because he was taken by surprise. He said, 'Do you want to play for Australia still?' I said, 'Yeah, a hundred per cent. But right now my daughter's sick.' Peter Nevill did a good job in my place, with seven catches and 45 runs, and Australia won the game easily. I sent him a bottle of champagne to celebrate his Test debut.

Mia was stable enough to fly home with Karina the day after the Test ended. They were going straight to Westmead, where Mia would be in the best possible hands so, as Karina and I had agreed, I told Darren and Rod I was available again to play out the rest of the series. We had a tour game against Derbyshire next up. I had a good relationship with Boof and the selectors, but as the game approached I felt as though they were talking to me differently, not in the usual relaxed way. When the team was announced, both Peter Nevill and I were in it. I knew what that meant — my Test career was over.

I asked Rod who was wicketkeeping in the game. Michael Clarke, who heard, said, 'Good question, Hadds. Rod?' Rod started to say we would split the keeping between us, but we all knew that's not how it worked. I said, 'Come on, Rod. I'm ready to go out there and do everything I need to, but just be straight. You already know who's playing in the Third Test and if it's Nev, he needs to keep in this game so he can get some more practice keeping in English conditions — you know, as a keeper, it's hard work. So just tell us.' He said he'd have to talk to the other selectors and went out to make some calls. Darren arrived and when Rod was done I went up to the two of them and said, 'So, what's happening for the Test?' Rod said, 'We're going with the winning team from last time.' I said, 'That's fine. So I'm dropped?' He fluffed around a bit, saying, 'No, we're just going the other way.' I tried again: 'Rod, just tell me I'm dropped so we can get on with it and I can go throw Nev some balls and help him get ready for this Test,' but he said again, 'No, no.'

There was a lot of protest when the news broke, with Matthew Hayden, Ricky Ponting, Shane Warne and Ian Healy among those who criticised the decision, saying it went against Cricket Australia's 'Family First' policy to drop someone after they'd pulled out of a single game for family reasons. They also said a lot of very nice things about the contribution I'd made to the game. I appreciated their comments, but I felt differently about what had happened. I didn't have a problem with being dropped. That's the way it goes in professional sport. Yes, my choice would have been to play out the Ashes — which, since we're fantasising, Australia would have won — and then retire on my own terms. But very seldom does professional sport deliver a fairy-tale ending.

No, what I objected to was simply not being told straight out. The end of a Test career is a big moment, however it comes about, and all I wanted was the kind of clarity I ended up getting from Boof, who confirmed that I was dropped and said it was purely based on performance (although he did say afterwards it was the hardest selection decision he'd ever made — and I knew he meant it — which was touching).

The thing that hurt me the most in the whole business was a quote Rod Marsh gave to the media in response to the outcry against the decision. He said, 'It was an amazingly hard call, but we have to try and do the best thing for the country and the selection panel believe that was the best thing for the team, for the country.' As he pointed out in the same interview, Rod had known me for two decades, since I was a teenager at the Cricket Academy. He knew that the team and my country meant everything to me. In fact one of the things I am most proud of as both a cricketer and a man is the comment made by Darren Lehmann and many of the guys I'd played with that I put the team first every time. So reading those words from Rod, which sounded as though he was saying I would put my own desire to play above what was best for the team or for Australia, well, it was like a knife to the heart.

With Mia stable and under observation in Westmead, I stayed on with the squad, continuing to train with Nev until the final game. Back in Australia, I made the formal announcement that I'd retire in September. It was pointed out to me that I was currently in equal position (with Greg Matthews) as the most capped NSW player ever and I was urged to delay the decision long enough to play just one more Shield game, thereby taking the record in my own right. But I would never take the field just to set a record or change my stats: that's not the legacy I want. My NSW team gave me a lovely send-off and I stepped away from the game a contented soul.

That's why the way my career ended is nothing more than a footnote. What counts are all the years in which I was blessed to have the chance to do what so many people dream about: all the games in which I gave everything I had for the teams I loved so much as we played our hearts out for this beauty of a country. The 'impossible' catches and the big centuries are part of it, of course, but so are all the tidy, flawless games behind the stumps that went by unnoticed, and the gritty 40s in game-changing partnerships too. And the endless laughs, and occasional well-earned tears, shared with blokes forever linked by a unique and precious bond.

That's what mattered to me in cricket and that's what was in my mind as I enjoyed the lap of honour Michael Clarke and I were given on a perfect sunny day in January 2016 at the SCG. That moment was all the more special because I shared it with the people who mattered most. Looking at my beautiful wife and children, so full of love and life, I gave heartfelt thanks to have them by my side as together we embarked on a whole new adventure: life after cricket.

EPILOGUE

ON HER RETURN FROM England, Mia was thoroughly checked at Westmead and allowed home, but two more bleeds soon afterwards made a necessity of the eight-hour shunt surgery we'd been hoping to avoid. It was sickening to think of her having to go through another huge procedure like that, but it was the lesser of two evils and we had the comfort of knowing she was once again in the capable hands of Dr Gordon Thomas. While she was on the operating table, Dr Thomas made some strategic moves to try to minimise the chances of future invasive procedures, removing her gallbladder and appendix and taking biopsies from the liver lesions (which confirmed they were benign).

Unfortunately, despite his good work, it looked as though Mia would have to go under the knife again just a few months later. She woke up in pain one morning in early January 2016 and by the afternoon was in hospital with what turned out to be a bowel obstruction. This can be an unavoidable side-effect of previous abdominal surgery, which leaves scar tissue the bowel catches on, leading it to twist the wrong way and get blocked.

The condition can't be left untreated, so when more than a week went past with no improvement, it seemed likely Mia would have to undergo surgery yet again, even though this was the last thing anyone wanted. But she was stable, so Dr Thomas continued to hold off and to our enormous relief after 11 days we got a minor miracle: the bowel unkinked itself and started working again.

Epilogue

At Zac's insistence, there had been an exception to my retirement from cricket: Twenty20. He was adamant that I had to stay on with the Sydney Sixers for at least one more summer and that sounded good to me. The 2015–16 Big Bash season was coming to a close when Mia went into hospital with the bowel obstruction, but to her absolute delight she was released in time to host a box at the SCG at the Sixers' final game of the season for some of the doctors who had saved her life.

We'd half-joked during her treatment that you could fill a room with her specialists, and now we did just that. Dr Luce Dalla-Pozza, Dr Gordon Thomas, Dr David Little, Dr Annabel Magoffin, Dr Craig Munns and their partners were all there, along with my parents and Karina's, and her sister, Danielle. It was a wonderful day and Mia, living testament to the extraordinary work of these wonderful, caring experts, was in her element.

Just a few weeks later she reached a milestone that had once seemed an impossible dream: she started school, just like any other five-year-old. In Mia's classic take-on-the-world fashion, she said a quick goodbye to me and Karina and headed eagerly in to her classroom without a backward glance.

Two years went by between the end of her treatment for cancer and the start of writing this book. With every passing month my memories of what she'd been through became less vivid, although I didn't realise quite how much they had faded until I opened the three *Mia's Journey* photo books Karina created using all those shots she took on her phone in hospital. She'd covered everything from diagnosis to the end of treatment, with full details of each step of the way. I'd accepted it when Karina said the books were an important record to provide answers for Mia if she wanted to know precisely what she'd been through, but I hadn't imagined myself ever wanting to look at them. Then one night I came home late; everyone was asleep, but I wasn't ready for bed. I went and sat in the lounge room and the books were right there. Once I'd started looking through them I couldn't stop.

All the emotions that had sunk under the surface rose up again. I felt sick as the pictures triggered one memory after another. I vividly recalled the awful sensation of holding Mia as a general anaesthetic hit: children don't flutter down into unconsciousness; one second they're looking up at you and the next they're lying seemingly lifeless. I never got used to it. I felt again the fear that iced my blood for months every time the phone rang when I was away from the hospital. I relived the anguish of looking at her, knowing she was in tremendous pain and not being able to do anything about it. And I felt my chest squeeze as I remembered those long, terrible nights in PICU sitting by her side willing her to fight as she hovered between life and death, murmuring to her, 'Daddy's here, Mia. Mummy and Daddy love you so much. Stay with us, Mia-moo, we need you,' sometimes feeling the tiniest squeeze of her hand on my finger in response, as a little tear slid down her face.

By the end of the third book I understood why Karina had been driven to make them and I appreciated the work she'd put in. Even so, I couldn't imagine myself ever opening them again. But as the most painful emotions began to subside, I realised that by capturing things at their worst, the books also showed vividly how far Mia had come.

She's still all too familiar with the Children's Hospital, but it has no fear for her. She says, matter-of-factly, 'That's where I used to live,' and when we go there for scans or clinic visits she looks forward to seeing the doctors and nurses and all the other people who continue to care so much about her and all the other children in their charge. Then, when she walks out those doors, she gets on with normal life, refusing to slow down or be limited by anything or anyone. She leaps in the air with excitement when it's time for swimming lessons or gymnastics and you'd never know she has a slight limp from the way she charges around the house, giggling and flashing that cheeky grin.

When her first school cross-country carnival came around, she could have used her limp as an excuse to sit out the event and no-one would have thought the worse of her, but that's not our

Mia. She lined up with all the other kindy kids, so cute in their sports uniforms. She took her first step — and went straight down on her face, along with four or five others. Then she picked herself up and took off again. She didn't even slow to a walk, but ran the whole way, trying her little heart out. Karina was helping out with the marshalling and she wasn't the only one among the gathered parents to shed a tear.

At the back of our minds is the ever-present awareness that Mia still has two and a half years of clear scans to go before she can be declared cancer-free, and even then she'll face numerous treatment-related challenges and risks for the rest of her life. But we will deal with those as they arise. In the meantime, we live life and cherish our children. We visit the site of our house-rebuild, finally underway under my dad's supervision. We enjoy going as a family to the boys' sport, watching as little Hugo heads straight past the bigger kids at soccer to score yet another goal or Zac charges across the cricket field to take a catch.

Karina and I don't know what the future holds. But guess what? No-one does. All any of us can do is make the most of what we have. As a cricketer, my goal was always to simplify: to take my technique back to basics and see the game in terms of its fundamentals. Well, sometimes life simplifies things for you in the most brutal way possible and that's what Mia's cancer did for us. When you have a child with a life-threatening illness, everything non-essential melts away; you understand like never before what's important and what's not. When all's said and done, family, love and accountability for your choices are what really matters. I hope I never forget that.

Anyway, enough philosophising; there's just enough time before dark for a quick game of backyard cricket, and it sounds like the kids have started without me ...

Brad Haddin, Sydney, August 2016

DANIEL LANE

IT DIDN'T TAKE LONG for Brad Haddin to prove he was carved from the same block of granite as some of Australia's toughest wicketkeepers — uncompromising scrappers such as Rod Marsh, Ian Healy and one of Brad's mentors, Steve 'Stumper' Rixon. When Phil Emery retired from the NSW Blues in 1999, news of Haddin's selection over Craig Glassock — considered by many as Emery's obvious heir — surprised a few of us in the media. Glassock had played a handful of games for NSW and, with the team in a state of transition — older players were moving on and the new breed was being ushered through — many believed the selectors would crave *some* experience. However, if there was any pressure on the young, seemingly cocky Haddin — who had already been earmarked as a special talent when he had captained Australia's Under-19s and represented the ACT Comets in the 1997–98 domestic one-day competition against the so-called 'big boys' — it didn't show.

It was obvious from watching Haddin perform in those formative matches for NSW that the 'keeper from Queanbeyan' was a 'goer'. While the Blues took some terrible beatings as they found their feet, there was plenty to like about what Haddin's teammates said about him. He didn't take a backwards step, he expected his bowlers to fight for their wickets, he took the 'game on' and liked to 'chat' to the batsmen from behind the stumps (whether it's true or not, one wonderful anecdote suggests that once led him to swallow five flies during a single innings!).

I saw first-hand the determination and energy that drove Haddin to greatness when he joined the old Thump Boxing gymnasium at Five Dock in Sydney's Inner West in 2004. I was a member there because it was the perfect place to let off steam from tight deadlines and the media grind. Brad was there for a different reason: to develop a level of fitness that would give him an edge over his rivals, all of whom would one day be contenders for Adam Gilchrist's place in the Australian team.

Like the other members, I watched as Haddin was put through fearsome one-on-one sessions by his trainer, Christian Marchegiani, a mutual friend. The program was designed to push Haddin deep into the *discomfort* zone and more often than not the relentless regimen of weights, agility exercises, shuffle runs, burpees, beep tests and other torturous drills left this star of Australian cricket hunched over a garbage bin, vomiting.

There were a few aspects of Haddin's approach to training that left an impression: most notably, he fought the natural instinct to collapse to the floor at the end of even the most gruelling session. I well remember the parade of younger players who'd accompany him to a session; while they spoke of their hunger and desire to play for Australia before training started, few were ever again sighted after their first taste of the 'tough stuff'.

As a journalist with an interest in what makes champions, I enjoyed talking to Haddin — who, it needs to be said, took weeks to drop his guard, through, I guess, the fear that his comments might end up in print — because he provided profound insights. Two things that stuck in my mind were his approaches to cricket and leadership, because both principles can be applied to life. He spoke of playing cricket with a sense of 'no fear', saying it's hard to achieve greatness in any field if you're forever looking over your shoulder for perceived threats. He also said over his regular post-training *macchiato* that his message to the players before a match was to be the person who made a difference out there. Both struck me as good creeds.

Once doctors said Haddin's daughter Mia was healthy enough for him to claw his way back into the Australian team, he provided raw insight into the emotionally draining battle he, his wife, Karina, and extended family had fought in an interview I did for *The Sun-Herald*. While his actions on the field and in the gym proved he was a warrior, listening to Haddin detail his little girl's battle exposed his vulnerability and fatherly tenderness. His decision to speak about the battle he and Karina had fought came after his heroic comeback to the Test team when he starred for Australia in the triumphant 2014 home Ashes series. However, he stressed there was no way he would've ever played cricket again had Mia needed him. 'I didn't think about cricket,' he said. 'I didn't think about coming back to the game ... It was [all about] making sure Mia had the best possible chance of surviving and that our other kids could live as normal a life as possible with everything that was going on.' As Haddin poured out his heart, I thought his emotionally charged words proved he was, first and foremost, his family's keeper.

Haddin proved he meant every word because he'll forever be remembered as the man who effectively walked away from the Australian cricket team during the next Ashes series that was staged in Britain. Fate once again dictated his daughter needed him more than his mates in their Baggy Green caps. While he says any parent would've reacted the same way, the fact is he was *the* parent put to the test.

Brad Haddin's entire career ought to be celebrated for the series of sacrifices that established him as a teammate who was selfless. After all, Haddin urged the national selectors to forgo him — the then vice-captain of the Aussie team — for the top job. Even though the Australian captaincy provides lucrative post-cricket opportunities, such as commentating, Haddin endorsed the much younger Steve Smith because he believed it was crucial that Cricket Australia prepared for the future. In a similar vein, he refused the opportunity to become the most capped player in the history of

NSW cricket by not doing what his teammates wanted: delay his retirement until he played one more match for the Blues. While they thought he was entitled to the honour, Haddin was adamant that to play that game would have been selfish — and unforgiveable. He realised he'd be bitterly disappointed in himself if he chased a personal milestone. 'It would worry me more being remembered for that — playing for a milestone — because that's not me,' he said. 'I wouldn't be playing to be a better player or making the environment better; it would be for personal reasons, and that would eat away at me for the rest of my life.'

Further testimony to his willingness to put others before himself was his taking Peter Nevill under his wing at the Eastern Suburbs District Cricket Club, and then NSW, even though it was clear the younger wicketkeeper, who'd moved to Sydney from Melbourne to improve his game, would one day be a direct threat to Haddin's place in the Australian team. Destiny decreed Nevill assumed Haddin's position behind the stumps when the selectors chose him to play in the Test *after* Brad returned from spending time with Karina by Mia's hospital bed. However, it says plenty for Haddin's qualities that it didn't cross his mind to ask his protégé to stand down and allow him to resume his place on the big stage. 'Nev was put in an uncomfortable position,' he says. 'I'm quite close to Peter and this was nothing to do with Peter ... It was a decision the selectors made. The selectors made their decision and that was fine ... I made myself vulnerable to being dropped because I walked away.'

Haddin's career statistics tell of a great achiever in Australian cricket, but the figures that note such things as his taking 262 catches in 66 Tests and scoring 3122 runs for the national one-day team fail to capture his epic tale of heart and courage. One of the great frustrations of being a journalist who has covered much of Brad Haddin's career is that he has *always* given the impression he'd prefer to have his teeth pulled than to talk about his personal triumphs. It's therefore been left to some of his former teammates to tell of the human moments behind the statistics and to document the actions of a teammate who made a difference:

Peter Nevill, Haddin's replacement as Australia's wicketkeeper
'It was obviously a difficult time for the Haddins when they were in London [and Mia was sick] but Brad was very supportive of me during that time. He could quite easily — and understandably — have shifted his entire focus away from cricket, but he still very much supported me during that Test match in London when I debuted. He and Karina sent a bottle of champagne to my room and their thoughtfulness in doing that during what was a terrible time for them is another example of the kind of people they are. He'd been such a great mentor to me in the nine years leading up to that match that we obviously had a wonderful relationship ... It was an unusual feeling [to replace him in that circumstance].

'Brad used to stress to me that as a wicketkeeper he did the basic things better than anyone and being able to do that is the key to wicketkeeping. It wasn't only the great catches and sharp stumpings that made him great; it was also the consistent things he did throughout his career.'

Steve Smith, 45th Test captain of Australia
'It was more or less Brad's idea that [the selectors] give the captaincy to me: he was the vice-captain at the time and he endorsed me for the job. He's a great man and it was tremendous during my first couple of games as captain to have him by my side to offer some guidance.

'I'll always remember Brad as one of the great team-men; a fierce competitor who wanted the best for whatever team he was playing for, be it Australia, NSW or the Sydney Sixers. Brad Haddin taught me plenty. I learned loads from listening to the way he spoke and watching the way he played the game.'

Peter Siddle, Australian fast bowler
'Brad was like the big brother of the team and we shared some good times together, and some bad times as well. Regardless of the circumstances, he was a great bloke to be around.

'Even though he wasn't the captain, I always looked up to Brad as a leader. The way he went about the game — he was competitive and aggressive — was extraordinary. When you talk about the Australian "way" of cricket, he stands alongside guys like Steve Waugh, Glenn McGrath, Ricky Ponting, Adam Gilchrist and David Boon — blokes who had a good crack.

'His decision to [stand down from the team to be with Mia] says what type of man he is, and it's that quality that allows me to know we'll be good mates for the rest of our lives.'

Nathan Lyon, Australian spin bowler

'Brad is one of the best teammates I've played alongside because he cares about you, and all good teammates put everyone else before themselves. He was exceptional in the way he carried himself on and off the field, and his professionalism was extraordinary.

'You always knew that Brad had your back in all areas of the game and that was a comfort. His willingness to lead from the front gave Australia a genuine edge. I think his efforts with the bat and gloves when we won the [2013–14] Ashes series 5–0 were incredible; he dug us out of trouble on so many occasions.

'While the public was captivated by Mitchell Johnson's performance in that series — and Mitch was on fire — Brad's efforts were acknowledged by his teammates. Watching him take the game on and change the momentum gave us the courage as the bowling unit to go out and take wickets.'

Mitchell Johnson, former Australian fast bowler

'We played a lot of cricket together and we always got into a lot of scraps together because Brad was one of those guys who'd back his mates 100 per cent. That quality made him one of the best team players imaginable.

'I admired that he was a very strong character who'd stand up for what he believed in. If there was something he didn't think was quite right, he'd speak up and get it out there. We looked up to him because when Brad spoke he was honest; he wasn't fearful of saying what he thought. He was an open book and it was good to have that kind of voice in the team.'

Ryan Harris, former Australian fast bowler

'Brad's legacy is that he proved the importance of passion. He was obviously great at what he did, but he also led so well from the front it really made a difference.

'When he returned to the Australian team [from helping to care for Mia in 2012–13] he obviously wasn't the captain, but he let the younger players know what it meant to play for Australia and what you needed to do to be a top player. He brought them into line and became a godfather figure in his own way.

'I admired that if there was an elephant in the room he was the person who'd bring it up because he realised that might help the team. He wasn't always right — and Brad will admit that — but he always raised points that needed to be discussed. He was brutally honest and enjoyed challenging the younger guys.

'When Mia [was sick] he kept it very quiet because he didn't want the detail to affect the team's preparation. We grew up in an era where the Baggy Green was everything, but what Brad proved is that family overrides everything.'

CAREER RECORD

of

BRADLEY JAMES HADDIN

Born 23 October 1977 (Cowra, NSW)

Right-hand batsman
Wicketkeeper

Compiled by Ross Dundas

CAREER SUMMARY

Grade	M	Inn	NO	Runs	HS	0s	50	100	Avg	Stk-Rt	Ct	St
First-class Career	184	300	39	9931	169	20	56	17	38.05	66.08	608	40
Test Cricket	66	112	13	3265	169	8	18	4	32.98	58.45	262	8
Touring First-class	24	31	5	954	129	2	4	2	36.69	69.03	62	8
Sheffield Shield	94	157	21	5712	154	10	34	11	42.00	70.89	284	24
International Limited-Overs	126	115	16	3122	110	2	16	2	31.54	84.22	170	11
Domestic Limited-Overs	96	95	6	3094	138*	8	18	6	34.76	94.36	128	35
International Twenty20	34	29	6	402	47	2	–	–	17.48	114.53	17	6
Indian Premier League	1	1	–	18	18	–	–	–	18.00	163.64	–	–
Pakistan Super League	8	8	4	188	61*	1	3	–	47.00	138.13	8	–
Big Bash League	16	16	1	462	76	2	4	–	30.80	129.78	5	2
Twenty20 Cricket	78	73	12	1468	76	6	9	–	24.07	125.14	50	16

SYMBOLS AND ABBREVIATIONS USED IN THE TABLES

*	Not out (unless otherwise indicated)
M	Matches
Inn	Number of innings
NO	Not out
HS	Highest score
0s	Ducks
Avg	Average
Stk-Rt	Strike rate
Ct	Catches taken while fielding/keeping wicket
St	Stumpings made while keeping wicket

FIRST-CLASS CAREER

Debut 1999–2000 New South Wales vs Queensland, Brisbane

BY SERIES

Season	Venue	M	Inn	NO	Runs	HS	0s	50	100	Avg	Stk-Rt	Ct	St
1999–2000	Australia	11	21	1	643	86	1	6	–	32.15	68.48	23	3
2000–01	Australia	9	15	1	397	93	1	3	–	28.35	72.03	26	3
2000–01	India	1	2	–	32	24	–	–	–	16.00	78.05	1	–
2001–02	Australia	10	18	2	515	102	3	3	1	32.19	77.56	27	1
2002–03	Australia	11	17	3	497	117	1	1	1	35.50	76.46	30	2
2003–04	Australia	6	11	2	351	76	–	3	–	39.00	73.43	18	4
2004–05	Australia	12	19	3	916	154	–	5	2	57.25	83.27	36	3
2005	England	1	1	–	94	94	–	1	–	94.00	97.92	2	–
2005–06	Pakistan	2	3	–	58	34	–	–	–	19.33	–	1	1
2005–06	Australia	9	13	1	617	116	1	4	1	51.42	70.27	23	1
2005–06	Australia	10	18	3	813	139	2	4	2	49.00	71.25	42	3
2007–08	Australia	7	9	–	489	123	–	1	3	54.33	61.82	31	2
2007–08	West Indies	4	7	1	215	64	–	1	–	35.83	51.31	19	2
2008–09	India	5	8	1	197	37	–	–	–	28.14	38.10	15	–
2008–09	Australia	5	8	–	422	169	–	1	1	52.75	62.61	13	–
2008–09	South Africa	4	7	–	201	63	–	1	–	28.71	64.01	18	1
2009	England	5	8	1	310	121	–	1	1	44.29	70.29	17	–
2009–10	Australia	8	13	3	370	88	1	2	–	37.00	70.34	33	1
2009–10	New Zealand	2	3	1	71	48	–	–	–	35.50	79.78	9	–
2010–11	Australia	8	14	3	504	136	–	5	1	45.82	53.62	24	2
2011–12	Sri Lanka	4	6	–	106	35	1	–	–	17.67	52.48	16	–
2011–12	South Africa	3	6	1	82	55	2	1	–	16.40	48.52	10	–
2011–12	Australia	8	11	2	202	80	3	1	–	22.44	48.33	28	1
2012–13	Australia	7	11	2	468	114	–	2	2	52.00	63.67	19	3
2012–13	India	1	2	–	51	30	–	–	–	25.50	47.22	4	1
2013	UK	9	14	2	411	113	1	3	1	34.25	59.56	43	3
2013–14	Australia	6	10	1	561	118	–	6	1	62.33	73.82	27	–
2013–14	South Africa	3	5	1	26	13	1	–	–	6.50	40.63	13	–
2014–15	UAE	2	4	–	45	22	1	–	–	11.25	38.79	2	1
2014–15	Australia	5	8	3	129	55	1	1	–	25.80	69.35	22	1
2014–15	West Indies	3	3	–	31	22	–	–	–	10.33	68.89	7	1
2015	England	3	5	1	107	35	–	–	–	26.75	53.50	9	–
Total		**184**	**300**	**39**	**9931**	**169**	**20**	**56**	**17**	**38.05**	**66.08**	**608**	**40**

BY OPPONENT

Opponent	M	Inn	NO	Runs	HS	0s	50	100	Avg	Stk-Rt	Ct	St
Derbyshire	1	1	–	32	32	–	–	–	32.00	72.73	–	–
ENGLAND	20	35	2	1366	136	1	11	3	41.39	61.53	79	1
England Lions	1	2	1	32	25*	–	–	–	32.00	78.05	2	–
England XI	1	–	–	–	–	–	–	–	–	–	2	–
Indian Board President's XI	2	3	–	66	34	–	–	–	22.00	51.56	3	–
Indians	1	2	–	83	60	–	1	–	41.50	81.37	4	–
India A	1	1	–	15	15	–	–	–	15.00	65.22	2	–
INDIA	13	22	6	429	55	2	1	–	26.81	47.51	56	2
Ireland	1	1	–	2	2	–	–	–	2.00	22.22	6	1
Jamaica Select XI	1	1	–	64	64	–	1	–	64.00	69.57	3	2
Kent	1	2	1	46	35	–	–	–	46.00	46.94	4	–
NEW ZEALAND	6	9	1	365	169	–	1	1	45.63	66.00	22	1
New Zealanders	1	1	–	14	14	–	–	–	14.00	82.35	1	–
PAKISTAN	5	9	–	115	41	2	–	–	12.78	60.85	19	2
Pakistan A	3	5	–	187	129	1	–	1	37.40	62.32	4	1
Queensland	21	36	4	1449	139	4	9	3	45.28	75.51	66	5
Scotland	1	1	–	113	113	–	–	1	113.00	71.52	4	1
Somerset	1	2	1	90	52*	–	1	–	90.00	84.91	2	–
SOUTH AFRICA	11	19	1	495	94	2	3	–	27.50	57.83	40	1
South Africa A	1	2	–	6	6*	1	–	–	6.00	20.69	4	–
South African Board President's XI	1	2	–	36	23	–	–	–	18.00	70.59	5	–
South Africans	1	1	1	20	20*	–	–	–	–	105.26	4	1
South Australia	17	25	3	1075	113	1	7	1	48.86	69.58	64	4
SRI LANKA	3	5	–	90	35	1	–	–	18.00	51.43	10	–
Sri Lankan Board XI	1	1	–	16	16	–	–	–	16.00	59.26	6	–
Tasmania	18	29	4	967	114	3	4	3	38.68	68.63	44	2
Victoria	20	36	5	1277	154	–	7	3	41.19	66.68	55	7
West Indian Board President's XI	1	1	–	1	1	–	–	–	1.00	8.33	1	–
West Indians	1	1	–	37	37	–	–	–	37.00	94.87	1	1
WEST INDIES	8	13	3	405	88	–	2	–	40.50	58.70	36	1
Western Australia	18	31	5	944	116	2	7	1	36.31	74.33	55	6
Worcestershire	2	1	–	94	94	–	1	–	94.00	97.92	4	1

BY CAPTAINCY

Captaincy	M	Inn	NO	Runs	HS	0s	50	100	Avg	Stk-Rt	Ct	St
As Non Captain	157	257	33	8139	169	18	47	13	36.33	64.20	519	32
As Captain	27	43	6	1792	139	2	9	4	48.43	76.59	89	8

BY INNINGS

Innings	Inn	NO	Runs	HS	0s	50	100	Avg	Stk-Rt	Ct	St
First Innings	103	10	4085	139	4	24	8	43.92	67.56	236	8
Second Innings	73	4	2760	169	4	14	8	40.00	65.17	154	10
Third Innings	84	17	2109	116	10	12	1	31.48	68.87	104	13
Fourth Innings	40	8	977	80	2	6	–	30.53	58.05	114	9

BY VENUE

in Australia	M	Inn	NO	Runs	HS	0s	50	100	Avg	Stk-Rt	Ct	St
Adelaide	17	29	7	1290	169	2	8	2	58.64	67.36	62	4
Albion	1	2	1	68	50*	–	1	–	68.00	95.77	5	–
Bankstown	2	4	1	237	114	–	1	1	79.00	75.24	7	2
Blacktown	1	1	–	10	10	–	–	–	10.00	45.45	–	–
Brisbane	16	28	1	1176	139	2	8	2	43.56	68.09	55	2
Cairns	1	1	–	15	15	–	–	–	15.00	65.22	2	–
Canberra	1	2	–	106	73	–	1	–	53.00	65.03	4	–
Darwin	1	2	–	129	129	1	–	1	64.50	62.32	3	–
Hobart	11	18	1	319	41	2	–	–	18.76	79.35	28	3
Lismore	1	–	–	–	–	–	–	–	–	–	1	–
Melbourne	11	20	2	688	117	1	5	1	38.22	64.60	32	2
Newcastle	2	4	1	115	50	–	1	–	38.33	81.56	7	1
North Sydney	1	2	–	95	87	–	1	–	47.50	73.08	4	–
Perth	13	24	2	709	94	3	7	–	32.23	71.62	60	3
Richmond	3	6	–	96	40	–	–	–	16.00	95.05	12	1
St Kilda	2	3	1	240	154	–	1	1	120.00	66.30	6	–
Sydney	48	70	13	2601	123	3	14	7	45.63	68.50	134	12
Total	**132**	**216**	**30**	**7894**	**169**	**14**	**48**	**15**	**42.44**	**69.06**	**422**	**30**

in England	M	Inn	NO	Runs	HS	0s	50	100	Avg	Stk-Rt	Ct	St
Canterbury	1	2	1	46	35	–	–	–	46.00	46.94	4	–
Cardiff	2	3	–	150	121	–	–	1	50.00	71.77	7	–
Chester-le-Street	1	2	–	17	13	–	–	–	8.50	60.71	6	–
Derby	1	1	–	32	32	–	–	–	32.00	72.73	–	–
Leeds	1	1	–	14	14	–	–	–	14.00	60.87	6	–
Lord's	2	4	–	122	80	–	1	–	30.50	50.41	9	–
Manchester	1	2	1	73	65*	–	1	–	73.00	67.59	7	–
Nottingham	1	2	–	72	71	–	1	–	36.00	48.32	6	–
Taunton	1	2	1	90	52*	–	1	–	90.00	84.91	2	–
The Oval	2	4	–	65	34	1	–	–	16.25	56.03	8	–
Worcester	3	3	1	126	94	–	1	–	63.00	91.97	6	1
Total	**16**	**26**	**4**	**807**	**121**	**1**	**5**	**1**	**36.68**	**64.05**	**61**	**1**

BY VENUE (continued)

in India	M	Inn	NO	Runs	HS	0s	50	100	Avg	Stk-Rt	Ct	St
Bangalore	1	2	1	68	35*	–	–	–	68.00	39.77	2	–
Delhi	2	3	–	49	24	–	–	–	16.33	64.47	3	–
Hyderabad	1	1	–	34	34	–	–	–	34.00	39.08	2	–
Mohali	2	4	–	97	37	–	–	–	24.25	40.08	8	1
Nagpur	1	2	–	32	28	–	–	–	16.00	35.56	5	–
Total	**7**	**12**	**1**	**280**	**37**	**–**	**–**	**–**	**25.45**	**42.04**	**20**	**1**

in Ireland	M	Inn	NO	Runs	HS	0s	50	100	Avg	Stk-Rt	Ct	St
Stormont	1	1	–	2	2	–	–	–	2.00	22.22	6	1

in New Zealand	M	Inn	NO	Runs	HS	0s	50	100	Avg	Stk-Rt	Ct	St
Hamilton	1	2	–	60	48	–	–	–	30.00	84.51	6	–
Wellington	1	1	1	11	11*	–	–	–	–	61.11	3	–
Total	**2**	**3**	**1**	**71**	**48**	**–**	**–**	**–**	**35.50**	**79.78**	**9**	**–**

in Pakistan	M	Inn	NO	Runs	HS	0s	50	100	Avg	Stk-Rt	Ct	St
Rawalpindi (KRL)	1	1	–	15	15	–	–	–	15.00	–	–	–
Rawalpindi (RCS)	1	2	–	43	34	–	–	–	21.50	–	1	1
Total	**2**	**3**	**–**	**58**	**34**	**–**	**–**	**–**	**19.33**	**–**	**1**	**1**

in Sri Lanka	M	Inn	NO	Runs	HS	0s	50	100	Avg	Stk-Rt	Ct	St
Colombo (PSS)	1	1	–	16	16	–	–	–	16.00	59.26	6	–
Colombo (SSC)	1	2	–	65	35	–	–	–	32.50	54.62	3	–
Galle	1	2	–	24	24	1	–	–	12.00	47.06	1	–
Pallekele	1	1	–	1	1	–	–	–	1.00	20.00	6	–
Total	**4**	**6**	**–**	**106**	**35**	**1**	**–**	**–**	**17.67**	**52.48**	**16**	**–**

in South Africa	M	Inn	NO	Runs	HS	0s	50	100	Avg	Stk-Rt	Ct	St
Cape Town	3	6	1	81	42	1	–	–	16.20	62.79	9	–
Centurion	1	1	–	0	0	1	–	–	0.00	0.00	4	–
Durban	1	1	–	5	5	–	–	–	5.00	50.00	6	1
Johannesburg	2	4	–	171	63	–	2	–	42.75	59.38	9	–
Port Elizabeth	1	2	–	10	9	–	–	–	5.00	27.03	4	–
Potchefstroom	2	4	1	42	23	1	–	–	14.00	52.50	9	–
Total	**10**	**18**	**2**	**309**	**63**	**3**	**2**	**–**	**19.31**	**56.49**	**41**	**1**

in Scotland	M	Inn	NO	Runs	HS	0s	50	100	Avg	Stk-Rt	Ct	St
Edinburgh	1	1	–	113	113	–	–	1	113.00	71.52	4	1

in United Arab Emirates	M	Inn	NO	Runs	HS	0s	50	100	Avg	Stk-Rt	Ct	St
Abu Dhabi	1	2	–	23	13	–	–	–	11.50	38.33	1	–
Dubai	1	2	–	22	22	1	–	–	11.00	39.29	1	1
Total	**2**	**4**	**–**	**45**	**22**	**1**	**–**	**–**	**11.25**	**38.79**	**2**	**1**

BY VENUE (continued)

in West Indies	M	Inn	NO	Runs	HS	0s	50	100	Avg	Stk-Rt	Ct	St
Bridgetown	1	2	1	77	45*	–	–	–	77.00	51.68	7	–
Greenfields	1	1	–	64	64	–	1	–	64.00	69.57	3	2
Kingston	2	3	–	56	23	–	–	–	18.67	41.79	11	–
North Sound	2	3	–	41	33	–	–	–	13.67	51.90	4	–
Roseau	1	1	–	8	8	–	–	–	8.00	80.00	1	1
Total	**7**	**10**	**1**	**246**	**64**	**–**	**1**	**–**	**27.33**	**53.02**	**26**	**3**

BY BATTING POSITION

Position	Inn	NO	Runs	HS	0s	50	100	Avg	Stk-Rt
Opener	6	1	83	41	–	–	–	16.60	72.17
3th	4	–	112	40	–	–	–	28.00	116.67
4th	4	–	63	34	1	–	–	15.75	82.89
5th	14	3	329	113	3	2	1	29.91	60.26
6th	89	14	3516	139	3	20	8	46.88	68.99
7th	165	20	5539	169	11	34	8	38.20	64.53
8th	18	1	289	41	2	–	–	17.00	56.12

BY TEAM

Team	M	Inn	NO	Runs	HS	0s	50	100	Avg	Stk-Rt	Ct	St
Australia A	7	9	–	354	129	1	–	2	39.33	67.89	17	4
AUSTRALIA	66	112	13	3265	169	8	18	4	32.98	58.45	262	8
Australian XI	14	18	4	483	94	1	3	–	34.50	66.71	36	3
New South Wales	97	161	22	5829	154	10	35	11	41.94	71.12	293	25

HIGHEST SCORES

Score	Team	Opponent	Venue	Season
102	New South Wales	Queensland	Sydney	2001–02
117	New South Wales	Victoria	Melbourne	2002–03
154	New South Wales	Victoria	St Kilda	2004–05
114	New South Wales	Tasmania	Sydney	2004–05
116	New South Wales	Western Australia	Sydney	2005–06
129	Australia A	Pakistan A	Darwin	2005–06
139	New South Wales	Queensland	Brisbane	2006–07
123	New South Wales	Queensland	Sydney	2007–08
100	New South Wales	Tasmania	Sydney	2007–08
113	New South Wales	South Australia	Sydney	2007–08
169	AUSTRALIA	NEW ZEALAND	Adelaide	2008–09
121	AUSTRALIA	ENGLAND	Cardiff	2009
136	AUSTRALIA	ENGLAND	Brisbane	2010–11
114	New South Wales	Tasmania	Bankstown	2012–13
108*	New South Wales	Victoria	Sydney	2012–13
113	Australia A	Scotland	Edinburgh	2012–13
118	AUSTRALIA	ENGLAND	Adelaide	2013–14

HOW DISMISSED WHEN BATTING

Innings	Not Out	Bowled	Ct Fieldsman	Ct Keeper	LBW	Stumped	Run Out
300	39	49	118	49	35	7	3

TEST CAREER

Debut 2007–08 vs West Indies, Kingston

BY SERIES

Season	Opponent	Venue	M	Inn	NO	Runs	HS	0s	50	100	Avg	Stk-Rt	Ct	St
2007–08	WI	West Indies	3	6	1	151	45*	–	–	–	30.20	46.18	16	–
2008–09	India	India	4	7	1	163	37	–	–	–	27.17	37.91	13	–
2008–09	NZ	Australia	2	3	–	194	169	–	–	1	64.67	68.07	5	–
2008–09	S/Africa	Australia	3	5	–	228	94	–	1	–	45.60	58.61	8	–
2008–09	S/Africa	South Africa	3	5	–	165	63	–	1	–	33.00	62.74	13	1
2009	Eng	England	4	6	–	278	121	–	1	1	46.33	69.50	15	–
2009–10	WI	Australia	3	5	2	224	88	–	2	–	74.67	67.88	14	–
2009–10	Pak	Australia	3	5	–	70	41	1	–	–	14.00	95.89	17	1
2009–10	NZ	New Zealand	2	3	1	71	48	–	–	–	35.50	79.78	9	–
2010–11	Eng	Australia	5	9	1	360	136	–	3	1	45.00	54.88	8	1
2011–12	S/Lanka	Sri Lanka	3	5	–	90	35	1	–	–	18.00	51.43	10	–
2011–12	S/Africa	South Africa	2	4	–	76	55	1	1	–	19.00	54.29	6	–
2011–12	NZ	Australia	2	3	–	100	80	–	1	–	33.33	55.87	8	1
2011–12	India	Australia	4	5	2	86	42*	1	–	–	28.67	48.04	18	–
2012–13	India	India	1	2	–	51	30	–	–	–	25.50	47.22	4	1
2013	Eng	England	5	10	1	206	71	1	2	–	22.89	49.40	29	–
2013–14	Eng	Australia	5	8	–	493	118	–	5	1	61.63	71.55	22	–
2013–14	S/Africa	South Africa	3	5	1	26	13	1	–	–	6.50	40.63	13	–
2014–15	Pak	UAE	2	4	–	45	22	1	–	–	11.25	38.79	2	1
2014–15	India	Australia	4	8	3	129	55	1	1	–	25.80	69.35	21	1
2014–15	WI	West Indies	2	2	–	30	22	–	–	–	15.00	90.91	6	1
2015	Eng	England	1	2	–	29	22	–	–	–	14.50	50.00	5	–
Total			**66**	**112**	**13**	**3265**	**169**	**8**	**18**	**4**	**32.98**	**58.45**	**262**	**8**

BY OPPONENT

Opponent	M	Inn	NO	Runs	HS	0s	50	100	Avg	Stk-Rt	Ct	St
England	20	35	2	1366	136	1	11	3	41.39	61.53	79	1
India	13	22	6	429	55	2	1	–	26.81	47.51	56	2
New Zealand	6	9	1	365	169	–	1	1	45.63	66.00	22	1
Pakistan	5	9	–	115	41	2	–	–	12.78	60.85	19	2
Sri Lanka	3	5	–	90	35	1	–	–	18.00	51.43	10	–
South Africa	11	19	1	495	94	2	3	–	27.50	57.83	40	1
West Indies	8	13	3	405	88	–	2	–	40.50	58.70	36	1

BY INNINGS

Innings	Inn	NO	Runs	HS	0s	50	100	Avg	Stk-Rt	Ct	St
First	39	4	1355	118	2	9	1	38.71	60.14	103	–
Second	25	1	843	169	1	3	3	35.13	58.95	56	1
Third	33	7	718	94	4	3	–	27.62	61.95	55	4
Fourth	15	1	349	80	1	3	–	24.93	46.91	48	3

BY VENUE

in Australia	M	Inn	NO	Runs	HS	0s	50	100	Avg	Stk-Rt	Ct	St
Adelaide	6	10	5	497	169	1	2	2	99.40	65.14	19	1
Brisbane	6	9	–	433	136	–	3	1	48.11	54.67	22	1
Hobart	2	4	–	69	41	–	–	–	17.25	97.18	9	1
Melbourne	6	10	1	276	65	1	3	–	30.67	57.50	20	1
Perth	5	9	–	371	94	1	4	–	41.22	71.07	28	–
Sydney	6	9	2	238	75	–	1	–	34.00	70.41	23	–
Total	**31**	**51**	**8**	**1884**	**169**	**3**	**13**	**3**	**43.81**	**63.52**	**121**	**4**

in England	M	Inn	NO	Runs	HS	0s	50	100	Avg	Stk-Rt	Ct	St
Cardiff	2	3	–	150	121	–	–	1	50.00	71.77	7	–
Chester-le-Street	1	2	–	17	13	–	–	–	8.50	60.71	6	–
Leeds	1	1	–	14	14	–	–	–	14.00	60.87	6	–
Lord's	2	4	–	122	80	–	1	–	30.50	50.41	9	–
Manchester	1	2	1	73	65*	–	1	–	73.00	67.59	7	–
Nottingham	1	2	–	72	71	–	1	–	36.00	48.32	6	–
The Oval	2	4	–	65	34	1	–	–	16.25	56.03	8	–
Total	**10**	**18**	**1**	**513**	**121**	**1**	**3**	**1**	**30.18**	**58.63**	**49**	**–**

in India	M	Inn	NO	Runs	HS	0s	50	100	Avg	Stk-Rt	Ct	St
Bangalore	1	2	1	68	35*	–	–	–	68.00	39.77	2	–
Delhi	1	1	–	17	17	–	–	–	17.00	48.57	2	–
Mohali	2	4	–	97	37	–	–	–	24.25	40.08	8	1
Nagpur	1	2	–	32	28	–	–	–	16.00	35.56	5	–
Total	**5**	**9**	**1**	**214**	**37**	**–**	**–**	**–**	**26.75**	**39.78**	**17**	**1**

in New Zealand	M	Inn	NO	Runs	HS	0s	50	100	Avg	Stk-Rt	Ct	St
Hamilton	1	2	–	60	48	–	–	–	30.00	84.51	6	–
Wellington	1	1	1	11	11*	–	–	–	–	61.11	3	–
Total	**2**	**3**	**1**	**71**	**48**	**–**	**–**	**–**	**35.50**	**79.78**	**9**	**–**

in Sri Lanka	M	Inn	NO	Runs	HS	0s	50	100	Avg	Stk-Rt	Ct	St
Colombo	1	2	–	65	35	–	–	–	32.50	54.62	3	–
Galle	1	2	–	24	24	1	–	–	12.00	47.06	1	–
Pallekele	1	1	–	1	1	–	–	–	1.00	20.00	6	–
Total	**3**	**5**	**–**	**90**	**35**	**1**	**–**	**–**	**18.00**	**51.43**	**10**	**–**

in South Africa	M	Inn	NO	Runs	HS	0s	50	100	Avg	Stk-Rt	Ct	St
Cape Town	3	6	1	81	42	1	–	–	16.20	62.79	9	–
Centurion	1	1	–	0	0	1	–	–	0.00	0.00	4	–
Durban	1	1	–	5	5	–	–	–	5.00	50.00	6	1
Johannesburg	2	4	–	171	63	–	2	–	42.75	59.38	9	–
Port Elizabeth	1	2	–	10	9	–	–	–	5.00	27.03	4	–
Total	**8**	**14**	**1**	**267**	**63**	**2**	**2**	**–**	**20.54**	**57.17**	**32**	**1**

BY VENUE (continued)

in United Arab Emirates	M	Inn	NO	Runs	HS	0s	50	100	Avg	Stk-Rt	Ct	St
Abu Dhabi	1	2	–	23	13	–	–	–	11.50	38.33	1	–
Dubai	1	2	–	22	22	1	–	–	11.00	39.29	1	1
Total	**2**	**4**	**–**	**45**	**22**	**1**	**–**	**–**	**11.25**	**38.79**	**2**	**1**

in West Indies	M	Inn	NO	Runs	HS	0s	50	100	Avg	Stk-Rt	Ct	St
Bridgetown	1	2	1	77	45*	–	–	–	77.00	51.68	7	–
Kingston	2	3	–	56	23	–	–	–	18.67	41.79	11	–
North Sound	1	2	–	40	33	–	–	–	20.00	59.70	3	–
Roseau	1	1	–	8	8	–	–	–	8.00	80.00	1	1
Total	**5**	**8**	**1**	**181**	**45***	**–**	**–**	**–**	**25.86**	**50.28**	**22**	**1**

BY BATTING POSITION

Position	Inn	NO	Runs	HS	0s	50	100	Avg	Stk-Rt
4th	1	–	0	0	1	–	–	0.00	0.00
5th	1	–	8	8	–	–	–	8.00	266.67
6th	9	–	148	42	1	–	–	16.44	64.63
7th	92	13	3009	169	4	18	4	38.09	38.09
8th	9	–	100	23	2	–	–	11.11	36.50

HOW DISMISSED WHEN BATTING

Innings	Not Out	Bowled	Ct Fieldsman	Ct Keeper	LBW	Stumped	Run Out
112	13	19	46	20	10	2	2

PLAYER OF THE MATCH AWARDS

Start Date	Opponent	Venue	How Out	Runs	Balls	Catches
8/11/2008	New Zealand	Adelaide	c Fulton b Redmond	169	(222)	3

SHEFFIELD SHIELD CAREER
Debut 1999–2000 New South Wales vs Queensland, Brisbane

BY SEASON

Season	M	Inn	NO	Runs	HS	0s	50	100	Avg	Stk-Rt	Ct	St
1999–2000	10	19	1	560	86	1	5	–	31.11	66.91	19	3
2000–01	8	14	1	360	93	1	3	–	27.69	70.31	25	2
2001–02	9	17	1	495	102	3	3	1	30.94	76.74	23	–
2002–03	10	17	3	497	117	1	1	1	35.50	76.46	28	2
2003–04	6	11	2	351	76	–	3	–	39.00	73.43	18	4
2004–05	11	18	3	902	154	–	5	2	60.13	83.29	35	3
2005–06	9	13	1	617	116	1	4	1	51.42	70.27	23	1
2006–07	8	15	3	669	139	1	4	1	55.75	73.44	37	3
2007–08	7	9	–	489	123	–	1	3	54.33	61.82	31	2
2009–10	2	3	1	76	44	–	–	–	38.00	61.79	2	–
2010–11	3	5	2	144	61*	–	2	–	48.00	50.70	16	1
2011–12	2	3	–	16	16	2	–	–	5.33	26.67	2	–
2012–13	7	11	2	468	114	–	2	2	52.00	63.67	19	3
2013–14	1	2	1	68	50*	–	1	–	68.00	95.77	5	–
2014–15	1	–	–	–	–	–	–	–	–	–	1	–
Total	**94**	**157**	**21**	**5712**	**154**	**10**	**34**	**11**	**42.00**	**70.89**	**284**	**24**

BY OPPONENT

Opponent	M	Inn	NO	Runs	HS	0s	50	100	Avg	Stk-Rt	Ct	St
Queensland	21	36	4	1449	139	4	9	3	45.28	75.51	66	5
South Australia	17	25	3	1075	113	1	7	1	48.86	69.58	64	4
Tasmania	18	29	4	967	114	3	4	3	38.68	68.63	44	2
Victoria	20	36	5	1277	154	–	7	3	41.19	66.68	55	7
Western Australia	18	31	5	944	116	2	7	1	36.31	74.33	55	6

BY CAPTAINCY

Captaincy	M	Inn	NO	Runs	HS	0s	50	100	Avg	Stk-Rt	Ct	St
As Non Captain	74	123	15	4251	154	9	25	9	39.36	68.48	212	19
As Captain	20	34	6	1461	139	1	9	2	52.18	78.97	72	5

BY INNINGS

Innings	Inn	NO	Runs	HS	0s	50	100	Avg	Stk-Rt	Ct	St
First Innings	53	6	2233	139	2	14	5	47.51	71.69	113	5
Second Innings	38	2	1647	154	2	9	5	45.75	69.35	79	6
Third Innings	45	8	1298	116	5	9	1	35.08	74.55	40	7
Fourth Innings	21	5	534	62*	1	2	–	33.38	64.57	52	6

BY VENUE

in Australia	M	Inn	NO	Runs	HS	0s	50	100	Avg	Stk-Rt	Ct	St
Adelaide	11	19	2	793	93	1	6	–	46.65	68.84	43	3
Albion	1	2	1	68	50*	–	1	–	68.00	95.77	5	–
Bankstown	2	4	1	237	114	–	1	1	79.00	75.24	7	2
Blacktown	1	1	–	10	10	–	–	–	10.00	45.45	–	–
Brisbane	10	19	1	743	139	2	5	1	41.28	79.47	33	1
Canberra	1	2	–	106	73	–	1	–	53.00	65.03	4	–
Hobart	7	13	1	213	40*	2	–	–	17.75	72.95	16	1
Lismore	1	–	–	–	–	–	–	–	–	–	1	–
Melbourne	5	10	1	412	117	–	2	1	45.78	70.43	12	1
Newcastle	2	4	1	115	50	–	1	–	38.33	81.56	7	1
North Sydney	1	2	–	95	87	–	1	–	47.50	73.08	4	–
Perth	8	15	2	338	70*	2	3	–	26.00	72.22	32	3
Richmond	3	6	–	96	40	–	–	–	16.00	95.05	12	1
St Kilda	2	3	1	240	154	–	1	1	120.00	66.30	6	–
Sydney	39	57	10	2246	123	3	12	7	47.79	67.63	102	11

BY BATTING POSITION

Position	Inn	NO	Runs	HS	0s	50	100	Avg	Stk-Rt
Opener	6	1	83	41	–	–	–	16.60	72.17
3th	4	–	112	40	–	–	–	28.00	116.67
4th	2	–	50	34	–	–	–	25.00	80.65
5th	8	–	137	66	3	1	–	17.13	49.64
6th	71	14	3199	139	1	20	8	56.12	70.22
7th	60	6	2018	154	6	13	3	37.37	72.12
8th	6	–	113	41	–	–	–	18.83	72.90

HOW DISMISSED WHEN BATTING

Innings	Not Out	Bowled	Ct Fieldsman	Ct Keeper	LBW	Stumped	Run Out
157	21	24	59	26	23	3	1

INTERNATIONAL LIMITED-OVERS CAREER

Debut 2000–01 vs Zimbabwe, Hobart

BY OPPONENT

Opponent	M	Inn	NO	Runs	HS	0s	50	100	Avg	Stk-Rt	Ct	St
Afghanistan	1	1	1	20	20*	–	–	–	–	222.22	1	–
Bangladesh	5	4	–	37	16	–	–	–	9.25	50.00	4	–
Canada	1	1	–	88	88	–	1	–	88.00	104.76	2	–
England	15	13	1	361	54	–	1	–	30.08	91.16	19	1
India	19	17	5	425	87*	–	3	–	35.42	77.98	16	–
Kenya	1	1	–	65	65	–	1	–	65.00	82.28	1	–
New Zealand	17	16	1	692	110	1	3	2	46.13	91.78	27	–
Pakistan	19	17	5	321	42	1	–	–	26.75	76.61	35	2
Sri Lanka	15	14	2	260	50	–	1	–	21.67	77.84	16	2
South Africa	17	17	–	395	78	–	4	–	23.24	90.18	18	2
Scotland	1	–	–	–	–	–	–	–	–	–	2	–
West Indies	9	8	1	275	70	–	2	–	39.29	88.42	24	1
Zimbabwe	6	6	–	183	49	–	–	–	30.50	69.32	5	3
Total	**126**	**115**	**16**	**3122**	**110**	**2**	**16**	**2**	**31.54**	**84.22**	**170**	**11**

BY INNINGS

Innings	Inn	NO	Runs	HS	0s	50	100	Avg	Stk-Rt	Ct	St
First Innings	77	11	2089	109	–	11	1	31.65	81.19	104	5
Second Innings	38	5	1033	110	2	5	1	31.30	91.09	66	6

BY VENUE

in Australia	M	Inn	NO	Runs	HS	0s	50	100	Avg	Stk-Rt	Ct	St
Adelaide	9	7	1	163	50	–	1	–	27.17	71.49	18	1
Brisbane	6	5	2	189	88*	–	1	–	63.00	93.10	9	1
Darwin	3	2	–	19	16	–	–	–	9.50	43.18	3	–
Hobart	7	6	–	139	42	–	–	–	23.17	107.75	6	1
Melbourne (MCG)	15	13	2	300	49	–	–	–	27.27	82.64	19	1
Melbourne (Docklands)	1	1	–	1	1	–	–	–	1.00	25.00	3	–
Perth	7	7	1	189	63	–	1	–	31.50	85.14	14	–
Sydney	13	11	3	341	109	–	1	1	42.63	103.02	13	3
Total	**61**	**52**	**9**	**1341**	**109**	**–**	**4**	**1**	**31.19**	**87.99**	**85**	**7**

in Bangladesh	M	Inn	NO	Runs	HS	0s	50	100	Avg	Stk-Rt	Ct	St
Mirpur	2	2	–	18	10	–	–	–	9.00	60.00	1	–

in England	M	Inn	NO	Runs	HS	0s	50	100	Avg	Stk-Rt	Ct	St
Lord's	2	1	–	13	13	–	–	–	13.00	100.00	1	–

BY VENUE (continued)

in India	M	Inn	NO	Runs	HS	0s	50	100	Avg	Stk-Rt	Ct	St
Ahmedabad	2	2	–	82	53	–	1	–	41.00	64.06	4	–
Bangalore	4	4	–	262	88	–	3	–	65.50	88.81	4	–
Jaipur	1	1	1	1	1*	–	–	–	–	100.00	1	–
Kochi	1	1	1	87	87*	–	1	–	–	126.09	–	–
Mohali	1	1	–	24	24	–	–	–	24.00	150.00	5	–
Mumbai	1	1	–	19	19	–	–	–	19.00	50.00	–	–
Nagpur	3	3	1	80	55	–	1	–	40.00	77.67	5	–
Pune	1	1	–	10	10	–	–	–	10.00	71.43	1	–
Ranchi	1	1	–	3	3	–	–	–	3.00	75.00	–	–
Total	**15**	**15**	**3**	**568**	**88**	**–**	**6**	**–**	**47.33**	**85.03**	**20**	**–**

in Malaysia	M	Inn	NO	Runs	HS	0s	50	100	Avg	Stk-Rt	Ct	St
Kinrara	5	5	1	174	70	–	1	–	43.50	86.14	12	–

in New Zealand	M	Inn	NO	Runs	HS	0s	50	100	Avg	Stk-Rt	Ct	St
Auckland	4	4	–	145	53	1	1	–	36.25	87.88	6	–
Hamilton	2	2	–	148	110	–	–	1	74.00	97.37	4	–
Napier	1	1	–	12	12	–	–	–	12.00	75.00	1	–
Wellington	2	2	–	23	17	–	–	–	11.50	88.46	2	–
Total	**9**	**9**	**–**	**328**	**110**	**1**	**1**	**1**	**36.44**	**91.36**	**13**	**–**

in Netherlands	M	Inn	NO	Runs	HS	0s	50	100	Avg	Stk-Rt	Ct	St
Amstelveen	2	2	–	15	10	–	–	–	7.50	34.88	4	–

in Sri Lanka	M	Inn	NO	Runs	HS	0s	50	100	Avg	Stk-Rt	Ct	St
Colombo (PIS)	4	3	1	55	42	–	–	–	27.50	55.00	5	1
Colombo (SSC)	1	1	–	9	9	–	–	–	9.00	42.86	–	–
Hambantota	2	2	–	12	7	–	–	–	6.00	44.44	3	–
Pallekele	1	1	–	12	12	–	–	–	12.00	66.67	1	–
Total	**8**	**7**	**1**	**88**	**42**	**–**	**–**	**–**	**14.67**	**53.01**	**9**	**1**

in South Africa	M	Inn	NO	Runs	HS	0s	50	100	Avg	Stk-Rt	Ct	St
Cape Town	1	1	–	15	15	–	–	–	15.00	44.12	1	–
Centurion	2	2	–	10	9	–	–	–	5.00	90.91	2	–
Durban	2	2	–	76	53	–	1	–	38.00	89.41	2	1
Johannesburg	1	1	–	62	62	–	1	–	62.00	96.88	3	–
Port Elizabeth	2	2	–	91	78	–	1	–	45.50	108.33	3	1
Total	**8**	**8**	**–**	**254**	**78**	**–**	**3**	**–**	**31.75**	**91.37**	**11**	**2**

in United Arab Emirates	M	Inn	NO	Runs	HS	0s	50	100	Avg	Stk-Rt	Ct	St
Abu Dhabi	4	4	–	64	36	1	–	–	16.00	68.82	1	–
Dubai	3	3	1	65	40	–	–	–	32.50	76.47	5	–
Sharjah	1	1	1	23	23*	–	–	–	–	85.19	3	–
Total	**8**	**8**	**2**	**152**	**40**	**1**	**–**	**–**	**25.33**	**74.15**	**9**	**–**

BY VENUE (continued)

in West Indies	M	Inn	NO	Runs	HS	0s	50	100	Avg	Stk-Rt	Ct	St
Kingstown	1	1	–	50	50	–	1	–	50.00	96.15	3	–

in Zimbabwe	M	Inn	NO	Runs	HS	0s	50	100	Avg	Stk-Rt	Ct	St
Harare	5	5	–	121	49	–	–	–	24.20	72.46	2	1

BY BATTING POSITION

Position	Inn	NO	Runs	HS	0s	50	100	Avg	Stk-Rt
Opener	47	1	1562	110	2	10	2	33.96	81.31
3th	5	–	145	49	–	–	–	29.00	87.35
5th	4	1	98	41	–	–	–	32.67	103.16
6th	11	1	347	87*	–	3	–	34.70	79.95
7th	42	10	847	70	–	3	–	26.47	84.03
8th	6	3	123	43	–	–	–	41.00	148.19

HOW DISMISSED WHEN BATTING

Innings	Not Out	Bowled	Ct Fieldsman	Ct Keeper	LBW	Stumped	Run Out
115	16	24	50	6	6	3	10

HIGHEST SCORES

Score	Team	Opponent	Venue	Season
109	Australia	New Zealand	Sydney	2008–09
110	Australia	New Zealand	Hamilton	2009–10

PLAYER OF THE MATCH AWARDS

Start Date	Opponent	Venue	How Out	Runs	Balls	Catches
02/10/2007	India	Kochi	not out	87*	(69)	–
08/02/2009	New Zealand	Sydney	run out (McCullum)	109	(114)	1
09/03/2010	New Zealand	Hamilton	st Hopkins b Vettori	110	(121)	2

DOMESTIC LIMITED-OVERS CAREER
Debut 1997–98 Australian Capital Territory vs South Australia, Canberra

BY SEASON

Season	Team	M	Inn	NO	Runs	HS	0s	50	100	Avg	Stk-Rt	Ct	St
1997–98	ACT	6	6	–	205	89	–	2	–	34.17	102.50	5	–
1998–99	ACT	3	3	–	165	133	–	–	1	55.00	97.06	4	–
1999–2000	NSW	6	6	–	170	70	1	2	–	28.33	101.19	7	4
2000–01	NSW	10	10	–	252	69	–	3	–	25.20	108.15	12	6
2001–02	NSW	10	10	–	360	120	1	2	1	36.00	104.96	20	5
2002–03	NSW	11	10	–	171	70	2	1	–	17.10	78.44	17	3
2003–04	NSW	7	7	1	76	22	1	–	–	12.67	71.70	8	1
2004–05	NSW	7	7	1	366	120	–	2	1	61.00	100.00	8	4
2005–06	NSW	9	9	–	193	65	1	1	–	21.44	79.75	23	5
2006–07	NSW	9	9	3	406	115	–	1	1	67.67	104.10	6	3
2007–08	NSW	6	6	1	314	138*	1	2	1	62.80	93.73	5	2
2009–10	NSW	2	2	–	40	27	–	–	–	20.00	78.43	4	–
2010–11	NSW	3	3	–	126	70	1	2	–	42.00	87.50	2	–
2011–12	NSW	1	1	–	32	32	–	–	–	32.00	82.05	2	–
2012–13	NSW	5	5	–	213	125	–	–	1	42.60	80.68	4	2
2013–14	NSW	1	1	–	5	5	–	–	–	5.00	50.00	1	–
Total		**96**	**95**	**6**	**3094**	**138***	**8**	**18**	**6**	**34.76**	**94.36**	**128**	**35**

BY OPPONENT

Opponent	M	Inn	NO	Runs	HS	0s	50	100	Avg	Stk-Rt	Ct	St
ACT	1	1	–	70	70	–	1	–	70.00	120.69	1	1
NSW	1	1	–	6	6	–	–	–	6.00	37.50	–	–
QLD	17	17	–	410	88	2	3	–	24.12	87.61	31	7
SA	18	18	1	395	125	4	2	1	23.24	82.46	24	4
TAS	17	17	3	637	138*	1	3	2	45.50	105.12	17	8
VIC	18	17	2	708	133	1	5	1	47.20	98.20	14	6
WA	24	24	–	868	120	–	4	2	36.17	93.23	41	9

BY CAPTAINCY

Captaincy	M	Inn	NO	Runs	HS	0s	50	100	Avg	Stk-Rt	Ct	St
As Non Captain	82	81	5	2659	138*	7	16	5	34.99	94.36	102	28
As Captain	14	14	1	435	120	1	2	1	33.46	94.36	26	7

BY INNINGS

Batting in Each Innings	Inn	NO	Runs	HS	0s	50	100	Avg	Stk-Rt	Ct	St
First Innings	47	2	1584	125	4	8	3	35.20	94.79	53	17
Second Innings	48	4	1510	138*	4	10	3	34.32	93.91	75	18

BY VENUE

in Australia	M	Inn	NO	Runs	HS	0s	50	100	Avg	Stk-Rt	Ct	St
Adelaide	11	11	1	249	125	4	1	1	24.90	89.25	17	2
Albion	1	1	–	12	12	–	–	–	12.00	109.09	2	–
Bankstown	5	5	–	161	120	–	–	1	32.20	118.38	7	1
Bendigo	1	1	–	89	89	–	1	–	89.00	97.80	1	–
Brisbane	9	9	–	297	88	–	2	–	33.00	84.62	20	4
Canberra	9	9	1	359	133	–	2	1	44.88	105.59	8	2
Coffs Harbour	3	3	–	29	15	1	–	–	9.67	48.33	2	3
Devonport	1	1	–	70	70	–	1	–	70.00	145.83	3	–
Drummoyne	2	2	–	14	10	–	–	–	7.00	73.68	3	1
Hobart	6	6	3	229	138*	–	–	1	76.33	110.63	6	3
Homebush	3	3	–	49	36	–	–	–	16.33	58.33	1	2
Hurstville	1	1	–	70	70	–	1	–	70.00	93.33	–	–
Melbourne	4	4	–	69	27	–	–	–	17.25	73.40	4	–
Newcastle	1	1	–	20	20	–	–	–	20.00	71.43	1	1
North Sydney	13	13	–	477	120	2	3	1	36.69	101.49	17	6
Perth	13	13	–	375	70	–	2	–	28.85	86.61	25	2
Richmond	1	1	–	7	7	–	–	–	7.00	36.84	–	–
St Kilda	1	1	–	17	17	–	–	–	17.00	62.96	–	–
Sydney	10	9	1	436	115	1	4	1	54.50	99.09	10	7
Wangaratta	1	1	–	65	65	–	1	–	65.00	97.01	1	1

BY TEAM

Team	M	Inn	NO	Runs	HS	0s	50	100	Avg	Stk-Rt	Ct	St
ACT	9	9	–	370	133	–	2	1	41.11	100.00	9	–
NSW	87	86	6	2724	138*	8	16	5	34.05	93.64	119	35

BY BATTING POSITION

Position	Inn	NO	Runs	HS	0s	50	100	Avg	Stk-Rt
Opener	39	–	1260	133	2	9	2	32.31	92.92
3rd	6	1	117	96*	2	1	–	23.40	99.15
4th	31	3	1137	138*	3	4	3	40.61	93.66
5th	9	1	350	125	–	2	1	43.75	92.35
6th	7	1	149	70	–	1	–	24.83	107.97
7th	2	–	18	18	1	–	–	9.00	112.50
8th	1	–	63	63	–	1	–	63.00	108.62

HOW DISMISSED WHEN BATTING

Innings	Not Out	Bowled	Ct Fieldsman	Ct Keeper	LBW	Stumped	Run Out
95	6	10	55	10	4	1	9

HIGHEST SCORES

Score	Team	Opponent	Venue	Season
133	Australian Capital Territory	Victoria	Canberra	1998–99
120	New South Wales	Tasmania	Bankstown	2001–02
120	New South Wales	Western Australia	North Sydney	2004–05
115	New South Wales	Western Australia	Sydney	2006–07
138*	New South Wales	Tasmania	Hobart	2007–08
125	New South Wales	South Australia	Adelaide	2012–13

INTERNATIONAL TWENTY20 CAREER

Debut 2005–06 vs South Africa, Brisbane

BY OPPONENT

Opponent	M	Inn	NO	Runs	HS	0s	50	100	Avg	Stk-Rt	Ct	St
Bangladesh	2	1	–	6	6	–	–	–	6.00	66.67	–	–
England	1	1	–	1	1	–	–	–	1.00	50.00	–	–
India	5	5	2	29	8	–	–	–	9.67	96.67	2	1
New Zealand	3	2	–	62	47	–	–	–	31.00	134.78	4	–
Pakistan	6	5	–	59	25	–	–	–	11.80	98.33	1	2
Sri Lanka	5	5	–	73	35	1	–	–	14.60	108.96	2	2
South Africa	5	3	2	20	16*	1	–	–	20.00	100.00	4	–
West Indies	6	6	2	146	42	–	–	–	36.50	139.05	4	1
Zimbabwe	1	1	–	6	6	–	–	–	6.00	50.00	–	–
Total	**34**	**29**	**6**	**402**	**47**	**2**	**–**	**–**	**17.48**	**114.53**	**17**	**6**

BY INNINGS

Innings	Inn	NO	Runs	HS	0s	50	100	Avg	Stk-Rt	Ct	St
First Innings	17	3	214	37*	1	–	–	15.29	118.23	9	4
Second Innings	12	3	188	47	1	–	–	20.89	110.59	8	2

BY CAPTAINCY

Captaincy	M	Inn	NO	Runs	HS	0s	50	100	Avg	Stk-Rt	Ct	St
As Non Captain	32	27	6	363	47	2	–	–	17.29	115.61	16	6
As Captain	2	2	–	39	24	–	–	–	19.50	105.41	1	–

BY VENUE

in Australia	M	Inn	NO	Runs	HS	0s	50	100	Avg	Stk-Rt	Ct	St
Brisbane	2	1	–	22	22	–	–	–	22.00	200.00	2	–
Hobart	1	1	1	37	37*	–	–	–	–	231.25	1	–
Melbourne	1	1	–	1	1	–	–	–	1.00	33.33	–	1
Perth	1	1	–	35	35	–	–	–	35.00	116.67	1	1
Sydney	2	2	–	21	15	–	–	–	10.50	131.25	1	–
Total	**7**	**6**	**1**	**116**	**37***	**–**	**–**	**–**	**23.20**	**152.63**	**5**	**2**

in Bangladesh	M	Inn	NO	Runs	HS	0s	50	100	Avg	Stk-Rt	Ct	St
Mirpur	4	3	1	29	15*	–	–	–	14.50	126.09	3	–

in England	M	Inn	NO	Runs	HS	0s	50	100	Avg	Stk-Rt	Ct	St
Nottingham	1	1	–	16	16	–	–	–	16.00	94.12	–	–
The Oval	1	1	–	24	24	–	–	–	24.00	126.32	–	–
Total	**2**	**2**	**–**	**40**	**24**	**–**	**–**	**–**	**20.00**	**111.11**	**–**	**–**

in India	M	Inn	NO	Runs	HS	0s	50	100	Avg	Stk-Rt	Ct	St
Mumbai	1	1	1	5	5*	–	–	–	–	125.00	–	–
Rajkot	1	1	–	5	5	–	–	–	5.00	166.67	1	1
Total	**2**	**2**	**1**	**10**	**5***	**–**	**–**	**–**	**10.00**	**142.86**	**1**	**1**

BY VENUE (continued)

in New Zealand	M	Inn	NO	Runs	HS	0s	50	100	Avg	Stk-Rt	Ct	St
Christchurch	1	1	–	47	47	–	–	–	47.00	130.56	–	–
Wellington	1	–	–	–	–	–	–	–	–	–	3	–
Total	**2**	**1**	**–**	**47**	**47**	**–**	**–**	**–**	**47.00**	**130.56**	**3**	**–**

in Sri Lanka	M	Inn	NO	Runs	HS	0s	50	100	Avg	Stk-Rt	Ct	St
Pallekele	2	2	–	7	7	1	–	–	3.50	70.00	–	–

in South Africa	M	Inn	NO	Runs	HS	0s	50	100	Avg	Stk-Rt	Ct	St
Cape Town	1	1	–	6	6	–	–	–	6.00	50.00	–	–
Centurion	2	1	1	16	16*	–	–	–	–	123.08	2	–
Durban	2	2	2	9	5*	–	–	–	–	75.00	–	–
Johannesburg	1	1	–	0	0	1	–	–	0.00	0.00	–	–
Total	**6**	**5**	**3**	**31**	**16***	**1**	**–**	**–**	**15.50**	**77.50**	**2**	**–**

in United Arab Emirates	M	Inn	NO	Runs	HS	0s	50	100	Avg	Stk-Rt	Ct	St
Dubai	2	1	–	24	24	–	–	–	24.00	88.89	–	1

in West Indies	M	Inn	NO	Runs	HS	0s	50	100	Avg	Stk-Rt	Ct	St
Bridgetown	4	4	–	30	15	–	–	–	7.50	107.14	1	1
Gros Islet	3	3	–	68	42	–	–	–	22.67	100.00	2	1
Total	**7**	**7**	**–**	**98**	**42**	**–**	**–**	**–**	**14.00**	**102.08**	**3**	**2**

BY BATTING POSITION

Position	Inn	NO	Runs	HS	0s	50	100	Avg	Stk-Rt
Opener	3	–	86	47	–	–	–	28.67	117.81
3rd	3	–	46	25	–	–	–	15.33	127.78
4th	5	–	73	42	–	–	–	14.60	90.12
5th	1	–	24	24	–	–	–	24.00	126.32
6th	4	–	62	35	1	–	–	15.50	131.91
7th	11	5	90	37*	1	–	–	15.00	112.50
8th	2	1	21	15*	–	–	–	21.00	140.00

HOW DISMISSED WHEN BATTING

Innings	Not Out	Bowled	Ct Fieldsman	Ct Keeper	LBW	Stumped	Run Out
29	6	2	15	2	–	3	1

HIGHEST SCORE

Score	Team	Opponent	Venue	Season
47	Australia	New Zealand	Wellington	2009–10

BIG BASH TWENTY20 CAREER

Debut 2011–12 Sydney Sixers vs Brisbane Heat, Sydney

BY SEASON

Season	M	Inn	NO	Runs	HS	0s	50	100	Avg	Stk-Rt	Ct	St
2011–12	2	2	–	76	76	1	1	–	38.00	124.59	–	–
2012–13	7	7	–	186	59	–	1	–	26.57	114.11	3	2
2015–16	7	7	1	200	72	1	2	–	33.33	151.52	2	–
Total	**16**	**16**	**1**	**462**	**76**	**2**	**4**	**–**	**30.80**	**129.78**	**5**	**2**

BY OPPONENT

Opponent	M	Inn	NO	Runs	HS	0s	50	100	Avg	Stk-Rt	Ct	St
Adelaide Strikers	2	2	1	76	54*	–	1	–	76.00	116.92	–	1
Brisbane Heat	3	3	–	134	76	–	1	–	44.67	136.73	–	1
Hobart Hurricanes	2	2	–	94	72	–	1	–	47.00	151.61	–	–
Melbourne Renegades	1	1	–	0	0	1	–	–	0.00	0.00	–	–
Melbourne Stars	2	2	–	41	39	–	–	–	20.50	128.13	1	–
Perth Scorchers	2	2	–	10	10	1	–	–	5.00	100.00	1	–
Sydney Thunder	4	4	–	107	59	–	1	–	26.75	121.59	3	–

BY INNINGS

Innings		Inn	NO	Runs	HS	0s	50	100	Avg	Stk-Rt	Ct	St
First Innings		7	1	182	72	1	2	–	30.33	129.08	2	1
Second Innings		9	–	280	76	1	2	–	31.11	130.23	3	1

BY CAPTAINCY

Captaincy	M	Inn	NO	Runs	HS	0s	50	100	Avg	Stk-Rt	Ct	St
As Non Captain	6	6	1	158	72	1	2	–	31.60	146.30	2	–
As Captain	10	10	–	304	76	1	2	–	30.40	122.58	3	2

BY VENUE

Venue	M	Inn	NO	Runs	HS	0s	50	100	Avg	Stk-Rt	Ct	St
Adelaide	2	2	1	76	54*	–	1	–	76.00	116.92	–	1
Brisbane	1	1	–	16	16	–	–	–	16.00	106.67	–	1
Homebush (Stadium Aus)	1	1	–	18	18	–	–	–	18.00	105.88	1	–
Homebush (RAS)	1	1	–	13	13	–	–	–	13.00	118.18	–	–
Melbourne (MCG)	1	1	–	39	39	–	–	–	39.00	139.29	–	–
Melbourne (Docklands)	1	1	–	0	0	1	–	–	0.00	0.00	–	–
Sydney	9	9	–	300	76	1	3	–	33.33	136.99	4	–

BY BATTING POSITION

Position	Inn	NO	Runs	HS	0s	50	100	Avg	Stk-Rt
Opener	8	–	201	76	2	2	–	25.13	130.52
3th	4	–	130	59	–	1	–	32.50	114.04
4th	3	1	89	54*	–	1	–	44.50	139.06
5th	1	–	42	42	–	–	–	42.00	175.00

HOW DISMISSED WHEN BATTING

Innings	Not Out	Bowled	Ct Fieldsman	Ct Keeper	LBW	Stumped	Run Out
16	1	5	8	2	–	–	–

HIGHEST SCORE

Score	Team	Opponent	Venue	Season
76	Sydney Sixers	Brisbane Heat	Sydney	2011–12

COMPARISONS

MOST DISMISSALS IN TESTS

Wicketkeeper	M	Dismissals	Catches	Stumpings	Dis/Inns Kept
MV Boucher (S/Africa)	147	555	532	23	1.975
AC Gilchrist (Aus)	96	416	379	37	2.178
IA Healy (Aus)	119	395	366	29	1.763
RW Marsh (Aus)	97	355	343	12	1.950
MS Dhoni (India)	90	294	256	38	1.771
BJ Haddin (Aus)	66	270	262	8	2.109
PJL Dujon (WI)	81	270	265	5	1.800
APE Knott (Eng)	96	269	250	19	1.545
MJ Prior (Eng)	79	256	243	13	1.753
AJ Stewart (Eng)	133	241	227	14	1.709

MOST DISMISSALS IN A TEST SERIES

Wicketkeeper	Year	Versus	M	Dismissals	Catches	Stumpings	Dis/Inn Kept
BJ Haddin (Aus)	2013	v Eng in Eng	5	29	29	0	2.900
RW Marsh (Aus)	1982–83	v Eng in Aus	5	28	28	0	2.800
RC Russell (Eng)	1995–96	v Aus in Aus	5	27	25	2	3.857
IA Healy (Aus)	1997	v Eng in Eng	6	27	25	2	2.250
MV Boucher (S/Africa)	1998	v Eng in Eng	5	26	25	1	2.600
AC Gilchrist (Aus)	2001	v Eng in Eng	5	26	24	2	2.600
AC Gilchrist (Aus)	2006–07	v Eng in Aus	5	26	24	2	2.600

ACKNOWLEDGEMENTS

KARINA AND I ARE keenly aware that not all families have been as fortunate as ours; that made us initially reluctant to share our journey. Having done so, we hope that our story strikes a chord.

My good friend Peter Lovitt bore the brunt of the media requests when Mia was first diagnosed and, with the help of my management, Neil Maxwell, Dominic Thornely and Judie Andersen, and my literary agent Jane Burridge, led me to the book world and helped me navigate it to create something that I can be very proud of. My gratitude also goes to the supportive HarperCollins team, especially Helen Littleton, Scott Forbes, Darren Kelly and James Kellow, who were wonderful in encouraging me to share my story in my own way.

My exceptional writer, Hazel Flynn, captured the nature of my childhood and the legacy I left when I retired from the game 38 years later, in part by poring over scrapbooks full of newspaper articles my mum collected and the diaries and photo albums Karina created of Mia's journey. This book could not have been written without her dedication and hard work.

I've learned so much over the years from coaches Steve Rixon and Trevor Bayliss, and continue to do so. They have become valued friends as well as mentors.

I like working with people I admire and trust, and I like accountability. When cancer enters your life these things take on a much deeper meaning. No professional anxiety, including walking out to bat at the MCG on Boxing Day, can be compared to the fear induced by hearing the words 'your child has cancer' and knowing you can't change the situation. Luckily, when it happened to us we found ourselves surrounded by people who genuinely cared for Mia and our family. We can't thank Dr Prakash and the staff at the Cabarita Family Practice and the doctors, nurses and staff at Westmead Children's Hospital enough for the expert care and support they provide. They give every child the best possible chance of a positive outcome, and their opinions and insights continue to give us great comfort (and help me sleep at night).

I'm not sure I will ever be able to fully express my gratitude to Karina's parents, Marg and Phil, for the gift they gave Karina and me when we needed it most. They sat beside Mia's hospital bed, raised a newborn baby and chased a toddler around without hesitation. As for Danielle, we still couldn't live without her skills in the technology department. Zachary, Mia and Hugo are the luckiest kids in the world to have the Castle family in their lives.

Peter and Michelle Comerford have been part of my life from the very start and, together with their daughters, Emily and Olivia, have followed my career through its ups and downs and offered continuous support, as have Mia's godparents, Paul and Sarah Byrom.

My grandparents, Mar and Pa and Nanny and Poppy, were my biggest fans, always insisting it wasn't my fault if I dropped a catch or played a silly shot, and I'm forever grateful for their belief in me.

My brothers, Mike and Chris, are the two best friends I could ever have. They have been there and enjoyed all the highs and the lows and given me unwavering support. I'm looking forward to being able to spend more quality time with Mike and Amy and my three nieces Molly, Georgia and Jemima, and I can't wait to see what the future holds for Chris and Jenna. We have a strong bond that will never be broken.

My love and thanks to my wife, Karina, who has supported me and celebrated with me when times have been good and showed the most extraordinary strength of character when they were anything but, living the truth of our marriage vows. Together we have created the most amazing little family and my children, Zac, Mia and Hugo, are the source of my greatest inspiration and happiness.

Last but not least, I owe Mum and Dad everything. They spent endless hours driving me to training sessions, trial matches and games, and sitting in the stands watching me, come rain or shine. They have given me unconditional love and support my whole life and were the rock I could lean on when things seemed at their worst. It is from them I learned my most valuable lesson in life — that family comes first.